Holocaust Education and the Semiotics of Othering

The Representation of Holocaust Victims, Jewish "Ethnicities" and Arab "Minorities" in Israeli Schoolbooks

Nurit Peled-Elhanan

Holocaust Education and the Semiotics of Othering

The Representation of Holocaust Victims, Jewish "Ethnicities" and Arab "Minorities" in Israeli Schoolbooks

Nurit Peled-Elhanan

First published in 2023
as part of the *The Learner* Book Imprint
doi: 10.18848/978-1-957792-08-8/CGP (Full Book)

Common Ground Research Networks
2001 South First Street, Suite 201L
University of Illinois Research Park
Champaign, IL
61820

Copyright © Nurit Peled-Elhanan, 2023.

All rights reserved. Apart from fair dealing for the purposes of study, research, criticism or review as permitted under the applicable copyright legislation, no part of this book may be reproduced by any process without written permission from the publisher.

Library of Congress Cataloging-in-Publication Data

Names: Peled-Elhanan, Nurit, author.
Title: Holocaust education and the semiotics of othering: the
  representation of Holocaust victims, Jewish "ethnicities" and Arab
  "minorities" in Israeli Schoolbooks / Nurit Peled-Elhanan.
Description: Champaign, Illinois: Common Ground Research Networks, 2023. |
  Includes bibliographical references and index. | Summary: "The book
  addresses the representation of three groups of "others" in Israeli
  schoolbooks: Holocaust victims, presented as the stateless persecuted
  Jews "we" might become again if "we" lose control over the second group
  of "others" - Palestinian Arabs - who are racialized, demonized and
  Nazified, and presented as "our" potential exterminators. The third
  group comprises non-European (Mizrahi and Ethiopian) Jews, portrayed as
  backward people who lack history or culture, requiring constant
  acculturation by "Western" Israel. Thus, a rhetoric of victimhood and
  power evolves, and a nationalistic interpretation of the "never again"
  imperative is inculcated, justifying the Occupation and oppression of
  Palestinians and the discrimination of non-European Jews. Advocating a
  multidirectional memory, the book proposes an alternative Hebrew-Arabic,
  multi-voiced and poly-centered curriculum that would relate the untold
  accounts of the people whom the pedagogic version of history seeks
  exclude. Instead of traumatizing and urging vengeance, it will encourage
  discussion and celebrate diversity and hybridity"-- Provided by
  publisher.
Identifiers: LCCN 2023009119 (print) | LCCN 2023009120 (ebook) | ISBN
  9781957792064 (hardback) | ISBN 9781957792071 (paperback) | ISBN
  9781957792088 (pdf)
Subjects: LCSH: Textbooks--Israel. | Curriculum change--Israel. |
  Education--Aims and objectives--Israel. | Semiotics--Social
  aspects--Israel. | Other (Philosophy)--Israel. | Holocaust victims. |
  Palestinian Arabs--Israel. | Mizrahim--Israel. | Jews,
  Ethiopian--Israel.
Classification: LCC LB3045.6.P45 2023 (print) | LCC LB3045.6 (ebook) |
  DDC 940.53/18071--dc23/eng/20230313
LC record available at https://lccn.loc.gov/2023009119
LC ebook record available at https://lccn.loc.gov/2023009120

In memory of Prof. Gunther Kress
Who taught me how to read images.

Table of Contents

Introduction	3

Part I
The Othering of Holocaust Victims

Chapter 1	29
Representing the Holocaust	
Chapter 2	49
Holocaust Instruction	
Chapter 3	59
Visual Representation of the Holocaust in Israeli Schoolbooks: Transposition, Transformation and Transduction	
Chapter 4	83
Symbols and Icons	
Chapter 5	107
The Pedagogy of Horror	
Chapter 6	133
Individual Victims as Specimens of Categories	
Chapter 7	169
The Question of Pornography	
Chapter 8	193
The Historical Recount	
Chapter 9	207
The Representation of the Holocaust in Israeli Schoolbooks: Conclusion for Chapters 1-8.	

Part II
The Othering of Jewish Ethnicities and Palestinian Minorities

Chapter 10	215
The Othering of Palestinians	
Chapter 11	251
The Nazification of Palestinians	
Chapter 12	261
The Othering of Arab Jews	
Chapter 13	275
They Say Our Color is Sad	

Part III
Epilogue: The Other is Me

Chapter 14: 287
   A Summary of the study
Chapter 15: 293
An Alternative Joint Narrative

Index 317
Bibliography 359

There must be some limit to the burden of remembering that we impose on our children and grandchildren.

J.M. Coetzee, *Elizabeth Costello* p. 18

Introduction. Scope and Methodology

This book examines the representation of Holocaust victims and Israeli Jewish and non-Jewish minorities in Israeli schoolbooks. It serves to expand the scope of my previous study, (Peled-Elhanan 2012) of the representation of Palestinians in Israeli schoolbooks, published between 1994 and 2009.[1]

Scholars claim that Israeli attitude toward its "others" is closely linked to the dominance of the Holocaust in Israeli consciousness.[2] Therefore, the study explores the semiotic resources used in textbooks to represent Holocaust victims, and traces a connection between "Holocaust rhetoric" and the depiction of the "others", namely the groups that have been deemed marginal or superfluous, and have been subjected to prejudice and discrimination, albeit for different reasons and to different degrees.[3]

The book has two main parts: the first discusses the multimodal representation of the Holocaust and its victims in Holocaust and history schoolbooks; the second part discusses the semiotic means by which contemporary Palestinian "minorities" and Jewish "ethnicities" are depicted in schoolbooks of history, geography and civic studies. The common denominator of Holocaust victims and contemporary "minorities" or "ethnicities" is that they are all perceived and presented as groups of "others", in distinct categories, devoid of history and individuality.

Context and Summary

The Israeli Interpretation of Never Again!

> Memory of suffering does not assure the life-long dedication to the fight against inhumanity, cruelty and pain as such, wherever they happen and whoever are the

---

1. Peled-Elhanan, Nurit. 2012. *Palestine in Israeli School Books Ideology and Propaganda in Education*. London: I.B. Tauris.
2. Segev, Tom. 1993. *The Seventh Million: The Israelis and the Holocaust*. New York: Hill and Wang; Zuckerman, Moshe. 1993. *Shoah in the Sealed Room. The Israeli Press during the First Gulf War*. Published independently (in Hebrew); Zertal, Edith. 2005. *Israel's Holocaust and the Politics of Nationhood*. Translated by Chaya Galai. Cambridge Middle East Studies series. New York: Cambridge University Press; Bashir and Goldberg, 2019. *The Holocaust and the Nakba*; Goldberg, Amos and Alon Confino. 2020. "To understand Zionism, we must listen to the voices of its victims." In: *972 Magazine. Independent Journalism from Israel-Palestine*.
3. Two important studies that employ multimodal discourse analysis to which I refer repeatedly in this book are Chouliaraki, L. 2006. *The Spectatorship of Suffering*. London, England: Sage; and Van Leeuwen, Theo. 2000. "Visual Racism." In Reisigl M. & R. Wodak Eds, *The Semiotics of Racism: Approaches in Critical Discourse Analysis*. Vienna, Austria: Passagen Verlag.

sufferers. [...] We cannot be sure whether the lasting legacy of the Holocaust was not the very opposite of that hoped for by many, and anticipated by some: the moral re-awakening or ethical purification of the world as a whole or any of its parts. (Bauman 2000, 12)

Scholars have frequently maintained that Israel's interpretation of the post-Holocaust Slogan *Never Again!* is key to understanding certain central sentiments and actions of Israeli society.[4] Among these are the constant fear of extermination and the general feeling of victimhood, that dominate Israeli social, political, and educational discourse[5]; the conviction that every expression of hostility toward Israel may lead to a new Holocaust;[6] the overriding importance attached to maintaining a Jewish majority, and the inculcation of uncritical admiration of the military from a very early age,[7] or the creation of what sociologist Baruch Kimmerling called cognitive militarism: "a world view in which civil society adopts, wholesale, the way of thinking of the military. Civilians are military in waiting, civil institutions are constantly preparing for the possibility of war, war is the horizon of both thinking and planning, problems are conceived as security issues, and victory is always the aim." (Cited in Illouz 2021).[8]

In his ground-breaking article *The Need to Forget*, Holocaust historian Yehuda Elkana[9] asserts that "two nations, metaphorically speaking, emerged from the ashes of Auschwitz: a minority that asserts, 'this must never happen again,' and a frightened and haunted majority that asserts, 'this must never happen to us again.'" The two interpretations of the post-Holocaust slogan, Never Again to us! Vs. Never again to anyone! correspond to the distinction made by De-Koven

---

4. Zertal 2005, Segev 1991, Naveh 2017.
5. Oren, Neta, Rafi Nets-Zehngut, and Daniel Bar-Tal. 2015. "Construction of the Israeli-Jewish Conflict-Supportive Narrative and the Struggle over Its Dominance." *Political Psychology* 36, no. 2.
6. Zuckermann, Moshe. 1993. "Shoa in the Sealed Room: The Holocaust in the Israeli Press during the Gulf War"; Raz-Krakotzkin, Amnon. 2019. "Walter Benjamin, the Holocaust and the Question of Palestine." In Goldberg, Amos and Bashir, Bashir. 2018. *The Holocaust and the Nakba*. Foreword by Elias Khoury. Afterword by Jacqueline Rose. Columbia University Press.
7. Gur Ziv, Hagit. *Militarism in Education*. Babel pub.
8. Illouz, Eva. 2021. "Holocaust, Militarism and Machiavelli's Advice: How Fear Took over Israel. "https://www.haaretz.com/israel-news/.premium.HIGHLIGHT.MAGAZINE-holocaust-militarism-and-machiavelli-s-advice-how-fear-took-over-israel-1.9415093.
Illouz observes, "In Israel of today, fear is so dominant that even those running against Netanyahu resort to the use of blunt security language. Kahol Lavan leader Benny Gantz, who sought to position himself as the moral alternative to Netanyahu, boasted that during the 2014 war, when he was the IDF chief of staff, he sent parts of the Gaza Strip "back to the Stone Age" and boasted that 1,364 Palestinians were killed in the hostilities." (ibid.)
9. Elkana, Yehuda. "The need to Forget." *Ha'aretz*, March 2, 1988.

Ezrahi (2015)[10] between centrifugal and centripetal Memory. Centrifugal memory is an open and creative memory, at times comical as in Benigni's film *Life is Beautiful*, whereas centripetal memory is sacrificial in nature, leading toward a melancholic dead-end. "Centrifugal" impulses surface "when one turns one's back on Auschwitz and substitutes other points of departure both into the past and into an open-ended future." The "centripetal" gaze, on the other hand, "is directed at the gas chambers and privileges the avenging forces, while handicapping genuine ethical struggles in the present. It gives rise to historical absolutes, avenging spirits, and apocalyptic politics" (p. 348).

De-Koven Ezrahi proceeds to argue that Israel appears to have succumbed to centripetal memory, "with its mythic projection and apocalyptic nature."(ibid.) In spite of Israel's educational slogan, *The Other is Me!*[11] which demands complete identification with (unknown) others, and the curricular requirement to teach tolerance and acceptance of others,[12] "to foster an awareness of the need to examine all information critically; and to cultivate the student's ability to understand the positions of those different from him or her",[13] Israeli scholarship suggests that the state's education system has thus far chosen to adhere to a centripetal memory that leaves only two options: to sacrifice or be sacrificed, to kill or to be killed. This stance is "deaf to the cosmopolitan, to the late modernist, and to the postmodernist discourses of empathy and responsibility." (De Koven Ezrahi 2015, 350).

The divergent interpretations of Never Again! also correspond to the distinction made by Dominick LaCapra between two forms of remembering the Shoah and writing about it: acting out and working through. Acting out corresponds to the discourse of "Never again to us," and is likely to generate a rhetoric of victimhood and its twin facet - the rhetoric of power.[14] This rhetoric is manifested in textbooks through discourse, genre, modality, and visual elements. By contrast, working through the trauma reflects a universal perspective regarding history and humanity. This approach tends to promote "a committed exchange

---

10. De-Koven Ezrahi, Sidra. 2015. "A Personal Postscript." In *Marking Evil: Holocaust Memory in the Global Age*. Edited by Amos Goldberg and Haim Hazan. The Van Leer Jerusalem Institute, 345-354.
11. *The Other is Me*. Israeli Ministry of Education. http://cms.education.gov.il/EducationCMS/Units/ui/
12. Naveh, *Past in a Storm*.
13. Cited in Naveh 2019. Ministry of Education, *Tochnit Halimudim Behistoria Lebeit Hasefer Hamamlachti Lekitot Vav-Tet* [History Curriculum for the National School System: Grades 6-9] (Jerusalem: Ministry of Education, 1992), 11.
14 Naveh, Eyal. 2018. *Past in Turmoil Debates over Historical Issues in Israel*. Hakibbutz Hameuhad Pub.; Bauer, Yehuda. 1996. "The influence of the Shoah on the founding of the state of Israel." In *Fundamental Changes in the People of Israel following the Shoah*, edited by Yisrael Gutman. Yad Va-Shem Pub .503-509 (Hebrew); Bauer, Yehuda. 2013. "The Shallowness of Israeli Air force planes flying above Auschwitz." *Haaretz*, October 6, 2013.

with the past in a critical manner," for "it is not apodictic or ad hominem but argumentative, self-questioning and related in mediated ways to action."[15]

Bashir and Goldberg (2019, 59) explain that one necessary component of working through is empathy towards the suffering of others, which "Never again to us!" does not allow. Empathy "confronts a tendency to fetishize a national redemptive narrative in cases of massive collective trauma, which violently excludes any otherness in a kind of scapegoat mechanism."

Fear as a Unifying Element

Sociologist Eva Illouz (2021) maintains that Israeli-Jewish consciousness is based on fear: "The genocide of Europe's Jews ascribed an almost metaphysical meaning to antisemitism, making the hatred of Jews appear to be eternal, inevitable and total, a part of the order of the universe." The great enemies have taken various shapes, but all were part of one endless chain of evil: Amalek, the Romans, the Christian Inquisition, Polish farmers who waged pogroms, all seem part of a historic chain whose pinnacle was Hitler. "That is how the central narrative that shapes modern Jewish consciousness was created: The world started being defined by its intention and determination to destroy the Jews."

The fear of existential threats has been absorbed into the Israeli "normalcy", as Historian Moshe Zuckerman (2023)[16] argues. Illouz contends that living in the shadow of major historical traumas, and having been mentally and emotionally trained to live in fear, Israelis do not possess and cannot acquire the political maturity of truly democratic citizenry, for they will always yield to their fear. Their perception of the world as enemy, she maintains, gradually shaped the Zionists' attitude toward Arab-Palestinians, whose anti-colonialist resistance is attributed to hatred of Jews, both by politicians and in textbooks.

Majoritarianism

> Majoritarianism thrives where majorities become seized of the fantasy of national purity, in that zone where quantity meets but does not completely define quality [...] These majorities are obsessed with the anxiety of incompleteness, which creates the frustration and rage that drives those forms of degradation that shock us most, from Germany to Rwanda, from Kosovo to Mumbai (Appadurai 2006, 159).

---

15. LaCapra, Dominick. 1996. *Representing the Holocaust. History, Theory, Trauma*. Cornell University Press.
16. Zuckerman, M. and Zimmerman, M. 2023. Thinking Germany – an Israeli dialogue. Tel Aviv. Resling Publishers.

Historian Raz-Krakotzkin (2019, 134) [17] notes that Israeli commemorative practices of the Holocaust "foster the perception of the 'rebirth' of the Jewish nation, i.e., Israel's establishment and existence, as a state in which the threat of annihilation is always imminent. The main lesson learned from the Holocaust thus transcends the need for a state or a haven, demanding that the Jews arm themselves to the teeth and take cover behind walls and a nuclear arsenal of ambiguous composition and proportions. [...] Paradoxically," he concludes, "the aspiration to 'normalization' perpetuates the sense of emergency and anxiety."

This anxiety engenders the need to maintain a Jewish majority at all costs, which is often expressed explicitly in schoolbooks, and legitimates the ongoing ethnic cleansing of Palestine (Peled-Elhanan 2012).

Anthropologist Arjun Appadurai (2006, 60) [18] lists four elements that comprise "the anxiety of incompleteness," all of which pertain to contemporary Israel. These are:

- A forced and artificial feeling of "we-ness."

- Social uncertainty

- A striving for national purity

- Majoritarianism

These elements are intertwined in Israel. The artificial "we-ness" of Jewish groups that have nothing in common apart from their faith, is fragile and may collapse at any moment. The social uncertainty stems from the unequal conditions and statuses of the various groups, and the competition between people of different identities - the ultra-orthodox, *mizrahim* (Jews from Muslim countries), Russian immigrants, Ethiopian Jews and illegal Israeli settlers - for political and cultural recognition and hegemony. These struggles generate contesting narratives of national memory, sacrifice, and victimhood (Loshitzky 2006, 328).[19] However, the one element that unites these antagonistic camps is fear of the enemy within and without, and the aspiration for national completeness and "purity", derived from the belief that only a Jewish majority and a powerful Jewish army can prevent another Holocaust, this time to be perpetrated by the Arabs.

---

17. Raz-Krakotzkin, Amon. 2019. "Benjamin, the Holocaust, and the Question of Palestine." In: Bashir and Goldberg 2019.
18. Appadurai, 2006. *Fear of Small Numbers.*
19. Loshitzky, Yosefa. 2006. "Pathologising Memory from the Holocaust to the Intifada." *Third Text* 20 (3/4, May/July, 2006): 327–335. Third Text ISSN 0952-8822 print/ISSN 1475-5297 online.

Majoritarianism explains why Israel has always refused to consider the return of Palestinian refugees, and why this issue is never discussed in any educational or political context. Psychologist Ofer Grosbard (2003, 57-58)[20] attributes this refusal to what he calls "the shudder", "a feeling of constant existential threat that derives from the Jewish past of pogroms and persecutions that culminated in the Holocaust. [...] That shudder makes it hard for us to discern where there really is an existential danger, and where, on the other hand, we distort reality and refuse to see things in a different light than our difficult past dictates." Grosbard defines "the deepest Israeli problem, the shudder," as the "difficulty to believe that it is really possible, more or less within the 1967 borders, to live a normal life [...]. We have a deep feeling that we can only live through struggles and the use of force." This is due to the fear of becoming a threatened minority once again. "This is a deep psychological problem of a country that feels small and weak whenever it is not fighting. When we struggle and fight, we are less able to feel the shudder and the fear. Confrontation and muscle-flexing play a well-known role in allaying the deepest anxieties - a negative role, of course." The "anxiety of incompleteness" and the "shudder" haunt the majority of Israelis, or rather the dominant Jewish group, which feels "incomplete" and therefore insecure in the wake of the Holocaust and the annihilation of East European Jewry, as Eyal Naveh (1999) explains in his history schoolbook.[21] This anxiety engenders the perception of non-Jewish minorities as a demographic and a security threat and of the Jewish "ethiciities" (i.e., Arab and Ethiopian Jews) as a threat to the "Western" culture of the state.

Summary of the Book

The first eight chapters of the book address the problematics of Holocaust representation and the different ways in which Holocaust victims are depicted in Holocaust and history schoolbooks. These chapters focus on the photographs and on the verbal texts in which they are embedded. The study shows that in their transposition from Nazi archives and private albums to Israeli schoolbooks, the photographed individuals do not regain their subjectivity, and become icons, symbols and specimens of categories, that lack any personal traits or history. The photographs are often abstracted from their original context and the subjects are stripped of their human dignity and of their story. They are mostly used to authenticate the Zionist Holocaust narrative. In this narrative, the Holocaust becomes the "distillation of history, and Zionism its ultimate conclusion [...]

---

20. Grosbard, Ofer. 2003. *Israel on the Couch. The Psychology of the Peace Process*. Albany: State University of New York Press.
21. The *Twentieth Century: On the Threshold of Tomorrow*. For 9th grade. Tel Aviv Books Publishers.

though no room is made for the annihilated themselves" (Raz-Krakotzkin 2003, 166). The exterminated Jews have become "a huge mass of anonymous objects (The six million), in which the Jewish individuals have become part of the practice of non-remembrance through the routinized fetishism of Holocaust "memory". (Zimmerman and Zuckerman 2023, 11). Zuckerman (2023) argues that Zionist Israel betrayed the real Jewish victims by turning them into an ideology of victimhood.

In schoolbooks, as in the general social, cultural and political discourse, the focus is removed from the people themselves, and is placed on a concept or a class of people. The function of schoolbook images is to represent Holocaust related concepts: hunger, starvation, labeling (the yellow badge), hanged partisans, humiliated Jews or Mengele's victims. Hence, although the photographs are traumatizing and constitute what Holocaust historian Hannah Yablonka (2010/2021)[22] calls "the pornography of evil" the students are prompted to think about Holocaust sufferers conceptually and to categorize them as they would categorize phenomena in any other subject matter.

The traumatizing images of atrocity, which the schoolbooks display, are ruled by what Marianne Hirsch (2001, 26) terms "the murderous National Socialist gaze", and therefore the Nazi perspective often comes across as objective and factual. The present study suggests that Israeli schoolbooks are trapped in this gaze and reproduce it not only through the photographs, but also in the texts and in the questions that accompany the photographs. Thus, the textbooks often prompt young students to adopt the Nazi gaze and Nazi logic, which presents the victims as ultimate "others".

This representation of Holocaust sufferers is blatantly at odds with the way Israeli children are educated to respect Holocaust victims, to refer to them as "holy martyrs" and to remember them with awe. Schoolchildren in Israel are required to "adopt" a Holocaust victim, learn about him or her, prepare an identity card for them, and light a decorated candle to commemorate them. This activity, called "Name and Candle," is performed at home, together with other family members, to ensure that "Holocaust victims will not be erased from memory and Holocaust deniers will not prevail." The aim is "to create a family tradition of remembrance."[23] Notably, all children, whatever their origin and family history, are expected to fulfil this assignment, since the Holocaust is considered the most powerful means of unifying all Jewish Israelis (Naveh 2017).

The juxtaposition of such initiatives with the traumatizing photographs, the inculcation of the Nazi perspective through schoolbook texts, and the detailed

---

22. https://www.haaretz.co.il/news/education/2010-03-22/ty-article/0000017f-f43b-d47e-a37f-fd3f98a00000. Alfasi, Moran. February 7, 2021. "Coffee with Hannah Yablonka." https://www.onlife.co.il/general/21956
23. https://meyda.education.gov.il/files/noar/candle-and-name.pdf

pornography of evil and suffering the schoolbooks expose, attest to an interest on the part of the rhetors and designers of the curriculum, to "punch the children in their guts" as the inspector general Avraham Green declared in the 1990s (quoted in Miron 1994)[24], to traumatize them and thereby guarantee their loyalty to the state of Israel, and "not to let the fire of vengeance die out." However, this vengeance is not directed toward the German persecutors and their collaborators in Europe, but toward Palestinian colonized subjects and citizens.

The representation of Holocaust victims

The "othering" of Holocaust victims and survivors is to be found in early Zionist discourse, and especially in the words of the first Prime Minister, David Ben Gurion who forged the Israeli nation and construed its social ideology. He introduced the idea that there are Jews who are not-us, whom we do not want to become, and whom we do not want to have among us. Ben Gurion claimed, regarding holocaust victims, "these are not the Jews we want to be", which has evolved into: these are the Jews we will never be again! (Segev 2019)[25]. He stated publicly, "call me anti-Semitic but I must say this. We are choked with shame by what is going on in Germany and Poland, that Jews do not dare to struggle. We do not belong to this people; we revolt against such a Jewish people. We do not want to be such Jews."[26] Before their extermination they were, according to Ben Gurion, "the selected members of the nation," who should have built the Jewish state. However, Ben Gurion claimed, the Jews became victims because they did not listen to the Zionist call that urged them to migrate to Palestine, and for that he despised them and blamed them for their own catastrophe. According to him and to other Zionist leaders, most of the European Jews who survived the war and were brought to Israel in the years that followed were not a proper replacement for the exterminated ones. They were broken people, penniless refugees, and most of them had no interest in and no capacity for settling the land as pioneers or defending it as soldiers (Segev 2019). They disappointed Ben-Gurion as "human material" and he referred to them as "human debris." He often expressed his aversion toward them: "Among the survivors of the German concentration camps," he said, "were people who, were they not what they were—hard and bad and

---

24. Miron, Dan. 1994. "Between Books and Ashes. On the Holocaust Literature of Ka-Tzetnik." In *Alpayim* 10, 1196-224. Reprinted in Miron, Dan. 2005. *The Blind Library: Mixed Prose 1980-2005*. Hemed Books, Yediot Aharonot Publishers, 147-183 (Hebrew).
25. Segev, Tom. 2019. *A state at Any Cost*. Farrar, Straus and Giroux; Illustrated edition.
26. Segev, Tom. 2001. *One Palestine, Complete: Jews and Arabs Under the British Mandate*. Paperback – Illustrated. Picador Publishers.

egotistical people—would not have survived, and everything they endured purged their souls of all good." (Segev 2019, 448). Therefore, he believed, the Holocaust was a crime against the future State of Israel: "I see the terrible historical significance of the Nazi slaughter not as the frightening number of Jews who were massacred but rather as the extermination of that select part of the nation that alone, among all the Jews, was capable and equipped with all the characteristics and abilities needed for the building of a state," he wrote (Segev 2019, 446).

Segev notes that over the years Ben Gurion repeated this thesis any number of times: "More than Hitler wounded the Jewish people he knew and hated, he devastated the Jewish state, whose arrival he did not anticipate."(ibid.) With these words, Ben Gurion defined all the Israelis as Holocaust victims as well, and to this day Israeli teachers often remind children, "We are all Holocaust survivors."[27] Holocaust Historian Omer Bartov (1996, 178) phrases it as follows: "Just as the state can be traced back to the Holocaust, so too the Holocaust belongs to the state: the millions of victims were potential Israelis. And more: all Israelis are potential victims in the past, the present, and the future."

The connection between the Holocaust and the state of Israel is often expressed by students on school trips to the extermination camps, where they enter wrapped in Israeli flags. This connection is explained in a text reproduced in the final 2020 Hebrew Language examination for immigrant Jewish students from Ethiopia, in the Moshav Herev La'Et. The examination includes only texts about the Holocaust and its remembrance, which the newcomers have to read and discuss. One paragraph from a text written by Mor Cohen, an art student who works as a guide in Yad Vashem Museum, states as follows: "The trip to Poland is not only a learning excursion but also a pilgrimage […]. At its end we find solace and hope for life, expressed in the Israeli flags the students wrap around themselves, while singing the national anthem Hatikva."[28]

This is the message conveyed by soldiers who enter the camps in military uniform, followed by a display of Israeli air force planes,[29] enacting the other facet of the rhetoric of victimhood, namely the rhetoric of power, which is clearly expressed in the Teacher's Guide for second grade (2020):

> The students will understand that during WWII the Jews did not have a state. The establishment of the state of Israel guarantees our security and safety. We are in

---

27. Burg, Avraham. 2008. *The Holocaust Is Over; We Must Rise from its Ashes*. New York: St. Martin Press.
28. https://meyda.education.gov.il/files/Pop/0files/ivrit_habaah_lashon/chativat_elyona/bagrut-win/Poland.pdf
29. Segev, Tom. *The Seventh Million*; Naveh, Eyal. 2017. "Holocaust, army and faith."

conflict with the neighboring countries and with all the Arab countries, but now we can defend ourselves.[30]

Pre-school teacher Ruthie Katzav, who was quoted and lauded in Israeli papers on Holocaust Day 2019, also expressed this notion:

> What is a Holocaust? A Holocaust is a huge disaster, a huge disaster. And this disaster happened to the Jewish people when they were scattered all over the world, in other countries. Not in the Land of Israel but in other, different countries all over the world. Jews can travel and visit other countries, but every Jew should know that Israel is his only true home.[31]

Jews living outside Israel are still considered to be living in "exile."[32]

The Representation of Palestinians

The schoolbooks reflect Israeli socio-political discourse in which the Holocaust is used to legitimate the occupation of Palestine and the discrimination of Palestinian citizens, by using the Holocaust as an example of what might happen to Jewish Israelis if they are not alert and allow the Palestinians to threaten Israel's existence, or rather replace the Nazi exterminators. This view was already voiced by Prime Minister David Ben Gurion in 1951, when he justified the demand for reparations from Germany. The goal of the agreement, he argued, was to prevent the Jews from returning to the situation they were in before the Holocaust: "We do not want the Arab Nazis to come and slaughter us," he said. (Segev 2019, 481).
[33] Sociologist Zygmunt Bauman (2000,12) explains rather cynically this

---

30. http://meyda.education.gov.il/files/moe/shoa/chika.pdf
31. https://www.ynet.co.il/articles/0,7340,L-5502051,00.html
See also https://vimeo.com/136484147
32. In a letter inviting college teachers to attend a lecture on the occasion of International Holocaust Day, 2021 about Karen Gershon, a Holocaust survivor and a well-known British poet and writer, we were informed that Gershon chose to settle in England after the war. Then, upon the invitation of Israeli president Shazar, she migrated to Israel and lived there for six years before returning to England "to live in exile" (*galut*). When I asked the lecturer (an American Jewish anthropologist and writer who married an Ethiopian Jew and lives in Israel, lecturing and writing children's books about diversity and differences, mainly about "accepting the other" https://en.sw.huji.ac.il/people/naomi-shmuel),who wrote the letter, why she chose the word "exile", she replied, "perhaps I should have said *gola* (diaspora)." Upon my insistence that England was the writer's chosen home she replied: "Each to their own ideology but England is not her country." This assertion attests to the very deep conviction among Zionists that every Jew who lives outside Israel is in exile, whether s/he knows it or not (email correspondence with Naomi Shmuel, January 21, 2021).
33. Sources used by Segev: Carlebach 1951; Ben-Gurion, Golda Meir, and Mark Dvorzhetski to the Mapai Central Committee, Dec. 13, 1951; Ya'akov Sharett 2007, pp. 253, 221ff., 237ff.

Nazification: "The ancestors are pitied, but also blamed for allowing themselves to be led, like sheep, to the slaughter; how can one blame their descendants for sniffing out a future slaughterhouse in every suspicious-looking street or building or – more importantly still – for taking preventative measures to disempower the potential slaughterers?" Bauman (2000, 14) observes that the Israeli "hereditary victims" are the flawed children, who feel they live in a world that "contains the possibility of another Holocaust [...] a world populated by the Jew-hating murderers who would not stop short of including them among its victims if given a chance and not having their blood-soaked hands tied."

Sociologist Julia Resnik (2003, 314) observes that since the *intifada* (Palestinian popular uprising) of the 1980s, and given the growing legitimacy accorded the Palestinian cause by the world since the 1990s, the Jewish victim syndrome has become ever more entrenched in Israeli political life, clearly serving to counterbalance Palestinian political demands and to dismiss their moral claims as insignificant when weighed against the tragedy of the Holocaust. Thus, a national memory that underscores the tragedy of the Holocaust is invoked to confront Palestinian claims to their land and encourage their exclusion.[34] This discourse has been transposed to education. As educational philosopher Ilan Gur-Ze'ev (1999)[35] argued, the ethnocentric lesson drawn from the official account of the Holocaust in schools molds the Zionist subject by denying the "other"- the Palestinians and their suffering.

In order to insure the state's security against the Palestinians, they are treated as "human weeds", people who are deemed superfluous or "the elements of the present reality that neither fit the visualized perfect reality, nor can be changed so that they do." (Bauman 1989, 65). Bauman explains that regimes that strive to build a nationally pure state, where racism activates social engineering, can be equated metaphorically to a gardener who wishes to design the perfect garden. "All visions of society-as-garden define parts of the social habitat as human weeds. Like all other weeds, they must be segregated, contained, prevented from spreading, removed and kept outside the society boundaries; if all these means prove insufficient, they must be killed."

These practices, that were prevalent in settler colonial states such as Australia, South Africa, the USA, reached a monstrous peak in Nazi Germany, and are still prevalent, to a lesser extent, in all nation states, especially in settler-colonial states such as Israel (Wolfe 2012, Pappe 2012).

The on-going Nazification of Palestinians in Israeli schoolbooks is addressed in Chapters 10-11.

---

34. See Raz-Krakotzkin, Amnon. 1994. "Exile within sovereignty: toward a critique of the 'negation of exile' in Israeli culture." *Theory and Criticism* 5. 1-113 (Hebrew).
35. Gur-Ze'ev, Ilan. 1999. *Philosophy, Politics and Education in Israel*. University of Haifa and Zamora-Bitan Publishers (Hebrew).

The representation of Jewish "ethnicities"

Chapter 12 discusses the representation of Mizrahi or Arab-Jews in Israeli schoolbooks, and chapter 13 addresses the portrayal of Ethiopian Jews in these books. The present study does not compare these groups of people who came from different corners of the world, with different histories and different languages, but only the way they are perceived and represented in Israeli schoolbooks.

Since the European Jews they expected were lost, the Zionists had to seek out other Jews to fill up, at least a bit, at least physically, the empty space left by the victims of the Holocaust. These Jews were found in Muslim countries, yearning for Zion, but they were considered a-priori a poor substitute for the murdered Jews of Europe. "The divine presence withdrew from the eastern Jewish communities and they had little or no influence on the Jewish people," said the Prime Minister Ben Gurion (Segev 2019, 448). They had no place in the Zionist dream of resurrection. The lands they came from were perceived as replete with ignorance, poverty and slavery, and had fallen far behind the European nations, who had experienced rapid progress. (ibid). The fact that European culture and progress may have led to Auschwitz was never mentioned.

Mizrahi Jews were brought to Israel in large numbers before and especially after the inception of the state. They were put in camps, where Holocaust survivors were first lodged as well, surrounded by barbed wires and disinfected with DDT. Later they were transferred to makeshift tent settlements, which were not fit for human life, and then to poverty stricken neighborhoods and remote villages (Segev 2019). They were viewed as breeders of the new Jews who would forget their provenance, their culture, their languages and their religious customs, to become the new Israeli Sabras, strong, fearless and loyal to their state. (Segev 2019).

Historian Raz-Krakotzkin (2004) explains that the abhorrence expressed by the dominating Ashkenazi group of anything eastern, oriental, or non-Western, underlies their attitude both towards Holocaust victims and survivors who were referred to as "eastern Jews", and towards the Jews who were brought from Muslim countries, and were perceived as primitive Orientals, who had lived outside history and were in pressing need of cultivation. Ben Gurion conflated Holocaust survivors and Mizrahi Jews as one problematic mass for the young state, claiming that both groups were inferior to proper Israelis. He emphasized time and again that Zionist Jews in Palestine, who are a mixture of biblical heroes with European culture, have nothing in common with them. Both Holocaust survivors and non-European Jews were Jews, he said, "only in the sense that they are not non-Jews." (Segev 2019, 451). "We came here as Europeans," he exclaimed, "our roots are in the East and we are returning to the East, but we bear European culture with us. We will not want to cut off either our ties or Palestine's ties to European culture" (ibid.) Although Ben Gurion came to regret his racist words years later, his first impressions defined the Israeli stance toward Holocaust victims and survivors and towards non-Western Jews, and persist to this day, three generations after the great Aliya, in schoolbooks as in the society at large. He defined the problem of Mizrahi Jews as a "racial" one, suggesting that in Israel, "an ostensibly 'superior' race, the Ashkenazi race, stands out and in practice leads the nation, as opposed to an eastern race of 'inferior level.' "(Segev 2019, 451). As Bauman explains, social gardening, based on national purity "has no room for anything except the dominant culture." (1989, 92).

Other Zionist leaders such as Ze'ev Jabotinsky who declared, "We, the Jews, have nothing in common with what is called 'the East,' thank God," expressed the same perception over the years. (Segev, Ibid.) Prime Minister Golda Meir said in 1964, addressing the Zionist Federation of Great Britain and imploring them to immigrate to Israel, that Israel needs civilized people, for it has brought Jews from countries with a civilization of the 16th century: Morocco, Iran, Egypt etc., and she doubted that they could be elevated to a suitable level. Prime Minister Ehud Barak called Israel "a villa in the jungle" in an interview published in the New York Review of Books (June 13, 2002), where he described the people of the Middle East in the following words:

"They are the products of a culture in which to tell a lie [...] creates no dissonance. They don't suffer from the problem of telling lies that exists in Judeo-Christian culture." Years later, he apologized.

Yaakov Sharet, the son and biographer of the second Prime Minister Moshe Sharet, expressed these views in 2021:

> The Holocaust and Stalin's spiritual genocide changed the structure and the demographic complexity of Israel. Only when it was clear that those who should have come are gone, they brought other Jews. I do not underestimate them, they are Jews like me and you, but their background was different. They came from Muslim countries, different religious background, huge tribal families and the admiration of the patriarch. They came to Israel and changed everything. To this day, their coming causes problems and repercussions.[36]

While Palestinians are portrayed as potential exterminators - a race of primitive predators who will never change and are, therefore, a threat on the Jewish-Israeli physical existence - the Arab Jews are presented as a threat to Israeli Eurocentric culture. These Jewish "ethnicities" as they are termed in the social and political discourse, are not represented as "weeds" but as wild flowers that need to be "lovingly cultivated" (Bauman 1989), hence as people who constitute a civilizing burden for Israel. Just how entrenched this conception is emerges in the following letter sent by the chief pedagogical officer in the Ministry of Education, the

---

36. Haaretz. September 18. 2021 in an interview with Ofer Aderet.

educational psychologist Yaakov Katz, to journalist Akiva Eldar (2004), regarding critical studies of Israeli schoolbooks, including my own. Katz received his Ph.D. from Witwatersrand University in Johannesburg in 1985, during the Apartheid era, has held several senior positions in the Israeli Ministry of Education, in religious colleges and in Bar Ilan religious university. He resigned from the ministry following accusations of embezzlement. [37] These biographical details are significant because of the similarity between Israel and Apartheid South Africa, with respect to our topic of discussion. As Lawrence Davidson (2012, 65)[38] points out, "Israelis like South African whites before them like to think of themselves as an isolated western enclave in a non-western world. The result of both cases is not integration with the West but rather self-imposed isolation that allows for the preservation of racist and ethnocentric attitudes, outdated imperialism and colonialism, attitudes that are long unpopular in the west."

Prof. Katz's letter reads as follows:

> It is our view that one must understand that the leaders of the state have always seen Israel, ever since its establishment, as a Jewish democratic advanced state, as having a distinct Western orientation despite its heterogeneous population. Jews from Muslim countries or those who live in the periphery have, like the Arab citizens, equal rights in our Western state and no one can expect that the education system should distort this reality only to create a false and artificial feeling of equality. The real equality and the real sense of belonging are nourished by the state's being a Jewish democratic state, which grants equal rights to all its citizens, without blurring its significant Western orientation.

The letter divides Israeli citizens into "our Western state" and all the "others," who include both Jewish and Muslim minorities, both natives and immigrants, to whom "we," the dominant minority group of "whites," grant certain rights but not full equality, in order to preserve our western character. This Eurocentric orientation, expressed to this day in schoolbooks and educational curricula, consistently adheres to the perception of a divided population in which "peripheral" elements are naturally segregated and regarded as "others." These include the Palestinian citizens of Israel and the Jews whose families originate from Muslim countries, as well as the Ethiopian Jewish citizens. They should not, according to Katz, seek to impose on the Western state a false, distorted, and artificial concept of equality, which cannot be realized because of their non-European provenance.

Although Katz's letter dates from 2004, the racist attitude he expresses has not changed much as recent studies prove. [39] Educational and financial gaps

---

37. May 11, 2006. https://www.ynet.co.il/articles/0,7340,L-3249516,00.html
38. *Cultural Genocide*
39. Kashti or, Haaretz. June 11, 2021. https://www.haaretz.com/israel-news/.premium-when-it-comes-to-education-israel-s-ashkenazi-mizrahi-divide-is-still-growing-1.9894471.

between Ashkenazi and Mizrahi Jews have not changed much in the last three generations. [40]

All these groups are equally portrayed as homogenous populations without history and without culture, apart from some folkloristic customs; as the Mizrahi Jews before them, Ethiopian Jews are seen as people who need to make a "leap to the 21st century" as one schoolbook puts it, [41] and whom Israel must help to pave their way "back" to proper Judaism. As Inbar Peled (2018, 12)[42] argues in her thesis *The Racialization of Ethiopian Jews in Israeli Law*, "The religious system that questions the Jewish provenance of Ethiopian Israelis has direct influence on their citizenship, but also on their exclusion from different citizenship spheres, such as education." However, the Israeli state insists on engineering its society, forge people's nature and mold all the Jewish citizens in the image of the mythological Zionist Western Israeli patriot.

The idea that Israelis must negate the Jewish Exile, just as Ben Gurion "forgot that he was Polish" (Segev 2019) is still promoted through education, along with the idea that Palestine had not had any life or history for the millennia "we" were not there. (*The Mediterranean Countries*, 54)

The educational message of the schoolbooks studied in the present work is that there are people who are worthy of belonging to the dominant group and people who are not worthy. The worthy ones must dominate the unworthy ones, "lovingly" cultivate them, or distance and eliminate them if they are deemed superfluous or dangerous. All the unworthy "others" are perceived not as individuals but as phenomena, and may be described in categories, of which each individual is but a sample. They do not enjoy the privileges of the worthy ones, even in their representation.

Hovering above the state is "the ghost of the Holocaust [which] appears self-perpetuating and self-producing" (Bauman 2000, 15). The holocaust ghost produces the Israeli rhetoric of victimhood and power that is promoted in schoolbooks, and teaches that "life is about surviving, to succeed in life is to outlive the others" (Bauman ibid.), both physically and culturally.

The condescending stance towards Holocaust victims and survivors, and the colonialist racist attitude and discriminatory practices towards non-Jewish and non-Western citizens, have been extensively discussed in history, sociology and

---

See also: Cohen Yinon, Noah Lewin-Epstein and Amit Lazarus 2019. Mizrahi-Ashkenazi Educational Gaps in the Third Generation. February 2019. *Research in Social Stratification and Mobility* 59 (2019) 25–33.
40. Kashti or, Haaretz. June 11, 2021. https://www.haaretz.com/israel-news/.premium-when-it-comes-to-education-israel-s-ashkenazi-mizrahi-divide-is-still-growing-1.9894471.
41. Avieli-Tabibian, K. 2009 *Journeys in Time: Building a State in the Middle East*. Tel Aviv: The Center for Education Technology. 239; See also Naveh et al. 2009, 300
42. *From Michael Brown to Yosef Salamsa: The Racialization of Ethiopian Jews in Israeli Law*. Unpublished dissertation for Masters in Law. Toronto University. Faculty of Law

literary texts, some of which will be mentioned throughout the present work, as it explores the multimodal representation of these groups in Israeli textbooks.

Chapter 14 reviews the main conclusions to be drawn from the analysis, and chapter 15 proposes to deconstruct the official "pedagogic" narrative and introduce, in a joint narrative, other versions and other interpretations, which Homi Bhabha (2000) calls "performative", and are to be found not only in official texts but in stories, art, folklore, in social practices and in the memories of people, especially those who are exiled in their own country, and are expected to forget their history. Hence, the joint curriculum should be multi-voiced and polycentric, and abandon the ideological writing of history, with its Eurocentric perspective[43] under the guise of "facts that speak for themselves".

The joint narrative would follow the principles of multidirectional memory (Michael Rothberg 2009, 22-23)[44], based on an interaction between Holocaust memory and other traumatic memories of slavery, decolonization, racism, and dispossession such as the Nakba. Multidirectional memory may lead to a multidirectional ethics, and combine "the capacious open-endedness of the universal with the concrete, situational demands of the particular."(ibid.) The public articulation of collective memory by marginalized and oppositional social groups can provide resources for other groups to articulate their own claims for recognition and justice (Rothberg ibid.).

In the joint curriculum, the Middle East should be presented not as a hostile entity to be conquered but as the cradle of all three major monotheistic civilizations that co-exist on the land of Israel/Palestine, and as the cultural provenance of most Israelis. It should offer a dialogic discourse that calls for discussion, and for openness rather than closure.[45]

Methodology

As in my previous studies,[46] I adopt a Social Semiotic approach to the analysis of textbooks and the methods of Multimodal Discourse Analysis,[47] to examine the

---

43. I adopt Stam and Shohat's definition of Eurocentrism: "Eurocentrism as the discursive precipitate of colonial domination, a kind of vestigial mental grid or epistemic machinery that enshrined colonialism's hierarchical stratifications, rendering them as natural, inevitable, and even 'progressive.'" (2014. 387)
44. Michael Rothberg, *Multidirectional Memory: Remembering the Holocaust in the Age of Decolonization*. Stanford: Stanford University Press, 2009.
45. Holquist, M. 2009. *Dialogism: Bakhtin and His World*. Psychology Press, USA, Routledge.
46. Peled-Elhanan, Nurit. 2009a. "The Geography of Hostility Discursive and Semiotic Means of transforming Realities in Geography School Books." *Journal of Visual Literacy* 27, no.2. 179-208; Peled-Elhanan, Nurit. 2009b. "Layout as punctuation of semiosis: some examples from Israeli schoolbooks." *Visual Communication* 8 (1).

semiotic means used in communication.[48] Since the representation of Holocaust victims and of contemporary "others" in schoolbooks reflects the prevalent social attitudes toward them (Resnik 2003, 298)[49], the semiotic expression of these attitudes and practices, be it a written, visual, or any other type of sign, is best analyzed in social-semiotic terms.

Carey Jewitt (2016, 146) summarizes the benefits to be gained from a Social semiotic study as follows:

> Social semiotics sets out to understand how representations are produced by and contribute to cultural settings, that is, to get at their social function and meaning potential in the communicative landscape. Their textual features are analyzed in order to comment on social relations, power, signification, the interests of sign makers, the imagined audience, and the social purposes realized by texts.

Social Semiotics assumes that all signs are made to function in communication (Kress 2010). Meanings and knowledge are *made* in signs or sign-complexes in distinct ways in specific modes, none of which are arbitrary (Kress 1993).[50] Signs are motivated by interest and ideology and are shaped by their history and current usage in a given culture (Kress 2010).[51] The meaning of every sign - be it verbal or visual, including color and layout - is determined not only by the sign's inherent qualities but also by the way it interacts with the other signs, by its

---

Peled-Elhanan, Nurit. 2010. "Legitimation of massacres in Israeli school history books." In *Discourse and Society*. Sage Publishers.
Peled-Elhanan, Nurit. 2014. "The De-Humanization of Palestinians in Israeli Schoolbooks: A Multimodal Analysis." In *Visual Communication*, edited by D. Machin, Boston, MA: Degruyter Publishing House. 327-340.
47. Kress, Gunther. 2012. "Multimodal discourse analysis." In *The Routledge Handbook of Discourse Analysis*. Edited by James Paul Gee and Michael Handford. Routledge. 35-50; Jewitt, Carey and Berit Henriksen. 2016. "Social Semiotic Multimodality." In: *Handbuch Sprache im multimodalen Kontext*, edited by Nina-Maria Klug. De Gruyter; Machin, David. 2013. "What is multimodal critical discourse studies?" *Critical Discourse Studies*, 10 (4). 347-355; Machin, David and Andrea Myar. 2012. *How to do Critical Discourse Analysis a Multimodal Introduction*. Sage Publishers; Van Leeuwen, Theo. 2013. "Critical Analysis of Multimodal Discourse." In *The Encyclopedia of Applied Linguistics*. Edited by Carol Chapelle. Wiley-Blackwell. 1-6.
48. Kress, Gunther & Theo van Leeuwen. 2006. *Reading Images The Grammar of Visual Design*. Routledge; Van Leeuwen, Theo. 2005. *Introducing Social Semiotics*. London and New York: Routledge; Van Leeuwen, Theo. 2008. *Discourse and Practice. New Tools for Critical Discourse Analysis*. Oxford Studies in Sociolinguistics.
49. Resnik, Julia. 2003. Sites of memory' of the Holocaust: shaping national memory in the education system in Israel. Nations and Nationalism 9 (2). ASEN 2003. 297–317.
50. Kress, G. 1993. "Against Arbitrariness: The Social Production of the Sign as a Foundational Issue in Critical Discourse Analysis. *Discourse in Society* 4(2). 169–191.
51. Kress, Gunther. 2010. *Multimodality: A Social Semiotic Approach to Contemporary Communication*. London: Routledge.

location in a certain site (e.g. a page in a schoolbook) at a certain moment, by its material features, and by its metaphoric qualities.[52]

Keith Jenkins (1991, 86)[53] asserts that "History is never said or read innocently for it is always for someone." The texts of history schoolbooks are not only "for" someone but also for something. They serve a social purpose. Therefore, every sign they contain should be conceived as being motivated by the interests, perspectives, values, and positions of the sign maker regarding the intended message and its recipients. These can be inferred from the text and testify to educational purposes and power relations.

The social semiotic approach is conducive to the analysis of textbooks because it is "not a pure theory or a self-contained field [...] it does not offer ready-made answers but rather provides ideas to formulate questions about human meaning making through sign making. [...] Social Semiotics only comes into its own when it is applied to specific instances and specific problems and it always requires immersing oneself not just in semiotic concepts and methods as such but also in some other field [...] interdisciplinarity is an absolutely essential feature for a social semiotic analysis" (van-Leeuwen 2005, 2).

A wide-ranging multidisciplinary literature serves as the theoretical foundation for the present study. It includes, besides history and multimodality, cultural studies and post-colonial studies,[54] everyday racism,[55] anthropology,[56] ethnography[57] and sociology,[58] multiliteracies (the London Group), and dialogue (Holquist 2009).

---

52. Forceville, Ch. 2016. "Pictorial and multimodal metaphor." In *Handbuch Sprache im multimodalen Kontext [The Language in Multimodal Contexts Handbook]*, edited by Nina-Maria Klug and Hartmut Stöckl. Mouton de Gruyter.
53. Jenkins, K. 1991. *Re-thinking History*. London: Routledge.
54. Appadurai, A.2006. *Fear of Small Numbers, an Essay on the Geography of Anger*. Duke University Press; Mbembe, Achilles. 2001. *On the Post Colony*. University of California Press.
55. Essed, Philomena. 1991. *Understanding Everyday Racism. An Interdisciplinary Theory*. SAGE Series on Race and Ethnic Relations; van Leeuwen, T. and R. Wodak. 1999. "Legitimizing Immigration Control: A Discourse-Historical Analysis." *Discourse Studies* 1(1). 83–118; Reisigl Martin and Ruth Wodak. 2001. *Discourse and Discrimination: Rhetorics of Racism and Antisemitism*.
56. Hertzog, Esther 1999. "Immigrants and Bureaucrats: Ethiopians in an Israeli Absorption Center." *New Directions in Anthropology*, vol. 7. New York, Oxford: Berghahn Books. Salamon, Hagar. 2003. "Blackness in Transition: Decoding Racial Constructs through Stories of Ethiopian Jews." In *Journal of Folklore Research* 40, no. 1 (Jan. – Apr.). Indiana University Press. 3-32.
57. Heath, Shirley Brice and Brian V. Street. 2008. *On ethnography: approaches to language and literacy research*. Teachers College Press, Teachers College, Columbia University.
58. In this study, I shall rely mainly on the sociological studies of Julia Resnik, Zygmunt Bauman, Yosefa Loshitzky, Arjun Appadurai and Ben-Eliezer, Uri. 2004. "Becoming a Black Jew: Cultural Racism and Anti-Racism in Contemporary Israel." *Social Identities* 10, no. 2.

"Rhetoric is the Politics of Communication" (Kress 2012)

The social semiotic theory of communication adopts a rhetorical approach (Kress 2012). Hence, the two principal considerations to be taken into account when studying multimodal texts such as schoolbooks are **rhetoric** and **design**. Both are socially motivated, rooted in specific instances and in a specific culture. Every representation reflects the intentions of both the rhetor and the designer of the complex sign, which may be a single phrase, or visual sign, a page, a double spread, or the entire book. The rhetor and the designer may or may not be the same person, but it is the rhetorical considerations that dictate the design, especially when academic material is re-contextualized for educational purposes. The task of the rhetor is "to assess and describe the salient aspects of the environment of communication" (Kress 2012, 41), in order to establish the conditions for communication: who are the participants and what are their characteristics? In the present study, the participants may be teachers and seven-year-old schoolchildren or high school students, who will soon be drafted into the army to maintain a regime of occupation. The rhetor's intent and purposes, or his/her agency, shape the actions of the designer, "whose agency in turn shapes the realization of the rhetor's intent."(ibid.) In other words, design "assumes the prior action of the rhetor. The designer "has the task of turning the rhetorical assessment of the environment, of the audience and of the means for materializing these into a design most likely to meet the political aims of the rhetor," maintains Kress (2012, 47).[59] Design is a response to questions such as, what mode is apt here? Kress (2020, 45) asserts that "the choice of mode represents a semiotic positioning, arrived at by the communicational requirements both of the initial maker of a sign or sign-complex, and the interpretative semiotic work of the person who engages with the prompt." In the case of schoolbooks, the initial maker is the rhetor-educator, and those who engage with the prompt are the students.

Bezemer and Kress (2008, 183) explain that "for the designer of the learning resource the question becomes one of aptness of the level of specificity-generality and arrangement for the specific occasion". The "occasion" includes the subject matter and the audience, which in this study comprises Israeli students from three to eighteen years old. The choice of mode of representation has implications for pedagogy. It "strongly sets the 'ground' for engagement and learning."(ibid.). In one mode actors are foregrounded, in another, actors can be backgrounded; in one mode, reading paths may be set by the learner, in another by the designer. Thus, the designer's epistemological commitment differs from that of the rhetor. The designer has to show for instance, what each element or character looks like, the

---

59. Gee, James Paul Ed. The *Routledge Handbook of Discourse Analysis*. Routledge.

relative proportions and the distance between two elements. These are necessarily part of the designer's considerations (ibid. 2008, 177).[60]

The interest that motivates the re-contextualization or the creation of the new signs for educational goals is "professionally shaped," (Kress 2020, 35), and "it is one means by which power enters into the transposition of meaning." It is power that transforms content and meaning in accordance with ideological and pedagogical norms that pertain to the way schoolchildren are encouraged to relate to the new signs and to the way the new signs - such as photographs in textbooks - are designed to affect them. Therefore, when one considers any act of sign making, one must always inquire into the power position of the rhetor and the designer with their audience.

A further question one should ask is what are the semiotic requirements of the content to be communicated, in our case the representation of Holocaust victims and of "minorities" in Israel?

The Multimodal Discourse Analysis (MMDA) of textbooks should expose both the rhetorical and the design considerations of the writers and editors of the textbooks, which determine the *criterial features* (Kress 2020)[61] of every sign on which they wish the students to focus, as well as the non-criterial features they prefer the students to ignore.

The Nature of Schoolbooks

Schoolbooks are a perfect example of what Kress (2000, 132-133) calls the "momentary congealing of semiosis," or "a punctuation of semiosis," for they bring "the process of semiosis [...] which is always multimodal [...] to a temporary standstill in textual form."[62] This means that textbooks reflect the interpretation of reality by the powers that be at the moment of their publication. Holocaust textbooks, being a punctuation of the official semiosis, reflect the current position taken by the state regarding the post-Holocaust slogan *Never Again!* a position that would inevitably be reflected in the representation of the Holocaust itself, but also in the representation of contemporary "others," and would justify their integration and their "cultivation," or else their distancing and elimination.

---

60. Writing in Multimodal Texts: A Social Semiotic Account of Designs for Learning *Written Communication* 2008. 25. 166
61. Beyond Words: Translation and Multimodality
62. Kress, G. 2000. "Text as the Punctuation of Semiosis: Pulling at Some Threads." In *Intertextuality and the Media*, edited by Meinhof, U.H. and J. Smith. Manchester: Manchester University Press. 132-155.

As Basil Bernstein (1996, 39)[63] maintained, "Pedagogic communication is often viewed as a carrier, a relay for ideological messages and for external power relations."

Ideological Common Ground and Basic Assumptions

As "any fully functioning semiotic resource," every text "must have the potential to meet three demands: to represent states of affairs in the world (ideational function), to represent or establish relations between reader and writer, speaker and listener (interpersonal function), and to represent all this as a message-entity, namely as text which is internally coherent and coheres with its environment (textual function)." (Kress 2010, 87).

All schoolbooks around the world must obey a certain perception and rules of representation dictated by the state. These determine the choice of facts and their arrangement as well as the paper time devoted to each event and personality. Furthermore, they shape the speech acts of the text, or in Barthes' words, determine what the text will say with what it says.

Schoolbooks in general do not simply represent the factual state of affairs, for they are required to create a "usable past" (Wertsch 2002) for future citizens, and are less concerned with reproducing the facts. They serve to shape compliant readers who will question neither the basic ideological assumptions of the educational discourse nor the facts that the book provides them. The books are designed to be reader friendly by presenting their subject matter in a coherent, engaging and attractive manner, especially when, as in the Israeli case, schoolbooks are trade books and teachers can choose what they like. However, all textbooks must be authorized by the Ministry of Education. This means that they must share an ideological common ground that rests on several indisputable basic assumptions (Fairclough 2003) that underlie the national master narrative. Upon this ideological common ground (Fairclough, 2003) all facts are constituted and all narratives are fashioned. Fairclough divides the fundamental ideological assumptions into three groups. The first contains **existential assumptions**, which relate to what exists or to the current state of affairs. In the Israeli political and educational discourse, what exists beyond doubt is antisemitism and the Jews' "historical" and "natural" rights to the entire land of Palestine and Israel, which is termed the Land of Israel.

The second group contains **propositional assumptions**: what can be the case? These assumptions trace an irrefutable scenario. The assumption common to all Israeli books is that Palestinian citizens and occupied subjects constitute a

---

63. Bernstein, Basil. 1996. *Pedagogy, symbolic control and identity*. London: Taylor and Francis.

demographic problem and a security threat, which could become fatal if not controlled.

The third group contains **value assumptions:** What is good and desirable? A Jewish state with a Jewish majority, and Israeli control. None of these basic assumptions has changed since early Zionism (Pappe 2017).

Schoolbooks are both hypertexts and intertexts: "intertexts," because they both refer to other texts and transform or re-contextualize texts of different genres. They are "hypertexts" in Gérard Genette's [64] sense of hypertextuality, which denotes any relation that a certain text B bears with a previous text A (the hypotext) from which it is derived or onto which it is "grafted." Images, like verbal texts, are always intertextualized with other texts. As Burgin (1982,144) [65] explains, "The intelligibility of the photograph is no simple thing; photographs are texts inscribed in terms of what may be called 'photographic discourse,' but this discourse, like any other, is the site of a complex 'intertextuality,' an overlapping series of previous texts 'taken for granted' at a particular cultural and historical conjuncture. These prior texts are presupposed by the photograph and are autonomous; they serve a role in the actual text but do not appear in it."

Israeli schoolbooks are derived from and grafted onto the dominant Zionist sociopolitical hypotext and their respective disciplinary hypotexts. Israeli schoolbooks comprise a "supra-disciplinary" [66] genre that combines various discourses and draws on different disciplines. Alongside the historical narrative or the geographical descriptions, one finds artistic visuals, poems, extracts from novels and maps accompanied by legitimating excerpts from the scriptures. For example, the chapter about animal and human reproduction in a science book is legitimated by the phrase: "And God blessed them, saying, be fruitful, and multiply, and fill the waters in the seas, and let fowl multiply in the earth." (Genesis 1:22).

Therefore, regarding every scholarly text and especially textbooks, one must ask the questions Edward Said asks: 'Who writes? For whom is the writing being done? In what circumstances?" And add Kress' (2010) question, for what purpose and from what position of power?

The Schoolbooks

The study examines general history and Holocaust schoolbooks, as well as civic studies and geography schoolbooks. The analysis focuses on "what is to be

---

64. Genette, Gérard. 1982. *Palimpseste: La littérature au second degré*. Paris: Editions du Seuil, 12-14.
65. Burging, Victor. 1982. "Looking at Photographs." In *Looking at Photographs*, edited by V. Burgin. Macmillan.
66. De Beaugrand, Robert. 1980. *Text, Discourse, and Process: Toward a Multidisciplinary Science of Texts*. Ablex.

communicated and on the means available for materializing the meanings at issue and the means most apt in terms of the social environment" (Kress 2012, 47), which in our case is the Israeli Jewish mainstream school. Although the present book focuses mainly on junior high school and high school schoolbooks, the books I examined are for all school levels: elementary school, junior and high school. I also investigated the Holocaust curriculum for pre-school, published by Yad Vashem and titled *Down Memory Lanes*. [67]

It is worth noting that three of the Holocaust schoolbooks (two schoolbooks by Mishol, 2014 and one by Hertz, 2015) were published in Jewish colonies in the Occupied Palestinian Territories, but they are presented as if they were published in Israel. [68]

The Multimodal Schoolbook

All schoolbooks are multimodal. (Van Leeuwen 1992). The study of multimodal texts such as schoolbooks considers the page or the double-spread as a single semiotic unit that conveys meaning beyond or apart from the meaning of any of its parts. Every linguistic or visual semiotic resource plays a role in making the meaning of the text, and each part of the verbal text and the visual content contributes to the whole through its position and function, and is interpreted with respect to the whole.[69] As theoretical physicist and semiotician Jay Lemke (1998, 283)[70] explains, "Meanings are not fixed and additive (the word meaning plus the picture meaning), but multiplicative (word meaning modified by image context, image meaning modified by textual context), making a whole far greater than the sum of its parts."

Lemke (2004) observes that since language is typological by nature it can name, categorize and label, but people's look, their expressions or their gaze, and the way they relate to one another or to us as viewers belong to the realm of the visual, which is topological and can reflect movement and degree.

---

67. https://cms.education.gov.il/EducationCMS/UNITS/Moe/Shoa
68. The Holocaust schoolbooks that are used in most mainstream schools are: Gutman 2009. *Totalitarianism and Shoah*. Yad Va-Shem and Shazar Inst., Publishers; Bar Hillel and Inbar 2010. *Nazism and Shoah*. Lilach Pub.; Tabibian, Ketsia 2009. *From Peace to War*. Shoah Institute for Educational Technologies; Naveh et al. 2009. *Totalitarianism and Shoah*. Rehes Pub.; Mishol. 2014. *Nazism, War and Shoah*. High School Pub.; Keren, Nili. 1998. *Shoah: A Journey into Memory*. Tel Aviv Books Publishers. All these schoolbooks were examined in this study.
69. Halliday. 1985. *An Introduction to Functional Grammar*. Routledge. xiii
70. Lemke. 1998. "Multiplying Meaning: Visual and verbal semiotics in scientific text." In J.R. Martin & R. Veel, Eds., *Reading Science. Critical and functional perspectives on discourses of science*. London: Routledge, 87-113.

Part I

The Othering of Holocaust Victims

Chapter 1. Representing the Holocaust

While historians, literary critics, poets, writers and sociologists have extensively studied the powerful presence of the Holocaust as a defining element of Jewish Israeli identity at both the personal and national levels, and of the conduct of the Israeli state toward its minorities, subjects, and neighbors,[1] the multimodal representation of the Holocaust and of contemporary minorities in schoolbooks has yet to be studied. Scholars who have examined the representation of the Holocaust in history books, movies, museums and digital media have barely turned their attention to schoolbooks.[2] Numerous works of history,[3] sociology,[4] philosophy,[5] and literature [6] focus on the representation of the Holocaust. Numerous works in the fields of cultural studies, post-colonial studies, and racism, examine the relation between the Holocaust and other forms of racism and violence toward "others", both in general and in Israel, [7] and the representation of "others" in general [8] and in Israel.[9] All these studies are highly relevant to the realm of education and to the representation of the Holocaust and of discriminated "others" in Israeli schoolbooks.

The question is how should Holocaust victims be represented to children? Should they be represented in written texts, in photographs or in cartoons? Through poems, movies, or by historical documents? Should written testimonies

---

1. Raz-Krakotzkin, Amnon. 2013. "History Textbooks and the Limits of Israeli Consciousness."
2. For instance, Friedländer, Saul. 1992. *Probing the Limits of Representation: Nazism and the "Final Solution"*; LaCapra *Representing the Holocaust*; Shandler, Jeffery. 2017. *Holocaust Memory in the Digital Age*. Stanford, California: Stanford University Press; Holtschneider, Hannah K. 2011. *The Holocaust and Representations of Jews*. Routledge Jewish Studies Series. Taylor and Francis. Kindle Edition.
3. See, for example, the articles by Hayden White and Saul Friedländer, in *Probing the Ethics of Holocaust Culture*. 2016, edited by Claudio Fogu, Wulf Kansteiner, and Todd Presner. Harvard University Press; and the works of LaCapra, Amos Goldberg, Alon Confino, Idit Zertal, Tom Segev, and Moshe Zuckermann.
4. Bauman, Zygmunt; Kimmerling Baruch.
5. Zizek, Derrida, Benjamin, Adorno, Steiner, Arendt, Agamben.
6. Anthelme, Robert. 1947. *L'Espèce Humaine*. éditions de la Cité Universelle. (The Human Race. Marlboro Press, 1998); Levi, Primo. *Is This a Man*; Semprun, Jose. *L'Ecriture ou La Vie*; Duras, Margueritte. *La Douleur*; Perec, George. *W ou le souvenir d'enfance*; Kambanellis, Iakovos. *Mauthausen*.
7. Rothberg 2006, Goldberg and Hazan 2015, Goldberg and Bashir 2018
8. Appadurai, Bhabha, Shohat, Mbembe, Said, Essed.
9. Kimmerling, Baruch. 2001. *The Invention and Decline of Israeliness: State, Society, and the Military*, University of California Press; Wolfe, Patrick. 2016. *Traces of History. Elementary Structures of Race*. Verso Books.

be replaced by recorded interviews (Shandler 2017),[10] or be transducted into more animated contemporary forms of expression, such as the diary of Eva Heyman, which was transducted from a written document into fictitious Instagram blogs ("Eva's Story"), or from words to images as in *Ann Frank Graphic Adaptation*[11]. Are graphic novels such as Spiegelman's *Maus* or Michel Kishka's *The Second Generation – Things I have not told my Father?* Better for describing the Holocaust? There is no doubt that they are more successful.

Educators may also grapple with the issue of whether the Holocaust should be presented as an unexpected but somehow explainable phase of Western history, its culture, and religions,[12] or rather as a monstrous consequence of human nature,[13] a crazed fantasy of a single anti-Semitic man who cast a spell on the world, an interpretation which turns Hitler into an "entity that remains outside human perception and grasp" (Landau 2016, 36).

Many thinkers view Nazism as a continuation of European imperialism (e.g., Arendt 1979, 123), itself a product of industrialization and of the Enlightenment.[14] Modernity, they argue, paved the way for colonialism, which post-colonial thinkers such as Aimé Césaire and Franz Fanon regard as the precursor of Nazism.[15] However, contrary to Robert Young's remark that "It took a Césaire or a Fanon to point out that fascism was simply colonialism brought home to Europe,"[16] European thinkers too have traced the same continuity between the Enlightenment, colonialism and Nazism. In 1942, the German-American philosopher Karl Korsch[17] wrote: "The novelty of totalitarian politics […] is simply that the Nazis have extended to 'civilized' European peoples the methods hitherto reserved for the 'natives' or 'savages' living outside so-called civilization." Hannah Arendt traced the roots of totalitarianism in European imperialist and

---

10. Shandler, Jeffrey. 2017. *Holocaust Memory in the Digital Age: Survivors' Stories and New Media*. Stanford, California: Stanford University Press.
11. https://www.yadvashem.org/education/educational-materials/books/dear-diary.html
Ann Frank Graphic Adaptation Illustrated by David Polonsky 2018 Penguin.
12. Steiner, George. 1974. *In Bluebeard's Castle: Some Notes Towards the Redefinition of Culture*. Yale University Press; Literary critic Dan Miron observes that the Hebrew-writing author Haim Hazaz and poet Uri Zvi Greenberg found the origins of the Holocaust in Christianity.
https://www.haaretz.co.il/literature/prose/.premium-1.9463326
https://www.haaretz.co.il/literature/study/.premium-1.9391580
13. Canetti, Elias. 1984. *Crowds and Power*. Continuum. New York.
14. Adorno, Theodor W. 1997. *Can One Live After Auschwitz? A Philosophical Reader*, edited by Rolf Tiedemann, translated by Rodney Livingstone and others. 2003. *Cultural Memory in the Present*. Issue 5, Borders and Boundaries Series. Stanford: Stanford University Press.
15. Fanon, Franz. 1967. *Black Skin White* Mask, 33; Césaire, Aimé. 1972. "Discourse on Colonialism." *Monthly Review Press*. New York, 14.
16. Young, R.C. 2004. *White Mythologies*. Routledge, Abingdon, 39.
17. Notes on History: The Ambiguities of Totalitarian Ideologies In: New Essays. A Quarterly Devoted to the Study of Modern Society, Vol. 6 (1942), no 2 (Fall), p. 1-9

colonialist history,[18] And J.P Sartre exclaimed: "with us there is nothing more consistent than a racist humanism since the European has only been able to become a man through creating slaves and monsters."[19]

Modernity, as Zygmunt Bauman (1989) observes, and the belief that man, with the help of scientific means, can create a perfect society, offered the technology and the justification to engineer societies rationally, and hence to subjugate and eliminate entire populations considered worthless or dangerous,[20] or, as Arendt puts it, superfluous and dispensable.[21] "For the modern mind, says Bauman, the elimination of inferior and unworthy elements was an act of creation [...] Perfection could only be achieved by the purging of imperfections. The story of modernity, and particularly of its twentieth century denouement, was a chronicle of creative destruction. The atrocities that marked the course of what Eric Hobsbawm called the "short century," from 1914 to 1989, were born of a dream of orderliness purity, clarity, and the transparency of ultimate perfection" (Bauman 2013, 33. 34)[22]

The Final Solution, argue other scholars in the same vein, was the disastrous product of modern bureaucratic machinery, "the progressive bureaucratization of killing [that] has placed a steadily increasing distance between the perpetrators and the consequences of their decisions and actions" (Landau 2016, 9), an observation that echoes Adorno (2002).[23] In Landau's view (2016, 15), "bureaucracy is a human invention which can subjugate its inventor, undermine human conscience and allow individuals to abdicate personal moral responsibility. 'It's the system's fault, not mine!'"

---

18. Arendt, Hannah. 1951. *The Origins of Totalitarianism* (New York: Harcourt Brace).
19. Sartre, J.P. 1976a. *Critique of Dialectical Reason. I: Theory of Practical Ensembles.* Trans. Alan Sheridan Smith. London: New Left Books. 752.
20. Bauman, Zygmunt. 1989. *Modernity and the Holocaust.* Polity Press.
21. Arendt, Hannah. "The Jew as Pariah. A Hidden Tradition." *Jewish Social Studies* 6, no. 2 (April 1944). 99-122; see too *Eichmann in Jerusalem.*
22. "The Role of Modernity: What was it and is it about?" *Dapim: Studies on the Holocaust*, 2013. Vol. 27, No. 1, 40–73. Routledge. Taylor and Francis Group.
The short century ends in May 1989 when the new Russian Congress met for its first session, and newspapers, television and radio stations, were newly empowered by the lifting of press restrictions under glasnost. Perestroika. https://www.history.com/topics/cold-war/perestroika-and-glasnost
23. Horkheimer, Max and Theodor W. Adorno. 2002. *Dialectic of Enlightenment. Philosophical Fragments*, edited by Gunzelin Schmidt Noerr, translated by Edmund Jephcott. Stanford University Press.

Writing the Holocaust

> The extermination of the Jews of Europe is as accessible to both representation and interpretation as any other historical event. But we are dealing with an event which tests our traditional conceptual and representational categories. (Friedländer, 1992, 2-3)

Hayden White (2016, 51)[24] observes that the Holocaust was "a new kind of event that effectively brought under question the representational practices and modes of explanation both of modern historiography and the modern human sciences in general."

Turning to the means of representation, or to the question of design (Kress 2012), scholars still debate whether one should use conventional tools to represent the Holocaust, or rather post-modern tools of analysis to deconstruct it.[25] Should one use predominantly archives or personal testimonies,[26] historical or literary rendering?

Many Holocaust researchers, philosophers, writers, and poets believe that in writing about the Holocaust discourse itself, language itself, must evoke the rupture and the trauma, and must demonstrate that no known semiotic system can adequately convey the true horror of the Final Solution, which broke every rule and taboo and trampled upon every value of what we conceive of as humane. I shall address here the work of three prominent scholars. The first is Saul Friedländer who defined the Holocaust as an "event at the limits" (1992, 2–3). What turns the Final Solution into an event at the limits and renders it difficult to historicize is the very fact that "it is the most radical form of genocide encountered in history: the willful, systematic, industrially organized, largely successful attempt totally to exterminate an entire human group within twentieth-century Western society."[27]

Friedländer describes Nazi reality as "both absurd and ominous, [...] a world altogether grotesque and chilling under the veneer of an even more chilling normality".[28] One of the questions we need to address, maintains Friedländer (1988), is how to render adequately both the utter criminality of the Nazi regime

---

24. White, Hayden. 2016. "Historical Truth, Estrangement and Disbelief." In *Probing the Ethics of Holocaust Culture*.
25. Lyotard, Jean Francois. 1988. *Le Différend.*. University of Minnesota Press; Friedländer, Saul. 2016. "Epilogue." In *Probing the Ethics of Holocaust Culture*; Friedländer, Saul. 1992. "Trauma, Transference and 'Working through' in Writing the History of the 'Shoah.'" In *History and Memory* 4, no. 1 (Spring Summer), 39-59.
26. Friedländer, *Probing the Ethics of Holocaust Culture*.
27. Friedländer, Saul.1992. "Introduction." In *Probing the Limits of Representation*, edited by Saul Friedländer. p. 10
28. Friedländer, *Nazi Germany*. p. 5.

and its utter ordinariness: industry, state bureaucracy, institutions whose function was to support the state system, and which became criminal through and through. He explains, "The very disappearance of these psychological (or sociobiological) barriers concerning the 'scientific' mass killing of other human beings represents the first and foremost issue for which our usual categories of interpretation are insufficient."[29] Language as such, he observes, "imposes on the historical narrative a limited choice of rhetorical forms, implying specific emplotment, explicative models and ideological stances. These unavoidable choices determine the specificity of various interpretations of historical events." (1992, 10). Consequently, Friedländer perceives a "double dilemma" that language and narration confront when seeking to represent the Shoah. On the one hand, the traditional categories of conceptualization and representation may be insufficient, since language itself may be problematic: "language with its 'redemptive,' integrating character may very well be an insufficient instrument to explain the inexplicable and thereby imposes limits to any form of narrative." (ibid.)

On the other hand, Friedländer believes that "on the face of these events we feel the need of some stable narration" (cited in Machtans 2006, 205)[30].

Therefore, he recommends the writing of an integrated history of the Holocaust, which he adopts in his own books. Such writing consists of the convergence of German decisions and policies, the reactions of the surrounding world and the memories and perceptions of Jewish victims.[31] As he specifies in *The Years of Extermination* "The "history of the Holocaust" cannot be limited only to a recounting of German policies, decisions, and measures that led to this most systematic and sustained of genocides; it must include the reactions (and at times the initiatives) of the surrounding world and the attitudes of the victims, for the fundamental reason that the events we call the Holocaust represent a totality defined by this very convergence of distinct elements."[32]

The weaving of memories, conceptions and life stories into the historical narrative turns the victims from numbers in the statistics into subjective human beings, and transforms their stories from "mythic" to factual.[33] Friedländer deems it highly important to ensure the constant presence of the victims and to integrate

---

29. Friedländer, Saul. "The Shoah in Present Historical Consciousness." In Friedländer, *Memory, History*. Published by: Indiana University Press. 42–63.
30. Machtans, Karolin. 2006. "Friedländer's Historiography of the Shoah." In Martin L. and Claus-Christian W. Szejnmann Eds., *How the Holocaust Looks Like Today*. 203.
31. "Some Reflections on the Historicization of National Socialism." *German Politics & Society* No. 13, The Historikerstreit (February 1988). Berghahn Books. 9-21.
32. Friedländer, Saul.2008 *Nazi Germany and the Jews: The Years of Extermination: 1939-1945.* Phoenix. Kindle Edition. loc. 166.
33. Watch "Friedländer, Saul. 2007. The Years of Extermination: A History of the Holocaust." YouTube.

their voices into the historiographical discourse, because they are the ones who provide the individual perspective that can clarify and answer many questions that the organizational voice cannot explain as plainly, such as their own passivity. The same past, he adds, means different things to different historians, to Germans and to the victims whose "modes of historicization of the Nazi era is just as relevant and legitimate" (1988, 19). Friedländer emphasizes that "it is too often forgotten that Nazi attitudes and policies cannot be fully assessed without knowledge of the lives and indeed of the feelings of the Jewish men, women, and children themselves" (1998, 2).[34] The personal chronicles found in diaries and letters, "like flashes that illuminate parts of the landscape," tell us about events that are generally not recorded in official documents, and reveal the thoughts, the actions, the efforts to survive, and the hampering of the Nazis' plans. Moreover, they warn against easy generalizations and "scholarly smug detachment." Friedländer also recommends that authors consciously include themselves in the historical narrative, in the form of commentary. Such commentary, he argues, "should disrupt the facile linear progression of the narration, introduce alternative interpretations, question any partial conclusion, and withstand the need for closure" (1992, 53).[35] The multi-voiced history Friedländer proposes (Blatman 2015, 12) defies consensus and closure, because as French philosopher Jean-François Lyotard asserts, "The striving for totality and consensus is, […] the very basis of the fascist enterprise."[36]

The integration of victims' memories with the historian's reflective commentary seeks to question the redemptive closure of any master narrative. But as we shall see, Israeli schoolbooks suppress or exclude memories that do not fit into the Zionist master narrative of progress that underlies all their historical accounts and offers a redemptive closure. The expression *me-Shoah le-tekumah* (from Holocaust to resurrection) became a constitutive slogan of Zionist consciousness, and it remains so to this day, featuring in many schoolbook titles.

In terms of genre and style, Friedländer, referring to a Yad Vashem study that was published in an educational brochure, intimates that the rational and factual "textbook style" of the brochure and of historical writing in general, or the writing of history in a "business as usual" style, cannot begin to convey the events of the Holocaust.[37] (2016, 51). Studying the historical writing of Shaul Friedländer in

---

34. Introduction to *Nazi Germany and the Jews*.
35. Friedländer, Saul. 1992. "Trauma, Transference and 'Working Through.'" In "Writing the History of the Shoah." *History and Memory* 4, no. 1: 39-59; Friedländer, Saul. 2000. "History, Memory, and the Historian: Dilemmas and Responsibilities." *New German Critique*, 80 (Special Issue on the Holocaust). Duke University Press. 3-15.
36. Introduction to *Probing the Limits of Representation*, ed. Saul Friedländer Cambridge, MA: Harvard University Press, 1992. 5.
37. Friedländer, Saul. 1984. *Reflections of Nazism: An Essay on Kitsch and Death*. Harper & Row. The study cited is Brozsat, Martin. 1979. *Hitler and the Genesis of the "Final Solution."*

The Years of Extermination, Hayden White praises Friedländer for using "literary techniques, devices, tropes, and figures in order to close the gap between truth and meaning in Holocaust historiography without fictionalizing, aestheticizing, or relativizing anything." (ibid. 54). Such writing, he explains, does not turn history into fiction but saves it from "conventional professional historiography, with its fetishism of the facts and nothing but the facts." Friedländer does not "emplot" the events of the Shoah and does not provide any "denouement". By including victims' diaries and his own voice, he "narrates without narrativizing, maps a field but does not emplot a single course of events, and resists the imposition of stereotypical structures of meaning that would allow any "domestication" of the facts." (ibid. 53) The facts he relates remain "estranged" and "unbelievable," and avoid the risk of being "understood" through narrative logic. White concludes that "Friedländer's history of the Holocaust is presented in such a way as to frustrate normal narratological expectations in order to produce the effects (and affects) of "estrangement," on the one hand, and "disbelief," on the other." (ibid.55).

For Michael Rothberg (2000, loc. 130 kindle)[38] the question is, how to represent the "seemingly irresolvable contradictions between the event's "uniqueness" and its "typicality," its "extremity" and its "banality," its "incomprehensibility" and its susceptibility to "normal" understanding" to ourselves and to others. These others are mainly the late comers, the readers of the postmemory generation, "who inherit[ed] [...] the detritus of the twentieth century." (loc. 103). Unlike other historical events, the "Holocaust's public persistence in postwar societies through a consideration of the memorial, legal, and political processes, not only keeps the events present in collective memory, but testify to the active influence of those events in many spheres of contemporary culture." (loc. 296). Therefore, writers should take into account their audience and the culture where their texts circulate and design their representations accordingly.

Rothberg recognizes two approaches to writing about the Holocaust: the realist and the antirealist. The realists argue that the Holocaust is knowable and that this knowledge can be translated into a familiar mimetic universe. They "assert the necessity of considering the Holocaust according to "scientific" procedures and inscribing the events within continuous historical narrative," arguing that it is "a historical event embedded in history and should be explained in relation to other historical events." (loc. 138). The antirealists claim that "the Holocaust is not knowable or would be knowable only under radically new regimes of knowledge for it cannot be captured in traditional representational schemata." (loc. 139). The representatives of the realist tendency are Goldhagen's book *Hitler's Willing Executioners*[39], where "seemingly radical evil is situated

---

38. Rothberg, Michael. 2000. Representation. Kindle edition.
39. Publishers: Little & Brown Book Group.

within an explainable tradition and everyday life-world",5 Hanna Arendt's concept of the banality of evil and the thesis of Zygmunt Bauman on the "modernity" of the genocide, which argues that "genocide is indeed explainable with reference to the intersection of very ordinary sociological structures of the modern world."(loc. 154). These positions, Rothberg explains, are all realist for they use concepts such as "banality," "ordinariness," "detached, professional" science, and "modernity," and suggest that "the phenomena they describe (whose horror is in no way minimized by them) may be apprehended and comprehended according to already established techniques of representation and analysis." (loc. 157).

For the antirealist the Holocaust is an unpresentable event out of history. Proponents of the antirealist tendency are not historians but they "shape the dominant popular understanding of the events through their access to the resources of the public sphere." These include writers such as Elie Wiesel, who claimed that "the universe of concentration camps, by its dimensions and its design, lies outside, if not beyond, history. Its vocabulary belongs to it,"[40] and "Auschwitz cannot be explained nor can it be visualized"; Claude Lanzmann, who asserts that his film *Shoah* forgoes any attempt to represent the Holocaust and declares any attempt to understand the events "obscene" (loc. 159); and Ka-Tzetnik who affirmed:[41] "It is impossible to explain Auschwitz. There is nothing in human language that can explain it. One cannot explain the burning of one baby, how can one explain the burning of a million and a half babies?"

These three important and influential personalities expressed these views despite their self-imposed mission to tell the tale through art and literature.

In view of these contrasting positions, Rothberg maintains that writing about the Holocaust demands a type of narrative that differs from those of traditional realist discourses, because "the category of reality that it seeks to register and produce demands an alternative account of the relationship between writers, readers, and the event," (in: Friedländer, 1992, 11).

Rothberg suggests a third way, which he calls "traumatic realism". He (2000) terms 'traumatic' "the peculiar combination of ordinary and extreme elements that seems to characterize the Nazi genocide".[42] The "ordinary" is not only the factual style of the report but also the ordinary, bureaucratic and systematic way the extermination was carried out, and that textbook style reflects. However, Rothberg's recommended representation includes not only documentation, but self-reflexivity and a representation or a design that marks the absences, the traumatic losses and the gaps that exist in any rendering of traumatic events.

---

40. Elie Wiesel, 'Now we know', in Richard Arens (ed.), *Genocide in Paraguay* Philadelphia. Temple University Press. 1976. 165.
41. Interview with Ram Evron, May 1986. Israeli TV
42. Introduction to *Traumatic Realism*

Therefore, he maintains, the Holocaust is best approached through interdisciplinary means, and he even suggests a trans-disciplinary space of dialogue. He suspects that "perhaps the frequently intoned "impossibility" of comprehending the Holocaust arises in part from the preservation of traditional disciplinary boundaries and structures of knowledge. Questioning those structures will not produce some mythical "full" understanding, but it may open up alternative avenues for exploring the intersection of the psychic and the social, the discursive and the material, the extreme and the everyday." (loc. 182). Rotherg believes that attentiveness to the structure of representation "can also lead to new forms of knowledge beyond the realist and antirealist positions and outside of traditional disciplines". (Loc. 191).

Thus, traumatic realism mediates between the realist and antirealist positions in Holocaust studies and marks the necessity of considering how the ordinary and extraordinary aspects of genocide intersect and coexist. It is an attempt to produce the traumatic event as "an object of knowledge and to program and thus transform its readers so that they are forced to acknowledge their relationship to post-traumatic culture." (Loc. 1981). Rothberg concludes, "Because it seeks both to construct access to a previously unknowable object and to instruct an audience in how to approach that object, the stakes of traumatic realism are both epistemological and pedagogical". (Loc. 1876).

Dominique LaCapra also believes that one must employ a new rhetorical model when confronted by the Final Solution and urges historians to seek new categories whereby to analyze the Holocaust. While Friedländer recommends that authors provide their comments, and Rothberg encourages writers' self-reflexivity, LaCapra advocates "writing that involve(s) affect and may empathetically expose the self to an unsettlement, if not a secondary trauma, which should not be glorified or fixated upon, but addressed in a manner that strives to be cognitively and ethically responsible" (2014, 42).[43] LaCapra (2014, 41) believes that "being responsive to the traumatic experience of others, notably of victims, implies not the appropriation of their experience," which is frequently called "identification," but rather "empathic unsettlement." Identification seeks to blur the distance between the self and the other, either through appropriation or subjugation. The individual must either reduce the other to his/her own concepts or subjugate himself/herself to the concepts of the other (Goldberg 2019, 41). This is the guiding principle that leads to questions found in Israeli school assignments such as "what did the children feel on the way to the gas chambers?"[44] To which a nine-year old student responded, "I cannot know how they felt," expressing the impossibility to identify with Holocaust victims or with any other sufferer.

---

43. LaCapra, Dominick. *Writing History Writing Trauma.*
44. Geva, Sharon. *Haaretz* October 27, 2013.

Empathic unsettlement recognizes the fundamental, inherent otherness of the individual who experiences the trauma, but despite the recognition of this radical and ineradicable otherness, it calls for a sense of empathy toward the sufferers. From this standpoint, the Israeli educational slogan "The other is me!" should in fact be, "The other is not me but nevertheless I feel for him/her and empathize with them." Such a slogan should lead toward a universal position of empathy regarding suffering, as Chouliaraki (2006)[45] recommends.

Emphatic unsettlement, asserts LaCapra, should have stylistic effects or, more broadly, "effects in writing which cannot be reduced to formulas or rules of method" (ibid. p. 40), But "at the very least, [it] poses a barrier to closure in discourse and places in jeopardy harmonizing or spiritually uplifting accounts of extreme events from which we attempt to derive reassurance or a benefit". (ibid. 40-41). Needless to say, such writing generates a similar mode of reading, so that texts written by an empathically involved author encourage involvement and empathy on the part of readers.

In this study, I examine how schoolbooks confront all these dilemmas, seeking to reveal the rhetoric of textbooks and the interest of rhetors and designers regarding the representation of the Holocaust to children.

Different Modes of Representation

> There is no vessel that can transmit it to human language or even contain it. (Ka-Tzetnik, interview with Ram Evron 1986).

Scholars such as Agamben or Felman,[46] and writers of literature such as Primo Levi, Robert Antelmes, Jose Semprum, and Iakovos Kambanellis, who survived death camps, but also authors such as Marguerite Duras, David Grossman, and George Perec, who were not camp inmates but wrote about the Shoah, emphasize the problematic nature of testimony and the inadequacy of language to describe what cannot be understood in human terms, to structure that which has destroyed structure beyond the grasp of language.[47] All languages seem inadequate to relate the events of the Final solution, because language collapses in the face of the Shoah,[48] facts lose their factuality,[49] and metaphors break down. Polish-Israeli

---

45. *The Spectatorship of Suffering*.
46. Agamben Giorgio. 2002. *Remnants of Auschwitz: The Witness and the Archive*. Zone Books; Felman, Shoshana. 1991. "In an Era of Testimony: Claude Lanzmann's Shoah." *Yale French Studies*, no. 79. *Literature and the Ethical Question*. Yale University Press. 39-81.
47. Diner, Dan. 2000. *Beyond the Conceivable: Studies on Germany, Nazism, and the Holocaust*; Rothberg, Michael. 2000. *Traumatic Realism - the Demands of Holocaust Representation*. Minneapolis, London: University of Minnesota Press.
48. Primo Levi, Paul Celan.

poet Uri Zvi Greenberg[50] argued that what happened to European Jews cannot be equated through a simile to anything else since "their extermination is a naked primordial event that leaves no room for comparisons[...] The eyes of the words burst in the face of what they see [...]The words sink into silence from before there were words in the world [...] there are no more parables and all the words are shadows of shadows."[51]

This applies not only to the German language, with which Paul Celan and Gunther Grass grappled (Steiner 1988)[52], but to every language, and especially to the European languages of civilization and morals, of cultured literature and poetry. Yet these languages of extermination were those in which European Jews often expressed themselves. To Paul Celan, who chose to write in German, stripped of its Nazi character it was not simply the murderous tongue of the Nazis, but a language that sustained his only connection to a loving mother. He felt the (pre-Nazi) language of Goethe to be his only remaining home and echoed this feeling when he accepted the Bremen Prize in January 1958, stating that "only one thing remained reachable, close and secure amid all losses: language. Yes, language. In spite of everything, it remained secure against loss."(ibid.) Nevertheless, he succumbed to silence, according to George Steiner, when he killed himself.[53]

Israeli poets and authors of European origin, seeking to avoid the languages that dominated their disastrous past, speak of their difficulties in adopting the Hebrew language for their poetic expression. Author Aharon Apfelfeld, for instance, says in an interview for the documentary *From One Language to Another* [54] that he writes German in Hebrew, while Poet Avot Yeshurun "experiences his own Hebrew voice as uncannily foreign" (Gluzman 2017, 69).[55]

Many consider literature to offer a better tool than history for the representation of the Holocaust events, both for the general public and for children. Alongside the "textbook style" by which the horrors of the Holocaust are rendered, Israeli school curriculum has always included poems and literary pieces. One schoolbook (Popovsky et al. 2008) teaches the Shoah through letters, poems

---

49. Nichanian, Marc. 2016. "The Death of the Witness or The Persistence of the Differend." In *Probing the Ethics of Holocaust Culture*, 141.
Agamben, Giorgio. 2002. *Remnants of Auschwitz. The Witness and the Archive*. MIT Press.
50. Miron, Dan. 2020. *Haaretz*, December 27, 2020.
51. https://www.haaretz.co.il/literature/study/.premium-1.9391580?lts=1614756812077
52. Steiner, George. 1988. "The Long Life of Metaphor: An Approach to the Shoah." In *Writing and the Holocaust* 1. Berel Lang, Ed. New York: Holmes & Meier.1-4.
53. For an analysis of Steiner's conceptions on the subject of Holocaust representation, see: Chatterley, Catherine D. 2011. *Disenchantment: George Steiner & the Meaning of Western Culture after Auschwitz*. Syracuse University Press.
54. Directed by Nurit Aviv, 2003.
55. Gluzman, Michael. 2017. "The Two Holocausts of Avot Yeshurun." In *Talking about Evil-Psychoanalytic, Social, and Cultural Perspectives*. Edited by Rina Lazar. Routledge. 69-80.

and short stories and another, adapted for children with special needs, turns factual documents into a fictitious child's diary.[56]

Literature is no doubt more impressive for children (and for many adults) than historical documents. An edifying example is the oeuvre of internationally acclaimed Israeli children's writer, Uri Orlev, who experienced the Shoah as a child, wrote in Hebrew, and succeeded in conveying children's experiences of the Holocaust to young readers all over the world through compelling stories featuring young heroes. His stories, as Rima Shikhmanter (2014),[57] notes, have no closure and do not convey any grand ideological or Zionist-political message, but extol human values of friendship, mutual aid, and survival. His protagonists both act out their tragedies and work through them; they mourn, fear, and move forward. The novels end when the story ends, when childhood ends. One of them - the only Holocaust novel that does it to this day, according to Shikhmanter - even conveys the message of peace, understanding, and love between Jews and Muslims, through the positive experience of the protagonist in Kazakhstan, to where he escaped and was warmly welcomed, by contrast to the cold, condescending welcome he received in the Israeli Kibbutz. Orlev's novels do not divide humanity into the evil (German/Arab) and the good (Jewish) people, but portray human beings as complex beings, endowed with both good and evil qualities. Writing for children, Shikhmanter observes, and from a child's point of view, allows Orlev the leeway to avoid the horror of the atrocities and yet engage his readers in the experiences of children during the Shoah.

The Holocaust and its social and cultural implications feature prominently in the fiction of postwar Israeli authors whose mother tongue is Hebrew[58], and in the poetry of the second and third generations.[59] From the early 1960, as the negative cultural attitude toward the survivors has changed, writers have been writing from a humanistic perspective that coped with the survivors' experience without ideological national commitments. (Oppenheimer 2010, 286).[60]

Given the impossibility of representing the final solution through any known semiotic tools,[61] some see silence as preferable[62] and contend with the dilemma it

---

56. *Toward Resurrection and Peace* 1999
57. Shikhmanter, Rima. 2014. "Limitations as Possibilities: Uri Orlev's Holocaust Narratives for Children and Young Adults." *Children's Literature*, Volume 42. Johns Hopkins University Press. 1-19.
58. For instance, Lili Perri (*Golem in the Circle*, 1966), Grossman, David. 2002. *See Under: Love. A Novel*. Translated by Betsy Rosenberg. Picador Pub. Amir Gutfreund. *Our Holocaust*. 2012. Nava Semel *and the Rat Laughed*. 2009. Published by ReadHowYouWant.com.
59. See Ofer, Dalia. 2009. "The Past That Does Not Pass: Israelis and Holocaust Memory." *Israel Studies* Vol. 14, No. 1, *Israelis and the Holocaust: Scars Cry out for Healing*. Indiana University Press. 1-35.
60. Oppenheimer Yochai. 2010. The Holocaust: a Mizrahi Perspective. *Hebrew Studies 51*.
61. Friedländer, 2016. *Probing the Ethics of Holocaust Culture*, Epilogue.
62. Steiner, George. 1998. *Language and Silence. Essays on Language, Literature, and the Inhuman*. Yale University Press. See too LaCapra. *Representing the Holocaust*. Loc. 1220 (Kindle).

imposes on those who swore to tell the story, such as the aforementioned writers Elie Weisel and Ka-Tzetnik. Elie Weisel declared that rather than writing about life in the camps, "we have actually written about something else, [...] about something that had only the physical appearance of the Holocaust. Actually, we have never been able to carry out an echo or a reflection, visual or otherwise, from that cursed universe."[63]

Polish-Israeli Holocaust writer Ka-Tzetnik argued that "there has not yet been created, in language, an explanation of that which happened there in Auschwitz. Sometimes I have to return to my previous books, the other ones, to see, and I shudder at the sight of the lines. Only words. I know that the paper would have burnt had it known how to transmit all this to language."[64] These writers believe, as does Lebanese-Palestinian writer Elias Khoury (2019, 1), who writes about the Palestinian Nakba, that "words lose all meaning because the silence of the victim becomes the only language befitting the horror of genocide."[65]

Visual Representation

The Use of Photographs

> Given that generations of individuals were not alive to experience the Holocaust firsthand, its visual representation thereby possesses a critical importance in the shaping of public consciousness. (Zelizer 2001)[66]

The problematics of the use of Holocaust photographs and their impact on viewers have been addressed by many scholars. Some argue that the decontextualized photographs create a new memory, one that is neither that of the victims nor that of the photographers. (Struk 2004, 213). Others argue that photographs merely feed the "desire for Holocaust"[67] and are no more than the "pornography of

---

63. Quoted in Irving Abrahamson, 1995. *Against Silence: The Voice and Vision of Elie Wiesel*, Volume 3. Holocaust Library publishers. 13.
64. TV interview with Ram Evron, May 1986. In fact, Ka-Tzetnik burned many versions of his own books. In 1993, at the age of 76, he managed to sneak out a rare copy of his first published work, a 1931 volume of poetry, from the National Library in Jerusalem, and a few days later sent its charred remains back to the director of the library along with a request to complete the task of burning all the "remnants" of the book, "just as all that was dear to me and my world was burned in the crematoria of Auschwitz." He also sneaked copies of his poetry from the Library of Congress in Washington and burnt them (Miron 1994).
65. Introduction to Bashir and Goldberg 2019.
66. Zelizer Barbie. *Visual Culture and the Holocaust*. p.1
67. Ball, Karyn. "Unspeakable Differences, Obscene Pleasures: The Holocaust as an Object of Desire." In *Women in German Yearbook* 19. University of Nebraska Press. 20-49.

evil";[68] that they generate a "horrid fascination," which makes the viewer want to see more and more of it.[69] Holocaust historian Hannah Yablonka, former head of the history curriculum, [70] worries that meaning is lost in the immensity of gruesome details. These scholars doubt the need for photographs,[71] wondering whether photographs can ever tell the whole truth, since they merely recreate the horror, reproduce the Nazi gaze, and thereby revictimize the victims. [72]

Other Holocaust scholars, despite voicing serious misgivings regarding the exhibition of Holocaust images of atrocity,[73] and recognizing the limitations of Holocaust photographs that are always partial and decontextualized, appreciate their importance in enabling viewers to imagine the unimaginable. They wonder how to read these photos and propose ways of looking at them and learning from them. [74] These scholars, who study images and the reception of Holocaust narratives in educational settings, agree that the insufficiency of language and of the conventional narrative genres of history writing calls for the use of images, especially for post-memory generations[75]. The aura of the Madonna evoked by a mother protecting her child, or from the posture and the silent plea of a girl who cradles her dead sister in her arms; the look in the eyes of the Last Jew of Vinnitsa as he sits on the edge of his own grave, above the corpses of his fellow Jews and family members; and the depths of despair and agony expressed in the dignified face of a woman who sells armbands in the ghetto, cannot be conveyed fully in words. Lilie Chouliaraki (2006, 81) believes that in order to grasp the full meaning of disastrous events we need a multimodal text, in which the images of suffering are embedded in the verbal texts, for it is the verbal–visual combination that

---

68. Holocaust historian Hanna Yablonka observes that other than displaying the "pornography of evil" there is no educational value in these technical details.
https://www.haaretz.co.il/news/education/1.1194213 2010 (Hebrew).
69. Baudrillard, Jean. 1984. *The Evil Demon of Images*, 27; Susan Sontag. 2004. On Photography, 20; Gourevitch, Philip. 1993. "Behold Now Behemoth. The Holocaust Memorial Museum: One more American theme park." *Harper's Magazine*, July issue, 55-62.
70. Interview (Hebrew) "The Necrophilic description is unnecessary"
https://www.onlife.co.il/general/21956
71 Lewis, 2001. Documentation or Decoration? Uses and Misuses of Photographs in the Historiography of the Holocaust Crane, Susan 2008. "Choosing Not to Look: Representation, Repatriation, and Holocaust Atrocity Photography." In *History and Theory*, Vol. 47, No. 3. 309-330.
Zelizer, Barbie. 1997. "La photo de presse et la libération des camps en 1945: Images et formes de la mémoire." *Vingtième Siècle. Revue d'histoire* 54 (Apr. -Jun.). Published by Sciences Po. University Press. 61-78.; Hirsch. 2001. *Surviving Images*.
72. Lewis 2001; Struk 2001. *Images of Women in the Holocaust*; Crane 2008.
73. Such as Barbie Zelizer, George Didi-Huberman (2012), Marianne Hirsch (2012), Sybil Milton (1986), and Wendy Lower (2021).
Lower, Wendy. 2021. *The Ravine: A Family, a Photograph, a Holocaust Massacre Revealed*. Apollo Publisher.
74. Georges Didi-Huberman, *Images malgré tout*. Paris, Éditions de Minuit, 2003.
75. Lewis, Chouliaraki, Zelizer, Struk, Crane, Milton and others are mentioned in this volume.

conveys the meaning, either on the screen or on the page. Chouliaraki shows that very often "it is the symbolic element in the meaning relationships between the visual and the verbal that ultimately, frames our engagement with the [...] event that the image stands for." (ibid.) From this perspective, the "constant presence of victims" and their voice recommended by Friedländer[76] should extend to their visual presence.

Didi Huberman (2012, 3) advocates watching the images of atrocity in order to imagine the unimaginable. To know, he says, we must imagine for ourselves. To remember, one must imagine, in spite of our inability to know how to look at these photographs today. The images do not say the whole truth and the events they depict are unimaginable, but that does not mean we can exempt ourselves: "It was impossible. Yes. One must imagine."

Didi-Huberman (2012) believes that the blurred and incomplete photos can help post-Holocaust viewers to confront reality by seeing it as if through a distorted mirror, as Perseus saw the reflection of the gorgon Medusa. Only by looking at her through the distorting mirror of his shield, could he confront and overcome her.

Photographer Margaret Bourke-White, who took pictures in extermination camps for Life Magazine, admitted she needed a shield through which to look at the horrors she was photographing: "Using the camera was almost a relief. It interposed a slight barrier between myself and the horror in front of me" (Quoted in Milton 1984, 60). She added, "I had to work with a veil over my mind. I hardly knew what I had taken until I saw prints of my own photographs".[77]

Didi-Huberman reminds us that even Holocaust survivors such as Jean Amery, Primo Levi and Ka-Tzetnik, Robert Antelmes or Jose Semprun, found it hard to watch these photos and could not connect them to their own experience in the camps. They did not see themselves as the Nazi photographers or executioners saw them and did not think these photographs represented them.

Marianne Hirsch (2001, 18)[78] studied Holocaust atrocity pictures and their possible effect on post-memory viewers. Post-memory consists not of events but of representations through which viewers, listeners and readers respond to the trauma of previous generations. Hirsch believes that much of our ability to remember depends on images. She agrees with Roland Barthes that photography enables direct access to past reality: "The encounter with the photograph is the encounter between two presents, one of which, already past, can be reanimated in

---

76. Friedländer, Saul. *Nazi Germany and the Jews: The Years of Extermination: 1939-1945*. Phoenix. Kindle Edition. loc. 166.
77. Goldberg, Vicky. 1989. *Margaret Bourke White*. Cleveland Museum of Art Publisher. p. 291
78. "Surviving Images: Holocaust Photographs and the Work of Postmemory." *The Yale Journal of Criticism*, Volume 14, Number 1. 5-37; *The Generation of Postmemory: Writing and Visual Culture After the Holocaust*. Columbia University Press.

the act of looking."[79]. Barthes maintains, regarding any photograph, that because of the physicality of photographs, in them "the past is as certain as the present, what we see on paper is as certain as what we touch."(ibid.) Hirsch adds that photographs, "do more than *represent* scenes and experiences of the past: they can communicate an emotional or bodily experience by evoking the viewer's own emotional and bodily memories. They *produce* affect in the viewer, speaking *from* the body's sensations, rather than speaking *of*, or *representing* the past." (2001, 12). Hirsch assumes that "this connection between photography and bodily or sense memory can perhaps account for the power of photographs to connect first- and second-generation subjects in an unsettling mutuality that crosses the gap of genocidal destruction." (ibid.)

Hence, the most relevant question regarding the use of Holocaust images in schoolbooks is, how do these images construct what we need to remember or rather, what meaning do we make of them at every generation and in every context?

All the above-mentioned scholars insist that when Holocaust photographs are shown they should be contextualized as far as possible and viewed along with an account of their circumstances or their phenomenology (Didi-Huberman 2012, Lower 2021). This contextualization must include place, date, the name and status of the photographers, and details of the event of photographing (Milton 1984; Lower 2021). Friedländer (2007)[80] regards the photograph as a "metonymic illustration" of what he calls integrated history. Addressing a specific photograph from September 18, 1942, showing David Moffie awarded his degree in medicine at the University of Amsterdam, he remarks, "On the left side of his jacket, Moffie displays a palm-size Jewish star with the word Jood inscribed on it […]. Shortly thereafter Moffie was deported to Auschwitz-Birkenau. He survived, as did 20 percent of the Jews of Holland; according to the same statistics, therefore, most of the Jews present at the ceremony did not."[81] Friedländer explains that this photograph "documents an act of defiance, on the edge of the occupier's laws and decrees […], an attitude widespread at Dutch universities since the fall of 1940" (ibid.). He believes that "from one simple snapshot the viewer gets the vast numbers of interactions between the German ideological hallucinations and Dutch administrative measures," between Dutch institutions and individual choices, along with the choices and decisions of Jewish institutions, "and at the center of it all, the fate of a Jewish individual." Hence, when the photo is "translated into

---

79. Barthes, Roland 1981. *Camera Lucida: Reflections on Photography*. New York. Hill and Wang.
80. The Years of Extermination: A History of the Holocaust. YouTube
https://www.youtube.com/watch?v=3AV3FuHwcps&t=11s
81. Friedländer, Saul. *Nazi Germany and the Jews: The Years of Extermination*: 1939-1945. Phoenix. Kindle Edition, 142-143.

words and narrated in its context, interpreted on various levels of significations, it can be seen as the metonymic illustration of integrated history." (ibid.)

Yvonne Kozlovsky-Golan (2017),[82] who studied the absence of North African and Libyan Holocaust victims from Israeli films and literature, asserts categorically that "what is not seen does not exist and what exists but has not been visually recorded and viewed is missing from the historical awareness of the public in the 20th and the 21st centuries" (p. 319). She cites two studies, conducted in 2006 and 2011, that found that both school and college students were far more affected by Holocaust photographs and movies, whether documentary or fictional, than by whatever was discussed in class or by what they read in textbooks. In fact, they hardly mentioned material they studied in school (p. 16). Kozlovsky-Golan attributes the lack of interest in North African Jewry during the Holocaust, and the scant knowledge about them, not only to the deliberate concealment of these victims by Israeli authorities, but also to the "invisibility" of that history and its absence from plastic arts and the screen.

As we shall see in the following chapters, Israeli schoolbooks fail to comply with the requirement to provide the details that can contextualize most photographs, even when this information is available. The photographs are often presented in a decontextualized manner, and do not facilitate empathy or any kind of connectedness on the part of the viewers, besides horror. In the schoolbooks addressed here, the images generally serve to illustrate the texts, although it is at times hard to divine what the picture is meant to illustrate. Many of the texts do not refer to the events depicted in the photos and many of the photographs embedded in the texts appear unrelated to them, either by topic, date, or location. Such layout conveys the idea that it does not matter where or to whom things had happened, as long as we know they happened. It distances viewers from the individuals who appear in the photographs and prompts them to see only the general picture they symbolize.

Transduction: from a diary to a blog, from a film to a dance

Kress (2012, 48) notes that "in a world of much greater variety and variability, the wide range of available modes increases the possibilities and potentials of apt representations of the world framed." Yet the examples addressed in this chapter also demonstrate how very conservative and sensitive adults are with regard to the semiotic modes deemed appropriate to represent the Holocaust.

An example of a written Holocaust testimony that was successfully transformed into a visible fictitious animated Instagram blog is the aforementioned

---

82. Kozlovsky-Golan, Yvonne. 2017. *Out of the Frame: The Absence of the Holocaust Experiences of Mizrahim from the Visual Arts and Media in Israel*. Tel Aviv: Resling (Hebrew).

diary of the Hungarian girl Eva Heyman (Eva's Story).[83] The blog has attracted millions of young people.[84] Based on the diary, the blog has attuned itself to the preferences of a young audience and its means of expression, first by replacing the page with the screen and then by translating the written language of the last century into the speaking register and style of young people today, complete with its slang and inflections. These changes have turned Eva into a contemporary teenage blogger who reports her seventy-year-old Holocaust experience on Instagram. The aim was to facilitate the identification of young people with her and arouse their empathy and their interest. While this format ignited debate, opposition, and no little indignation, it has done a better job of bringing the Holocaust into the lives of 21st century post-memory children than any written document has.[85]

Using the Holocaust in modern art productions is rarely received with sympathy. For example, a Holocaust-themed ice dance set to the soundtrack of Begnini's film *Life is Beautiful*, which recreates Begnini's Holocaust story, performed by dancers dressed as inmates of Nazi extermination camps. The performance was aired on November 29, 2016, on state-run Russian TV, and sparked a vehement debate. Its advocates argued that it offered an appropriate homage to the film and to the memory of the victims, whereas its opponents believe that it defiled the memory of the dead. Some said they imagined people watching it while ordering popcorn salted with tears.[86]

These examples show that the choice of mode is indeed crucial. TV mini-series such as *Holocaust* (NBC 1978) and films such as *Schindler's List* are received far more calmly than the Instagram blog of Eva or the Begnini's story transducted to a ballet on the ice.

However, all these example show that thus far the arts, whether graphic novels such as *MAUS* or *Ann Frank Graphic Novel*, literary novels, movies, TV series or documentaries, in spite of being controversial, have been more successful than history schoolbooks in conveying, and impressing upon the public, individual experiences of the Holocaust (as Rothberg notes in *Traumatic Realism*. Loc. 328). It is therefore quite clear that such transducted representations should find a place in a curriculum that seeks to render the Holocaust accessible to young students.

Consequently, an important question that arises is, to what extent the representation of the Final Solution should be "estranged", or "domesticated".

---

83. https://www.yadvashem.org/education/educational-materials/books/dear-diary.html
84. https://www.theguardian.com/world/2019/may/08/instagram-holocaust-diary-evastories-sparks-debate-in-israel.
85. For a discussion about Eva's Story see Nirit Anderman Haaretz 30.4.2019. "The creators of "Eva" explain why it is good to represent the Shoah through Instagram."
https://www.haaretz.co.il/gallery/cinema/2019-04-30/ty-article-magazine/.premium/0000017f-f7b4-d044-adff-f7fdc4850000 (Hebrew).
86. https://www.youtube.com/watch?v=cDd6YMufCYQ

(Hayden White 2016). Should Holocaust representation generate the sense of "another planet", along with another time, other species of humans, or represent the protagonists, both victims and murderers, as people like us. Holocaust author Ka-Tzetnik, who wrote about Auschwitz, in his early novels, as if it was another planet, conveyed a different, more domesticated, message in his final novel *Shivitti,* where he writes: "Wherever there is man there is Auschwitz, because Auschwitz was not created by Satan but by me and you, just as the [Hiroshima] 'mushroom' was not created by Satan but rather by me and you. The human being" (Hebrew version, 1987, 112-113).

In this vein, Ronnie Landau (2016), one of the few historians who have addressed the teaching of the Holocaust, recommends "reflecting for a moment on the whole history of how human beings have dealt death to one another" (p. 9), and suggests that "we must understand that the Holocaust, for all its freakishness, was a human event, all too human, which shows that humanity is eminently capable of doing anything that our technology makes possible, horrifyingly ready to perform unimagined acts of wholesale destruction and self-destruction" (p. 8). The Holocaust, he reminds us, raises profound and disturbing questions about the ease with which people, all of us included, can fall into a pattern of conformity and obedience to orders, particularly if those orders emanate from a source, which is deemed to possess authority. "Humankind is also, the Holocaust shows us, alarmingly prone, especially in the twentieth century, to replace personal ethical standards with collective ones that appear to exempt the individual from accountability" (p. 8).

Chapter 2. Holocaust Instruction

Holocaust instruction in Israel is compatible with its ever-growing presence in the public sphere and its transformation into the main component in the formation of the common denominator of national identity. Naveh (2017, 280).

Although most of the scholars who write about Holocaust representation do not address textbooks in particular, authors of schoolbooks would do well to consider these observations. As the above excerpts show, major scholars agree with Friedländer who rejects what he calls the "'textbook style" of "business as usual"[1] as an adequate mode of writing about the Holocaust. Yet it seems that the authors of Israeli schoolbooks still adhere to this style, probably because no clear conception has evolved, nor has any directive been issued as to how Holocaust schoolbooks should be written (Keren 2017). Exceptionally, in recent years an attempt has admittedly been made to devise a special curriculum for pre-school and first grades, *Down Memory Lane*, written in accordance with educational principles, such as the exclusion of atrocity images (Kadari-Ovadia 2019).[2] This curriculum focuses on (real or invented) individual stories of heroism and survival, mostly involving children, while providing only a very general context of WWII.

Holocaust education in Israel has undergone various phases. Although during the 1950s and 1960s "an environment of memory of the Holocaust" existed in Israel (Resnik 2003, 297), the Holocaust remained a private experience that attracted little public attention (Yablonka 1994).[3] The topic of the Holocaust was all but ignored in the Israeli national memory. The young state's major educational objective was to inculcate the values of heroism, military superiority, and self-determination. Preparing the young generation for the task of defending the country in the face of its enemies was the educators' main priority (Resnik 2003.). The Holocaust, during which millions of Jews were slaughtered almost without resistance, was the antithesis to the national ethos that the education system sought to consolidate. The victims and survivors were typically viewed with contempt, for they represented the weak diasporic Jews who went "like sheep to the slaughter." The Jews of the Diaspora seemed "as passive and weak and thus as contemptible. It was a common claim—instead of coming to Palestine, the Jews of Europe let the Nazis murder them, and thus undermined the Zionist project. A

---

1. Friedländer, Saul.1984. *Reflections of Nazism: An Essay on Kitsch and Death.*
2. Kadari-Ovadia, Shira. 2019. "How did the children feel on the way to the gas chambers?" Haaretz 2.5.2019.
3. Yablonka, Hanna. 1994. *Foreign Brothers* 1948-1952. Yad Ben Zvi Publishers (Hebrew).

dichotomy was drawn between "them," who embodied the contemptuous diasporic past and "we," the resurrected people of the future, the Zionists who had buried the past. (Naveh 2017, 276).

The recent diasporic past was erased and replaced by a different, ancient past, which consisted of the myth of Masada, along with its Zionist interpretation of "brave Jewish warriors standing up to the might of the Roman army. [This] was a much-needed antidote"[4] and seemed a far preferable national "memory," an example of a "beautiful death" worth imitating.

The European Zionist nationalist movement envisioned the creation of a modern state and the shaping of a "new Jew," who was to be European by culture and a warrior modeled on biblical heroes. The schoolbook *Values and Citizens* (2014) describes this new Jew by a quote from the story "Yehuda the Orchard's guard" by Yosef Luidor: "a young man of about 30, with a tremendous body and his prominent chest, broad shouldered, powerful and courageous. Standing still with his sandaled feet wide apart and his hands deep in his pockets, he resembled a steady rock whose roots are stapled deep in the ground."[5] The students are then required to draw the figure of this "new Jew," to point out his most salient features and to think why the Zionist leadership wanted to create such a new Jew. (p.371). The answer is that the Zionist muscly soldier-farmer was meant to be the negative of the "exilic Jew" (Zimmerman and Zuckerman 2023), the anti-thesis of the studious, weak and pale diasporic Jew, who perished in the Holocaust without fighting back. Jews in diaspora did not value muscles and physical bravery as much as they valued spiritual one (Boyarin 2000),[6] but the Jewish community in Palestine had nursed the expectation that their [Zionist] disciples in the Nazi ruled Diaspora would prove their worth, vindicate their Zionist education, and rebel, even if their rebellion was doomed. The Jews were expected to die a 'beautiful,' worthy Zionist death (Zertal 2005, 30). In this spirit, "A periodical aimed at young people interpreted the acts of the [Warsaw Ghetto] rebels as "a need to resurrect Masada - the symbol of Israel's heroism throughout the generations." (ibid.)

As part of the mission to preserve the memory of the Holocaust, the Law of Holocaust and Heroism Remembrance Day was enacted by the Knesset on May 18, 1953, and a subsequent law, passed in 1963, made the teaching of the Holocaust mandatory. Teachers, however, were reluctant to address a topic that ran counter to the dominant values, and tended to focus on heroism (Resnik, 2003). Heroic episodes such as the Warsaw Ghetto uprising or partisan resistance,

---

4. Stiebel, Guy. 2013. *The Guardian*, https://www.theguardian.com/world/2013/sep/22/israel-masada-myth-doubts
5. Luidor, Yosef. 1967. "Yehuda the Orchard's guard." In: Landau, Dov, editor, *Stories*. The Israeli Writers Association. Tel-Aviv. Masada Publishers.
6. "The Colonial Drag Zionism, Gender and Mimicry." In: Fawzia Afzal-Khan, Kalpana Seshadri-Crooks, Eds. *The Pre-Occupation of Postcolonial Studies* 2000:234-265.

with which Israelis could identify were emphasized disproportionately. Only "heroes" were taught about. Their images were exhibited everywhere and even heroic statues (which hardly resemble the original figures) that aroused identification, were erected and admired, (Naveh 2018, 173). Speaking at the ceremony held at Yad Vashem on the eve of Holocaust Memorial Day in 1964, Prime Minister Levi Eshkol declared, "the Jewish fight against the Nazis and the [Israeli] War of Independence were, in fact, a single protracted battle."[7] Historian Tim Cole (2006) believes this is the message conveyed by Yad Vashem's exhibition to this day.

This attitude has undergone a gradual change, and although the Holocaust commemoration day is still called Holocaust and Heroism Day, the mantle of heroism has been extended to the maintenance of day-to-day life and to those who survived.[8] Holocaust historian Daniel Blatman (2015, 12) notes that this change took place following the appearance of several studies, especially in Israel, which focused on Jewish endurance and resistance "not necessarily of a military or underground nature, but rather a determined struggle to maintain the continuity of life". These studies shattered the image of the passive Jews who "went like sheep to the slaughter," describing "the reactions of Eastern European Jews to persecution and their valiant attempts to survive." Blatmam cites Mark (Meir) Dworzecki,[9] who wrote in 1968:

> It was the purpose of the Nazis to deprive the Jew of his human visage, that is why the resistance of the anonymous masses must be affirmed in terms of how they held to their humanity, of their manifestations of solidarity, mutual help, self-sacrifice, and that whole constellation of manifestations subsumed under the simple heading of 'good deeds'.

The Eichmann Trial in 1961 ignited interest in the survivors and their stories, which were silenced and deemed irrelevant in the first decades of Israeli education. However, sociologist Julia Resnik (2003) believes it was Israel's initial setbacks in the 1973 Yom Kippur war and the fear of "being exterminated once again" that transformed the Holocaust into a highly important component of the school curriculum, a step deemed "an appropriate response to the crisis of national

---

7. Cited in Cole, Tim. 2006. "Nativization and Nationalization: A Comparative Landscape Study of Holocaust Museums in Israel, the US and the UK." *Journal of Israeli History: Politics, Society, Culture*, http://www.tandfonline.com/loi/fjih20
8. Feldman, Yael. 1992. "Whose Story Is It, Anyway? Psychology and Ideology in the Representation of the Shoah in Israeli Literature" in *Probing the Limits of Representation*, edited by Shaul Friedländer. Cambridge, Mass. Harvard UP. 223-239.
9. In Meir Grubstein (ed.), *Jewish Resistance during the Holocaust*, 174. Quoted in Daniel Blatman (2015, 12). "Holocaust scholarship: towards a post-uniqueness era". *Journal of Genocide Research* 17 (1). 21-43.

subjectivity unleashed by the War in 1973" (ibid., 297). The national "we-ness" was compromised by the failure to win this war as decisively as in 1967, and the conviction that the Jewish nation was in need of a state began to be questioned in view of the sacrifice demanded of the young generation in order to sustain it. Resnik relates that "the fact that some of the problems that surfaced in the wake of the Yom Kippur War were seen as 'failures of education' encouraged educators to explore new approaches to developing a national consciousness. Educators recommended stressing the pogroms against the Jews in Europe, the Holocaust, and Israel's ongoing wars against its neighbors as a strategy designed to renew national cohesion and identity. "Instead of solidarity based on religion or a common history, this new discourse promoted a collective memory based on the fate of the Jewish nation as victim, linking people through the fear rooted in the nation's tragic past" (ibid. 311). Consequently, Holocaust education was upgraded by the state as it sought "to shape national subjects that would voluntarily continue to live in Israel despite the security problems, and would be eager to defend the homeland with their lives" (Resnik 2003, 310).

In the discourse of a "state for a persecuted nation", that has manifested itself in the educational field since the 1970s, the former despised Jews, who perished dishonorably, became the potential "us" who may perish again (Naveh 2018, 175). The Holocaust came to be seen as the incentive for the establishment of the state of Israel, and its raison d'être. Since then the Holocaust has been taught as part of the Zionist narrative, offered as the foremost justification for establishing the state of Israel, and has gradually become the central event of Jewish history that defines Israeli identity (Oron 1993). [10] It has thereby replaced the event of the establishment of the State of Israel, and is gradually replacing Zionism, not only as the defining element of Israeli identity, but also as the ultimate criterion according to which all the actions of humankind are interpreted (Naveh 2017, 2018).[11] In other words, the Holocaust became the "chosen trauma" of Israeli Jews. Psychoanalyst Vamık D. Volkan[12], who coined the term, defines chosen trauma as the shared images of specific historical events in ancestors' times "during which a large group suffered loss or experienced helplessness and humiliation in a conflict with a neighboring group." (2015, 13). The term refers to the mental representation of the event that led the group to encounter immense

---

10. Oron, Yair. 1993. *Jewish-Israeli Identity*. Sifriat HaPoalim (with the Kibutzim College of Education), Tel-Aviv (Hebrew); Oron, Yair. 2005. *The Pain of Knowledge Holocaust and Genocide Issues in Education*. New Brunswick: Transaction.
11. Naveh, Eyal. 2017. "Holocaust, army and faith"; Naveh, Eyal. 2018. *The Past in a Turmoil*. Hakibbutz HaMeuhad Pub.
12. Volkan, Vamık D. 2001. "Transgenerational Transmissions and Chosen Traumas: An Aspect of Large-Group Identity." *Group Analysis* 34(1). Sage Publications. 79-97. Volkan, Vamık D. 2015. *A Nazi Legacy. Depositing, Transgenerational Transmission, Dissociation, and Remembering Through Action*. London, Karnac Books Ltd.

loss, and to feel helpless and victimized. While groups may have experienced any number of traumas in their history, only certain ones remain alive across centuries. For the Jews in the Diaspora and for orthodox Jews today, the chosen trauma is the destruction of the second Temple in 70 AD, commemorated by a day of fasting (9th of Ab), while for Zionist Israel it is the Holocaust, a colossal disaster that occurred four generations ago in another country, on another continent, experienced by the great-grandparents of some Israeli children. A chosen trauma indicates the group's failure to reverse narcissistic injury and humiliation inflicted on them (Volkan 2001, 2015). While the group does not choose to be victimized or suffer humiliation, it unconsciously "choose" to add a past generation's mental representation of an event to its own identity. Volkan (2015, 13) explains that these images from the group's past may become "most significant 'identity markers' for ethnic, national, religious, or political ideological large groups." The traumatic experiences and the damaged self-images associated with the mental representations of the traumatic event are "deposited," in Volkan's words, into the evolving self-representation of children of the next generations, as if these children will be able to mourn the loss or reverse the humiliation. Such depositing constitutes "an intergenerational transmission of trauma." If the children cannot deal with what is deposited in them, as adults they will in turn pass the mental representation of the event onto the next generation.

Volkan argues that fact and fantasy, past and present, are intimately and violently intermingled in the remembering of the chosen trauma.

"When a present-day conflict begins with current enemies, "chosen traumas" are reactivated along with entitlement ideologies. Entitlement ideologies refer to a shared sense of entitlement to recover what was lost in reality and fantasy during the collective trauma that evolved as a chosen trauma. The reactivation of "chosen traumas", along with entitlement ideologies within a society, creates a "time collapse" (2015, 16-17), that typically occurs when a chosen trauma is reactivated. The fears, expectations, fantasies, and defenses associated with a chosen trauma reappear when both conscious and unconscious connections are made between the past trauma and a contemporary threat. This process magnifies the image of current enemies and current conflicts. As we shall see in chapters 10-11, Palestinians are represented in schoolbooks, as in the socio-political discourse in Israel, as potential or actual Nazis. The current events of hostility reactivate a sense of victimization, and the sense of revenge becomes exaggerated, and may perpetuate otherwise unthinkable cruelty against others.

In Israel, all members of the Jewish group, even those whose ancestors were not affected by the Holocaust, share the mental representations of the annihilation of European Jewry. The important point is that the members of the group are linked together through sharing the chosen trauma. In other words, "the chosen trauma is woven into the canvas of the ethnic or large group tent, and becomes an inseparable part of the group's identity."(ibid.) A good example is the student who recently emigrated from Ethiopia and told her college teacher: "I wanted to feel Israeli so I went to Auschwitz."

Volkan shows that "leaders intuitively seem to know how to reactivate a chosen trauma, especially when their large group is in conflict, or has gone through a drastic change, and needs to reconfirm or enhance its identity."(ibid.) Chosen traumas are similarly recalled during the anniversary of the original event, and the ritualistic commemoration helps bind the members of the large group together (ibid.). In Israel, Holocaust Remembrance Day serves as an opportunity for politicians and prime ministers to stir up fear and animosity toward the country's co-citizens, subjects and neighbors.

As Holocaust historian, Hannah Yablonka observes, "We only teach our students that we are victims", or in Bauman's words "hereditary victims". She believes that this education has produced "generations who do not understand what normalcy is."[13] In an interview conducted in February 2021 she elaborated this statement by calling the constant preoccupation with Holocaust atrocities "necrophilia," and asserted that "this unending harping on the Shoah as the most important thing, has destroyed Zionism and turned Israel into 'an alternative to disaster' and nothing more." Yablonka believes that the stories of Holocaust survivors and the millennia of Jewish culture would provide lessons that are far more valuable for the younger generations.[14]

From Shoah to Resurrection

The primary message conveyed by Israel's educational system to this day is that antisemitism, which drove the Holocaust, is the reason for Israel's existence and its justification. From this discourse follows that only a Jewish state, wherein Jews form the majority, can guarantee security to each individual Jew in the world. This is the same message that Yad Vashem Museum conveys, as James Young contends: "the museum seems to be saying. 'That was *Galut* (exile), where Jews had no refuge, no defense, only death and destruction; this is Israel, its people are alive" and safe.[15] Holocaust historian Omer Bartov likewise observes, "The visitor [to Yad Vashem] should leave with the thought that had there been a Jewish state before the Holocaust, genocide would not have occurred; and since genocide did occur there must be a state."[16] Hence, the Holocaust is part of a narrative of progress and redemption. According to the Zionist view, the Jewish people "almost miraculously, arose like a phoenix from the ashes, and started anew

---

13. http://www.massuah.org.il/english/Product.aspx?product=536&category=9
14. Yablonka, Hanna. 2010. https://www.haaretz.com/1.5045991;
15. Young, James. 1994. *The Texture of Memory*. Yale University Press. 253.
16. Bartov, Omer. 1996. *Murder in Our Midst: The Holocaust, Industrial Killing, and Representation.* New York. 178.

immediately after the Holocaust, building a national home in the Land of Israel, despite the putatively immoral opposition of the Palestinian inhabitants of the land and the entire Arab world. (Bashir and Goldberg 2019).[17]

Israeli schoolbooks portray the Holocaust as a phase on the path toward redemption in the form of Zionism and the resurrection of the Jewish nation in the state of Israel. Schoolbook titles such as *From Holocaust to Resurrection* or *Toward Resurrection and Peace* attest to this perception. Friedländer mentions this propensity regarding Jewish historians as well (1992, 51).

In conclusion, "In this narrative, the establishment of the State of Israel was the inevitable and rightful due of the victims of Nazism, and the entire world, certainly Euro-Christian society, which bore responsibility for hatred of Jews and for the Holocaust, was duty bound to lend its support, as part of its obligation to make amends after World War II. Thus, the Holocaust is perceived as an event that has reached a conclusion and found its "solution". (Raz-Krakotzkin 2019, 104).

The Ka-Tzetnik Project

During the 1990s, Israel's Ministry of Education chose to distribute Ka-Tzetnik's controversial Holocaust novels to high school students. Ka-Tzetnik was the name writer Yehiel De-Nur gave himself (he objected to calling it a "pen-name") as the *chronicler* of Auschwitz (he refused to call himself an author of literature). The name derives from the German acronym KZ (Ka-Tzet) for Konzentrationslager—concentration camp. The inmates of the camps were referred to as Ka-Tzetniks and identified by number; De-Nur was Ka-Tzetnik 135633, and this was how he signed his works (Segev 1991, 2).[18] His first book *Salamandra* was one of the first Holocaust books to be published in Palestine. Subsequently, Ka-Tzetnik published *House of Dolls, Piepel, The Clock*, and *Phoenix over the Galilee* (in Hebrew titled as *a Phoenix from the Ashes*), all of which constitute *A Chronicle of a Jewish Family in the Twentieth Century*. The family apparently is his own. In all his books apart from *Phoenix over the Galilee*, he wrote about the brutal expulsion and ghettoization of Jews, and the daily routine at Auschwitz, describing sadistic acts in horrifying detail, including cannibalism and the sexual abuse of young girls and boys (Segev 1991, 2-3). Ka-Tzetnik's *Chronicles* was the first work to describe these horrors in a literary genre, and to inform the Israeli audience about "the planet Auschwitz." His books were avidly read by the first two generations (1950-1960) and were later made mandatory reading for a decade in high schools (1990-2000). Tenth grade students were asked to write a seminar paper on the

---

17. Bashir and Goldberg 2019. *The Holocaust and the Nakba*. Introduction.
18. Segev, Tom. 1991. *The Seventh Million*. Farrar, Straus and Giroux. Kindle Edition.

topic "The Holocaust and the Resurrection of Israel." Three such papers would receive an annual prize, the "Ka-Tzetnik Prize for Holocaust Consciousness."[19] However, in the early 2000s Ka-Tzetnik's books were deemed inappropriate for such a young audience and were removed from the curriculum by Nili Levi, the coordinator of literature studies at the Ministry of Education, who terminated the project. The reasons she gave were that unlike Primo Levi, Aharon Apfelfeld or Ida Fink, Ka-Tzetnik "throws" the reader into "another world" and erects a barrier between them. "Rather than inviting his readers to accompany him step by step on his terrifying journey, rather than showing his reader what happened from the sidelines, he simply casts him, alone, straight into the fire".[20] Ka-Tzetnik, argues phycologist Galia Heled, after interviewing teachers who taught the books, "does not seek to tell us what happened to him. Instead, he aspires to take his readers to the depths of the pit along with him." (2007, 127). Criticizing the remoteness of his style, writer Haim Be'er confides that he was "overwhelmed" by Ka-Tzetnik and felt he was being "raped" by this writing. These reactions demonstrate that both teachers and writers, who took issue with Ka-Tzetnik, advocated a "communicable" Holocaust, namely a narrative that does not "transgress the taboo against direct representation of the Holocaust" (Heled 2007, 128). However, this taboo, as we shall see, is transgressed in schoolbooks to this day.

Holocaust historian Amos Goldberg (2013) argues that the incommunicability of Ka-Tzetnik's writing consists of conveying the pain and the disaster in an unmediated way. He asserts that Ka-Tzetnik's works are infused with "the poetics of the block." This definition may have a double meaning, referring both to the poetics of the housing "blocks" in Auschwitz, where most of his plots are located, and a poetics that creates "blocked" texts, [21] which are one prolonged scream of pain that can neither be deconstructed or processed in any way, nor expressed differently. This writing, its qualities notwithstanding, lacks the communicating and therapeutic elements it should have contained. Thus, it fails to make the suffering accessible to the reader, nor does it alleviate the pain of the writer himself. (ibid. 72).

The teachers, writers and critics, continue to seek a "palatable" or a "communicable" representation of the Holocaust, as their criticism of Ka-Tzetnik shows. However, from Ka-Tzetnik's writings it would appear that he had no interest in making his suffering "accessible" or to "alleviate the pain" of himself or of others. In Kress's (2010) terms, Ka-Tzetnik is not a communicator. He does not seek to "communicate" his pain and trauma to his readers. He appears to be

---

19. Glasner-Heled, Galia. 2007. "Reader, Writer, and Holocaust Literature: The Case of Ka-Tzetnik." *Israel Studies* 12, no. 3. Indiana University Press. 109-134.
20. Nili Levi in Heled 2007,127
21. Goldberg, Amos. 2013. "Body, 'jouissance' and irony in the representation of the Holocaust." In *Pain in Flesh and Blood*, edited by Stav Shira and Orit Meital. Kineret-Zmora-Dvir Publishers.

concerned only with the designer's question, "what do I want to say and how am I going to say it?" rather than with the question of the rhetor or the communicator: "how am I going to communicate this to my audience in a way they can understand?" This is what moved literary critic Dan Miron to define his writing as immature and even "juvenile," because children's writing often lacks the sense of an audience (Britton 1975).[22] They are more "designers" than "rhetors" or communicators.[23] Yet, judging by the afore-mentioned observations of Ka-Tzetnik himself about the impossibility of writing about Auschwitz, one cannot but conclude that he chose to write about that which was incommunicable in an incommunicable way. He was writing a disaster, which can be done only disastrously, if at all. French philosopher Maurice Blanchot, whose book *Writing the Disaster* touches upon these issues, likewise speaks of the impossibility of writing about Auschwitz in some reader-friendly way. "How can one philosophize, how can one write in memory of Auschwitz, of those who told us, sometimes in notes buried near to the crematories: know what happened here, do not forget, and at the same time you will never know."[24]

Ka-Tzetnik's solution to this dilemma was to employ an "Auschwitz style" to describe Auschwitz, although as he intimated in the interview, this attempt was a failure. Nevertheless, in their papers - which unfortunately are never addressed in the studies about the project - the students connected to another aspect of his writing. Ka-Tzetnik's language is imbued with Jewish mysticism through which he makes his protagonists transcend the hell in which they live. This tends to render his telling even more impenetrable. Yet, the students focused on this aspect of his writing far more than on its "pornographic" content.[25]

The question relevant to the present study is why was Ka-Tzetnik chosen in the first place to represent the Holocaust in Israeli schools? Confronted with criticism from literary critic Dan Miron,[26] and from Holocaust historians such as Omer Bartov,[27] who found the books too "voyeuristic," pornographic and outright dangerous, the inspector general of the literary curriculum at the time, Avraham Green, argued that since we have no video evidence from Auschwitz, these books

---

22. Britton, J. 1984. Viewpoints: The distinction between participant and spectator role language in research and practice. *Research in the Teaching of English*. 18(3), 320–331.
23. Peled-Elhanan, Nurit. 2017. "Writing as Design Children's Multimodal Writing." In Archer, A. and Breuer E., Eds. *Multimodality in Writing*. Brill, 253-277.
24. Blanchot, Maurice. 1980. "Our Clandestine Companion." In *Political Writings, 1953–1993*. Translated by Paul Zakir. New York: Fordham University Press, 2010, 152.
25. *Instruction of the Shoah and the Resurrection of Israel in Ka Tzetnik's books*. Edited by Dorit Sharir. Unpublished document.
26. Miron, Dan. 1994. "Between Books and Ashes. On the Holocaust Literature of Ka-Tzetnik." In *Alpayim* 10, 1196-224. Reprinted in Miron, Dan. 2005. *The Blind Library: Mixed Prose 1980-2005*. Hemed Books, Yediot Aharonot Publishers, 147-183 (Hebrew).
27. Bartov, Omer. 1997. "Kitsch and Sadism in Ka-Tzetnik's Other Planet: Israeli Youth Imagine the Holocaust." In *Jewish Social Studies New Series 3, no. 2 (winter)*, Indiana University Press. 42-76.

were needed to "punch the children in their guts" (quoted in Miron 1994) with the reality of this other world, and therefore this was the right thing to do. Only this kind of encounter with the suffering of the Jews could inculcate in students the belief in the justification for founding a state for the Jews in Israel. In the teacher's guide to the Ka-Tzetnik project (p.18), Avraham Green referred to one of Ka-Tzetnik's books, *The Clock*, which portrays torture, displacement, and brutal murder in a most gruesome and horrifying manner, creating a "pornography of suffering" (Dean 2004),[28] as follows: "It is our duty to read this book in order to appreciate what we have today. The suffering of the exterminated gives us the moral right to demand and to have a sovereign state of our own. The lesson of the Holocaust demands of us not only to be prepared for and alert to every danger [...] but also to be right in whatever we do." Many Israelis viewed The Planet Auschwitz described by Ka-Tzetnik as justification for a Nationalist-Zionist reading of the Holocaust, as "symbolizing everything that Zionism was created to undo, and serving as the ultimate and absolute justification and legitimation for the foundation of the Jewish state." (Bartov 1997, 55). Israeli literary scholar Iris Milner likewise believes that Ka-Tzetnik's work "as a whole, represents the national salvation ethos as a substitute for divine salvation, and by that awards this salvation a transcendental dimension" (Milner 2008, 190).

---

28. Dean, Carolyne. 2004. *The Fragility of Empathy after the Holocaust*. Cornell University Press, Chapter 1. "Empathy, Suffering and Holocaust Pornography,"16-43.

Chapter 3

Visual Representation of the Holocaust in Israeli Schoolbooks: Transposition, Transformation and Transduction

> Each mark makes meaning by differentiating itself from other marks, altering its meaning as it travels from context to context (Jacques Derrida)[1]

The overarching question addressed in this chapter is this: what happens to Holocaust photographs once they are transposed to Israeli textbooks? More precisely, how are the photographed individuals presented in schoolbooks?

In his article *Beyond Words: Translation and Multimodality*[2] Gunther Kress (2020, 35) examines the transformation of verbal and visual signs that are transposed from one site to another. This transposition, he argues, creates newly made *motivated signs*. The signs are motivated first of all by *interest*, since "the *interest* of the sign-maker/meaning-maker determines what is taken as *criterial* about an entity. It determines what will be represented about that entity or phenomenon. That which is taken as *criterial* will be the *signified*." Hence, the three cardinal issues to be considered in studying the transposition of signs are interest, criteriality, and the newly made motivated sign.

Recontextualization: Changing Social Sites

Kress (2020, 38) observes, "Meanings made in any one (social) site are constantly and frequently remade in different sites, in different social and semiotic environments, or are *re-contextualized*." Recontextualization is, literally, moving

---

1. Quoted in Chouliaraki. 2004, 188. "Watching 11 September: The Politics of Pity". In: *Discourse & Society* SAGE Publications (London, Thousand Oaks, CA and New Delhi). www.sagepublications.com Vol 15(2–3). 185–198. Chouliaraki paraphrases Derrida, J. 1982. "Structure, Sign and Play in the Discourse of the Human Sciences." In: *Writing and Difference*. Chicago: Chicago University Press.
2. Kress, Gunther. 2020. "Transposing Meaning: Translation in a Multimodal Semiotic Landscape." In *Beyond Words: Translation and Multimodality*. Routledge.

meaning material from one context with its social organization of participants and its modal ensembles to another context, with its different social organization and modal ensembles. Selection of *meaning materials* plays an important role in recontextualization to pedagogical sites, because not everything in the originating context may be relevant in the new context. Meaning material always has a semiotic realization, thus recontextualization involves the re-presentation of the meaning materials in a manner suitable to the new context, in the light of the available modal resources. In every school subject, discourses produced in formal and informal sites outside school are transformed upon being transposed to the new pedagogical *site* and recontextualized in the *pedagogic discourse*. Sites can be defined by the social roles of the participants - sign makers and recipients, typically involved in the sites, as well as the modes, media, and genres typically used in these sites (Bezemer and Kress 2008, 184).[3] *Pedagogic discourse* is a composite of *instructional discourse*, or the content of a school subject, and *regulative discourse*, or the social relations, underlying a specific pedagogy (Bernstein 1996).Therefore, "pedagogic discourse cannot be identified with the discourses it transmits [...]. It is the pedagogic principle which appropriates other discourses and brings them into a special relationship with each other, for the purpose of their selective transmission and acquisition at school" (Bernstein 1996, 46). After the selection, there is the question of *foregrounding*. Some elements are foregrounded and others are backgrounded, as in the transformation of "carpentry" to the school subject "woodwork". What may be highly significant in the originating environment, say the commercial aspect in carpentry, may be far less so in the environment of recontextualization, the school. Hence, the assigning of *salience* concerns the content, the people and the actions that are foregrounded. The *modal* resources of the new context may differ from those of the original context, and the modal ensembles required for the audience of the new context may necessitate the *selection of modes* according to these needs, as exemplified in the case of transduction of photographs to drawings, discussed in the following section. The meaning materials are therefore selected according to what is deemed pedagogically relevant in the new site and modes are selected according to what is available and apt for the new site. What is being represented is guided by a complex rhetorical decision, derived from questions such as "what are the rhetor's interests? What is best for the audience in the new environment? How is the meaning material most aptly represented, and what modal resources are available in the new environment?" (Bezemer and Kress 2008, 185). Kress and Bezemer emphasize that "in recontextualization there is inevitably a *social repositioning*" (ibid., 186) according to the *social relations* that pertain and are (re-)constructed

---

3. Bezemer, Jeff, and Gunther Kress. 2008. "Writing in Multimodal Texts a Social Semiotic Account of Designs for Learning." In *Written Communication* 25. Sage Publications. 166.

between teacher and students, between them and the authors of the resource, and between them and those who are represented.

In the process of *transposition*, Kress (2020) explains, the meaning of the sign, in this case the photograph, is not preserved. Transposition creates new relations between the verbal and the visual texts, and new relations between the photo and its viewers, as well as between the semiotic and the "out of semiotic" (Chouliaraki 2004) or the social sphere into which the photo is transposed. As Kress makes clear (2020, 47), "the real issue looming is not the technology but the future shape of what we call 'the social'". Hence, the question of photographic meaning "is constantly to be referred to the social and psychic formations of the author/viewer, formations. [...] Whatever specificity might be attributed to photography at the level of the 'image' is inextricably caught up within the specificity of the social acts which intend that image and its meanings: news-photographs help transform the raw continuum of historical flux into the product 'news,' domestic snapshots characteristically serve to legitimate the institution of the family, and so on." (Burgin 1982 144,154).

The social context, in which images are created and viewed, facilitates certain interpretations and suppresses others. This is very similar to the attribution of meaning to textual documents, especially ancient or political ones, and to literary and poetic texts whose meaning changes from one era to another, and from one audience to another. One example is the study of the Holocaust from women's perspective (e.g., Jo-Ann Owusu, 2019)[4] which has yet to find its way into schoolbooks.

Photographs taken in the ghettos and camps by the official Nazi propaganda units, but also by Nazi amateurs, were intertextualized with anti-Semitic discourse and images and with Nazi racist ideology. The visuals in the reports about the ghettoes, many of them staged, reinforced anti-Semitic stereotypes by visually supporting biases such as the Jews' "lack of personal hygiene," and Jewish indifference to one another's suffering (Keilbach, 2009).[5]

In conclusion, since it is the social that determines the semiotic choices, and it is the social that is affected by them, the photos and the texts in which they are embedded should be seen as motivated by social interest and ideology. In the case of textbooks, the social-educational interest determines the semiotic choices of the sign maker or the designer of the page, the double spread or the entire book, as well as the *criterial features* of each photograph that make it apt or suitable to be presented in the educational texts.

---

4. Owusu, Jo-Ann. 2019. "Menstruation and the Holocaust." *History Today* 69 (5).
5. Keilbach, Judith. 2009. "Photographs, Symbolic Images, and the Holocaust: On the (im)possibility of depicting historical truth." *History and Theory, Theme Issue* 47. Wesleyan University. 54-76.; Milton, Sybil. 1984. "The Camera as a Weapon." In: *Simon Wiesenthal Center Annual Volume* 1, chapter 3.

The researcher, who examines these issues, encounters first of all the newly made signs themselves and asks, what was criterial in their making? On which features of the photograph did the sign maker want the viewers to focus? What do they signify? The answers to these questions help the researcher to address the important question: what motivated the making of the sign? What was the interest of the sign makers?

The following multimodal analysis addresses both the photos themselves, and how they were made, their functions and meaning in their original context and their use and role in the schoolbooks. It examines the way the students are prompted to look at the images. As we shall see in the following sections, Israeli schoolbooks generally use photographs of victims to illustrate the history of the Holocaust and to serve as evidence of the murder process, but do not dwell on their content or on the event of photographing. The students are prompted to view the photographed persons as symbols, icons, or specimen of categories and phenomena.

The Trajectory of Holocaust Photographs

> World War II was not only the most destructive armed conflict ever; it was also the most photographed (Wendy Lower 2021, 19).

Only a fairly small number of the abundant Holocaust photographs have become icons and symbols of the Shoah after the war, and these photographs crop up in most publications. Milton (1986)[6] notes that although more than two million photos are held in the public archives of over twenty nations, the quality, scope, and content of the images reproduced in scholarly and popular literature have been extremely repetitive. They are reproduced over and over again, their protagonists are often nameless and their context is often vague. As Janina Struk observes (2008, 112)[7]: "No one will probably ever know what exactly the majority of the images show, nor who the victims are. But pictures such as those [...] are widely displayed as reliable evidence of the Nazi Holocaust."

Most of the images of Holocaust victims, as historian Sybil Milton (1984)[8] reminds us, were not created by social activists or concerned cameramen. They were generally taken by the killers themselves, who used their cameras as weapons of aggression, or by the liberators, who used their cameras as weapons of retribution and justice.

---

6. Milton, Sybil. 1986. "Photographs of the Warsaw Ghetto." In *Simon Wiesenthal Center* Annual 3, 307.
7. *Images of Women in Holocaust Photography*.
8. Milton Sybil 1984: Camera as a weapon.

Following World War II, Holocaust photographs were expropriated from their original owners, and became the property of Holocaust museums and private collections all over the Western world, such as Yad Vashem Holocaust Museum or Getty. The liberation photographs belonged after the war to the US Army or to other Allied armies, which were designated as their new custodians (Milton ibid.). De-contextualized from their circumstances, nameless and dateless in many cases, these photographs became the property of new masters who used them for different purposes and endowed them with new meanings. Therefore, apart from trivial images, different viewers will find different meanings in each photo (Lewis 2001)[9]. Judith Keilbach (2009, 62) argues that "depending on the 'national' meaning of the Holocaust and the dimensions that one part of the population experienced, the use of pictures and their underlying motifs vary enormously. For example, the achievement of the Allied soldiers is emphasized by pictures showing the number of survivors, and the cleaning up of the camps." These photographs, implicitly and invariably, "take the soldiers' point of view, showing the unimaginable horror to which 'our boys' were exposed".

Holocaust images that to German Nazis appeared to be tokens of achievement were transformed, by their transposition to the museums, into criminalizing evidence and commemorating icons. The individuals who were photographed, generally for purposes of identification before or after they were killed, were transformed by this transposition from *Stücke* (pieces, units) as the Germans called them, into icons of victimhood and figures of memory. These icons have attained an almost mythic status (Brinks 2000)[10] and are used as such in Israeli textbooks.

Through their transposition from the museums to schoolbooks, these mirror-reflections of horror have been transformed from exhibition items to educational resources, or to means through which the state educates its young to remember. Hence, the same photograph can convey different meanings in different political moments and in different schoolbooks, depending on the book's pedagogic-political orientation, its target readership (students in religious or secular schools, middle school or high school), and whether it is issued under a left-wing or a right-wing government.

Nazi photographs illustrate the nature of the perpetrator's gaze as well as its connection to the perpetrator's deed (Hirsch 2001). When we confront perpetrator images, we cannot free ourselves from the gaze of the executioner. Hence the

---

9. Lewis, Bryan F. 2001. "Documentation or Decoration? Uses and Misuses of Photographs in the Historiography of the Holocaust." In: *Remembering for the Future -the Holocaust in an Age of Genocide*. Editors in Chief John K. Roth and Elisabeth Maxwell; Editor Margot Levy Volume 1, History.341-358.
10. Brink, Cornelia. 2000. "Secular Icons: Looking at Photographs from Nazi Concentration Camps." *History and Memory*, vol. 12, no. 1 (Spring/Summer 2000), 135-150.

importance of providing the phenomenological details of the photo to the observer.[11]

The Importance of Phenomenology

> If we knew what preceded that moment of death, what followed, and what happened to each person we see in the picture, we could unmask the killers and restore a semblance of life and dignity to the victims by restoring a voice to the voiceless. Wendy Lower (2021, 12)

Hirsch (2001)[12] studied the iconic atrocity photographs that were taken after the liberation of the camps, and divided them into two broad categories: subjects and objects. The subjects are human beings, dead or alive, portrayed in neat rows of bodies, haunted thin faces behind barbed wire, and electrocuted people on the fence, living skeletons trudging along on a death march, starving children laid out on the ground. The objects are what Hirsch termed *the accoutrements of atrocity*, such as wire fences, piles of shoes, clothes and spectacles, furnaces with or without the debris of bones, abandoned possessions, the courtyard where prisoners were counted and the deportations to gas chambers began, and the entire topography of atrocity. All these are *stock images*, namely a limited number of photographs that have become the tropes of the Shoah. They are all considered "icons of extermination" and they appear in most publications and museums. They have been continually re-contextualized in new discourses, in works of art, in museum brochures or leaflets for visitors, for students, or for children. Each site endows them with a different function and meaning.[13] As Sontag (2004, 39)[14] observes, "The photograph will have its own career blown by the whims and loyalties of the diverse communities that have use for it."

Art historian Didi-Huberman (2012)[15] contends that every Holocaust photograph is an act - an event - although the image is never complete by itself, never shows the whole. Photographs taken by victims, he maintains, can help the viewer understand who they were and what drove them to risk their lives and photograph the atrocities. Therefore, in order to gain some understanding of these images or of what they stand for one must unfold their phenomenology as far as

---

11. Hirsch, Marianne. 2001. "Surviving Images Holocaust Photographs and The Work of Post Memory." *The Yale Journal of Criticism* 14, no. 1. 5-37.
12. Surviving Images: Holocaust photographs and the work of post-memory. *The Yale Journal of Criticism*, Volume 14, Number 1, spring 2001. John Hopkins University Press. 5-37
13. Holtschneider, K. Hannah (2011). *The Holocaust and Representations of Jews* (Routledge Jewish Studies Series). Taylor and Francis, Kindle Edition. 60-61.
14. Sontag, Susan. 2004. *Regarding the Pain of Others*. Picador.
15. Didi Huberman, George. 2012. *Images in Spite of All*. London and Chicago: University of Chicago Press.

possible. His example is the four photographs taken probably by Alberto (also called Alekko or Alex) Errera in Birkenau.[16] These photos provided the unique evidence of the burning of people. Didi-Huberman defines the photographs - "wrest from hell" - as an act of resistance. The photos were taken from a hiding place behind a wall and therefore would always be partial, a "tear" as Huberman calls it, but also a "veil" since most of the scene is concealed and suggestive. While the "tear" gives us information about the situation that was photographed, the "veil" tells us a great deal about the photographers and the conditions in which they ventured to take the photographs. Other scholars agree that regarding Holocaust photographs one must inquire who took the picture, by what means, and in what circumstances, and as far as possible explore the thorniest question, namely, "who were the victims"? We generally know more about Nazi perpetrators because they left reports, than we do about their victims (Magilow and Silverman 2015, 26; Lower 2021).[17]

Hirsch (2001, 13) recalls the story *Traces* by Ida Fink. Fink describes a scene in which the heroine looks at a photo. "On the one hand, a blurred picture with a lot of white in it, depicting footprints and some wooden stalls in the snow. On the other, a narrative about the massacre of the children and their parents, the last in their ghetto. The two are incommensurable, illustrating the incommensurability of the crime and the instruments of representation, and even conceptualization, available to us. The absolute limits of representation." Hirsch notes that "perhaps the most haunting, arresting moment in Ida Fink's 'Traces' is the witness's question, 'I wonder who photographed it'?" Fink's story reminds us that "every image also represents, more or less visibly or readably, the context of its production and the very specific gaze of a photographer." (ibid.)

Other questions that pertain to the phenomenology of the photograph are was it staged by the Nazi photographers from the official propaganda units? Was it taken by an independent Nazi "tourist" to the ghetto, or by a Jewish prisoners or Jewish photographers such as Mendel Grossman and Hynrik Ross in Łódź, who risked their lives with every photo they took in seeking to record the last months or moments of Jewish life?[18]

Sybil Milton (1984), examined the chronological, geographic, and photo-historical context of images produced by Nazi, Jewish, neutral, and Allied cameramen, pointing out that every publication that makes use of these photographs should provide information about the following:

---

16. Didi-Huberman does not mention the photographer's name because it was revealed after he had published his book. Personal communication.
17. Magilow, Daniel H., and Lisa Silverman. 2015. *Holocaust Representations in History*. London: Bloomsbury Academic. Lower, Wendy. 2021. *The Ravine. A Family, a Photograph, a Holocaust Massacre Revealed*. Apollo Books. Head of Zeus.
18. https://www.wbur.org/artery/2017/03/29/henryk-ross-nazi-ghetto

1. The photographer's identity: Nazi, Jewish, neutral, or Allied liberator;

2. The date, location, and circumstances of the photograph, preferably including the image's position and context on the full roll of film;

3. The function of the photograph: officially commissioned combat photography, newsreel or magazine photojournalism, propaganda photo, or amateur snapshot; and whether the photograph was intended for publication or for private use.

4. The relationship between camera and subject: did the subject/s cooperate, were they under duress, or were they unaware of the camera, and was the scene posed, staged, or candid.

The differences between official Nazi photographs, Nazi amateur photographs, and Jewish or prisoners' photographs, are crucial. While Nazi official photographers staged propaganda films in the ghettos and the camps, that would justify the genocide for posterity,[19] Nazi amateur photographers also risked a lot when they took photographs. The war caught the Nazis in what Wendy Lower (2021, 19) labels a camera craze, that had prevailed in Germany since the 1920s. Joseph Goebbels, for instance, embedded fifteen thousand photojournalists in all theaters of the conflict, producing more than 3.5 million images." (ibid. 15). Soldiers were not allowed to take private photographs. Lower reports that "Second Lieutenant Max Täubner was found guilty of excessive barbarism unworthy of a man in uniform; his actions included "taking tasteless and shameless pictures", including one of a naked Jewish woman, and openly bragging about them to his wife and friends back in Germany [...] Täubner's crime was not murdering Jews, since the court affirmed their extermination. Rather, he was charged for his "barbarism" in producing and displaying atrocity photographs. His breaches of discipline and state security earned him a ten-year prison sentence. This is the only known German wartime trial of this kind."[20]

Scholars consider amateur photos to be an important historical source because they give us an outsider's view of ghetto life, without the intervention of Nazi propaganda staging. Lewis (2001) points out that one may find more evidence in an amateur snapshot taken as a record of "what was there" than in a photograph taken by an identified Nazi professional who served the cause of Nazi propaganda. Hanno Loewy (1989, quoted in Holtschneider 2011), who studied the provenance of 2400 photographs from Auschwitz Birkenau, points out that amateurs

---

19. See also Silver Ochayon, Sheryl. 2013. "Who Took the Pictures? The Ghetto Photography of Mendel Grossman in Lodz, as Compared With the Ghetto Photography of German 'Ghetto Tourists'." https://www.yadvashem.org/articles/general/who-took-the-pictures.html
20. Lower, *The Ravine*.

photographed everything, all the way to the gas chambers. Sybil Milton (1984, 4)[21] explains the importance of amateur photos as follows:

> ...in the Einsatzgruppen the killers and photographers were often one and the same. Their sadistic voyeurism led to the crassest violations of the victims' privacy; even the most personal moments of death and dying were no longer respected. But despite the violence and horror of some of these amateur images, this candid record represents an important historical source.[22]

Amateur photos are often accompanied by the photographers' impressions, which direct our attention to the criterial features that prompted them to shoot the photograph. Following is Heinrich Joest's photo of barefoot teenagers in Warsaw ghetto (Image 1). Joest was an amateur photographer, a hotel owner, and a Nazi soldier. On his forty-second birthday, he bought a camera and treated himself to a trip to the ghetto to observe those Jews he had never seen before. He spent an entire day in the ghetto, driven by a "horrified fascination," and took a hundred and forty one photos depicting all manner of misery, starvation, and death.[23] In his book, he declares, "Later when I looked at these pictures, I asked myself, how could you photograph something like that?" Jean Baudrillard (1984, 27)[24] maintains that atrocity images arouse "brute fascination" and seduce the viewer, but Joest was fascinated and seduced by the sights themselves. He admitted that he felt the urge to see more and more of them.

---

21. Milton, Sybil. 1984. *The Camera as Weapon: Documentary Photography and the Holocaust.*
22. The Einsatzgruppen were the "special action" squads that murdered more than a million Jews in Ukraine
23. Schwarberg, Gunther (Editor). 2001. *Joest, Heinrich. A Day in the Warsaw Ghetto.* Steidl Publishers.
24. Baudrillard, Jean. 1984. *The Evil Demon of Images.* Power Institute Publications, no. 3.

Image 1. "A group of destitute boys on a curb in the Warsaw Ghetto, 1941"; photographer Heinrich Joest. United States Holocaust Memorial Museum. Photograph Number: 32328[25]

The caption of the US Holocaust Memorial Museum does not mention the photographer, Joest. Joest commented on this photo as follows: "I was amazed to see how many boys had no shoes, even though it was already quite cold on this September day. After enlarging this photo, I later discovered, in the background, the Wehrmacht sergeant with his attendant, a soldier. I thought to myself that he intended to make some purchase in the ghetto, jewelry perhaps."

This commentary, which is excluded from the information given by the schoolbooks that include this photograph, reveals the criterial feature of the image in the eyes of the photographer: barefoot children on a cold autumn day, in a street where everyone else wears shoes.

Joest's "amazement" reveals his genuine or affected naïveté: why don't they wear shoes in cold September, when everybody else does? He also noted the military men whom the caption ignores. His interpretation of the military presence in the ghetto is rather odd, implying that he was unaware of its horrific cynicism: they probably came to buy cheap jewelry. After all, this is what one does when visiting a Jewish neighborhood, even while you lock them in a ghetto and starve

---

25. https://collections.ushmm.org/search/catalog/pa2425

them to death. In his comments Joest reveals his position as a "tourist" in the ghetto, a man who was not involved, was unaware of what was going on, and who came to take a peep and some photos, as many other Nazi soldiers did, and as tourists usually do in poverty stricken neighborhoods in India, or in hunger stricken areas in Africa.

In one Israeli schoolbook this photo bears the caption: *Boys of the Ghetto* (Gutman 2009), omitting the qualifier "destitute" from the caption given by the museum, as if the expression "boys in a ghetto" is telling enough. Each of these three captions draws our attention to different criterial features of the picture, to different meanings. Personally, I was drawn to the boy who sits on a log. His resourcefulness fascinated me and had I written the caption to this photograph I would have drawn the students' attention to him, because this is where he is transformed from a victim to a boy again, and students might be able to identify with him, a boy of their age, in another country, in another world.

A further detail with which the students can identify is the huge feet of these adolescents, since this is the age when boys' feet grow very rapidly, almost out of proportion, and this growth may explain why they are all barefooted. They have outgrown their shoes and their parents could not afford to buy them new ones. The adults around them, who wear shoes, no longer have this problem. Teenagers today, who change their shoes frequently and whimsically, can feel empathy or compassion towards these barefooted youngsters.

Holtschneider[26] (2011, 61) demonstrates the lack of details that exists in Holocaust museums, where the texts that accompany the photographs do not always reveal the purpose for which the photo was taken, and the uses to which it was put before its transposition to the museum. For example, in the Jewish Museum in Berlin the images about the activities of the Jewish Cultural Association (Jüdischer Kulturbund) are displayed without mentioning that these were also used for Nazi propaganda purposes, showing to the world that Jews in Germany apparently were able to conduct a thriving cultural life. (ibid. p. 121).

Sybil Milton takes historians to task for neglecting to draw attention to these important facets of photographs. She argues that still photography of the Holocaust has been used carelessly in historical literature. The origin or purpose of the photograph have seldom been deemed important or identified. Lewis (2001) notes that in the photographic archives at the United States Holocaust Memorial Museum, which serve as a source of photographs for Yad Vashem and for various publications, including schoolbooks, alongside every photograph is a preprinted form that provides relevant information. But against the item *photographer,* the most frequent entry is "No photographer recorded." Susan Crane observes that by

---

26. Holtschneider, K. Hannah. 2011. *The Holocaust and Representations of Jews*. Routledge, Jewish Studies Series.

definition, photographs are images taken out of context[27], the context of their production, the context of the scene they represent, and the context of the lives of any person living or dead who appears in them. Therefore, the more we reconstruct their phenomenology, the more we know them historically. Photographic historian Janina Struk's book *Photographing the Holocaust*, (2004) is an attempt to uncover the misuse and the irresponsible recirculation of Holocaust atrocity images. Struk, (p.2) recalls that when she asked an archivist about the provenance of a Holocaust image, she was met by a quizzical, impatient response. She was made to feel that it was "irrelevant and morbid" to inquire. If we all "know" what a Holocaust atrocity photograph conveys and no one doubts that it is genuine, then seemingly no-one needs to consider the tragic specifics, except perhaps the relatives of the dead. However, as Milton (1984) insists, emotion is not equivalent to scholarship and the irresponsible and inappropriate use of Holocaust photography must be supplanted by visually literate scholarship.

Without their phenomenology, many Holocaust photographs have lost their linkage to the events they depict, and it is therefore difficult to know "to what extent these photographs, which have been transformed into symbolic images by their repeated use, are able to depict or convey the historical truth." (Keilbach 2009, 55)

Israeli schoolbooks use Holocaust photos indiscriminately, be they authentic or staged by Nazi photographers, presenting them as factual and objective without specifying most of the background details even when these are available. They do not differentiate between amateur and official Nazi photos, or those taken by Jewish photographers, which are surprisingly rare in these schoolbooks, although their work is shown and discussed in the unit students learn for their final examination "How Can a Man", published by The International School of Holocaust Teaching in Yad Vashem[28]. In this unit, in a chapter called "Teaching the Holocaust through photographs," researcher Fancesca Rainiger explains the important details one must take into consideration when discussing, showing and looking at Holocaust photographs, demonstrating the work of Jewish photographer Hynrik Ross as an example. She insists that without the phenomenology of the photograph and the details that were mentioned above, one can never know the photographic event, and whether the photograph was "exploitative, reportorial, or memorial in nature" (Milton, ibid. p. 12).

Most photos in the textbooks are identified, if at all, only by their current institutional affiliation or "ownership," which reveals nothing about the photo's circumstances. They are often cropped or become parts of a collage, and readers

---

27. Crane, Susan. 2008. *Choosing Not to Look*, 325. See also Zelizer, Barbie. 2000. *Remembering to Forget, Holocaust Memory through the Camera's Eye.* 226-229.
28. https://www.yadvashem.org/he/education/video-toolbox/hevt-photographs.html#1

are generally left without information about the photographic event, the photographer, or the photographed subjects.

Since the phenomenology of Holocaust photographs is usually missing in Israeli textbooks, the students cannot tell whether the photographer was in a position to order the subject to smile, or to eat, to ignore a dying man or child in the street, to play the violin or to dance.

Staged Photographs - the Judenrat Building in Warsaw Ghetto[29]

Andrea Liss (1998)[30] notes that since the ghettos were strictly closed off to the outside world, except to the Nazis stationed there and to the new arrivals, the photographs that remain are double-edged; although they offer rare views of the ghettos, many were staged by the Nazis. These staged photographs were orchestrated to veil the mechanisms of the Final Solution and were targeted at the (largely unconcerned) free world, to project the lie that victims of the Nazis were safe, and even gainfully employed. The following example shows two photographs of the building of the Jewish council (the Judenrat) in Warsaw Ghetto, taken by two professional Nazi photographers - Albert Cusian and Erhard Josef Knobloch - employed by the army's Propaganda Unit 689. The photographs (Images no. 2 and no. 3) were transposed to Yad Vashem archives by the German Bundesarchive,[31] which claims to hold "more than twelve million pictures, aerial photographs and posters [...] of German history. Most of them focus on events and persons that happened and lived in the 20th century."

Several scholars, among them Sybil Milton, Andrea Liss, and Ulrich Keller, mention these official Nazi photographers. Stationed in Warsaw in 1941, PK Unit 689 took staged pictures depicting the "amusements of the ghetto elite". Yad Vashem researcher, Sheryl Silver Ochayon (no date mentioned), notes that the footage is remarkable for its cinematic falsification, as it juxtaposes the meticulously-staged scenes in which Jews are shown enjoying a life of luxury in the ghetto with scenes of poverty, starvation, and abject misery.[32] The PK unit operated under the auspices of Signal, the Nazis' main international propaganda magazine, which appeared in more than twenty foreign language editions and had a circulation of 2.5 million.[33]

---

29. The Judenrat was the Jewish council appointed by the Nazis to govern Jewish life and help execute the German policy of extermination.
30. Ibid., *Photography and Naming* pp. 1-13
31. https://www.bundesarchiv.de/EN/Navigation/Find/Photos/pictures.html
32. Sheryl Silver Ochayon, *Who Took the Pictures* https://www.yadvashem.org/articles/general/who-took-the-pictures.html#footnote13_8etk16m
33. Liss, Andrea. 1998. *Trespassing through Shadows: Memory, Photography, and the Holocaust.* Visible Evidence, Volume 3. Minneapolis London: University of Minnesota Press.

Milton[34] reports that Albert Cusian was stationed in Warsaw during 1939 and 1940 to chronicle the creation of the Warsaw ghetto. His equipment (p.48) "was a Leica camera with a 3.5 Elmar lens to capture the misery and suffering of the ghetto's inhabitants." Cusian, who was an eager photographer, reported as follows, "I photographed everything in sight. The subject matter was so interesting. I took pictures in the morgue and at the Jewish cemetery. Bodies of Jews who had died during the night were laid out on the pavements for collection in the morning. I'd wait until the collectors came and then took pictures of them." (Milton ibid.).

Image 2. Photographers: Albert Cusian and Erhard Josef Knobloch Propaganda-Kompanie 689: Warsaw, Poland, May 1941: Policemen and citizens at the entrance to the Judenrat building in the ghetto. Yad Vashem archive. 101366. 3955/273

In Avieli-Tabibian's schoolbook (*From Peace to War and Shoa* 2009) the caption under this photograph is "a couple leaving the Judenrat building, 1939," prompting us to focus on the couple, and in Naveh et al., 2009 (*Totalitarianism*

---

34. Milton, *The Camera as Weapon*.

and Shoah), the caption reads, "People at the entrance to the Judenrat building in Warsaw," with no date specified.

The photograph in Image 2 complies with the instructions given to official Nazi photographers of Warsaw Ghetto, to show how indifferent rich Jews were to their starving brethren, and to photograph people's suffering as proof of Jewish decadence rather than the result of the Germans' policy of starvation (Ulrich Keller 1984)[35]. The photographers never recorded Nazi crimes and portrayed Jewish misery as an element of Jewish lifestyle or Jewish nature. Since many of the propaganda photographs of these two photographers were manipulated and staged, as documented in the diary of Adam Czerniakow,[36] and were taken during a short span of time[37] it is quite likely that photograph no.2 (101366) that was transposed to Israeli schoolbooks, was also staged, for it shows two people who are too well dressed for the ghetto, and a little man emerging behind them from the building, wearing an oversized coat and bearing a frightened expression. The exceptionally well-dressed couple who ignore the dying man may enrage the viewer, although such sights are quite common all over the world. The couple belies the Jewish commitment, *One for all, all for one* and the slogan *Whoever saves a single soul saves an entire world*, upon which Israeli children are educated. From this perspective, the photograph connotes moral downfall.

The photograph appears to be the second of a pair of photographs that were submitted together to Yad Vashem and were allocated consecutive numbers:

The photographs ID card in Yad Vashem

Item ID	101365
Archival Signature	3955/273

Item ID	101366
Archival Signature	3955/274

The first photograph (101365) mentioned in this card is the following (Image 3):

---

35. Keller, Ullrich.1984. *The Warsaw Jewish Ghetto in Photographs*.
36. Czerniakow, Adam. 1999. *The Warsaw Diary of Adam Czerniakow: Prelude to Doom*. Edited by Raul Hilberg. Published in association with the United States Holocaust Memorial Museum.
37. Ulrich Keller explains that "while a prolonged or repeated presence of Propaganda-Kompanie 689 in Warsaw is a distinct possibility, the photographs reflect such uniform social, economic and weather conditions that they must have been taken in the span of a few weeks. On the basis of numerous factual picture details, it can safely be determined that the period in question is late winter and early spring, 1941."

Image 3. Warsaw, Poland: Two Jewish policemen at the entrance to the Judenrat building, May 1941. Yad Vashem Archive 101365. 3955/274

The credits written on the photo ID card are:

Photographer	PK 689 Photographers Knobloch & Cusian
Date of Accession	02/07/1993
Subjects	Jewish Police, Corpses, Ghettos, Buildings

The schoolbooks provide no information about the photographers and their work, and do not show the first photograph of the Judenrat building, without the couple and the little man. The photographs remain unattributed and in at least one case (Avieli-Tabibian, 2009) the photograph is misdated. The date given in the schoolbook is 1939, whereas only "in October 1940, the Jews of Warsaw, Poland's capital, were ordered to move to the Muranów district, just west of the city center. On the night of November 15, 1940, the Germans sealed off the Warsaw Ghetto." (Magilow and Silverman 2015, 26).

While for the Nazi Germans, the criterial feature of the photo was the good life some Jews were leading in the Ghetto, and their complete indifference to their brethren's suffering, the criterial feature which made it an apt choice for Israeli schoolbooks, must have been the building itself, since it is embedded in a subchapter dealing with the Judenrat. While the identity cards of both photos mention *Jewish Police, Corpses, Ghettos*, and *Buildings*, the captions in the Israeli schoolbooks refer only to the affluent people and to the building, without mentioning the "corpse" on the steps, thus prompting the students to ignore him and to focus only on the building, the policemen, and the well-dressed couple who pass by the dying figure and continue their conversation. Hence, what is lodged in the viewer's mind is the image that the German-Nazis sought to embed in us (Keilbach 2009).

Israeli schoolbooks that present Nazi propaganda photographs as objective and informative documentary sources, without divulging their phenomenology, transpose into the schoolbook texts the Nazi gaze uncritically and without reservation. The staged photograph becomes authentic, as the Nazis wished it to be seen.

Transduction: Changing Modes from Photo to Drawing

One of the modes employed to represent Holocaust victims to children is *transduction*. Transduction is the term used for the moving of semiotic material from one mode to another.

It "names a process in which ontological change takes place. That is, the source and the target mode have entities of a different kind: whether in terms of the *logics* (of *temporality* or *spatiality* as in transduction from writing to image) or of 'substance.' The signifier is transformed, however minutely, bearing the traces of its recent as well as those of all other uses." (Kress 2020, 46)

Kress explains that given this difference in material and cultural work performed in the process of transduction, there can never be a perfect translation from one mode to another. Hence, "We can ask about gains and losses in the process of modal change." (Kress and Bezemer 2008, 176). The prime example of transduction of Holocaust photographs into drawings is Art Spiegelman's graphic novel MAUS, in which he turned his father's Holocaust experience into a novel, transducting iconic and personal photographs into drawings. In doing so, he argued, he turned his father's story into literature but not into fiction (*Metamaus*, 125)[38] and put the dead into "little boxes", which, so he explained, gave "real tensile strength to the work." (ibid.73). The original three-page edition of *"Maus"*, published in *Funny Animals* in 1972, begins with a cartoon redrawing of the famous photograph of Margaret Bourke-White showing liberated prisoners in Buchenwald. Hirsch (2001)[39] comments that since the son was unable to imagine

---

38. Art Spiegelman 2011. Metamaus. Viking Pub.
39. Hirsch, M. *Surviving Images: Holocaust Photographs and the Work of Postmemory.*

his own father's past other than by way of repeatedly circulated and emblematic cultural images, that had become part of his own consciousness and his family album, he transducted them into drawings, thereby turning them into his own creation. Spiegelman furthermore turned the human beings into mice and cats, thereby foregrounding the essence of their existence in the camps. Cartoon drawings invariably represent the essence of what they depict (Van Leeuwen 2005). Individual differences are irrelevant from the point of view of the essential or general truth the sign maker seeks to convey. Newspaper cartoons, for instance, tend to have reduced articulation of detail, background, depth, light and shade, and no articulation of color and tonal gradation. By contrast, the articulation of these very parameters in news photographs is greatly amplified. Regarding their modality value, argues Van Leeuwen, cartoons are perceived as visual "opinions", and are considered to be less factual than photographs, which are believed to provide reliable documentary information. The cartoon turns reality into an imagined version of this reality, which is less shocking than photos. Thus, it renders reality imaginable.

Some authors and designers of textbooks probably believe that transducting Holocaust photos into drawings constitutes a double shield that makes it even easier for young readers to confront what the photographs show. Since it conveys a clear one-dimensional message and is less complex than the photo, the drawing does not actually document but foregrounds the atrocity, and helps create the traumatic post-memory with its clear message. Such considerations may have prompted the designers of the textbook for high-school students with special needs[40], to transduct iconic Holocaust photos into drawings, using a high contrast technique. The book does not mention who gave the designer permission to transduct the photos, and the captions under them, as we shall see, refer us back to the photographs themselves, as if there is no difference between the original photograph and the transducted drawing. One example is that of a woman armband seller of Warsaw ghetto, photographed by Joest.

---

40. *Toward Resurrection and Peace (1999)*

אישה בגטו וורשה מוכרת סרטי שרוול ובהם מגן־דוד
(אנציקלופדיה של השואה א', 62)

Image 4: *Toward Resurrection and Peace* (1999, 93). "A woman in Warsaw ghetto sells armbands with the Star of David. (Shoa Encyclopedia I, item 62a)". Copyrights: Ramot Pub. Tel Aviv University, Yahas Project. The Ministry of Education.

The photograph was taken by Joest on his birthday trip to the ghetto. It appears in most textbooks without credit, as an icon of ghetto misery.[41] Although the woman has no name and no history, Joest's comments contextualize her and tell us that the photo was not staged, and that the woman may not have been aware of being photographed: "This woman stood with closed eyes in front of a wall of tattered posters announcing a symphony concert with Szymon Pullman in the concert hall at Rymarska 12, and a program at the café Ogrod in Nowoliopki Street. She was selling padded armbands with the Star of David on them, which every Jew was required to wear. She looked as if she was about to topple over and die the next moment."

The tattered remains of posters on the wall, advertising cultural events and other entertainments, emphasize the tragedy, the collapse of Jewish life in the

---

41. *In The Ghetto of Warsaw: Photographs by Heinrich Joest*, 1st. edition.

ghetto, and the trajectory of this woman's life from an apparently normal existence, replete with cafes and concerts, to the brink of hell. However, in the schoolbooks Joest's text is omitted. In the drawing, the texts of the advertisements are rendered incomprehensible. From that, one may infer that it was the essence and not the details that were deemed important in the transduction. The interest of the designer must have been to show the woman on the background of destruction, where ads about cafes and opera have long lost their meaning and only torn shreds are left of them.

Image 5. Heinrich Joest. Warsaw Ghetto, Poland. September 19, 1941. Yad Vashem archive 2536_40.

Although the woman herself is changed and the photo is altered, the transduction bears traces of the original. The drawing resembles the photograph in some of its features, which are both concrete and conceptual, and were probably criterial for the book designer. These features are the armbands and the impression of misery. The essence of the image, the evocation of resignation and doom, is transposed, yet many details of the original are missing. In the photograph, the woman's person tells a story of starvation and emaciation, but above all of humiliation and despair. Her dignified expression despite the abject despair she evokes, her closed eyes, her beautiful hair, her elegant dress and coat, which accentuate her downfall and the tragedy of her fate, are effaced in the transducted version. These details, as Van Leeuwen explains, are superfluous to the drawing, because they add meaning that diverts attention from the essence of the photo. In the drawing, she looks younger and poorer, her cloths are shabby, and her eyes are open, staring blankly as if in demand. However, the reference to the original photograph in the caption indicates that the schoolbook's designer believed that the missing details do not alter the photo or its meaning.

The second example is another of Heinrich Joest's photographs, taken on his birthday trip to the ghetto.

Image 6. Heinrich Joest. 1941. Yad Vashem archives 2536/81.

Joest's original caption reads, "These were clearly sisters. If the younger one was dead, I could not say. She did not move."

All the textbooks that display this photograph have the same caption: "a *boy* dying in his sister's arms." (My bold).

The transduction (Image 7) may hint at the motivation, which could have been unconscious, for the dying girl's change of gender.

Image 7. *Toward Resurrection and Peace* (1999, 87)

The drawing transformed the older sister, who is a child herself, into an angry woman, a mother wearing a coat, heavy boots and an armband with the Jude inscription; the dying little girl becomes a young bald person, who seems to be alive and looking upward, perhaps toward heaven. The woman in the drawing looks out at us fiercely and demandingly. In the distance, behind them, we see six ghostly figures that presumably represent the six million exterminated Jews.

What was transposed into the drawing is apparently the cardinal criterial feature or the essence of the photograph in the eyes of the textbook designer, namely the Pieta posture. While the Pieta is not part of Jewish or Israeli culture it is part of the general culture that Israel pretends to share with Europe. This may have grasped the imagination of the designers of Holocaust and history textbooks, who transformed the dying little girl into a boy, and may have influenced the authorizing committees that have overlooked the change. Holocaust atrocity images that have become icons, as Judith Keilbach (2009, 62) observes, have acquired meaning by virtue of their motifs and specific composition, several of which echo conventions of Christian display, for example, the motif of "ecce homo" or of a "martyr." These Christian themes are prevalent in Israeli culture and popular psychology. In fact, Michelangelo's Virgin Mary bears more likeness to the girl in the photo than to the mother in the drawing. Both are gentle, resigned, and avert their eyes. One may also argue that the little girl holding her dying sister arouses much more empathy than the angry mother in the drawing does.

All the semiotic changes and transformations notwithstanding, the essence of the Pieta emerges, and the caption refer us to item b'468 in the Shoa Encyclopedia, as if it were a faithful reproduction of the photo. It is worth noting that B'468 (or the number 62a in the previous example) is not the photo's serial number, which is 2536/81 in the Yad Vashem Archive, but the page number in the encyclopedia, displaying the photograph as one in a series of photos of starving children in Warsaw Ghetto, without credit. As Janina Struk (2004) notes, in spite of copyrights laws Holocaust photographs are seldom credited. Milton (1986) remarks that such negligence and disregard for the precise reference of photos is a sign of irresponsibility, which attests to a tendency to use the pictures functionally and emotionally, rather than historically.

Kress (2020, 53) argues that the equation of the transduction and the original emanates from a "misleading notion of the transposition of meaning." He adds that teachers [and perhaps textbook authors as well] pay little heed to transduction, as if saying "I'm interested in knowledge; I'm here to teach history, not to worry about drawing or writing or whatever."

George Didi Huberman (2012, 120) strenuously objects to tampering with Holocaust photos, arguing that the result of graphic manipulation is that the document is "quite simply disfigured, despised, severed from its phenomenology at the very moment of pretending to give a synthetic representation of the event". From this point of view, perhaps the solution that Lissner[42] proposes could be a better one. Lissner believes transduction may offer a good alternative and commends the use of a dignified and respectful type of drawing rather than a degrading photo, especially of children, provided these drawings do not strive to reproduce the original photo, but rather function as symbols. He notes, "The graphic approach, using drawings, often symbolic ones, brings out a principle rather than a particular person." This is what Art Spiegelman did in MAUS.[43]

Another example is recent Israeli Holocaust literature for children, which has increased in volume in response to the Ministry of Education's 2013 decision to oblige teachers to teach the Holocaust to all students in schools and kindergartens. The picture books use Holocaust symbols and icons such as the yellow badge, the barbed wire fences, the striped uniforms of the camps' prisoners, the swastika, and other familiar images, in symbolic and metaphoric ways, "infusing the visual memory of the Holocaust through different channels and, at the same time, soften the horror by connecting it to positive, warm feelings." (Rima Shikhmanter 2014).[44] For instance, a subliminal visual representation of a barbed wire as bare

---

42. Lissner, Jorgen. 1981. Merchants of Misery. *New Internationalist*. June 1. 1981
43. Spiegelman, Art. 1980. *Maus, a Novel*. Row Publishers.
44. Shikhmanter, Rima. 2021. "Beyond the Yellow Badge Constructing a Visual Memory of the Holocaust in Israeli Picture Books, 1980-2020." A paper presented at the Eighth International

thorny trees creates "a double meaning of a threat and closure but also of magic and fantasy", and a promise of resurrection. These multiple meanings reflect the central theme of these books: "in all evil, one can find small islands of goodness." (ibid.)

Since schoolbooks are meant to teach the concepts that are conveyed through the photographs, such symbolic representation may serve this purpose much better than the drawings that pretend to be realistic.

Conference of The European Network of Picturebook Research hosted by The Program in Research of Child and Youth Culture, Tel Aviv University. October 3-4.

Chapter 4. Symbols and Icons

> Photos are markers of both truth-value and symbolism. (Barbi Zelizer, *Remembering to Forget*, p. 9)[1]

In the next three chapters, I examine some of the photographs that have become symbols, icons, or specimens of categories, and trace their use in schoolbooks. For schoolchildren, as for all post-memory generations, these photographs *are* the Shoah. Therefore, it seems important to understand what motivates schoolbook designers to show these images to young students, and to find out how they guide them to understand what they see.

Icons and Symbols

The photos we find in textbooks and which Israeli schoolchildren see every year during preparations for Holocaust Day, are chosen from the limited number of Holocaust stock images that have become the Holocaust itself or its simulacra for post-memory generations. This is because the real has disappeared. Equating the Holocaust to an earthquake, Lyotard (1984, *The Differend*) asserts that not only the landscape, the people, and the events were erased, but also the means by which one can describe or remember them. The few buildings left in Auschwitz have mostly been reconstructed, rearranged, and are often presented as different from their original function. As Dwork and van Pelt (1994, 239)[2] emphasize, "The guides who direct tourists through Auschwitz I, do not indicate that the building that they understand to be 'the place where it happened' is in fact a facsimile". Hence, the photos are the evidence. However, Zelizer believes that the images that have lost contact with their original circumstances, threaten, "to become a representation without substance" (Zelizer 1998, 201). As such, they can empower "both those who seek authentication of Nazi atrocities and those who deny them."

The stock images reproduced in most albums, museums and schoolbooks are the ones that have attained an almost mythic status in a world that has become ever more accustomed to seeing violence every day in color, live on the screen, from every corner of the world. Nevertheless, to this day all the atrocities are

---

1. Zelizer, Barbie. 1998. *Remembering to Forget: Holocaust Memory through the Camera's Eye*. Chicago: University of Chicago Press.
2. Deborah Dwork, Deborah and Robert Jan van Pelt 1994. "Reclaiming Auschwitz," in Geoffrey Hartman, ed., *Holocaust Remembrance: The Shapes of Memory*, Cambridge, MA. 236-37.

judged and evaluated against the Holocaust. "It is as if in the spring of 1945 the world lost a certain innocence, and the pictorial remains of that passage have become the leitmotivs for our reactions to all that we are presented." (Brink 2000, 136)[3]

These few images were transposed from Nazi archives and liberators' albums to public sites such as museums and to Holocaust history books. During the course of this transposition, the atrocity in the photos is "moved from the contingent and the particular to the symbolic and the general," (Zelizer 1998, 9). The atrocity is kept alive, foregrounded, and at the same time it is transformed into mere representation.

Cornelia Brink (2000,138)[4] explains that pictures that are classified as icons differ from those considered "documentary images" in that they provide little or no evidence of a specific time and place, anonymizing human beings, depriving them of their individuality as far as possible and placing them within aesthetic pictorial traditions to serve as illustrations. The photographed individuals become icons through abstraction and assume symbolic power since they are not really narrated themselves, but serve as illustrations of the overall story of extermination.

Relics of the camps, barbed wire, the entrance gate to Auschwitz-Birkenau, the camps' watch towers, barracks, crematoria, chimneys, and heaps of Zyklon B gas, became icons that evoke the Final Solution, or the image and the idea of the system of concentration and extermination camps, in which the mass murder of European Jews, organized by the state, was carried out (Brink 2000).

Turning photographs into icons and symbols is necessary as Judith Keilbach (2009)[5] maintains, if they are to form the building blocks of collective memory. As such, the images should not be complex. They must be conventional and simple or else become conventionalized through cropping or montage. In this way, they quickly direct the viewer to the intended meaning. Hannah Holtschneider (2011) notes that these are indeed the criterial features of Holocaust photos that render them suitable for presentation in Holocaust museums: "the curators rely on the accessibility of the images, their 'immediacy,' making a complex process of decoding and contextualization superfluous. Hence, while photographs are also treated as historical sources, their value as sources of historical knowledge is not explored" (p. 59). Holtschneider observes that unlike Anna Frank and a few other victims who are shown individually and have a story, all the others, whose story is

---

3. Brink, Kornelia. "Secular Icons: Looking at Photographs from Nazi Concentration Camps." *History and Memory*, Vol. 12, no. 1. 135-150.
4. Brink, Cornelia. 2000. "Secular Icons: Looking at Photographs from Nazi Concentration Camps." *History and Memory*, vol. 12, no. 1 (Spring/Summer). Indiana University Press. 135-150.
5. Keilbach, Judith. "Photographs, Symbolic Images, and the Holocaust: On the (im)possibility of depicting historical truth." *History and Theory, Theme Issue* 47, May 2009: 54-76 © Wesleyan University 2009 ISSN: 0018-2656

not told, are presented in the museums as "orphaned", and appear to be less valued. These photographs are not treated as historical documents that deserve to be labeled. On the contrary, they are chosen from the outset as examples of larger categories (p.60).

Through the photographs, the unknown victims of the Holocaust have gained "international prominence" (Ruth Ayab 2020).[6] They have become "The Boy from Warsaw ghetto," "The last Jew of Vinnitsa," or "The mother from Ivangorod."

It appears that the same criterial features render these photographs appropriate for inclusion in Israeli schoolbooks. Most of the photographed people are displayed not as individuals but either as icons, symbols, or indices (Pierce 1991, 251)[7]. In their transposition to schoolbooks, as in their transposition to museums, the photographed individuals lose their individuality and sometimes their provenance and the time of their death. The photograph loses its phenomenology or its context as an event. Whether they are shown en masse, from a distance, in blurred photos, or in close-up, Holocaust victims generally appear in Israeli textbooks as nameless, de-contextualized beings, devoid of personal history, even when this history is available.

Pierce explains that any sign can become a symbol, an icon, or an index. If it partakes in the character of the object or in the idea it represents, then it is an *icon*. People can be iconized for what they are (the last Jew to be murdered in Vinnitsa, Image16), for their action (the Boy Image 9), or for their function in the narrative or in a universal system of values (a mother protecting her child while being shot (images no.17, 18).

Holocaust photographs are not icons in the religious sense, though they are regarded as such (Brink 2000, 137)[8], especially in Israel where Holocaust victims are labeled "saints". They are what Vicky Goldberg[9] named *secular icons*. They are iconic in the sense that they offer an analogy between the event and its representation. They also function as (authentic) symbols for all the events that comprise the Holocaust, and which have been "canonized" into an easily recognizable collection of images of atrocity in the twentieth century.

Iconicity does not necessarily attach itself to a concrete reality. Instead, the photograph can represent an abstraction by becoming the key signifier of whichever generic condition it seeks to capture. Iconic Holocaust photos came to signify predominantly abstractions such as "cruelty," "hunger," "National

---

6. Ayab, Ruth. "Photographs of Disaster." In *Visual Studies*. Routledge, Taylor and Francis. 169-193.
7. Hoopes, J. Ed. 1991. *Pierce on Signs. Writing on Semiotic by Charles Sanders Pierce*. University of North Carolina Press, North Carolina: Chapel Hill.
8. Brink, Cornelia, 2000. *Secular Icons. Looking at Photographs from Nazi Concentration Camps*.
9. *The Power of Photography*, 1993.

Socialism," "genocide," or "racism."[10] All these are concepts attached to concrete human figures or to non-human objects.

A sign becomes a *symbol* when it is different from the object it signifies but is interpreted as connoting this object. For instance, the swastika bears different meanings in two different cultures.

An *index* is a sign that relates to a referent. For instance, the weathervane that points in the direction that the wind is blowing. *Indexical* meaning signifies by establishing some "physical" or direct connection to a phenomenon or an idea it refers to. The photographed persons may function as indices when they represent metonymically certain situations (starvation) or categories (yellow badge wearers) of which they are a specimen. Although the photos "can never impart comprehensive knowledge of the Holocaust, (no picture could)," says Judith Keilbach (2009, 68) "or become historical sources in themselves, [...] their actual depiction can refer to a wider context in a metonymic way."

Piotor Sadowski (2011) maintains that all "photography is indexical insofar as the represented object is 'imprinted' by light and the chemical process on the image, creating a visual likeness that possesses a degree of accuracy and 'truthfulness' unattainable in purely iconic signs such as painting, drawing, or sculpture."[11]

Chouliaraki (2006) notes that the three types of meaning (indexical, iconic and symbolic) are not, in practice, clearly distinct and often coexist in single portrayals of suffering. Although they are not purely symbolic, for they do not merely allude to something outside themselves, Holocaust atrocity pictures have acquired symbolic significance. The mother from Ivangorod, who protects her child with her body as she is shot, became the icon of German genocide of the Jewish people in the USSR, and symbolizes motherhood.

Scholars are not unanimous in their attitude towards the iconization of Holocaust photographs. Some maintain that the iconization of photos has rendered them banal and impaired their poignancy through overuse. As Sontag (2003, 82) claims, "shock can become familiar. Shock can wear off [...]. As one can become habituated to horror in real life, one can become habituated to the horror of certain images."[12] Barbie Zelizer (1998, 158)[13] regards the repetition and the re-surfacing of the same iconic pictures as "reducing what was known about the camps [and ghettos] to familiar visual cues that would become overused with time." Clément

---

10. Chouliaraki, "The Analytics of Mediation." In *The Spectatorship of Suffering*, 79-80.
11. Sadowski, Piotr. 2011. "The Iconic Indexicality of Photography." In *Semblance and Signification:* [Iconicity in Language and Literature 10]. Edited by Pascal Michelucci, Olga Fischer and Christina Ljungberg, 353–368.
12. Sontag, Susan. *Regarding the Pain of Others*. Farrar, Straus and Giroux. Kindle Edition.
13. Zelizer, Barbi.1998. *Remembering to Forget. Holocaust Memory through the Camera's Eye*.

Chéroux believes that Holocaust photographs are often "degraded from a document containing context to a symbol lacking substance." [14]
On the other hand, the iconic and symbolic images can serve to reinforce pre-existing knowledge. Hirsch (2001a) observes that while photographs generally shock us because they show something novel, Holocaust images shock not because they are novel but because we are familiar with their context. We know what the *Arbeit Macht Frei* sign means or meant, and we know what the railway lines symbolize or the registration post at the entrance to the camps, the watchtowers, the barbed wires, or the boxes of Zyklon B. They shock us each time we look at them because they reproduce the traumatic memories we have inherited or absorbed. For Jews, old railway lines will never have a meaning other than "transports", tall chimneys crematoria, barbed wires death camps. These have all become icons, indices, and symbols of the Genocide, transmitted from one generation to the next like memes. This is what Israeli children learn. "By triggering associations and calling upon existing archives of knowledge, the symbolic images may be able to transmit historical truth even though this truth cannot be depicted in the picture itself." (Keilbach 2009, 68). One example is the gate to the Auschwitz-Birkenau death camp with its ironic *Arbeit Macht Frei* inscription. The photograph was taken by Stanislav Mucha, a Polish photographer, seconded to a unit of the Red Cross (Keilbach, 2009, 73), shortly after Auschwitz was liberated (on January 27, 1945), as part of a status report on the circumstances the Allied army encountered. For the post-Auschwitz generations, whose memory is nourished by texts and photos, or by organized tours in Auschwitz-Birkenau, this gate symbolizes "the threshold that separates the human community from the 'planet Auschwitz.' The horror therefore lies not in the photo itself but in what one knows ahead of viewing it. However, the inscribed arch did not have a central position in the history of Auschwitz. Very few of the Jews deported to Auschwitz saw that gate. Most Jewish prisoners were taken by truck directly to Birkenau to be gassed. Moreover, the expansion of the camp in 1942 placed the gate in the interior of the camp, not at its threshold (Hirsch 2012, 115). "Yet our memory clings to the inscription above the gate as the modern version of Dante's 'Lasciate ogni Speranza' at the entrance of his Inferno." (Dwork and Jan van Pelt 1994, 236-237) [15]. Even Holocaust writer and former Auschwitz inmate Ka-Tzetnik regarded it as the symbol of the planet of death. Upon realizing that Auschwitz

---

14. See Chéroux, Clément. 2001. "Du bon usage des images." In *Mémoire des Camps: Photographies des camps de concentration et d'extermination nazi* (1933–1999). Edited by Clément Chéroux. Paris: Marval, 13.
15. "Reclaiming Auschwitz," in Geoffrey Hartman, Ed. *Holocaust Remembrance: The Shapes of Memory* (Cambridge, MA, 1994), 236-37. Quoted in Sidra DeKoven Ezrahi. 1995. "Representing Auschwitz," in: *History and Memory*, Vol. 7, No. 2 (Fall Winter, 1995). Indiana University Press. 121-154.

was not "another planet", and that the yawning soldier who guarded the truck on which he and others were led to the gas chambers could have been himself, he had a vision in which the inscription *Arbeit macht frei* was transformed into a different inscription, *SHIVITTI* [שיויתי] which is written on the holy arch in every synagogue, and symbolizes the Providence.[16] "For Art Spiegelman, the creator of the Holocaust graphic narrative *Maus*, as for all of us in his generation," suggests Hirsch (2012, 64), "the gate was the visual image we share, of the victims' arrival to the camp. The artist utilized it not only to render the narrative immediate and "authentic" but also as a point of access (a gate) for himself and for his post-memorial readers." (ibid).

The gate appears on many of the covers of Israeli schoolbooks that address the Holocaust, and in all the chapters that touch on the genocide, as *the* symbol of the extermination, irrespective of whether the book is written by a survivor of the camp or by a post-memory author. The photographs that appear at the end of these books are usually those of Israeli youngsters standing erect and proud under the gate and its inscription - the symbol of antisemitism and genocide - holding aloft the Israeli flag as a symbol of resurrection, redemption, and the Zionist victory over Nazism.

The Boy: A Cropped Image as a Symbol of Annihilation

Image 8. *Forcibly pulled out of bunkers.*[17] © National Archives, Washington, Stroop Report Image No 89835b. Yad Vashem Archives 26655. 1065/848

---

16. Ka-Tzetnik. 1999. *Shivitti, a Vision*. Gateways Books & Tapes, 2nd edition.
17. US Holocaust Memorial Museum. Holocaust encyclopedia.
https://encyclopedia.ushmm.org/content/en/photo/jews-captured-by-german-troops-during-the-warsaw-ghetto-uprising.

One example of an icon and a symbol is the photograph of the boy in Warsaw ghetto, his arms raised in a gesture of surrender. Marianne Hirsch (2002, 100)[18] believes that:

> If you had to name one picture that signals and evokes the Holocaust in the contemporary cultural imagination it might well be the picture of the little boy in the Warsaw ghetto with his hands raised.

This photo, taken by Franz Konrad, was one of fifty-two black-and-white images contained in a report submitted by Stroop, the SS general who oversaw the liquidation of the ghetto. The Stroop report described in minute detail how the uprising in the Warsaw ghetto (April 19 to May 16, 1943) was crushed. The photo's original caption read *Mit Gewalt aus Bunkern hervorgeholt* (Pulled from the bunkers by force), conveying a message of success and efficiency.

Hirsch (2012, 139)[19] notes that like all perpetrator photos, the entire image "is evidence not only of the perpetrator's deed but also of the desire to flaunt and advertise the evidence of that deed." The Stroop Report, she contends, was in fact a letter addressed to Himmler, a gift of "victoriously embraced cruelty." (ibid.). SS General Jurgen Stroop sought to show Heinrich Himmler how he had (on Himmler's orders) eradicated the Jewish ghetto in Warsaw. He gathered in a large book all the daily reports of the burning of the houses, and the step-by-step elimination of the resisting population, until the uprising was crushed. His report culminates with the account of the burning of the Great Synagogue in Warsaw, after which he could triumphantly claim: "The Jewish ghetto in Warsaw is no more." He added a title page with elegant calligraphy and bound the material in rich leather for presentation to Himmler. In addition, he appended to the material forty-nine (or fifty-four, in some of the three copies of the report) photographs bearing captions.

The original Stroop Report is kept at the Instytut Pamieci Narodowej (IPN) in Warsaw. The National Archives and Records Administration (NARA) in Washington, DC, hold a microfilm copy, made in September 1945, which was used as evidence during the Nuremberg trials (Struk 2004). Justice Jackson, in his opening address, declared: "I hold a report written with Teutonic devotion to detail, illustrated with photographs to authenticate its almost incredible text, and beautifully bound in leather with the loving care bestowed on a proud work. It is the original report of the SS Brigadier General Stroop, in charge of the destruction of the Warsaw Ghetto, and its title page carries the inscription 'The Jewish Ghetto

---

18. Hirsch, Marianne.2012. "Nazi Photographs in Post-Holocaust Art: Gender as an Idiom of Memorialization." In: *Crimes of War: Guilt and Denial in the Twentieth Century*. Edited by O. Bartov.
19. Hirsch, Marianne. *The Generation of Postmemory: Writing and Visual Culture After the Holocaust*. Columbia University Press.

in Warsaw no longer exists.' It is characteristic that one of the captions explains that the photograph concerned shows the driving out of Jewish 'bandits'; those whom the photograph shows being driven out are almost entirely women and little children." (Nazi Conspiracy 1, 143)[20]

The act of photographing the roundup, Hirsch notes, functions just like the exclamation mark in the title of the report *The Jewish Quarter of Warsaw Is No More!* This exclamation mark is "the sign of unredeemable annihilation, and it connects the perpetrator's gaze and to the perpetrator's deed." (ibid.) The boy, with his raised hands, mirrors that exclamation mark and has, once he was plucked from the photograph, become the symbol of unredeemable annihilation. [21]

Hirsch (2012,130) wonders about "the enormous cultural attraction to it, the obsessive manner in which it has appeared just about everywhere for several decades in the aftermath," and asks, "how can perpetrator images [...], evidence of photography's implication in the death machine, have come to play an important, even a prevalent, role in the cultural act of memorializing the victims? How, through what distancing mechanisms, have contemporary artists, even Jewish artists of the second generation, been able to incorporate them so widely into their memorial work?"

The answer is twofold. First, as Kress (2020) explains, when a sign - in this case a photograph - is transposed from one site to another, its meaning is not transposed but transformed, because it is re-contextualized in a different textual and social environment, and its function changes. Hence, this photo, produced as evidence of the successful crushing of the revolt, has served as proof of Nazi cruelty and Jewish bravery and victimhood upon being transposed to the files of the Nuremberg trials and to commemorating sites. The second part of the answer lies apparently in the special qualities of the picture, especially in its cropped state, which is more famous than the whole photograph. It is in its cropped version that the image of the Boy has attained the role of the "most famous Holocaust photograph" and has become a "secular icon." Extracted from the original photo, he became the icon of all Jewish children exterminated under Nazi rule.

---

20. *Nazi Conspiracy and Aggression.* 1946. Ed. United States Office of Chief of Counsel for the Prosecution of Axis Criminality. 8 vols. Washington: U.S. Government Printing Office, 1946-48.
A copy of the album was found in Stroop's home in 1945. The original title of the report is *Es gibt keine jüdischen Wohnbezirke in Warschau mehr*; it was published in German, with an introduction by Andrzej Wirth, in 1960. An English translation, *The Stroop Report*, was published in 1979. It is available on the web, for example at http://www.holocaust-history.org/works/stroop-report. Stroop was tried by the American military in Dachau in January 1947 and was sentenced to death, but was extradited to Poland, where, after a trial in a Warsaw court, he was executed in the city's central prison by hanging on March 6, 1952. Source: Peter Ohlin. "The Holocaust in Ingmar Bergman's 'Persona': The Instability of Imagery." In *Scandinavian Studies*, Vol. 77, No. 2 (Summer 2005). Published by University of Illinois Press on behalf of the Society for the Advancement of Scandinavian Study. 241-274.
21. Hirsch, *The Generation of Postmemory.*

The phenomenology of the photograph from which the boy was extracted is partly revealed in the book *The Boy – a Holocaust Story* by Dan Porat (2010). Although the boy was the object of his quest, Porat was unable to identify him or the women standing on his left. However, he describes the circumstances and the people linked to the image: the ghetto, the Jews of Warsaw, resistance fighters, the notorious commandant Jurgen Stroop and Franz Konrad, the Nazi photographer who confessed to have taken the picture. Porat furthermore tells the story of Josef Blösche, the soldier shown aiming his rifle at the boy, who was sentenced to death by an East German court in 1969 and executed by a firing squad. He chronicles the life of Stroop, who was convicted by a Polish court of the murder of 56,065 people and was hanged in 1952 along with his photographer Konrad.

Image 9: Front cover of Porat's book. Hill and Wang, 2010

Porat's book cover (Image 9) shows the phases of cropping by which the boy was de-contextualized and transformed into an icon and a symbol. The *criterial feature* of the cropped photo is neither the crushing of the uprising nor Stroop's liquidation of the ghetto, but the defenselessness of children in the face of cruel state forces such as the Gestapo or the Einsatzgruppen death squads. Standing among other victims, mostly fighters of the uprising, the boy is a real boy in a real situation, one of many children like him, some of whom appear in the same photograph. However, the cropped photo of the boy and the meaning it conveys in most of its reproductions and recontextualizations, "not only leave out, but actually deny, the original context of its production, by focusing on the boy himself, isolating him from the community within which he was embedded and removing the perpetrators from view" (Hirsch 2012, 76: infantilizing the victim.)

The cropped icon

Art historian George Didi-Huberman (2012, 34) argues that cropping makes photographs appear safe at the expense of erasing the event itself. He explains that the cropping helps us focus on the "main" parts, namely those that curators of exhibitions or designers of schoolbooks and commemoration albums are interested to show.[22]

The re-contextualized symbolic image of the child, (Keilbach 2009, 72) transforms both the documentary content and the meaning of the picture. Unlike the original whole, the symbolic cropped image lacks any evidence of the uprising itself, and significantly reduces the victims' diversity; it thereby fails to do justice to the uprising and to the numerous adult victims. "If any element of the original photograph is included in the cropped version, it is usually the one soldier standing behind the boy, aiming his gun at his back. This is how the boy appears in paintings in which the actual street scene is erased, and all that remains is a mythical encounter between innocence and evil." (Hirsch 2012, 76) [23]

The changes made by cropping, not only mask the circumstances and the environment in which the boy is shown, but also erase the visual signs that would allow readings other than that of the innocence and defenselessness of child victims. Mogilev and Silverman (2015)[24] warn, regarding the image of the boy,

---

22. The four photos from Birkenau taken clandestinely by Sonderkommando workers from within the gas chamber were cropped and retouched by various curators for different reasons before they were exhibited. The wall was cropped and the women's breasts were emphasized. See Struk, Janina. 2008. *Images of Women in Holocaust Photography*.
23. *The Generation of Postmemory*.
24. Magilow, Daniel and Lisa Silverman. 2015. "The Boy in the Warsaw Ghetto (Photograph, 1943): What Do Iconic Photographs Tell Us About the *Holocaust?*" in *Holocaust Representations in History: An Introduction. London*: Bloomsbury. 13–21.

against "the dangers of relying on an iconic photograph," contending that to understand a complex history, it is essential to know as much as possible about both the photograph's broader historical context and the specific circumstances of its creation.

Keilbach adds that the cropping of the picture serves the way (West) Germany dealt with its National-Socialist past. It allowed the Germans to feel guilty without requiring them to reflect upon their own involvement in the incidents, or to take any ameliorative steps. Cropped from the photograph and removed from the original scene, the boy no longer belongs to the Warsaw ghetto. Stripped of any political and social context, this symbolic image of a child raising his hands in surrender tells a horrific story of injustice, and the innocent child's face evokes a feeling of empathy and facilitates a sense of guilt "that lies outside any actual analysis of historical responsibility." (ibid.) Hirsch asserts further that the photo "infantilizes and universalizes the victim as an innocent child and, through a false sense of intimacy fostered by the close-up, reduces the viewer to an identificatory look that disables critical faculties" (Hirsch 2012,76). His cropped image turned the boy into a unique victim, and not one of many. He is threatened and unprotected in a hostile world and not in a specific ghetto in a specific moment in history. His image almost instantly acquired symbolic overtones within broader frames of reference that endowed it with national and even global significance (Keilbach, ibid.). This status is enhanced by his anonymity, although many people have pretended to be the boy.[25] As Israel Gutman, a researcher in Yad Vashem, whose textbooks are addressed here, said in a television interview on July 31, 1998, "we'll never know who the boy in the picture is. He is one of the last anonymous children from the Warsaw ghetto. He embodies all the victims, the eradication of all of them." Gutman added a Zionist tone: "This anonymous child is part of the founding myth of the State of Israel; he embodies the tragedy of the Shoah all by himself." (*The Photos of the Century*, 2000).[26]

---

25. In the 1980s, a man named Zvi Nussbaum, an ear-nose-and throat specialist living in Rochester, New York, claimed to be the boy. Nussbaum recalls, "So on 13 July 1943, we [Nussbaum, his aunt and his uncle] were at the Polski Hotel, the meeting place stipulated by the Nazis [for transportation to Palestine in exchange for Germans held there]. As we were about to leave, an officer read out a roll call, but I wasn't on the list. I saw my aunt and uncle getting into a lorry and I panicked. I ran towards them. That was when a soldier pointed his machine gun at me and ordered me to raise my hands." This account can be found in the video film and book, *The Photos of the Century*, compiled from the audio-visual series produced by Arte and the Capa agency in cooperation with Mission 2000.
However, scholars such as Dan Porat doubt that Nusbaum is the boy. Watch Porat on https://www.c-span.org/video/?296933-1/the-boy-holocaust-story
26. Robin, Marie-Monique. Arhundradets bilder. SvT - Swedish Television Corporation. July 31, 1998, rebroadcast on June 21, 2001. Cited by Ohlin (2005,250).

Semiotician Guy Gauthier [27] notes that symbols of previous times often undergo a process of devaluation before they may surface once again. However, the symbolic power of this boy's image has not faded at all, but has rather attracted more general interpretations over time. Since the message of this photograph, especially in its cropped state, is conventionalized - everybody knows what "hands-up" means and everyone is equally shocked at seeing a small boy with his arms raised in front of a large soldier - it is used to this day as a symbol of the cruelty of oppressive powers toward children in many conflict-ridden zones, or under totalitarian regimes.

Shown as being alone in the evil world, the boy of the Warsaw ghetto has become "everyboy" in a world where children are forced to confront state brutality, barriers and high walls, and are placed at risk of being killed for no reason, by an aggressive police officer or soldier. It is the innocence of these children and their small stature, along with their helplessness in the face of state brutality, that arouse viewers' emotions and empathy toward the child, whether he or she is Vietnamese, African, or Palestinian. The boy's image has become a universal "icon of loss," as painter Samuel Bak titled one of his paintings of him.

Images of children who are transformed into icons or symbols are often cropped from larger photos and presented in a de-contextualized manner (Ayab 2020). The Napalm-burned girl, the drowned Syrian toddler and others children have become the symbols of inhumaneness in wars. However, unlike the other child-victims who became symbols of state injustice and cruelty, the Warsaw ghetto boy *is not harmed yet*; he is about to be harmed and he innocently does what he was instructed to do and what he believes will save him. The murderous Nazi gaze is projected onto this pre-extermination photograph and as we look at him, we know, as did Barthes,[28] observing the photograph of the young Lewis Payne preparing to be hanged, that "*He is dead and he is going to die.*" Schoolchildren, like all other viewers, share, maybe for the first time, Barthes' feelings when looking at the photograph: "I observe with horror an anterior future of which death is the stake [...] the photograph tells me death in the future." That this took place in the Warsaw ghetto adds to the mythical aspect of the picture, for it is associated with heroism and resistance, and this boy, represented on his own, can thus be seen both as the ultimate victim and as the archetypal child hero (Keilbach, 2009).

Both textbook designers and artists frequently take the liberty of tampering with Holocaust pictures. Some painters who survived the Holocaust as children drew the boy with their own face instead of his, explaining that he expresses their feelings and represents them. When asked by the newspaper *Die Zeit* to submit a

---

27. *Initiation à la sémiologie de l'image*, 1979.
28. The photograph was taken by Alexander Gardner, 1865. *Camera Lucida* 1981, 96.

particularly meaningful photo of himself, the Yugoslav writer Aleksandar Tišma, himself a survivor, sent in the boy's picture instead. "There are no photos of me that I connect to an important memory," he wrote, "I send you instead the photograph of another that I actually consider as my own. I immediately saw that the boy with his hands up in the right-hand corner of the picture is me. It's not only that he looks like me, but that he expresses the fundamental feelings of my growing up: the impotence in the face of rules, of humanity, of reality[...] I recognize myself in him, in him alone."[29]

Ingmar Bergman used the entire photograph in his film *Persona*, and aroused curiosity regarding not only his motivation but also the photograph itself, especially the boy. Several commentators speculated about the reasons for Bergman's inclusion of the photograph in his film in an unexpected and unexplained way, and about the phenomenology of the picture. In the film, the heroine, Elizabet, who has fallen silent and ceased to communicate, and who has torn up her own son's photograph, finds this photograph by chance when she picks up a book, and the photograph falls from it. The movie does not explain who put it there and why. Critics felt that "there may be evidence here, but of what?" (Ohlin, 2005, 244).

Ohlin's (2005) observation about the relationship between photograph and viewer, in this case between the boy and the actress, is relevant to every Holocaust representation:

> The photograph looks back at the actress, as she looks at it, and while it seems to demand an answer, it remains actually mute. It invites a search for meaning, but the more deeply we penetrate it, the more it fragments and disintegrates. (p. 264)

Ohlin's interpretation derives from Barbie Zelizer's observation mentioned above, about Holocaust photographs becoming representation without substance. Ohlin maintains that this is precisely what *Persona* is all about: "how human beings, never mind photographs, can assume masks and become thereby representations without substance." (ibid.251)

Janina Struk (2004)[30] seconds this view by pointing out that the photograph of the boy in the Warsaw ghetto tells us nothing, except that the scene actually existed at a specific moment in time. This facilitates its iconization and its use for the representation of other catastrophes.

---

29. Hirsch, *Nazi Photographs in Post-Holocaust Art*, 141.
30. Struk, Janina. 2004. *Photographing the Holocaust: Interpretations of the Evidence*. London: I.B. Tauris.

The Boy as a Symbol of Palestinian Suffering

The boy from Warsaw Ghetto, cropped from the original photograph, symbolizes the killing of the young in all genocides. Hirsch comments, "If the victim is infantilized, then the perpetrator is hyper-masculinized, represented as the ultimate phallic, mechanized, supra-human evil." [31] Thus, Israeli soldier Noam Hayut becomes the soldier who aims his gun at the boy, when he meets the eyes of the girl at whom aims his rifle.

> For that girl, I embodied absolute evil. Even if I was not as cruel as the absolute Nazi evil in the shadow of which I had grown up, I didn't have to achieve its perfection and force in order to fulfill my role in her life. No. I was merely who I was, playing the role of absolute evil in the play of her life. As soon as I realized the fact that in her eyes I myself was absolute evil, the absolute evil that had governed me until then began to disintegrate. And ever since, I have been without my Holocaust. Ever since, everything in my life has taken on new meaning: the sense of belonging is blurred, pride has gone missing, belief has weakened, regret has grown strong, forgiveness has been born. (p. 63) [...][32]

The Palestinian girl, who saw Hayut as the "ultimate phallic, mechanized, supra-human evil", liberated him from his hereditary Holocaust, replacing it with her own.

The boy is often adopted as a symbol by Palestinians and Israelis who protest against Israel's colonization of Palestine (Rothberg 2011)[33]. People often compare Palestinian misery under Israeli rule to Jewish misery in the ghettos and make comparisons between besieged Gaza and the Warsaw ghetto, or between the West Bank areas surrounded by the wall that Palestinian masons built at Israel's behest and the Warsaw ghetto wall the Jews were forced to build by the German army. These comparisons often become an equation, as in Norman Finkelstein's photo essay that equates Gaza with the Warsaw ghetto in order to "render Palestinian suffering visible" (Rothberg, 532). The South African Jewish jurist Richard Goldstone, who headed the United Nations Human Rights Commission Fact Finding Mission after the Israeli onslaught on Gaza in 2009, declared, "Gaza is Israel's Warsaw" and forwarded a photo-essay with "parallel images of Nazis and Israelis".[34]

---

31. Hirsch, *Nazi Photographs in Post-Holocaust* Art. 143.
32. Courtesy of Hayut Noam. *The Girl Who Stole My Holocaust*
33. Rothberg, Michael. 2011. "From Warsaw to Gaza: Mapping Multidirectional Memory." *In: Criticism* Fall 2011, Vol. 53, No. 4. ISSN 0011-1589. C 2011 by Wayne State University Press, Detroit, Michigan, pp. 523-548.
34. Rothberg 2011, 526.

Others compare Gaza to Warsaw Ghetto without equating the two places. Ex-Israeli fighter pilot Yonatan Shapira, who has become a champion of peace, wrote on the remnant of the Warsaw Ghetto wall: "Let all the ghettos be liberated. Free Gaza!" Shapira explained to the IDF radio: "My action is not controversial, I am not equating Gaza to the monstrosity of Nazi death camps, but I am saying we must talk about the silence in Israel and in the world when people are confined in a ghetto-like place." [35]

Michael Rothberg points to the work of Israeli-British artist Alan Schechner in *The Legacy of Abused Children: From Poland to Palestine*, a 2003 digitally altered photograph and DVD projection[36]. In this work of art, the photograph of the boy from Warsaw and a well-known photograph of a Palestinian child seized by Israeli soldiers are embedded in each other. The boy from Warsaw holds in one of his raised hands the photograph of the Palestinian boy brutally hauled off by Israeli soldiers, and the cropped photograph of the Warsaw boy is pinned to the chest of the terrified, crying Palestinian boy, and covers the hand of the Jewish soldier who holds him.

Like Shapira, Schechner took "dissimilarity for granted, since no two events are ever alike," and then invoked the connections nonetheless (Rothberg 2011, 16). He was not seeking to equate the suffering of Jews in Warsaw ghetto with that of Palestinians in the West Bank, but rather to compare the injustice of the two situations and to portray the psychological condition of victimhood:

> Whilst I have no interest in comparing the two events to see which was the most horrific [...] I am interested in exploring the very real links between them (quoted in Rothberg 2011, 14).[37]

At the other end of the political arena are the Jewish settlers who, during Israel's "disengagement" from the occupied Gaza strip in 2005, wore yellow Star of David badges, and sent their children out in poses imitating the iconic Warsaw Ghetto boy, to confront Israeli soldiers whom they treated as Nazis. For them, being evicted from their homes in occupied Gaza was equal to the eviction of Jews from their homes in Nazi-ruled Warsaw. Thus, the suffering of the Holocaust, and the boy who raises his hands on his way to extermination, were appropriated for contemporary political ends (Rothberg 2011). In a work by Noa Abendt (Image 10), whose grandparents were Holocaust survivors, the photo was enlarged to

---

35. https://www.haaretz.com/2010-07-05/ty-article/idf-objector-sprays-free-gaza-graffiti-on-warsaw-ghetto-wall/0000017f-db51-db5a-a57f-db7beaf60000
36. Alan Schechner, *the Legacy of Abused Children: From Poland to Palestine* (2003). Still images from a looped projection.
https://www.nictoglobe.com/new/friction-research/gb-israel-turky/alan%20schechner/text.html
37. *Mapping Multidirectional Memory.*

human size and the face of the boy was cut out so that anyone can put their head in the hole and become the Boy. This conveys the message that we are all the Boy.

Image 10. Courtesy Noa Abendt.

The Boy as a symbol in Israeli Schoolbooks

Though Israeli schoolbooks often show the whole photograph of the Jews from Warsaw Ghetto who were pulled from the bunker by force, they never mention Dan Porat's findings about the photographed people and the uprising. They too use the cropped boy as a symbol. In Avieli-Tabibian (2009), the boy from Warsaw Ghetto appears alone, as an icon, devoid of context, at the top left corner of every page of the chapter titled *The Armed Struggle of the Jews*. Thus, the uprising is symbolized not by one of the fighters nor by anyone who could commemorate the resistance and the revolt, but by a photograph that was used by the Nazis as an icon of the unredeemable annihilation of Warsaw Ghetto and of Jewish life.

In Mishol (2014), we see the boy from Warsaw at the bottom of each page of the chapter on the direct shooting of Jews by the Einsatzgruppen in the Ukraine. Transposed to this textbook, the boy from Warsaw came to represent the exterminated Jews of another country.

The cropped picture that shows the boy alone features on many of the schoolbook covers as well: trodden under a gigantic boot (Gutman 2009), raising his arms in front of Hitler and Stalin under a huge yellow *Juden* badge (Inbar and Bar-Hillel 2010), or floating in murky air above the warlords and the machines of war (Mishol 2014). In all these portrayals, he is looking out at the viewer with the pleading, frightened, innocent look Kress and Van Leeuwen (2006) defined as a "demand." This look can be interpreted as a demand for responsibility or rather for response-ability in the sense that Levinas imparted to the term (Andrea Liss 1998, 112)[38]. Based on Andrea Liss' interpretation of Levinas, we can assume that the boy does not ask for comprehension because "in the Shoah's web of cruelty and incomprehension, the relations between the pictured victim and the photographer, and the pictured and contemporary viewers, were and still are so severely asymmetrical" (ibid.113). He does, however, make a plea for acknowledgement and responsibility. In Israeli discourse, his demand is often interpreted as a call for vengeance against all those who wish to exterminate "us" again, exemplified in the play written by Israeli playwright Hanokh Levin, *The Patriot*. In the play Mahmud, a little Palestinian boy, stands with his hands up, just like the boy from Warsaw, as an Israeli soldier holds a gun to his head. The Israeli soldier named Lahav (which is the Hebrew word for Blade), addresses his own mother as he aims the revolver: "He will avenge your blood and the blood of our murdered family, as then, mother, when your little brother stood alone in front of the German at night" (cited in Hirsch 2012, 144).

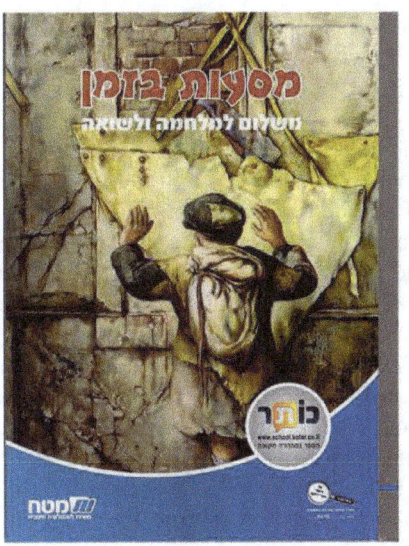

Image 11. Avieli-Tabibian 2009. (Samuel Bak, Icon of Loss, 2008, 152×122 cm). Courtesy of the Center of Educational Technologies.

---

38. Liss, Andrea. *Trespassing Through Shadows. Memory, Photography, and the Holocaust.*

Apart from serving as an icon in the chapter about the Warsaw ghetto uprising, in Avieli-Tabibian's Holocaust schoolbook (2009), a painting of the boy fills the entire front cover. The painting shows him from behind so that the viewer is placed in the position of the soldier Josef Blösche, who aimed his rifle at him. Since in Hebrew the front cover of a book is called its "gate," the student enters the book through this picture in the position of Blösche, through the symbol of Jewish annihilation. The painting was given a universal title, *Icon of Loss*. Bak has painted the boy dozens of times in numerous scenes, with or without a face, in a variety of cultural and religious contexts. In one of these the boy is nailed to the cross, and in another he carries the cross on his back along the Via Dolorosa in East Jerusalem, which may convey a double meaning: little Jewish Jesus or the (repenting) Jew. The paintings attest to the artist's multidirectional remembrance, "marked by transcultural borrowing, exchange, and adaptation" (Rothberg 2009, 254). The icon is disengaged, in Rothberg's words, "from exclusive versions of cultural identity" and demonstrates "how remembrance both cuts across and binds together diverse spatial, temporal, and cultural sites." It also points to the similarities of racial and religious wars, be they Jewish, Christian, or Muslim (Rothberg 2009, 11, 95).[39]

The designer of the schoolbook could have chosen any of Bak's paintings, but s/he chose the one in which he turns his back to us, placing us in the position of his potential or real killer. We see only his back covered with what resembles the yellow *Juden* badge, his knapsack and his raised hands. The boy faces a wall covered with the same yellow badge that covers his body; he is threatened from behind while coming up against the wall in front of him. This may be the wall that separated the ghetto from the Aryan section of Warsaw; or it may be the Wailing Wall in East Jerusalem, symbol of Jewish catastrophe and exile, which welcomes him at the moment he is caught by the Germans, just before his probable death, but blocks him instead of saving him. The painting is very different from the original photograph and yet it could never be mistaken for any image other than that of the boy from Warsaw ghetto. This reinforces his status as an icon.

With his back turned to us, the boy evokes the comparison, although once again not the equation, with another child who has become a symbol of his people's suffering, and who turns his back on the hostile world that persecutes him. This is the little Palestinian boy Handala, drawn in the late 1960s by Naji al-Ali.[40] Handala appeared for the first time in Al-Siyasa in Kuwait in 1969, two

---

39. Michael Rothberg, 2009.*Multidirectional Memory Remembering the Holocaust in the Age of Decolonization.* Stanford university press. Stanford, California.
40. Naji al-Ali was born in 1938 in Al-Shajara, Tiberias. He was a cartoonist. He died on [August 29, 1987, in Charing Cross Hospital, London. He was allegedly murdered by Israeli secret service agents in London.

years after the 1967 war and Israel's colonization of Palestine. He turned his back to the viewer in 1973, and vowed not to show his face until Palestine was free.

Unlike the boy from Warsaw, Handala does not raise his arms in surrender but waits with his hands folded behind his back. His body acquires the shape of the prickly pear, the symbol of Palestinian patience (*saber* means patience in Arabic), appropriated by the Zionists to symbolize the Israeli *sabra*, who is the "new Jew" - prickly on the outside and sweet on the inside. While the boy's knapsack and heavy boots tell us he was destined to continue his life as the wandering Jew, Handala's posture and bare feet declare that he is planted in the land. He is here to stay and has nowhere to go.

One cannot tell whether the painter had in mind this comparison with Handala, or whether the image was chosen to adorn the schoolbook's front cover for that reason. Interpretations of images reveal a lot about ourselves, our knowledge, and our affective tendencies and political views (Gauthier 1979, Kress 2020)[41]. Therefore, we have ground to believe that were they to see these images side by side, many viewers would be struck by the comparison between these two boys, the painted one who was a real boy destined to perish, and the fictitious one, who lives under the threat of annihilation. Both became the symbols of the persecution of their respective peoples, both turn their back to us when interpellated - one in fear, obeying a command to halt, the other in defiance, obstinately refusing to turn when we look at him, until his country is free. We, as spectators, are in the position of the killers who threaten both children from behind.

Image 12. A grafiti of Handala
Source: https://stevesalaita.com/renouncing-israel-on-principle/

---

41. Guy Gauthier (1979) *Initiation à la sémiologie de l'image*. 2nd Ed. Paris: *Les cahiers de l'audiovisuel* (published by the Service Audiovisuel de la Ligue Française de l'Enseignement et d l'Education Permanente)

Childhood in the Ghetto

If Auschwitz is unimaginable, we must give the same attention to an image as we do to what witnesses say (Didi-Huberman 2012, 3).

The criterial feature or the signified is often a concept (Kress 2020), of which human beings are merely the carrier. Children are frequently cropped from photographs in order to create symbols of abstract concepts. Here is an example:

Image 13. Willy Georg 1941: "Emaciated mother and twins. Starvation was also indicated by swollen limbs." *In the Warsaw Ghetto: Summer 1941* © IWM (HU 060701).

This photograph narrates a story about motherhood in the face of the German starvation policy. A starving mother stands guard over her twin daughters who are dressed impeccably in white socks and shoes that were scarce in the ghetto, as Joest showed (image 1). One of the girls wears a hat and a ribbon in her hair, and the other a beautifully tied head kerchief. The mother has even spread a cloth or a carton under them so they should not sit on the bare stone. The family is placed against a closed store, with iron bars and heavy locks. The mother may have dressed up the girls to attract attention and hopefully elicit some coins or food, while she herself stands aside, emaciated with swollen limbs. The mother and one of the girls look at us, or rather at the photographer, in demand, while the other girl looks at her sister with the same demanding look. Neither the viewers nor the twin sister can help. The Nazi photographer did not help them either.

Every photograph has two sorts of meaning or message: a *denoted* message, which is the *analogon* itself (Barthes 1981, 88), or the reality depicted in the photo; and a *connoted* message, which is the manner in which society communicates to some extent what it thinks of this reality. This image denotes starvation in Warsaw ghetto. It connotes a universal message about Nazism, racism, victimhood, motherhood, and the indifference of the outside world. All are expressed by the very fact that this photo exists.

In the schoolbook of Inbar and Bar-Hillel, *Nazism and Shoah* (2010), the chapter on starvation in the ghetto displays a cropped section of the photograph that shows only the twin girls, although the mother is the one who indexes the starvation the chapter is about. The cropping has "orphaned" the girls in order to turn them into an icon of something else, "childhood in Warsaw Ghetto."[42] The cropped girls do not narrate a story; they belong nowhere in particular, least of all to their mother, and they certainly do not represent other girls or children in the ghetto. They symbolize a "universal" state of lonely uncared-for children, which they are not. Although albums of amateur photographers such as Joest or Georg, and official albums such as that of Ewald Gnilka,[43] contain numerous photographs of solitary starving children in Warsaw Ghetto, on their own or in groups, that could symbolize this concept better, the textbook designer chose to crop this photograph and isolate the twins, literally tearing them away from their mother, to symbolize other children who were indeed isolated upon their parents' death or incapacity to care for them. The cropped photograph is placed alongside a text that addresses smuggling as one of the main sources of food in the starving ghetto, and

---

42. While in Hebrew the word "girls" (*yeladot*) and the word "childhood" (*yaldut*) are spelled the same way (without vowelization dots), I tend to believe the meaning here is "childhood," although "girls" would also turn them into an icon or a specimen.
43. Milton, Sybil. 1986. "Images of the Holocaust Part I." *Holocaust and Genocide Studies*, Volume 1, Issue 1. https://doi.org/10.1093/hgs/1.1. pp. 27–61

the tragic lot of little smugglers who were caught and killed by the German police. But the girls do not appear to be smugglers and their starving bodies are covered with beautiful clothes. We can only surmise why the designer chose this cropped image. Perhaps s/he simply found the girls cute, and cute lonely children arouse sympathy more easily than ragged, dirty, starving waifs, and are less shocking.

Image 14. Childhood/Girls in Warsaw ghetto. *Nazism and Shoah* 2010.
Lilach Publishers.

Didi-Huberman (2012, 34) is concerned that the iconic use of cropped pictures points to "inattentiveness" toward the pictures and the events they represent. Rather than cropping, Didi Huberman urges viewers to imagine the unimaginable and make, an "effort of archeological work [...] that will relate the pictures in a constant sequence of collisions and connections, fractions or transformations". He therefore recommends that the photographs be left intact. In a similar vein, Lewis (2001, 349)[44] speaks about "scholarly sloppiness" and argues that such tampering would never be permitted with verbal texts. He makes the important point that unlike textual quotations, where unannounced cutting would not be tolerated, "the cropped version of the photograph never carries a statement that it has been cropped from a larger photograph. In fact, despite the fact that a huge number of reproductions of Holocaust photographs are cropped in various ways, not one

---

44. Lewis, Bryan, F. 2001. "Documentation or Decoration." In *Remembering the Future*.

example has been found where the reader is informed that some cropping has taken place."

Lewis argues that cropping detracts from the documentary value of the photograph, especially if it is used as a historical resource for teaching purposes. "Given that the meaning of a photograph can be significantly changed by cropping out elements, particularly when supported by a carefully written caption, it is a practice judged to be unacceptable and unprofessional" (ibid.).

The practice of cropping a photo to turn suffering children into icons or symbols raises the question of ownership. Those who crop the photographs believe it is their owner's right because they possess the photographs and hence the photographed, having possibly paid for them or having appointed themselves to be their custodians. The respect accorded to authors of written texts, who have author-ity over their texts, is not extended to Holocaust photographers, who are either Nazis, unknown, or dead. The new "owners" thus feel free to alter the appearance and the meaning of the photograph, to suit their purpose when transposing them to their sites, including schoolbooks.

Chapter 5. The Pedagogy of Horror

> Pictures showing heaps of skeletons and tortured emaciated bodies was exceedingly important in 1945 but must be reconsidered after nearly forty years; the aim of illustration is not to shock but to inform. (Milton 1984, 1)
>
> Must the torment and deaths of millions be replayed in museums, books or magazines? (Struk 2008).

Upon considering the exposure of schoolchildren to photographs of atrocity one may ask, how can we read these photos and make children read them? Or even, should we look and make children look at these photographs? Do the atrocity photos act like clichés, empty signifiers that distance and protect the viewers from the event? Does the obsessive repetition of these photographs dull our response to contemporary instances of brutality, discarding them as something already known or, on the contrary, does their repetition in itself retraumatize, turning distant viewers into surrogate victims who, having seen the images so often, have incorporated them into their own narratives and memories, and have thus become all the more vulnerable to their effects? (Hirsch 2001, 8).[1]

Hirsch wonders, if these photographs cut and wound, if they enable memory, mourning, and working through (ibid. 5). She further asks if these images can enable a responsible and ethical discourse. She doubts whether one can see the human beings behind the atrocity, whether these photographs "lead us back to the prewar images of individuals, families, and groups, as they are shown in the Tower of Faces in Yad Vashem", and whether, as we project these two kinds of images unto each other - the beautiful prewar faces and the horrid photographs of torture and death, "do we see them as mutually implying each other, do we come to appreciate the extremity of the outrage and the incomprehension with which they leave anyone who looks?" (ibid. 16).

Janina Struk (2004)[2] argues that these images have become the sum total of what most people "know" about the Holocaust. They are certainly the sum total of what Israeli children know. This is where their importance lies. Nevertheless,

---

1. Hirsch, Marianne. 2001. Postmemory. Yale *Journal of Criticism*, Spring 2001.
2. Struk, Janina. 2004. *Photographing the Holocaust. Interpretations of the Evidence*. London: I.B. Tauris.

ponders Struk (2008, 115)[3] "If the images were taken by the Nazis to degrade their victims, are we not colluding with them by displaying them? Do we have a right to show people in their last moments before facing death to support propaganda, for whatever purpose? "

This question is of utmost importance in the context of education and Holocaust remembrance. Children are not naturally drawn to feel empathy or affiliation with tortured, brutalized or dying human beings. Former soldier and writer Noam Hayut describes his feelings as a child on Holocaust Memorial Day (2013, 19):

> It was the tormenting insight that I belong to this one miserable people. Why me? The question gnawed. Why was I born to this fucked-up people? A nation killed and slaughtered and raped as 'the whole world kept silent.' […] Why do I not belong to another people, any people? Why? […] When I wondered why I couldn't be born to another people, I imagined a perfectly normal place—just like my village, only its inhabitants were not hated or persecuted or killed or incinerated, as in the films shown on Holocaust Memorial Day.

Israeli schoolbooks contain more atrocity photographs than any other sort of image, as can be seen in this list of schoolbooks:

- *Nazism and Shoah*: 35 of 45 pictures are atrocity images.

- *Nazism, War and Shoah*: 48 out of 55 pictures are atrocity images.

- *Shoah and Memory*: 135 of 150 pictures are atrocity images.

- *Shoah - a Journey into Memory*: 81 of 100 pictures are atrocity images.

- *Totalitarianism and Shoah* (Gutman): 95 0f 110 pictures are atrocity images.

- *Toward Resurrection and Peace*, 1999 (Special Education): contains 44 anti-Semitic caricatures and seven atrocity photos transducted into drawings.

- *Destruction and Heroism, Nazism and the Holocaust* for grade 11: 52 atrocity images, 11 antisemitic caricatures.

---

3. Struk, Janina. 2008. "Images of Women in Holocaust Photography." *Feminist Review*, No. 88, *War*. Published by: Palgrave Macmillan Journals. 111-121.

The dominance of atrocity pictures in Israeli textbooks, raises the question, how do they portray the East European Jew? What does Jewishness look like in these books that are meant to teach children to remember? Atrocity pictures present Jewishness as something ugly, destitute, brutalized, and humiliated, with a few exceptions that portray bravery or distinction. They are not dignified and do not inspire reverence.

As Landau argues (2016, 8), Holocaust teaching "can help socialize and even civilize our students," but, it can also "titillate, traumatize, mythologize and encourage a purely negative view of all Jewish history, of Jewish people and indeed, of all victim groups".

Images of Extermination

Once photographs are transposed to schoolbooks, they become teaching material. And the question is what do they teach? This section addresses three photographs of Jews shot in the Soviet Union when direct shooting was applied, during the "Holocaust by Bullets"[4]. The photographs have become icons of atrocity and are used as such in Israeli schoolbooks.

The Massacre at Liepaja

Image 15. Yad Vashem Archives 85D02

---

4. Father Patrick Desbois . 2009. *The Holocaust by Bullets: A Priest's Journey to Uncover the Truth behind the Murder of 1.5 Million Jews*

The photograph of The Massacre at Liepaja shows four women and a little girl in their undergarments, standing huddled together as they wait to be shot.[5] The girl is leaning on one of them and the women are holding one another. No one embraces the little girl. Hirsch and other scholars repeatedly argue that viewers who look at the photo of these women today cannot help but reproduce or appropriate the Nazi gaze:

> In the brutally frontal image, the camera is in the exact same position as the gun and the photographer in the place of the executioner who remains unseen. The victims are already undressed; the graves have been dug. The area surrounding the women is already strewn with bodies. Displayed in their full vulnerability and humiliation they are doubly exposed in their nakedness and their powerlessness. They are shot before they are shot. (Hirsch 2001, 24).

The photo is one of several, taken by the Germans at a massacre at Liepaja in Latvia during which 3,000 people were murdered in a single "action."[6] The caption in Keren (1999) reads: "Murder of Jewesses in Leipaja, Latvia," and the students are asked a question about the killers, not about the victims of the "action" of murder: "Why in your opinion did the Germans document their victims before murdering them"?

The question prompts the students to adopt or at least understand Nazi logic. Gutman (2009, 226) displays the same photo alongside another photo of the same or different women, photographed from behind, on the edge of the mass grave piled with bodies, into which they are to fall after being shot. Both pictures illustrate a chapter that explains the transition from shooting to killing in gas trucks. Above the photos, we find the heart-breaking testimony of a woman who survived the massacre. She describes the murderers as being particularly vindictive and sadistic, and reveals that they asked her, "Who should we shoot first, you or your daughter"?

Following this testimony, the students are asked two questions about the killers:

> 1. How is the encounter between Germans and Jews in the ghettos different from their encounter during the actions of the Einsatzgruppen? Where was it harder for the Germans to ignore the suffering of the Jews?

---

5. Keren (1999, 57).

6. https://www.vintag.es/2018/04/liepaja-massacres.html Through the Untold Stories, YadVashem. https://www.yadvashem.org/untoldstories/database/murderSite.asp?site_id=572

2. What can we learn from the photos? [...] Were the murderers acting as obedient automatons or did they actively initiate the torture of their victims and feel proud of it?

The questions posed by both Keren and Gutman transform the status of the photographs from icons of genocide into indices of German soldiers' emotions and logic. The students are prompted to focus not on the women but on the murderers, and try to understand their motives, their feelings, and the difficulties they encountered during the Holocaust of bullets. It is they who are given agency and a voice. The women merely serve to illustrate the unfortunate predicament of the German soldiers.

The Last Jew in Vinnitsa

Image 16. "The Last Jew in Vinnitsa". Yad Vashem Photo Archives 2626/4

Yad Vashem's Caption reads: "German soldiers of the Waffen-SS and the Reich Labor Service look on as a member of an Einsatzgruppe prepares to shoot a Ukrainian Jew kneeling on the edge of a mass grave filled with corpses. Date 1941 – 1943. Locale- Vinnitsa, [Podolia; Vinnitsa] Ukraine." United States Holocaust Memorial Museum, courtesy of Sharon Paquette. Photograph Number: 64407."[7]

The Last Jew from Vinnitsa (Image16), sitting on the edge of the mass grave and waiting to be shot, has become the icon of National Socialist cruelty and of the Einsatzgruppen massacre in the Soviet Union. The photo shows a young man being shot at the edge of a ditch full of corpses, while Nazi soldiers observe the spectacle.

The photograph is one of many "icons of destruction." It marks the individual presence of the last Jew, who probably did not know he was the last, as a reminder of the catastrophe and one of its traces. The man has no "Jewish" characteristics. He is dressed like any other European man and can therefore represent all the victims.

The historical facts about Vinnitsa, which do not appear in any schoolbook, are detailed by Holocaust historian Shaul Friedländer (1997, 361).[8] The Germans occupied the *oblast* (region) of Vinnitsa between mid-1941 and 1943. Friedländer reports, "Once Hitler decided to move his forward headquarters to Vinnitsa (in the Ukraine), the Jews of the area had to disappear." The Jews of Vinnitsa were murdered in two stages: "The majority of Vinnitsa's roughly 15,000 Jews were murdered in two large-scale murder operations, in mid-September 1941 and in mid-April 1942. About 1,000 skilled workers were spared during these massacres. Half of them were incarcerated in a Vinnitsa labor camp, and the other half were deported to a Zhitomir labor camp. They were used for various works, including the construction of Hitler's 'Werewolf' - forward headquarters near Vinnitsa. Most of these forced laborers were murdered in the summer of 1942 after the construction of the 'Werewolf' was completed. Vinnitsa was liberated by the Red Army on March 20, 1944."

According to different sources the original photograph was either found in an Einsatzgruppe member's photograph album or removed from the pocket of a dead soldier; written on its backside was "Last Jew of Vinnitsa," now used as the image's label.

The photograph was circulated by United Press International (UPI) in 1961 during the trial of Adolf Eichmann in Israel. UPI had received it from Al Moss (b. 1910), a Polish Jew who acquired it in May 1945, shortly after he was liberated

---

7. https://www.yadvashem.org/untoldstories/database/index.asp?cid=686
8. Friedländer, Saul. *Nazi Germany and the Jews: The Years of Extermination*: 1939-1945. Phoenix. Kindle Edition.

from the Allach concentration camp by the US 3rd Army. Moss, who was living in Chicago in 1961, wanted people "to know what went on in Eichmann's time."[9]

Judith Keilbach (2009, 68) contends that the photograph cannot in any way claim to represent, in the sense of being commensurate with, the crime it purportedly depicts. It cannot refer to its incomprehensible, inconceivable referent, namely the extermination of Soviet Jewry, not even to the murder of the last eighty Jews of Vinnitsa. However, as an icon it displays representatives of the three major groups that constituted the Holocaust "protagonists": the victim, the killer, and the on-lookers. It embodies the entire scope of atrocity: the absolute power of the murderer, the total helplessness of the victim, and the indifference or curiosity of the on-lookers. However, although the man is helpless, he is not entirely passive. His gaze, directed straight into the eyes of the photographer and into our eyes, is an act of defiance and demand. In Chouliaraki's (2006, 90) words, this victim is "placed in an active relationship with the spectators."

The photograph was displayed from 1971 to 1994 in the Reichstag building in Berlin as part of an exhibition titled Questions on German History. Writer Glenn Paterson saw it there on his visit to the Reichstag and could not put it out of his mind. The photo has haunted him for many years. Paterson wrote in The Guardian (2014) that what struck him most of all was the man's look:

> I say I encountered this photograph. Actually, I was stricken before it. It was clear what was about to happen, yet the expression on the victim's face was not one of terror, but rather of disgust that this thing was being done to him, that these people were capable not just of doing it, but of watching it being done.[10]

Hannah Arendt was impressed by the bland expressions of the executioner and the on–lookers, who, in her view, could have been watching a barber at work rather than witnessing the heartless extermination of innocents. Arendt observes that in this photograph one sees the death of human empathy, which is one of the earliest and most telling signs of a culture about to descend into barbarism.

Israeli textbooks do not discuss the photo and its trajectory, nor the impression it made on Patterson or on Arendt; they do not provide any information about Jewish life and its extermination in Vinnitsa, and assign different dates and locations to the photo, giving it general titles befitting an icon. For instance, Gutman and Shatzker (1990, 107) locate the murder in Russia without a date. Inbar and Bar Hillel (2010) specify neither the date nor the place of the execution, and use the photo as an icon of "Jews killed by the Einsatzgruppen who were active mainly in the Ukraine." In Avieli-Tabibian 2001 the photo's caption reads, "The vale of killing, Vinnitsa Ukraine," without a date, drawing our

---

9. https://digital.kenyon.edu/bulmash/1085/ https://rarehistoricalphotos.com/last-jew-vinnitsa-1941/
10. *The Guardian*, Saturday October 25, 2014.

attention to the terrain rather than to the man. In this schoolbook, the double spread looks eclectic. The photo of the Last Jew features on the left page usually saved for new information. On the right-hand page, which is always reserved for known or given factual material (Kress and Van Leeuwen 2006), we find a document that lists Jews murdered in Lithuania, sent by the murderers from Kovno (930 km. from Vinnitsa) on November 1, 1941. To the left of the Last Jew we find the poem *Ponar*, dedicated to the murdered Jews of Ponar (841 km. distant from Vinnitsa). The poem is superimposed on a testimony of a survivor of the massacre in Zagorodka, near Pinsk in Belarus (501km. from Vinnitsa and 362.5 km. from Ponar), delivered at the Eichmann Trial in Jerusalem in 1961. Had the names of the places and the distances between them been mentioned in the schoolbook, the students could have conceived the scale of the mass murder.

The four visuals grouped together - a photograph of slaughter, a list of casualties, a poem, and a testimony, each drawn from a different far-flung place, constitute a semiotic unit that sums up the mass murder of Soviet Jews by direct shooting, and the last Jew of Vinnitsa represents them all. However, historians would not readily agree that a certain case in one location could represent other cases in other places: "Neither Kovno, nor Treblinka, nor Wannsee, nor Babi Yar can alone represent the others." (Landau 2016, 13)[11]. Yet in this schoolbook, the Last Jew of Vinnitsa is abstracted from his own history and provenance, and becomes an icon of the entire genocide.

The question put to the students is, "Why did the mass murder begin with the German invasion to the Soviet Union"? This question also prompts the children to adopt or understand Nazi logic.

In a later version of Avieli-Tabibian (2009, 215-216), the same caption is attached to the photo, "The vale of killing, Vinnitsa," but a rough date is added: 1941-1943, covering the period of the mass murder of Jews in the Soviet Union, and enhancing the power of the photo as an icon. In this version, the photo is placed alongside some lines of a letter written in October 1941 by a murderer policeman, Walter Matner, to his wife, regarding the mass murder of Jews in Mogilev, Belarus, located 611.8 km. from Vinnitsa:

> When the first truck arrived my hand trembled a bit but you get used to it and when the tenth truck arrived I visioned in great calm and shot with confidence men women and children, knowing I have two babies at home and that this mob would have done the same if not worse to us had they had a chance. The death we gave them was a nice death compared with the tortures endured by thousands and thousands in the cellars of the Ga PA O. (Browning 1995, 340).[12]

---

11. Landau, Ronnie. 2016. *The Nazi Holocaust: Its History and Meaning*. I.B. Tauris Publishers.
12. Browning Christopher. 1995. *The Path to Genocide: Essays on Launching the Final Solution*.

This document gives the killer agency, which may have been Browning's intention, yet Browning and his thesis are not discussed in the schoolbook, which provides only a reference to the book, which probably conveys nothing to the students. The schoolbook treats the policeman Walter Matner as a person Israeli students can identify with: he feels, he thinks, he weighs the pros and cons, and makes "rational" decisions regarding the killing of civilians.

The questions to the students prompt them to ponder the letter but not the picture, and to focus on the personalities of the murderers rather than the look in the eyes of the victim, as they are encouraged to understand Walter Matner and his motives:

> What are the arguments the writer uses in order to justify the murders he participated in?

The question is not *whether* such murders could be justified but simply *how* they were justified, without inverted commas, which creates the assumption that they can indeed be justified. All the students are asked to do is find out how.

Words like *justification* and *legitimacy* regarding Nazi actions crop up frequently in this chapter, although they evoke value systems that were destroyed by the Germans and therefore cannot be applied to Nazi mass extermination. The human propensity to use known signifiers to describe the unknown is widespread and stems from the fact that we understand things by comparing them to other things that seem similar in some way. Yet as Friedländer argues, when we seek to explain the Holocaust according to known norms or logic, we arrive at the limit of representation (Friedländer 1990). The use of the word 'argument' assumes that this issue is debatable, that there were or can be arguments for and against the extermination of people, and that some arguments can convincingly justify such an action, according to certain norms or logic.

However, as Diner argues[13], the very nature of the Nazi project makes its logic inherently impossible to follow; it demolishes rationality. "The Nazi system, and its annihilative purpose, emerges as neither rational nor irrational, but rather as counterrational."(2000, 137). Diner studied the efforts of the Jewish councils, the Judenrat, to understand the Germans' logic in order to anticipate their actions and exert a moderating influence on them. These leaders of the dying communities tried to think like the Nazis but failed. Diner observes that this very subject matter acts to deactivate our ability to understand. (ibid.)

When describing Nazism and the Final Solution, he argues, "Historians must accept a cancellation of basic principles of rationality before venturing on their

---

13. Diner, Dan. 2000. "Historical Understanding and Counterrationality." In *Beyond the Conceivable: Studies on Germany, Nazism, and the Holocaust.* EBSCO Publishing: eBook Academic Collection (EBSCOhost). 137.

enterprise."(ibid.) German "rationalization" for the mass killing, to which the school children are asked to adhere in the questions we have seen so far, cannot be justified or legitimated by any argument or means of justification and legitimation known to people prior to the Holocaust, or by the language that purports to be the same after the Holocaust. The mass murder was "rationalized" by a reasoning that distorted all logic and shattered all layers of understanding, and it therefore calls for other forms of expression, other words. As Adorno insists (2004,367)[14]: "After Auschwitz there is no word tinged from on high, not even a theological one, that has any right to exist unless it underwent a transformation."

The schoolbook chapter proceeds with the following sub-chapter: (p. 216): "Arguments that legitimate the murder of Jews in the Soviet Union." The sub-chapter reproduces the decree ordering the killing of Jews in Bialystok, on July 1941. The decree (p. 117) portrays the German murderers as sensitive human beings and includes the following instructions:

> The battalion and company commanders are especially responsible to provide for the spiritual care of the men who participate in this action. The impressions of the day are to be blotted out through the holding of social events in the evenings. Furthermore, the men are to be instructed continuously about the political necessity of the measures.

The question regarding this entry is this: "The second part [of the decree] deals with the murderers. What is written about them? What can you conclude from that"?

The obvious conclusion to be drawn is that the German soldiers were human beings like any others, soldiers like any other soldiers, with a sensitive soul, who nevertheless were persuaded to commit the most awful crimes out of obedience and patriotism. This message delivered to young Israelis about to enlist in the army and to help maintain a colonial regime can make a crucial impact. The questions can thus be read as encouraging students to ponder their own future conduct as occupying soldiers.

Finally, the students are asked the following questions (p.117):

> - According to the decree, what is the justification for killing Jews?
>
> - Why, in your opinion [literally, "according to you"], was it necessary to provide justification for the murders?

The principal message that these questions convey is that one can grasp the Holocaust in rational terms, find arguments that justify it in accordance with our

---

14. Adorno, Theodor 1966/2004. *Negative Dialectics*. Routledge.

values, in accordance with what we believe to be reasonable and rational, with what we were taught and teach about right and wrong, about human rights, and about killing innocent people.

Below the letter of Walter Matner and the photo of the last Jew from Vinnitsa, we find a lengthy report about the massacre at Mogilev (611.8 km. distant from Vinnitsa). Thus, the photograph of the last Jew of Vinnitsa comes to represent the Mogilev massacre. Four long pages of lists of murdered Jews follow, all taken from *Ordinary Men* by Christopher Browning, who transposed them from Nazi archives. These lists date every massacre and specify the exact number of murdered people, for example:

> Battalion 314 shot 367 Jews in a "cleansing action."
>
> Battalion 45 shot 61 Jews, and the "police squadron" (mounted police) [shot] 113 Jews.
>
> Police Regiment South shot 1,324 Jews.
>
> Battalion 320 provided the "cordon" while the Staff Company of the HSSPF shot 15,000 Jews at Kamenets, Podolsky on August 26-27, and another 7,000 on August 28.
>
> Battalion 320 shot 2,200 Jews in Minkovtsy." Etc.

Adorno (1966) remarks: "To quote or haggle over the numbers is already inhumane."[15] These Jewish victims, represented by The Last Jew of Vinnitsa, were reduced by the Germans to lists and numbers, and remained so in the schoolbook. Lists constitute a part of the language of bureaucracy, "a form of organizing human action which is governed by impersonal procedures"' (Van Leeuwen 2008, 47). These lists of massacred Jews were compiled to demonstrate that the mission had been accomplished, but also to stress the magnitude of the "danger" that had been eradicated. Lists and numbers cannot evoke empathy for they annihilate the sufferers, but they do "suggest that such horror can happen to anyone and therefore that viewers or readers should not feel too safe themselves." (Holtschneider 2011, 51). They are sure to evoke such fear among Israeli children, who are regularly reminded from an early age, that this is what happened to Jews in the "other countries," when they did not have a state of their own and a strong army. Yet fear fails to evoke pity or mourning.

---

15. Education after Auschwitz A radio-talk on April 18, 1966.

Naveh et al. (2009) embed the photograph of the last Jew of Vinnitsa in a testimony concerning "killing into death pits" in Pohost Zagorodsky, Belarus, 529 km. from Vinnitsa. The caption reads: "Murder into Death Pits: by the method of direct shooting in its various forms hundreds of thousands of Jews were murdered up until December 1941, around a million and a half in all the stages of the Final Solution." Naveh et al. omit the later rounds of massacres in Vinnitsa, in April 1942 and in summer 1942, during which this photo must have been taken, if indeed this was the Last Jew of Vinnitsa.

In Mishol (2014), the photo appears under the title: "The Killing Pits," unlinked to any specific time or place. This page also carries photos of executions committed in Lithuania, Riga, and during Operation Barbarossa in general. To the left is a map of the final solution in the USSR. The date given is 1941. At the bottom of this, and all the other pages of this part of the book, the boy from the Warsaw ghetto, with his arms raised in surrender, features as an icon of Jewish annihilation.

In Hertz (2015), the photo also appears as part of the discussion of Operation Barbarossa, dated 1942. The precise location – Vinnitsa - is not mentioned. Following the photo, the book reproduces the testimony of Herman Graebe at the Nuremberg Trials. Graebe witnessed the massacre of the Jews of Dubno (305 km. from Vinnitsa) on October 5, 1942, but since the book does not mention the event to which Graebe refers, it appears that his testimony is linked to the photo from Vinnitsa. The witness describes how the killer of 20 people, including a family of eight, sat smoking on the edge of the pit after completing his task. The book then asks:

> Do you think the way the murders were handled and the conduct of the murderers impacted the scale of the murder?

The question prompts the students to consider the efficiency of the method of direct shooting, or rather its "handling."

Presenting the Germans as the main protagonists of the events, and the "paper time" allotted to their thinking, feeling and reasoning, reveal an interest to foreground the murderers as regular human beings, in line with Browning's approach. Browning introduced a new kind of perpetrator history, which focuses on the "little men," the soldier at the bottom of the hierarchy of the "machinery of destruction," who personally carried out the millions of executions (Friedländer 1990, 27).[16] Browning acknowledged that his attempt to understand the behavior of the killers involves an element of empathy, but insisted that "understanding is not forgiving" (ibid. p. 36). Yet, as mentioned above, Browning's views on these "ordinary men" are not addressed in the textbooks, nor presented as a theory. His

---

16. *Probing the Limits of Representation.*

views could be extremely pertinent to Israeli students, in relation both to the Holocaust and to the Palestinian catastrophes - the Nakba (1948) and the Naksa (1967) - perpetrated by Israeli pre-state militia and the Israeli army, and in relation to the ongoing military regime that governs the Palestinians in the occupied territories, of which the students are about to become a part.

Adorno (ibid. *Education*) likewise suggested that the sentiments and reasoning of the German killers should be studied in depth in order to understand how such personalities were formed, so as not to replicate the conditions that had enabled the Holocaust to happen. The schoolbooks, however, ignore the debates that concern the proper ways to represent the perpetrators, and the limits of representation.

To summarize, the last Jew of Vinnitsa is transformed, in the transposition of the photograph to schoolbooks, into an icon of the mass of anonymous Jews who were murdered by the German killing squads, and are represented by numbers. The photo gains its symbolic value by being abstracted from its circumstances, its provenance, and its history, and serving as an icon for events that took place on different dates and at different locations, far distant in time and space from Vinnitsa. The Last Jew of Vinnitsa is barely noticed by the texts woven around him. The captions refer only to the "killing", the "pits", the "vale", or "the murderers" of other "Jews," but not to the person gazing at us. The few testimonies about the other massacres, that are meant to add a dramatic or authentic touch to the lists, refer mainly to the behavior and to the state of mind of the German killers. From an historical point of view, Janina Struk cautions against the kind of presentation[17], arguing that,

> Pictures, often of unrelated events, sometimes taken thousands of miles apart, are placed side by side and give us the impression that there was some continuity in the events they portray. It is, in effect, a fiction and fiction invites fantasy (Struk 2004, 213).

---

17. *Photographing the Holocaust*, 2004

The Ivangorod Mother

Image 17. Einsatzgruppen murdering Jewish civilians in Ivangorod, Ukraine, 1942. Credit: Jerzy Tomaszewski, Poland. Yad Vashem Archive, Photo Collection 143DO5

Another photograph that "made history," was widely disseminated and is immediately recognizable, is the photo of the Ivangorod mother being shot by German soldiers as she protects her child with her body (Struk, 2011)[18]. The mother, cropped from a larger image, was transformed into an icon of the murder of Soviet Jews by direct shooting. The complete image appears to be the one reproduced over two full pages in the book *We Have Not Forgotten.*[19] The photo, which contains other people and various objects, was thought to be a snapshot taken by a German soldier. In addition to the German soldier, the woman and the child, the image clearly shows a group of four or five people crouching to the right of the mother, alongside a number of shovels; on the extreme left of the photo, the ends of a number of rifle barrels are also visible (Lewis, 2001). Lewis cites several books in which this photograph is cropped in different ways, adding that the picture most widely used today is the one cropped by Yad Vashem. He writes as follows:

---

18. Struk, Janina. 2011. *Private Pictures, Soldiers' Inside View of War.* London: I.B. Tauris.
19. *1939-1945. We Have Not Forgotten.* 1960 League of Fighters for Freedom and Democracy. Polonia Publishing House.

> The most extreme cropping has been found in Yad Vashem's publication *The Holocaust;* most of the uniformed German has been cropped out, leaving mainly the rifle and much of the woman has been cropped. The resulting image has been enlarged to fill a page, and the consequent reproduction quality is quite appalling. But then, many of the important images reproduced in this publication, despite being produced by a recognized authority on the Holocaust, have been brutally and pointlessly cropped, making this particular work a prime example of bad practice. (2001:348).[20]

Lewis explains the cropping was done for the purpose of iconization, arguing that,

> the complete image is more complex: the interplay of the various elements, the ends of rifles, the German in uniform, the line of fire of the rifle, the woman and child, the apparent movement of the woman, the body at the feet of the German, the small grave near the feet of the German, the group of people to the right of the photograph, the variety of shovels, as well as the presence of the photographer, combine to make a straightforward reading impossible.

Lewis believes that "it is a good example of the ways in which meaning can be affected, even changed, by the cropping of a photograph." (ibid.)

The cropped photo's criterial features are both concrete and conceptual, as in most icons: the shooting and the act of "mothering". While the Last Jew of Vinnitsa is iconized for what he is - a helpless Jew staring defiantly ahead before being shot - the woman is iconized for her universally appreciated act of "mothering," which is "the act of giving care to a child" (unlike "fathering," which signifies only the act of begetting a child, Van Leeuwen 2008, 42). She is no doubt aware that her act of protection is futile, yet all mothers can identify with her. Her act evokes the most universal quality of humanity, asserts Chouliaraki (2006, 144). The killer and the two rifles behind him symbolize the height of male evil. Hence, this image contains all the ingredients of a myth. The visual juxtaposition of the two themes - the frail helplessness of the mother and child against German violence - demonstrates the contrast between humanity and inhumanity. This photo not only reports on a shocking possibility, but actually induces the shock. It raises the most fundamental moral question: how can a young mother and a baby be condemned to death? In so doing, it drives the viewers to demand that justice be restored (Chouliaraki 2006).

The trajectory of the photograph is detailed by freelance documentary photographer and writer Janina Struk (2011), as following: In 1942 in Nazi-occupied Warsaw, a Polish post office clerk working for the resistance, opened a letter sent by a German soldier to his family. It contained a photograph that so

---

20. Lewis, Bryan, F. 2001. "Decoration or Documentation." In *Remembering for the Future.*

shocked the man that he forwarded it to the Polish underground. On the back of the photograph, the soldier had written in German: 'Ukraine 1942, Jewish Action, Ivangorod.' The photo fell into the hands of 16-year-old Jerzy Tomaszewski, who worked in the darkroom of one of the largest photography shops in central Warsaw, called Fotoris. One of his tasks was to pass on evidence of German atrocities to London, so that the Allies could publicize Nazi crimes committed in Eastern Europe. The Germans brought into the shop their private photos that featured girlfriends, social occasions and sometimes images of Jewish ghettos, deportations, executions, and other atrocities. "The Germans loved photography," Tomaszewski told Janina Struk (2011, 80). Tomaszewski and the other Polish workers were encouraged to chat with their German customers, to divulge as much information about the pictures brought in by them as possible: where they were taken, by whom, and exactly what they showed. "We had to be careful because it was highly dangerous work," Tomaszewski related, "but we were young and we didn't always understand the danger, or the importance, of the work we were doing." Himself a photographer and a member of the nationalist Polish wartime underground AK (Armia Krajowa), Tomaszewski sent a duplicate of the photograph to London and kept the original in his personal archive. "Jerzy Tomaszewski, observes Struk, a man who had risked his life by placing his trust in the value of pictures, by smuggling, taking, and collecting them, had never questioned their importance." (ibid.) He also photographed the Warsaw uprising and was wounded there. His story and the photographs he took during the uprising, which do not appear in Israeli schoolbooks, show strong young people on a mission, unrecognizable as the defeated, bedraggled, frightened figures shown in Nazi photos. He was one of the three editors commissioned by the Polish Foreign Office to compile the book *1939–1945: We Have Not Forgotten* (1960), in which the Ivangorod photograph first appeared in its two forms: the uncropped photograph of the killing is inside the book, and on the book's cover the photograph appears "severely cropped so that only the soldier and the woman and child were visible" (Struk 2011, 86).

More than sixty years after the war, Jerzy Tomaszewski allowed Janina Struk to view the precious and terrible evidence, from which she made a perfect copy. Struk writes about the cropped picture as follows (ibid. 95):

> Somewhere near the small town of Ivangorod in Ukraine, a German soldier points his weapon at a woman with a child in her arms. She has turned away from the soldier and wrapped herself around the child. Her foot is lifted from the ground as though she might be moving away from the soldier or perhaps the shutter has caught the moment the bullet has hit her.

Struk mentions certain "confusing" objects in the original photo. Apparently, these objects were deemed less suitable for iconization to those who cropped it, although, as Journalist Fisk insists, they provide context to the photograph. Didi-

Huberman (2012, 65) encourages viewers of Holocaust images to see the image "as an amalgam, an impurity, with visible things mixed with confused things, illusive things mixed with revealing things, " because the image is *"neither all nor nothing.* If the image were 'all,' then no doubt we would have to say that there are no images of the Shoah. But it is precisely because *the image is not all* that it remains legitimate to establish the following: there are images of the Shoah, which, even if they do not say everything (and still less "the all") of the Shoah, are nonetheless worthy of being looked at and examined as characteristic facts and as fully fledged testimonies of this tragic history."

Robert Fisk (2011)[21] follows this path, believing that unlike the cropped iconized part of the photo, the scrutiny of the entire photo, unclear as it is, enables the picture to tell a story, which gives us a wider look, and a deeper understanding of the Holocaust.

The "confusing" elements are likely to be the people on the right, who are apparently bending over a dead body on the edge of a ditch that was probably a mass grave they themselves had dug. "It may be" writes Fisk, "[…] that the soldier is actually shooting at the four men and that one of the other two rifle barrels is firing at the woman with the child. The shadows on the ground to the left suggest there may have been many more killers shooting at that moment. But what struck me was the nature of the earth on the right of the picture." Struk notes an "indistinguishable object" on the right, which to Fisk appeared to be a wooden stake. "'You will dig your own mass grave, up to this point.' Is that what the Germans ordered their victims to do? But then, reader, observe carefully, I discovered what is clearly a metal shovel, upside down, its shaft behind the stake. It is identical to other shovels in other execution pictures I have seen. Had the four men been digging their own graves?"

The Ivangorod picture shows all the important components of the scene: the killing, the cadavers, the field of slaughter and the diggers of the grave. And we, the viewers, "take on the photographer's view of the event as he stands among the perpetrators, collaborators, and other onlookers, probably including more Jewish victims waiting to be killed." (Lower 2021, 15)

---

21. https://www.independent.co.uk/voices/commentators/fisk/robert-fisk-ukraine-1942-what-are-we-seeing-6264646.html

Image 18. The cropped photo of Image 17. Yad Vashem Archive 65779.

Fisk attempts to trace the trajectory of the photograph after it was discovered, although no one knows the details of the photographing event; he follows Didi-Huberman's instruction to all viewers of Holocaust atrocity images: Imagine!

Fisk exemplifies in his report the importance of the photograph as testimony. He reports, "The photograph has also been the subject of controversy and its authenticity disputed for various political and ideological reasons." When the photograph was published in the *We Have Not Forgotten* collection, issued by the Soviet-installed Polish Communist regime after the war, a right-wing West German newspaper, *Deutsche Soldaten Zeitung*, ran a headline above it that read "Achtung Fälschung" (Beware Falsification). The reasoning was that the man pointing the rifle at the young woman and her child was not wearing a German uniform or using a German rifle. Then, a former member of Hitler's Einsatzgruppen, the "special action" squads that murdered more than a million Jews in Ukraine, authenticated the photograph, explaining that the soldier in the picture was wearing a German Einsatzgruppen uniform and holding a standard Einsatzgruppen rifle. Years later, at an exhibition of German atrocity photographs taken in Eastern Europe, held in Dresden, an old man stared at the pictures for a long time and then began to cry. As he rushed from the exhibition hall, he shouted: "It's me...it's me."

Robert Fisk emphasizes the relevance of such photographs to present times:

> In her book, Struk asks why soldiers take pictures of their own cruelty. There are countless authenticated pictures of German troops grinning as they stand next to hostages who have been hanged, crowding round mass graves to watch the execution of Jews, Soviet commissars, hostages, men and women. [...] Somehow, I can imagine the terrible, excited conversation. 'Hey, Hans! On your left, they are shooting Jews. Get your camera. Look at that woman run!' SNAP.

Or was the cameraman an off-duty killer? We shall probably never know. But the tradition, of course, continues. Look at the videos Americans took of their murder victims in Iraq.

Fisk's reflections and Struk's story about the discovery of the picture endow the photograph and its trajectory with a perspective that the cropped picture lacks, because icons do not provide context, they only convey a very general message. Photographs are cropped to bypass the "scrutinizing" that Fisk and Didi-Huberman deem necessary to imagine the event captured in them, and to be informed by it. However, even in its cropped state and devoid of the phenomenological details, the image displays a victim who is "humane" and exhibits humane behavior we can relate to and admire. Chouliaraki (2006, 106) explains that "the human quality of the sufferers is semiotized as their capacity to act [...] to say or do something about their condition, even if this power is simply the power to evoke the beneficiary action of others".

The agency of the sufferers is visually manifested in different ways, in a gaze, such as that of the last Jew of Vinnitsa; or it may appear as "condition", where the sufferer symbolizes a "universal" human state of existence, such as motherhood (ibid.). The mother from Ivangorod possesses a "conditional agency" that implies that she is only able to act in a limited and ineffective way, but her human agency touches, shocks and destabilizes every viewer.

Schoolbooks usually present the cropped photo in its iconized state, sometimes devoid of details of time and place. None of them discusses the photo and its trajectory, or the reactions of other viewers to the photograph. They use this photograph, like that of the last Jew of Vinnitsa, to discuss the method of direct killing and its "shortcomings", and to explain the transition to gas trucks as a more efficient means of exterminating the Jews. In the first edition of his schoolbook (*Shoah and Memory* 1999) Gutman places the cropped image directly below the heading: "Searching for alternatives to direct shooting," thereby prompting readers to focus their interest on the method of killing rather than on the mother and child, or on the crime committed. In Inbar and Bar-Hillel (2010, 212), the cropped image forms part of a collage, which is the "gate" to the chapter on the final solution (Image19). The caption reads, "Einsatzgruppen - murderers in action," which also prompts the reader to focus on the killers. The photo is overlapped by a famous photograph of Churchill and Roosevelt, and faces a photograph of a British naval vessel in the Mediterranean Sea. It is connected by a diagonal vector to a photo of a wooden bunk, where prisoners slept crowded in Auschwitz. The diagonal vector creates a narrative or a chronological connection between the shooting and the extermination camp, where Jews were gassed after the method of direct shooting was found to be inefficient or not efficient enough. This page thus displays two axes: the war and the warlords versus the victims whom these warlords failed to save.

Image 19. *Nazism and Shoah* 2010. Lilach Publishers.

In the schoolbook *Destruction and Heroism* (Hertz 2015) the cropped photo of the mother from Ivangorod appears on each page of the chapter on the Holocaust, and is thus transformed into a symbol of the entire process of extermination. It reappears in the sub-chapter on the Final Solution at the top of the page, alongside a photograph of an inscription a murdered Kovno Jew wrote in Yiddish with his blood, as he lay dying on the floor of his kitchen: "Jews Revenge!"

Although the two murders were committed and recorded in two different locations 692 km apart, Ivangorod in the Ukraine and Kovno in Lithuania, in this layout it seems that the call for revenge from Kovno pertains to the murder of the mother and the child in Ivangorod, and hence to all the murders of Jews across the USSR. The poem about the massacre in Ponar, Lithuania, 726km. distant from Ivangorod, is placed under both photos, across the entire width of the lower part of the page, uniting them. The story of the poem is recorded in the schoolbook, no doubt because it has become part of the Israeli Holocaust canon. The poem was written by two different poets in Vilnius, Lithuania. The first poet, Leon Volkovisky wrote the first stanza in Polish, set to the music of a lullaby composed by his 11-year-old son who survived and became the famous Israeli pianist Alexander Tamir. The father titled the poem *Chiho Chiho* in Polish and later *Shtiler, Shtiler* in Yiddish, which means Silence, Silence, as it begins with the line: "Silence, silence son, be quiet, here the graves are growing..." The father was subsequently murdered in one of the "actions" conducted in Vilnius ghetto, and the one verse he wrote was translated into Yiddish by the poet-partisan Shmerke Kacharjinsky, who added further verses. The poem was later retitled *Ponar* because it is dedicated to the Jews murdered in Ponar. It was often read and sung in Vilnius Ghetto and is one of the poems read out on every Holocaust Day in Israel, in Hebrew. The trial of Adolph Eichmann in Jerusalem in 1962 concluded with a reading of *Ponar*.

The three items (two photos and a poem) are thus detached from their original contexts and recontextualized in the schoolbook, where they form a new complex sign that functions as a myth; and like many other myths, it represents horrendous injustice, sacrifice, noble humanity and the call for eternal revenge. The newly made sign combines three constitutive elements of our life: the feminine motherhood; the masculine - both the Nazi murderer and the Jewish call for revenge; and the spiritual poetry that commemorates people's suffering caused by human barbarity. They also connote the concept of the human spirit that endures "in spite of everything": motherhood manifested to the last breath; a call for revenge written in blood by a dying man; and poetry composed by those who were about to be executed. This is why these photos became what photography historian Vicky Goldberg (1991,145) termed "secular icons," namely photographs that possess intense symbolic impact through representations that inspire a degree of awe, mixed with dread or compassion, and that seem to encapsulate such complex phenomena as the power of the human spirit and universal destruction.

Since the word "revenge" is written in Hebrew letters, Israeli readers may regard it as a call addressed to them directly, which urges them to become indignant (Keilbach 2009) and to seek revenge. But as Boltanski (1999, 116),[22] notes, a viewer of these photographs, seeking revenge today, actually does no more than "quench his own desire to persecute, to satisfy his taste for violence and destruction or, in Sade's terms, to give vent to his natural propensity for crime." He feels summoned to take action: "to cast his eyes on the unfortunate and look evil in the face without immediately turning away, to allow himself to be taken over by the horrific." (ibid.) As Hayut (2013) and Burg (2008) explain in their autobiographies, and as soldiers from Breaking the Silence often testify, for Israelis the call of revenge is directed not at the Germans and their collaborators, but at present day potential exterminators, namely the Arab-Palestinians. This echoes Volkan's observations, that the reactivation of the chosen trauma is never directed against those who generated it, because it may occur generations after the original event took place: "as the chosen trauma passes from generation to generation it changes function, and may be reactivated against other, current enemies." (1998, 9)[23] This reaction reinforces Struk's observation (2004), that watching Holocaust atrocity images does not necessarily educate against war.

The Verbal Text

The verbal texts within which this photo is embedded prompt readers to focus on another aspect altogether, namely the technical flaws of the method of direct shooting. In Hertz (2015, 108), the text begins thus:

> The method of direct killing had its shortcomings: it was slow, wasted a lot of ammunition (at least one bullet per person) and was hard to conceal. The explosive sounds of shooting were heard from afar. The method presented certain hardships as far as the German soldiers were concerned as well: the work was dirty and required direct contact between murderer and victim. Hitler quite likely issued the order to extend the extermination of the Jews to other parts of Europe already at this stage [...] This is why the Germans searched for more effective alternatives for the mass murder of the Jews."

The expository, seemingly dispassionate reasoning style of this analysis of the method of killing and its flaws shifts the focus abruptly from the inconceivable

---

22. Boltanski Luc 1999. *Distant Suffering. Morality, Media and Politics.* Cambridge University Press.
23. Transgenerational Transmissions and Chosen Traumas. Opening Address XIII International Congress International Association of Group Psychotherapy. August, 1998

cruelty and suffering shown in the photo of the murder in Ivangorod, the poem Ponar and the call for revenge written in blood, to the German killers and their logistical problems. The shift is so unsettling and surprising that one is moved to wonder about its educational purpose, and about the interest or the motivation of those who introduced it. What we experience here is the interplay between the extreme nature of the subject matter and the "normality" of the text, which, as mentioned above, is considered problematic by scholars such as Friedländer, Dan Diner, Michael Rothberg, LaCapra or Adorno. By noting that the method of direct shooting "had its shortcomings," the text asserts that it was not perfect but not altogether bad. It presented "certain hardships." We gain the impression that the rhetor of the schoolbook seeks neither to invalidate nor reject the method of direct killing, nor to find fault with its planners and executioners, but rather to adopt an objective and neutral position on the matter; to examine the method technically, and weigh its pros and cons, so as to convince readers that gassing was a better alternative. After all, direct shooting did produce impressive results, as Browning's list shows and as the photographs of mass graves prove. Thus, the schoolbook text reproduces the Nazis' pattern of thought and operation.

Saul Friedländer (1984)[24], as was already mentioned, calls this writing "bureaucratic, rational and factual" or the "historiography of business as usual," which, he asserts, is typical of textbook writing. Sentences such as "the method of direct killing had its shortcomings," or "the method presented certain hardships," or "this is why the Germans searched for more effective alternatives for the mass murder of the Jews", simulate a sphere where human extermination is logical, and where people can become superfluous and dispensable.

In the second version of his textbook, Gutman (2009, 228) explicitly invites readers to view the photo of the Ivangorod shooting through Nazi eyes. The photograph is embedded in a text about the "search for alternatives to direct shooting." Below the photo, there is a question: "What were the reasons that drove the Nazis to seek alternatives to the direct shooting of Jews according to this photograph?" This question, which also appears in the final History examination (matriculation) in winter 2022, explicitly directs the students to adopt the perpetrators' gaze along with their murderous logic. It prompts students to consider the photo of the woman, who is trying in vain to protect her child with her body, not as criminalizing evidence, as a devastating shocking image of the darkest evil and the loftiest expression of motherly devotion, but as an example of a rather sloppy method that needs to be improved, as proof of the waste of ammunition, inefficiency, and disturbing experience on the part of the German soldiers.

---

24. Friedländer, Shaul. 1984. *Reflections of Nazism: An Essay on Kitsch and Death*. Harper & Row.

Students may be drawn to calculate how many bullets the German murderer had to spend on this woman and her child. At least two. But what if the child moves? What if the mother starts running? Maybe three bullets. Maybe four. What if she falls on him and covers him with her body? Would the soldier kick her away in order to kill the child? These questions may arise because of the book's failure to mention that "According to common Nazi protocol, bullets were not to be wasted on Jewish children. They were instead left to be crushed by the weight of their kin and suffocated in blood and the soil heaped over the bodies," as Wendy Lower who investigated the photograph of the killing of a mother and two children in Miropol, makes clear (Lower 2021, 14, 17).[25] The students may ask themselves more humane and unanswerable questions as well, such as "What thoughts ran through this mother's mind as she was forced to march to this site with her child? Did the boy try to run away, shocked and confused? Was the father killed first, before their eyes or is he one of the diggers in the distance?" (Lower ibid.)

Instead of addressing the photograph, the books emphasize the inefficiency of the method of direct shooting that was an unnecessary hassle for the German soldiers, who only sought to do their duty, and for whom physical contact with the victims was terribly annoying. They conclude that gassing was a far more efficient method. In this way, students are taught the bureaucratic thinking and the industrialization of mass murder, along with the total indifference to human life and human expressions of despair and helplessness.

Bar-Hillel and Inbar (2010, 228-229) show, in the sub-chapter "The Transition to Gas Trucks," another photo of direct shooting, that shows very clearly and convincingly how inefficient it was: two soldiers aim at one victim, although next to this photograph, on the lower right of the page - the part of the page reserved for the "given" and the "real" - we find a photo of a mass grave suggesting that the "harvest" of direct shooting was quite impressive. The heading of the double spread reads, "No one escaped!" (Image 20).

---

25. Lower, Wendy. 2021. *The Ravine. A Family, a Photograph, a Holocaust Massacre Revealed*. An Apollo Book. Head of Zeus.

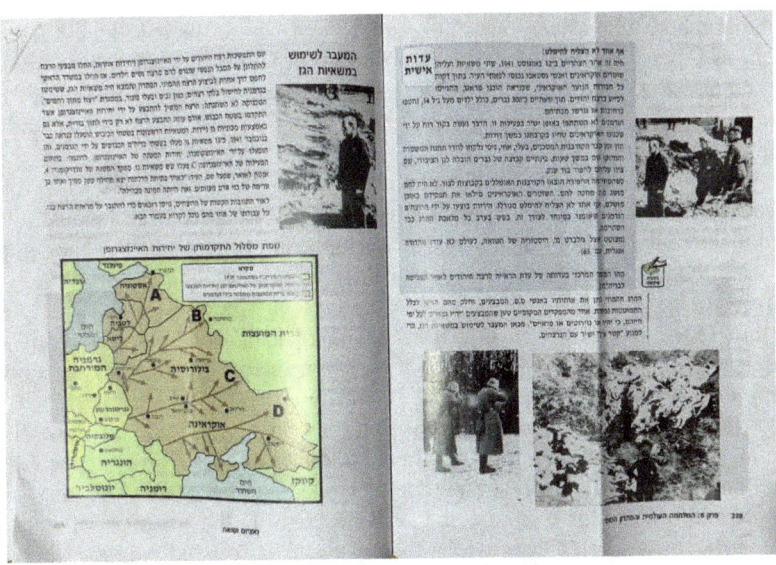

Image 20. Nazism and Shoah, pp. 228-229. Lilach Publishers.

On the left page, above a cropped segment of the photo, that shows only the victim and the gun pointed at his head, the heading reads: "The transition to gas trucks." The main text explains once again how inconvenient direct shooting was for the German soldiers. A map shows us the immensity of the area the Germans wanted to cleanse of Jews. Indeed, this mission could not have been accomplished by direct shooting. The map enhances the sense of objectivity established by the text that relates the facts seemingly without evaluation or judgment.[26]

Summary

The three photos of the women who are about to be shot in Liepaja, the last Jew in Vinnitsa and the Ivangorod mother, show nameless individuals being murdered. We are told that they are shot because they are Jews, but since they carry no Jewish "object signs" (term coined by Roland Barthes) on them, such as a hat, side-locks or any other indication of being Jewish, they can represent any oppressed minority that the ruling powers have decided to eliminate. This is one of the features that turned them into icons. We look at them from the position of the

---

26. On the functions of maps, see Chouliaraki 2006; Peled-Elhanan 2012; Momonier. 1991. *How to Lie with Maps.*

photographer, who knew very little about them, as did their killers, but regarded them as superfluous people to be disposed of. For us as viewers, these individuals are humanized, not only because we know they were innocent victims of racism, but because we are caught in the gaze of the man and the women, and in the mother's act of protection.

The photos were supposedly taken by individuals as souvenirs, or as tokens of a successful mission and a special adventure. Transposed to Holocaust museums and albums, they were transformed from souvenirs to icons of the Nazi genocide. Transposed to Israeli schoolbooks, their iconic status is preserved, albeit narrowed. For Israeli students and teachers these are not only icons of helplessness in the face of power, of injustice, or of racism, but specifically of Jewish helplessness in foreign lands, where Jews had no state of their own nor a powerful army to protect them.

In the books studied here, these victims have also become illustrations of the inefficiency of the method of direct shooting, as they were for the Germans. The photographs themselves are not discussed in the books, are not narrated. Readers know nothing about the victims or of the history of the places and the communities from which they were taken to be killed, as if they had no life before their death. Nothing is told about the trajectory of the photographs, even though this information is readily available, and tells a story of Heroism. The students are prompted to reflect upon the narrative of the "Holocaust with Bullets" in what Chouliaraki (2006)[27] terms the *agoraic* mode: to deliberate, to reason, eschewing the *theatrical mode*, which is a more emotional way of relating to suffering and the sufferers. The agoraic mode leaves the viewers detached as far as possible from the sufferers themselves. The theatre mode on the other hand, calls for empathy and relies on viewers' participation in the psychological and emotional states of the sufferers. None of the texts studied here prompts the readers to adopt the latter orientation. Rather, they are expected to observe the victims' misfortune dispassionately, and judge it objectively, from a German military point of view.

In the final history examination of winter 2020, Israeli high school students were given specific questions regarding the "psychological distress" of the German soldiers during the Holocaust of Bullets and were asked to enumerate the reasons and the justifications for the passage to gas.

---

27. In the chapter "The humane sufferer and the agora"

Chapter 6. Individual Victims as Specimens of Categories

> Only the abstract Jews could be subjected to genocide [...]. For genocide to be possible personal differences must first be obliterated and faces must be melted into the uniform mass of the abstract category. (Zygmunt Bauman 1989, 227)

> Without knowing more about the people in the pictures, the viewer cannot 'rescue' them from oblivion [...] The viewer becomes involved in seeing those murdered in the same way as their murderers did: as a collectivity. (Loewy 1996, 267f in Holtschneider 2006, 59).

Persons can be represented generically as classes, or specifically as identifiable individuals. The classification of people, as Kress and Hodge (1979, 63) point out, is a bidirectional instrument of control: "control over the flux of experience of physical and social reality [. . .] and society's control over conceptions of that reality." Classification creates "a kind of second-order reality, a conception of reality," which is determined by the interest and ideology of the classifier. Human beings can be represented either in terms of their unique identity, as nominated individuals, in which case we speak of *individualization*, or in terms of identities and functions they share with others, in which case we speak of *categorization*. And it is always interesting to observe in a given discourse, which social actors are categorized and which are nominated (Van Leeuwen 2008). Individual Holocaust victims, perpetrators, or rescuers who were chosen to appear in textbooks as subjects, are always named and generally look rather "like us." Prime examples are Anna Frank the victim, Hitler the perpetrator, Anielewicz the hero of the Warsaw Ghetto uprising, Raoul Wallenberg the rescuer, and numerous politicians. As scholars have shown, we are more likely to be empathic toward and to care about the sufferers who are construed as individuals and are presented as persons like 'us', well dressed, with agency, a name, and a voice (Rabinowitz 2001, 76; Chouliaraki 2006). When people are represented in this way, we feel closer to them and tend to respect them more.

When people are categorized, they are defined by their belonging to or affiliation with a certain group, according to criterial features in which the classifier is interested. (Van Leeuwen 2008, 46).[1] Van Leeuwen enumerates different strategies of (mis-) representing people. These include collectivization, exclusion, suppression and backgrounding, genericization, functionalization, and impersonalization. This chapter demonstrates how these strategies are used in the

---

1. Van Leeuwen, 2008. *Discourse and Practice*.

representation of Holocaust sufferers. To the Germans, their victims were nothing but *Stücke*, namely pieces or units of categories. Indeed, victims on whom experiments were conducted were referred to by the Nazi scientists as "specimens" of a certain "human material."[2] They materialized this conception by erasing people's names and identity and tattooing numbers on their arms, which became their sole means of identification. But the victims were further categorized. For example, in the leather-bound Auschwitz album that contains a hundred and ninety three photographs, showing the arrival and selection of Jews deported from Hungary, the pictures are sorted into systematic categories such as "deployable men," "deployable women," "non-deployable men," and "non-deployable women" (Keilbach 2009, 64).

Functionalization depicts people as nameless characters who fulfill functional roles, and do not become "points of identification" for the reader or the viewer (Van Leeuwen 2008). In the schoolbooks studied here, some adults and children are mentioned by name but most of them are not. The omission of names reflects the interest of the designers to use the photographed victims as representatives of categories. Since viewers are scarcely able to look at Holocaust photos as indications of individual lives and histories, they tend to see them as their murderers did, as samples of categories classified by their function in the Final Solution, such as "prisoners," "smugglers," or "Mengele's twins." The sufferers are thus classified according to their function in the narrative.

Genericization is effected by the use of an indefinite article in descriptions, for instance a humiliated Jew, a begging or a dying child, can be substituted by any other humiliated Jew, begging or dying child. In the case of schoolbooks, Genericization is the outcome of a decision made by the rhetor not to nominate the photographed person. This has nothing to do with who the photographed person is. For example, the small girl who looks straight into our eyes (Keren 1999, below. Image 25), wearing the yellow badge, is identified generically in the schoolbook as "a German girl wearing a badge," although she is not anonymous. Her name is recorded in Yad Vashem's archives as Hannah Lehrer. Hence, her presentation as an anonymous child, or as a specimen of the category "badge wearers", must be the outcome of a deliberate decision. In the Israeli schoolbooks studied here, most photographed victims are presented as such in the captions.

Categorization symbolically removes the photographed individuals from the readers' world of immediate experience and presents them as distant "others" rather than as people with whom "we" have something in common. Categories of people may also be denoted by general nouns, or by grammatical metaphors, such as "medical treatment", that appears below the photograph of a physician (Image

---

2. About, Ilsen. 2001. "La photographie au service du système concentrationaire national-socialiste 1933-1945. In: *Memoires des Camps: Photographies des camps de concentration et d'extermination nazi* (1933–1999). Edited by Clément Chéroux. Paris: Marval.

30); or "sights of hunger in the ghetto," (Image 32) indexed by a dying child lying in a street in Warsaw ghetto; "childhood in the ghetto," (Image14) indexed by the two little twin girls sitting on the pavement. The grammatical metaphors prompt us not to consider the photographed doctors, beggars, or dying children as particular human beings in whom we should be interested, and to regard only the criterial features that led to their categorization: the white coat of the doctor, the tiny dying body in the street, the rags of the little beggars, or the yellow badge on Hannah Lehrer's chest.

As in advertisements, the "categorized" people are presented as types. In advertisements people are shown as desirable models of current styles of beauty or as stereotypes of some class of people, and their individuality is hidden behind that which categorizes them - the hairdo, the makeup, the dress, the status accessories, stereotypical facial characteristics, function or fate: doctors, children, immigrants, casualties, the man in the street, etc. (Van Leeuwen 2008).

Bureaucracy categorizes people according to various criteria, as does education and the military. Science likewise categorizes people, plants and other living creatures into "families," types and kinds. People are often represented as part of a group by virtue of some criterial feature, such as fishing, agriculture, industry, their being refugees, or immigrants. The criterial feature that qualifies them for a specific representation may be their age, their occupation, their provenance, their appearance, or their gender, among other traits. Scientific study allocated tigers, cats, lions, leopards, and pumas from all over the world to the same "family" according to criteria that interested scholars. Human beings, dolphins, and other "mammals" comprise another such "family."

Racist discourse operates in many ways like the discourse of science and bureaucracy. It classifies or divides reality according to categories made up by discourse. Racist discourse classifies all Jews as belonging to the same "species" owing to their religion, although they come from different places, differ in their looks, and speak different languages, as Primo Levi realized when he was deported to Auschwitz and met, for the first time, Jews from other countries (*Is That a Man*). It categorizes Black people based on their color, homosexuals for their sexual preference, and immigrants for their "non-belonging." Refugees are called in French "sans papiers" (without documents) regardless of who they are, where they come from or what they do.

In advertisements, in science, in the bureaucracy and in racist discourse people can be visually represented not merely as stereotypes but as "specimens" of certain classes, with no need for verbal identification. In schoolbooks too, the "specimens" index others who belong to the same category according to the criteria defined by the book's rhetor and are often presented anonymously in the captions.

Armband Sellers, Beggars and Little Smugglers

As explained above, the creation of new signs by the transposition of signs such as photographs from one site to another is driven by interest that is often professionally shaped (Kress 2020). The designer's choice of images for a schoolbook may be attuned to the students' age or faith. Let us examine photographs that appear in three schoolbooks written by the same author for different ages (ages 12-14 and ages 16-18) and for different religious orientation (secular and orthodox).³ The schoolbooks for younger and religious students show images that are all less disturbing than those shown to the secular older students.

Image 21 *Journey into the Past*, 2001 for grades 7-9; *Journey into the Past selected chapters*, 2007 for religious state high school. Courtesy of the Center for Educational Technologies.

---

3. The books are: For younger students (aged 12-14, Avieli-Tabibian 2001) *A Journey into the Past: the 20th Century in Favor of Liberty;* for older religious students (aged 16-18, Avieli-Tabibian 2007): *A Journey into the Past: Selected Topics in History. The 19 and the 20th Century;* The book for 16–18-year-old secular students (Avieli-Tabibian 2001a): *The Age of Horror and Hope.*

Image 22. *The Age of Horror and Hope* for grades 10-12.
Courtesy of the Center for Educational Technologies.

In both examples, the pictures are embedded in a text addressing the Judenrat - the Jewish council appointed by the Nazis to govern Jewish life and help execute the German policy of extermination. The Judenrat leaders were often accused of being obsequious, or even of collaborating with the Nazis, since they complied with their requirements, provided lists of "workers" for the extermination industry, regulated daily life, made decisions pertaining to work, food, and health, and thereby determined who would live (for a short while longer) and who would die. The texts reveal the dilemmas faced by these people who had to make impossible choices as they sought to govern a starving community destined to perish. As historian Dan Diner (2000, 136)[4] explains, "The councils, bereft of any alternative, directed the Nazi engendered reversal of all values - the ethics of ends and means and the associated assumptions of rationality - against themselves, and against the Jewish communities entrusted to their care." Some Judenrat officials were tyrannical; some were corrupt and took care of their own, while others were helpful. None of these leaders could repeal the death sentence pronounced by the Germans on all the Jews. Some were men of principle, like Adam Czerniakow of the Warsaw Ghetto who committed suicide when ordered to furnish victims for transports, knowing where these transports led. His tragedy is merely mentioned, not discussed in the textbooks for younger and religious students. A more detailed report appears as a side note in the margin of the page for older students. On the page for younger and religious students, the text relating the life story of another "elder" and head of a Judenrat, Haim Romkovsky of Łódź, who was murdered in Auschwitz, is also placed in the margin. The suicide of Czerniakow from Warsaw and the murder of Haim Romkovsky of Łódź illustrate the dire predicament within which the Judenrat functionaries operated, and from which they could escape only through death.

The images in all three textbooks illustrate the same themes, demonstrating various ways of coping within the regime of starvation imposed by the Germans, and the life the Judenrat was regulating. However, the photographs differ in the degree of horror they evoke. In the schoolbooks for younger and religious students, we see three photos of children: an armband seller, little beggars, and little smugglers being arrested by the Gestapo. The armband seller is smiling, looking straight at the photographer and at us. He is placed at the right-hand top spot - the "ideal given" spot - on the page (Kress and Van Leeuwen 2006) and is the first picture to be seen. Since the source of the photographs is not mentioned, we cannot know whether the boy smiled naturally or was ordered to smile, and why he looks so healthy and is dressed better than the other children. Context may be extremely important here, for as Didi-Huberman (2012) observes, a girl who smiles in a French film is not the same as a girl who smiles in a Nazi film. A well-

---

4. Diner, Dan. 2000. *Beyond the Conceivable: Studies on Germany, Nazism, and the Holocaust*

dressed, healthy smiling boy, who sells racist armbands in the Warsaw ghetto, is not just any healthy smiling boy. He may have been an "actor" in one of the Nazi propaganda films for which children were well fed and well-dressed a few days before the shooting. Milton (1984) notes that the photographed subjects in the ghettos were always vulnerable to the whims of the Nazi photographer, even if he was an amateur. Even the private photographs, that often reveal compassion rather than disgust, she says, show compliant subjects. Nazi photographer Willy Georg[5], who served as an official photographer in the ghetto but took private photographs as well, reported in 1980, when he dared publish his photographs, that the Jewish subjects in the Ghetto, who knew he was a Nazi, were too scared to object and too eager to please. Some of them even smiled, touched their hats in respect, or showed off their children.[6]

The boy's smile and wellbeing create the illusion of contentment and amiability that form a screen through which the picture is less difficult to observe. However, we cannot forget that while he is smiling at the invisible photographer and at the schoolchildren who see him in their textbooks, he is destined to die. We know this, but he does not. We know that every Holocaust photograph conveys this catastrophe.

---

5. *In the Warsaw Ghetto: Summer 1941*, by Rafael F. Scharf and Willy Georg. April 1, 1993. Aperture.
6. https://wearethemuseumcollective.wordpress.com/2015/03/29/in-the-warsaw-ghetto-photographs-by-willy-georg/

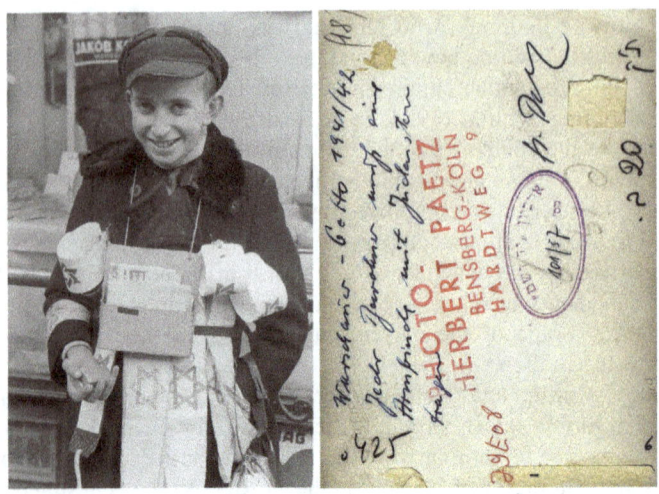

Image 23a: Warsaw, Poland, 1941-1942. A boy selling armbands in the ghetto. Item ID: 95259. Yad Vashem Archive: 29E08.[7]

Image 23b: Warsaw, Poland, Children begging in the ghetto, 1940-1943. Yad Vashem Archive. Item ID: 2955. Archival signature: 933/140.[8]

---

7. https://photos.yadvashem.org/photo-details.html?language=en&item_id=95259&ind=4
8. https://photos.yadvashem.org/photo-details.html?language=en&item_id=2955&ind=8

Image 23c: Warsaw, Poland. German soldiers searching a Jewish boy who is attempting to smuggle goods into the ghetto. Yad Vashem Archive. Item ID: 29548. Archival signature: 4613/454.[9]

The photo beneath the young armband seller shows starving children in the street,[10] directly below the note on the suicide of Adam Czerniakow. The little beggars were photographed by the two official Nazi photographers, Albert Cusian and Erhard Josef Knobloch of Propaganda-Kompanie 689, whose photographs have often been criticized for being implicitly or explicitly anti-Semitic (Keller 1984)[11]. However, the schoolbooks show the photographs without mentioning the photographers, their propaganda unit, or the fact that many of their photographs were staged. In some Holocaust albums these children appear separately, which indicates that the photographers may have grouped them together to enhance the impression of neglect, misery, and destitution. Nevertheless, the children, though nameless and voiceless in the photos, do have a face and a gaze. Two of the beggars look straight into the camera and therefore into the viewers' eyes, and their gaze commands rapport with their suffering. One of the children is crying in terror, not for help, but out of sheer misery, or so it seems, for she does not make eye contact with the photographer. Another child speaks, as if imploring or demanding something, while a third puts on his best smile. This last one appears alone in Joest's album, with the same smile, in the midst of what Joest terms a "good" street, full of people and merchandise. However, this child's smile is different from that of the armband seller. It is not the proud smile of a healthy boy

---

9. https://photos.yadvashem.org/photo-details.html?language=en&item_id=29548&ind=0
10. Yad Vashem Archive 933/140
11. Keller, U. Ed. 1984 *The Warsaw Ghetto in Photographs.* Yad Vashem Photo Archive 933/7/17

who stands upright and has a purpose,[12] but rather the smile of a beggar, crouched in the street, who has nothing to lose, and is beseeching the photographer with the only thing he has to offer - his smile. Both he and the boy who implores make eye contact with the photographer, and it is not hard to guess what they are demanding. The baby that one of them holds enhances the sense of disaster and urgency.

A straight vector descends from the armband seller to the beggars and may suggest a relation of opposition. Between them, we find the note about Czerniakow's suicide - the leader who should have cared for the children but could not and therefore abandoned them.[13] A diagonal vector connects the band seller to the photo of the little smuggler apprehended by the Gestapo, suggesting a relation of similarity and difference: both found ways to make a living and provide for their families, although one was relatively safe while the other was risking his life. Thus, the page is laid out to show all three photographs connected by invisible vectors that tell the story of ghetto children. However, the photo of the little smuggler stands out from the others. It is placed in a special yellow "window" in the bottom left corner of the page, usually displaying the "new real" (Kress and Van Leeuwen 2006) according to Hebrew reading. The photograph is placed alongside the famous poem dedicated to the anonymous little smuggler, by the poet Henryka Łazowertówna,[14] who was murdered in the Treblinka extermination camp in August 1942. This arrangement iconizes the little smuggler, for as a rule, "songs and poems stabilize collective memories" (Wertsch 2002, 52), and turn narratives into myths (Barthes 1957). The frame that singles him out, and the poem that glorifies this little thief, allocate him a place of honor in the mythical hall of fame, alongside fictional and mythical little boys such as the heroes of De Amici's stories, or little Hans Brinker who saved his country from a flood by sticking his finger in the dyke. The smuggler is the hero of whom either historian Emanuel Ringelblum or journalist Peretz Oputchinski (the textbooks disagree on the attribution), the chroniclers of the Warsaw ghetto archive Oneg Shabbat, wrote, "After the war is over, we should erect a monument to the memory of the unknown smugglers."[15]

The photo of the little smuggler has undergone multiple transformations in its transposition to the schoolbook. From a Nazi propaganda film[16] to an Israeli schoolbook, from a thief being caught, as the Nazis showed him - calling him an

---

12. On the meaning of postures and gestures, see Canetti. 1960. *Crowds and Power*.
13. In his book, *The Ghetto Fights* Marek Edelman describes the anger he and other people felt toward Czerniakow, who killed himself and abandoned them.
14. https://www.jhi.pl/en/articles/warmth-and-lightness-of-style-henryka-lazowertowna,5178
15. In his book, *Jewish-Polish Relations during the Second World War* (p. 82) Ringelblum attributes this saying to "attorney Leon Berensohn who was a counsel for the defense of the fighters of independence during the partition of Poland".
16. See Yael Harsonsky, *Film Unfinished*

outlaw gangster - to an eternal child-hero, an icon of bravery and self-sacrifice, which connotes German racist cruelty toward children. His capture by the Gestapo and probable torture and murder shortly after the photograph was taken, endow him with eternal glory. He has become a figure of memory.

The direct vector that connects the smuggler to the little beggars who lie exhausted in the street, captioned generically as "children in rags in the streets of Warsaw," points to a relation of contrast, and glorifies the smuggler still more. While the other children surrendered to their fate or to hunger, he fought to the end. The smuggler, like other mythical brave and selfless children, died thinking (so the poem tells us) about his mother, who would be unable to serve food to her children. Note the woman who appears to support him while trying to save his merchandise.

To conclude, the books for younger and religious students focus on children: the cunning child who found a job and earns a living; the brave self-scarifying boy forever mythologized and glorified by a poem; and the desperate children who are the ultimate victims of the Germans' policy of starvation. The tone of the text about the Judenrat, in which these photos are embedded, is positive and makes no mention of the corruption and the eagerness of some Jewish leaders to obey the Germans.

In the textbook for older secular students (grades 10-12), *The Age of Horror and Hope*, the same themes appear, in almost the same text, but it is more critical of the Judenrat, and addresses questions of nepotism and corruption alongside the commendable actions taken by these councils, and the dilemmas they faced. The photos show both children and adults and the layout portrays the situation in the ghetto in a more realistic manner, eschewing the sympathy aroused by the smile of the little armband seller and the mythologized little smuggler. The changes in the choice of photos and their positioning in the layout create a different impression. The photo of the little smuggler is again placed in the bottom left corner depicting the "new real", or the new reality of the ghetto that depended on these small smugglers for food. But this time, the boy is embedded in a text that addresses the starvation policy and the ways Jews coped with it. His capture signifies nothing but death and more hunger. He is not placed in a special frame, nor is he glorified by a poem, and his name remains forever unknown. He is depicted as a specimen in the category of smugglers who forfeited their lives for a turnip.

The most striking difference between the books is to be found in the photographs of the armband sellers. The seller is an adult, the woman photographed by Joest whom we saw transduced in another book (Image 5). She stands in stark contrast to the smiling boy of the book for younger and religious students, and judging by her expression, and by Joest's comments, we may conclude that she did not pose willingly, as the boy may have done, or even consciously.

On the opposite side of the page is a photo of two adult beggars (Image 24), taken by Joest as well, who wrote, "One woman was leaning against the wall [...] unconscious. The other one was looking at me as if asking me to help her." The armband seller did not look at him, she was past human contact, but the beggar who tried to assist her friend or sister, is humanized by a gaze that Joest interpreted as an appeal for help.

Image 24. Heinrich Joest. Yad Vashem archival signature 2536/78

While the photos on these pages, like the photos in the other books, depict three ways to survive in the ghetto - "working," smuggling food, and begging, all of which lead to eventual death - in the book for high-school secular students we are shown death's dominion more clearly and cruelly. In a later edition of the same book,[17] the layout is different: although the woman armband seller remains in the same place, she is connected by a diagonal vector to a photo of the Judenrat building from which the aforementioned well-dressed couple emerge, ignoring the half-dead figure who lies on the steps (Image 2). The vector connecting the Judenrat building to the starving armband seller signifies either a causal relation or opposition. The woman armband seller is the product of Nazi policy implemented by the Judenrat.

---

17. *Journeys in Time: from Holocaust to War and Peace,* 2009

The Badge as a Criterial Feature

Image 25. Keren 1999. Courtesy of Mapa Pub. Tel Aviv Books.

Image 25a. Hanna Lehrer's photo: Yad Vashem Photo Archive 14081189

The woman band seller also features in Keren (1999), *Journey into Memory*, in a chapter titled "The Nazis devise plans to uproot and isolate the Jews." In the top right section of the page - the first item to be seen according to Hebrew reading, or the "given" part of the layout that generally establishes the given reality, (Kress and Van Leeuwen 2006) we find a photo of a shop destroyed during Kristallnacht, the vandalizing act against Jewish property and against Jews that ushered in state-approved violence. A well-dressed mother and child, who seem untouched by the pogrom, pass by it.

The photo of the woman band-seller appears on the top center of the page and is probably the most salient image in the double-spread, given its placement and the horrific human image it presents. The caption reads: "This woman found herself a way to make a living by selling armbands." This somewhat cynical caption seeks to individualize the woman, to portray her as someone who makes her own decisions and acts accordingly, even cunningly perhaps. It contradicts Joest's impression of the woman who "looked as if she was about to topple over and die the next moment." Her face and veiled eyes tell us, as does the photographer Joest, that she was not a woman "who found a way to make a living," but rather the ultimate victim of the circumstances into which she was thrown by German racism. Alongside her photo is a drawing of a Star of David, alluding to the badges she is selling and signaling that this is the criterial feature of the photo, and the reason it was chosen.

A diagonal vector connects the armband seller to a little girl who is positioned directly below the ruined shop, at the real-given spot on the page. She wears a badge with the Star of David. The vector signifies that the woman and the girl are of the same order; two parts of a taxonomy whose criterial feature is the badge, although one is old and the other is young, one lives in Warsaw, Poland, and the other in Germany, and they would probably not have understood each other's language had they met. The badge that defines the girl and was the criterial feature for choosing her photograph, is likewise placed beside her photo, magnified and in color, emphasizing its prominence as the feature that should be the focus of attention. The caption includes questions: "A Jewish girl from Germany with a yellow badge. When was the yellow badge used to identify Jews in the past? What is the difference between past usage and that of the Nazis?"

These questions clearly divert the focus from the little badge bearer to the badge itself. That is why her name and history are not mentioned. Her function is to feature metonymically as a specimen of her category, and not as an individual worth remembering and commemorating. In the archive of Yad Vashem, she is identified as "Hanna Lehrer, 6 years old, a Munich Jew, who wears both her personal golden Jewish star around her neck and the mandated Yellow Star badge identifying her, isolating her, and alienating her from other Germans. Hanna was later sent to Riga, Latvia, where she was killed."[18]

Whereas the woman was photographed by an independent amateur photographer, Hanna's photo served to identify her on the ID cards the Germans issued for Jews. Van Leeuwen (2008, 42) observes that *identification* entails defining social actors not in terms of what they do, but in terms of what they, more or less permanently or unavoidably, are. Yet this function of the photograph is not specified in the schoolbook either. Marianne Hirsch (2001, 25) notes that "the very fact of their existence may be the most astounding, disturbing, incriminating thing about these photographs" that were taken for "identification, visibility, and surveillance, not for life but for the death machine that had already condemned all of those thus marked, with an enormous J in gothic script." (ibid. p 27). Hirsch notes that (like the photos required for a USA visa today) these pictures had to show the full face with the left ear uncovered, as a telltale identity marker.

All the photographs pertaining to the Final Solution, argues Arendt, are misleading because we see that which was not totally destroyed, or had not been destroyed yet.[19] However, Holocaust photographs of children and adults taken from ID cards, index extermination (Hirsch ibid. 74). Gazing at them, we know that the photographed victims were already killed by "the murderous Nazi gaze of the photographer that condemned them." The students who look at the picture of a living girl after she has died do not see her dead, though death emanates from the photograph. Once little Hanna was photographed, and was on her way to being murdered, she was transformed into a specimen of the category of *Jewish children to be burned*. The Israeli schoolbook classifies her as a specimen of a different category, that of the *yellow star bearers*. In both cases, she is used functionally. Had the students known Hanna's name or short life story, she would have aroused their feelings and diverted their attention from the badge to her person.

This schoolbook rhetor does not always choose to conceal the murdered children's names. On the first page of the chapter titled "The Murdered", we find a photograph of a boy and a girl of Hanna Lehrer's age. The caption reads, "Anna Klein, six years old and her brother Jon, three years old, as they were photographed in 1942. Both were murdered in Auschwitz, two of 1,500,000 children who were exterminated in the Shoah".

Here Kress's concept of interest becomes crucial. What was the interest of the rhetor not to mention Hanna Lehrer's name and the fact that she too was one of the 1,500,000 children who were exterminated in the Shoah, but to mention the names of Anna Klein and her brother Jon, and their fate, which was identical to that of Hanna? We must conclude that the children served different functions in

---

18. Yad Vashem / United States Holocaust Memorial Museum Photo Archive.
19. Arendt, Hannah. 1958. *The Origins of Totalitarianism*. New York, 446.

the book, different interests. Individual tragedy is always more touching than a collective disaster. Anna and Jon Klein personify the 1,500,000 exterminated children. They make the immense number more tangible for the students, more engaging, and perhaps more shocking or saddening, reminding them that this unimaginable number is composed of cute little children. They serve to materialize the atrocity of the Final Solution by individualizing it and reminding readers that children had names before they were turned into specimens of murderous categories, before becoming numbers and pieces of flesh to be dispatched into the furnace.

Image 26. Studio portrait of Anna (6) and Jon (3) Klein. United States Holocaust Memorial Museum, courtesy of Artur (Arieh) Klein. Photograph Number: 63683 (https://collections.ushmm.org/search/catalog/pa1154259)

We are not told whether Anna and Jon wore a badge at any time, or whether they were ever photographed by the Germans, although we may assume they were. Of their life story only their ages are communicated to us, and the fact that they were killed. No details of their life or provenance are given, thus turning Anna and Jon into indices. Hirsch (2012, 231) observes that the indexical nature of such photos enhances their status as harbingers of death and, at the same time, their capacity to signify life. Life is the presence of the children facing the camera; death is the radical break, the finality introduced by the past tense and the knowledge that they will die, that they have died, transmitted by the presence of the photograph in this chapter.

Neither Hanna's nor the Klein siblings' characters and lives had anything to do with the choice to mention or not to mention their names and fate. The decision as to whose identity would be foregrounded and whose would be suppressed was semiotic. Both the siblings and Hanna represent all the other children in their category. Upon her transposition to the schoolbook, anonymous Hanna remains a specimen of the category to which she was assigned by the Germans. The photo of Anna and Jon acquires a different meaning when transposed from the family album to the schoolbook, as they are transformed from unique cherished children into an index of a million and a half exterminated boys and girls. The function of their photo in the schoolbook is to trigger emotion, and mentioning their names and ages seems sufficient to endear them to us, so we can pity and mourn them. Looking at them, we cannot accept the fact that they were ruthlessly murdered. Had the readers known that Hanna Lehrer was murdered as well, they would have been equally devastated, but Hanna's criterial feature is her badge. We are not told her age or that she was killed. The educational message conveyed here is that some children get to have their names mentioned and some do not, and this has nothing to do with whom they really are, but merely reflects the interest of those who choose them for their rhetorical purposes.

Partial Information and Deleted Identity: The Misrepresentation of Masha Bruskina

One of the functions of the historian as mediator is to ascribe meaning to documents, whether textual or visual, using captions, context, and all the available and relevant documents and materials (Lewis 2001). As the examples above demonstrate, the recontextualization of history in educational texts and the transposition of photographs to schoolbooks, involve the deletion of information or parts of it, motivated by rhetorical interests. The following instance of partial information emerges in the portrayal of the hanging of two adolescents. The girl is already dead, while her comrade is having the noose placed around his neck by a

German hangman.[20] This way of killing, as Mercedes Camino (2022, 4)[21] explains, began in Poland and was due to the Nazi classification of Slavs and Jews as *Untermensch*, "which was translated into a brutal display of power that included public executions, and the ever-present spectacle of dangling corpses."

The photograph of the hanging is one of eight photos of the execution of seventeen-year-old Russian communist Masha Bruskina and her friends, on October 26, 1941.

Masha Bruskina, who was subsequently celebrated as "the heroine of Minsk," (Hirsch 2012, 149),[22] was one of three communist resisters who were paraded through the streets of Minsk and publicly hanged. The gruesome photos of their humiliation and execution were published after the war, but only the two boys were identified; the girl executed with them was denied an identity, and especially a Jewish identity, until 1968, when Russian filmmaker Lev Arkadyev initiated an investigation into the "unknown girl."[23] Eyewitnesses who provided detailed descriptions about her not only identified Bruskina, but also spoke about her remarkable demeanor on the day of her execution.[24]

Masha Bruskina was born in Minsk in 1924 to a Jewish family. She was a member of the school committee of the Leninist Young Communist League, the Komsomol. In June 1941, shortly after her graduation and the German occupation of the Belorussian capital, she moved with her mother into the Minsk ghetto. Masha soon escaped to the city's "Aryan side," lightened her hair, and took on her mother's maiden name, Bugakova. She volunteered as a nurse at the hospital which the occupying German forces had requisitioned as an infirmary for wounded Soviet prisoners of war. Masha joined a local resistance cell organized by Kiril Trus and Olga Shcherbatsevicha. She used her position at the hospital to smuggle medical supplies and photographic equipment to the Soviet underground. She helped other resistance members to spirit Soviet prisoners of war away to

---

20. https://www.tate-images.com/DK0558-Photograph-from-the-public-hanging-of-Masha.html
21. Camino, Mercedes. 2022. "War, gender, and lasting emotion: letters and photographs of Masha Bruskina and Olga Bancic, 1941–44." In: *Women's History Review*. 27 Jun 2022. Taylor and Francis Online. 1-26.
22. *The Generation of Post Memory*
23. Arkadyev and Dikhtyar, 'The Unknown Girl', *Yiddish Writers* 1 (1987). 161-204; Bill Keller, 'Echo of '41 in Minsk: Was the Heroine a Jew?', *New York Times*, 15 September 1987 (https://www.nytimes.com/1987/09/15/world/echo-of-41-in-minsk-was-the-heroine-a-jew.html). Miller, *One by One by One* (New York: Touchstone, 1990); Tec and Weiss, 'A Historical Injustice: The Case of Masha Bruskina', *Holocaust and Genocide Studies* 11, no. 3 (1997). 366-377; reprinted as 'The Heroine of Minsk: Eight Photographs of an Execution', *History of Photography* 23, no. 4 (1999). 322-30.
24. For a discussion of these photographs, see Tec, Nechama and Daniel Weiss 1999 Published online: 2015. "The Heroine of Minsk Eight photographs of an execution." *History of Photography*. Volume 23, Issue 4. Taylor and Francis. 322-330

safety, and to redeploy captured Soviet officers, with significant combat experience, to the ranks of the growing partisan movement.

In early October 1941, a Soviet prisoner-patient denounced the resistance group to the German authorities. Masha and several members of her cell, including leaders Kiril Trus and Olga Shcherbatsevicha and her sixteen-year-old son, Volodya, were arrested. On October 26, 1941, Masha, Kiril, and Volodya were paraded through the streets of Minsk to the chosen place of execution. Masha walked proudly wearing the placard that read: "We are the partisans who shot German troops[25], and looked straight at the photographer/executioner's camera. She was very conscious of her appearance and the way people saw her. In a letter to her mother on October 20, 1941, she wrote: "I am tormented by the thought that I have caused you great worry. Don't worry. Nothing bad has happened to me. I swear to you that you will have no further unpleasantness because of me. If you can, please send me my dress, my green blouse, and white socks. I want to be dressed decently when I leave here." (Hirsch ibid. 347).[26] She wanted to dress in her best clothes on the day of her execution and did not want her tortured dying face to be seen. "When they put her on the stool," recalled eyewitness Petr Pavlovich Borisenko, "the girl turned her face toward the fence. The executioners wanted her to stand with her face to the crowd, but she turned away and that was that. No matter how much they pushed her and tried to turn her, she remained standing with her back to the crowd. Only then did they kick away the stool from under her." Therefore, by showing her hanged figure facing the camera and the spectators of her execution, Israeli schoolbooks transmit a clear message that her dying wishes are not to be honored. According to Camino (2022) turning her back to the spectators was Bruskina's last act of defiance, the only one available to her: refusing to face a photographer. "Her attitude thus foregrounds that the decontextualization of these images means, to perpetuate the perpetrators' gaze." As Susan Crane observes (2008, 322), "With atrocity images, we have tended toward preservation as if by moral imperative, but if that choice means retention of, indeed conservation of, the Nazi gaze, we should reconsider the alternatives". Camino adds, "Bruskina's last action sought to prevent her last moments from becoming a public spectacle, reclaiming for a moment the privacy that the violence of the execution, perpetuated by the photographs, sought to destroy. That Bruskina turned her back repeatedly when the noose was placed around her neck corroborates the degree to which the photographs completed the violence of the hangings […].

Masha and her friends were hung by the 707 Infantry Division of the Wehrmacht with assistance given by the Second Schutzmannschaft Battalion of

---

25. https://commons.wikimedia.org/wiki/File:Bundesarchiv_Bild_146-1972-026-43,_Minsk,_Widerstandsk%C3%A4mpfer_vor_Hinrichtung.jpg
26. For a discussion of this letter see: Mercedes Camino. 2022.

Lithuanian auxiliaries, led by Antanas Impulevičius-Impulėnas. In fact, it was one of these Lithuanians who photographed the proceedings." (Camino 2022, 7). In the present study, out of respect for her dying wish I did not reproduce the photograph that appears in the schoolbooks.

Although the story of Masha and her friends is well known and the photograph became the iconic image of the Great Patriotic War, as the 1940s Soviet partisan resistance movement came to be known,[27] Bruskina's life story is not mentioned in any of the schoolbooks studied here. Israeli schoolbooks show the photo of the hanging without providing any details of the victims or their circumstances. The biography of Masha Bruskina may explain this rhetorical decision. Masha was a communist, not a Zionist, and risked her life to save Russian soldiers, not to help Jewish victims. Contrary to the inscription on the placard she wore on her neck the day of her death, Masha was not involved in armed resistance and was not a partisan. However, the state of Israel commemorates Masha Bruskina as a Zionist-Jewish partisan. A street in the illegal Jewish settlement of Pisgat Zeev was named after her and a monument glorifying her as a Jewish Partisan was erected in the Youth Village Hakfar Hayarok. In a short film which introduces the monument, the guide praises her Zionist spirit and says, pointing at the statue, "she is finally home, in her homeland Israel, and will forever be an inspiration to Israeli youth and soldiers."[28]

The caption under the photograph in Gutman (1999/2009) reads, "Hanged partisans in Minsk October 1941. On the left; the Jewess Masha Bruskina, seventeen." This caption prompts readers to assume mistakenly that Masha was executed for being a Jewish partisan. Her comrade Volodya, who was hanged next to her, and is seen crying for her in the photo, remains anonymous. Thus, he is classified implicitly as non-Jew, and therefore as someone whose identity is irrelevant in an Israeli schoolbook. This partial information clearly serves an interest or a principle, according to which the victims' names and faith are either mentioned or not, and biographical details such as Masha's can be foregrounded or suppressed. For Gutman the criterial feature for displaying Masha's image was her Jewish origins. She is classified as "one of us" - a heroine of the kind that Israel admires. Thus, the schoolbook validates the false Nazi accusations written on the placard she wore around her neck before and after she died. The readers of this schoolbook cannot possibly know who she really was, but they learn to admire and commemorate Jewish partisans who resisted the Germans and did not march to the gas chambers like sheep to the slaughter.

Ironically, her Jewishness is also the reason why Masha remained anonymous in her native country, Belarus, until 2008, nearly two decades after the dissolution

---

27. Heberer, Patricia. *Children during the Holocaust*, 344-346.
28. https://www.youtube.com/watch?v=kyXRuXalGXM

of the USSR, when her identity was accepted officially (Camino 2022). Even today, as Camino notes (p. 13), "her ethnicity is nowhere acknowledged in Belarus, which preserves the USSR's narrative of disregarding the suffering of 'nationalities', claiming genocide for Belarusians and other Slavic peoples."

Another Holocaust textbook in which the photo of these hanged youngsters appears, is Popovsky et al. (2008). In this schoolbook, the photograph bears a caption: "Jewish partisans were executed all over Europe." This caption, which is also the heading of the sub-chapter, commemorates Jewish partisans' bravery and self-sacrifice through a photo that, in reality, shows non-partisans of whom only one was Jewish. While in Gutman, the identity of Volodya is concealed and can only be guessed, in Popovsky et al. the caption of the photo transforms him from a communist Russian into a Jew. The photo of the hanging appears in a chapter devoted to the Hungarian-Jewish parachutist Hannah Senesz, who was executed at the age of twenty three in Hungary, having been sent there from her kibbutz in Palestine by the Zionist leadership, on a "rescue" mission which one textbook (Barnavi 1998) terms "suicidal."[29] The object of this mission was to produce a national myth "to the effect that the labor movement had gone to the rescue of Jews in the Holocaust," and "as in previous cases that was the principal good it did." (Segev 2019, 338). The chapter in Popovsky et al. (2008, 65), tells the story of Senesz's brief life in Hungary and in the Kibbutz Sdot Yam, and includes two of her well-known poems and numerous photographs, but not the photograph of her execution. I dare say that if such a photograph exists, her family would never allow it to be exhibited. A cropped photo of a happy Hannah Senesz in the kibbutz in Palestine[30] is displayed next to the photo of the hanging of Masha and Volodya, with the caption: "Hannah Senesz was executed by shooting in November 1944." By juxtaposing the two photos of Senesz and of the unnamed adolescents identified as Jewish partisans, the book creates a "covert taxonomy" (Kress and Van Leeuwen 1995) indicating that the photos are of the same order. Both pictures show young "Jewish partisans" who were executed by the Nazis. However, readers are prompted to focus on one photograph only, that of Hannah Senesz, whose life story and poems take up the entire chapter. Given that these photos serve as teaching resources, we may conclude that by placing the two photos next to each other, and prompting viewers to consider only one of them, the book

---

29. See Baumel, Judith Tydor. 1996. "The Heroism of Hannah Senesz: An Exercise in Creating Collective National Memory in the State of Israel." *Journal of Contemporary History* 31, no. 3. 521-546.
30. https://www.alamy.com/english-hannah-senesh-people-of-israel-original-image-name-location-between-1942-and-1943-date-qsp1942-00-00t000000z8p13191942-00-00t000000z9p13261943-00-00t000000z9-hannah-senesh-memorial-center-via-the-pikiwiki-israel-free-image-collection-project-image352020901.html?imageid=52353E28-AF77-4ECD-BBDC-DDBD5D0F92D1&p=1249410&pn=1&searchId=f6f8d3d8a3ce290d3668f5c360cf39a7&searchtype=0

conveys yet again, that some victims matter more than others, some deserve to be commemorated and remembered and some do not.

Had they told Masha's story, the writers could have drawn an interesting comparison between the two young girls who gave their life for a cause. Such a comparison could address the universal adolescent propensity toward idealism and self-sacrifice in the service of great ideals. Both girls were attached to their mothers, as their letters to them prove. Both letters express the daughters' sorrow for abandoning their mothers, and try to comfort them. A letter from Hannah to her mother was found in her clothes after her execution:

> Beloved mother! I can only tell you this: million thanks. And I would like to ask your forgiveness if I may. You alone will understand why there is no need for any more words...
> With infinite love
> Your daughter, Hannah[31]

It is worth mentioning that in Soviet schoolbooks, as in the Israeli schoolbooks mentioned here, Bruskina was also listed as 'unknown', despite the widespread use of her photographs (Camino 2022). Thus, in all three systems of education: the Soviet, the Israeli and the Belarussian, the national ideology dictated the misrepresentation of Masha Bruskina.

Indetermination, Anonymization, and Irreverence

> *Indetermination* occurs when social actors are represented as unspecified, "anonymous" individuals or groups, *determination* occurs when their identity is, one way or another, specified. (Van Leeuwen 2008, 46).

In all the cases discussed in this chapter, we find a mixture of determination and indetermination. Unlike Hanna Lehrer, Masha Bruskina is not completely anonymous, but both of them are rendered stripped of their identity and decontextualized from their circumstances. Masha is partly determined by Gutman, who informs readers of her name, age and her Jewish affiliation, but divulges nothing about her actions or political devotion to the communist party, nor the cause to which she was dedicated until death. She remains totally anonymous in Popovsky et al.

---

31. My translation. A faulty translation can be found here: https://www.kveller.com/hannah-senesh-was-a-jewish-heroine-with-thanks-to-her-mother/

Anonymization through Captioning

As we saw in the previous examples, captions indicate the interest of the sign maker and the criterial features of the sign on which viewers are guided to focus. Van Leeuwen (2005, 230)[32] summarizes the relations between photo and caption in the following table, and shows that images can extend words and vice versa, through similarity (similar content in words and image), through contrast, or through complement.

Image–text relations

Elaboration	Specification	The image makes the text more specific (illustration)
		The text makes the image more specific (anchorage)
	Explanation	The text paraphrases the image (or vice versa)
Extension	Contrast	The content of the text contrasts with that of the image
	Similarity	The content of the text is similar to that of the image
	Complement	The content of the image adds further information to that of the text, and vice versa ('relay')

In this section, I examine instances in which the caption neither complements the image nor contrasts with it, but rather bears no relation at all to it, and thus alters its meaning. In the following examples, we come across a different form of anonymization, whereby the anonymized person's name and story are attributed to someone else. Thus, they often "strip the picture of its referential power" (Zelizer 2000, 120)[33]. Zelizer refers to atrocity photographs taken by the liberators of the camps, which were given captions after the event, mostly by people who were not present at the time. Consequently, as in Israeli schoolbooks, some captions located the same event in different places and on different dates, as is the case with The Last Jew of Vinnitsa, and by doing so they changed history. To the newspapers,

---

32. *Introducing social semiotics*
33. Zelizer, Barbie, 2000. *Remembering to Forget: Holocaust Memory through the Camera's Eye.* 2nd Edition. University of Chicago Press Bunko.

155

observes Zelizer (p.120), "it mattered little whether a stack of bodies was in Ohrdruf or Buchnwald. What mattered was that it happened. The image thus functioned to provide proof of atrocity even if the location (or date) of the atrocity was incorrect". As we have seen in previous chapters, Israeli schoolbooks adopt the same practice.

Both Roland Barthes and Walter Benjamin focus on the relations between caption and image. In *A Small History of Photography* (1931),[34] Benjamin points out that written information is required in order to read photographic images that claim authenticity (by contrast to photography used in art or advertising), because photographs show too little reality, since they omit structures and context. Those need to be supplemented by the caption. When showing reality that is no longer explicit, "will not the inscription become the most important part of the photograph?" he asks (ibid.). Barthes regards captions not as signposts helping the reader to perceive the photograph as "evidence for historical occurrences," as Benjamin perceives them,[35] but as a way to select and anchor meaning. Barthes underlines photographs' polysemic meaning and their plenitude, and believes they provide an overflow of information (1981, 87). The accompanying text, he maintains, limits the polysemic meaning of the images and ascribes meaning to them amidst a "floating chain" of signifieds.[36] Barthes defines the relationships between text and image as either *anchorage* or *relay* (1977, 38)[37]. By anchoring them, words elucidate pictures, or as Van Leeuwen (2005, 229) puts it "The text directs the reader through the signifieds of the image, causing him to avoid some and receive others, and 'remote-controls' him towards the meaning chosen in advance". In relaying, "text and image stand in complementary relationship and are both fragments of a more general syntagm to which each contributes its own distinct information" (ibid.).

Lewis (2001, 348) points out that many photographs taken by the Germans acquired their racist meaning only by virtue of the caption, and that a different caption could have evoked compassion and sympathy toward the same photographed sufferers. This information is important for students who need to know whether the caption is part of Nazi propaganda or was attached by the current agency that "owns" the picture, or by the textbook writer, for each is guided by different interests. Lewis (2001:349) contends that misleading

---

34. Benjamin, Walter. 1979. "A Small History of Photography." In Benjamin. *One Way Street and Other Writings*. London and New York: Verso. 255. Quoted in Keilbach. 2009. *Photographs, Symbolic Images, and the Holocaust*, p. 57.
35. Benjamin, Walter. 2004. "The Work of Art in the Age of Mechanical Reproduction." In *Film Theory: Critical Concepts in Media and Cultural Studies*, ed. Philip Simpson, Andrew Utterson, and K. J. Sheperdson, I. London and New York: Routledge. 242.
36. Barthes, Roland. 1991. "Rhetoric of Image." In *The Responsibility of Forms*. Berkeley and Los Angeles: University of California Press. 28.
37. *Image, Music, Text.*

and incorrect captions "are a serious issue, for a number of reasons. Not least, they misinform the reader. They indicate sloppy scholarship, and if that is apparent in the use of images and their captions, the reader is entitled to ask whether it carries over into the main text. But incorrect captions also give revisionist historians an opportunity to discredit the photographic evidence of the Holocaust."

Let us now delve into some examples.

1. Settela as the boy Avram

In Popovsky et al. (2008), the events of the Shoah are related through personal stories and poems. Genocide researcher Yair Oron (2005)[38] commends this book for being personal and engaging, and highly informative. He concludes that this kind of teaching will draw pupils toward the poems themselves, and will spark their interest in the broader historical context surrounding the events depicted in the lyrics. Like other scholars, Oron believes that acquainting readers with a particular life story prompts them to identify with a specific individual, and that this is the best way to engage them with Holocaust history - the era, and its victims. As an example, he offers Kambanellis' poem from the Mauthausen Trilogy *The Song of Songs* "Have you Seen my Beautiful Beloved", which appears in the schoolbook and evokes a personal identification with the specific figure of the girl whom the author mourns.

Another poem in the book is "On the Boy Avram," by Israeli poet laureate Nathan Alterman. The boy Avram, who returned home after the war, hides under the staircase, afraid to climb it and find his slaughtered family. Literary scholar Sidra De-Koven Ezrahi suggests that the boy Avram has reversed roles with the biblical father Avram (Abraham), because in this poem it is the father who was sacrificed by fire. The boy in the poem is orphaned from both his biological and his heavenly father, therefore the poet removed from his name the letter H, that signifies God, and that God added to the biblical Avram, to change his name to Avraham. Nevertheless, Avram cannot give up and must go on, for "the command that had thundered upon Avram the father thunders now upon Avram the boy."[39]

The poem is analyzed meticulously over five pages. All the details about the poet, the period and the biblical sources that inspired the poem, are explained. Attached to the poem, on each of the five pages, is the iconic photograph of the child looking through a slot in the cattle wagon that carried victims to the extermination camps.[40]

---

38. Oron, Yair. 2005. *The Pain of Knowledge: Holocaust and Genocide Issues in Education.*
39. Ezrahi, Sidra DeKoven. 1980. *By Words Alone: The Holocaust in Literature*, p. 105
40. https://www.hmd.org.uk/resource/anna-maria-settela-steinbach/

Image 27. Westerbork, Holland, A Gypsy girl Settela Steinbach staring out of a deportation train, 15/05/1944. Yad Vashem Archive. 100528. 1570

On the final page, the face of the child without the wagon appears under a huge Israeli flag, which covers the entire sky like Providence itself, apparently symbolizing the triumph of Zionism over National Socialism (Image 28). The photographed child, transposed to the Israeli textbook and attached to the poem, represents the boy Avram. However, this nine-year-old child is a girl, and she is not Jewish – she is a Sinti from Holland, who had nothing in common with the flag of Israel, nor with Hebrew mythology or with Zionism. She did not return home after the war and was not hiding under the staircase when her photo was taken; she was locked in a cattle wagon on the way to her extermination, and was murdered in the gas chamber in Auschwitz with her mother and nine siblings, in the night between 2-3 of August 1944. Her name is Anna Maria (Settela) Steinbach. [41]

By failing to mention the child's name, gender or biography, the book prompts readers to ignore the photographed human being, and to focus instead on the criterial feature that motivated the choice of photo - a child victim of the Holocaust. The students who peer at her are prompted to identify with the boy Avram and his plight, but not with her. They are prompted to identify with the Israeli flag flying above her head, but not with her people.[42]

---

41. https://www.hmd.org.uk/resource/anna-maria-settela-steinbach/
https://www.yadvashem.org/blog/remembering-settela.html
42. Wagenaar, Aad. 1994. *Settela: The Girl Who Got Her Name Back*.

Image 28. *Identity and Identification* 2008, 107. Center for Educational Technologies

The girl Settela, who for years was thought to be Jewish, became one of the most ubiquitous icons of the Holocaust and features in albums, books, and films (e.g., *Night and Fog*), one of which was made in 1944 by the Nazi commander of the Westerbork transit camp in Holland, and directed by Rudolf Breslauer. However, by the time the schoolbooks studied here were published, Settela's identity was already known. Nevertheless, in Popovsky et al., she stands for a Jewish boy, and Avieli-Tabibian (2007:149) presents her photo bearing the caption: "A Jewish girl peeping from a truck on the way to the extermination camp".

Keren (1999) also uses the photo of Settela, but the criterial feature of the photo in her schoolbook is not the girl but the wagon. After telling Settela's true story, the text proceeds to reproduce the poem "Here, in the sealed wagon," written by Holocaust survivor and Israeli poet Dan Pagis, who uses allegorically another biblical story, that of Eve and her two lost sons, Cain and Abel. The poem constitutes part of the caption below Settela's photograph and prompts students to see the girl as representing Eve or one of her lost boys, or not to see her at all.

2. Impersonalization and Irreverence: Rabbi Moshe Hagerman

The following example from Keren (1999,103), is the famous photo of Rabbi Moshe Hagerman being humiliated by German policemen, on Bloody Wednesday

---

https://www.brabantremembers.com/persecution/het-meisje-met-de-hoofddoek-vindt-haar-naam/?lang=en in his town Olkusz, Poland. The photo is placed without its context in a chapter titled: "Religious faith tested by the Holocaust." It tells the stories of various rabbis and the ways they chose to lead the Jewish believers in the ghetto, during deportations and executions, and in the death camps. Yet the only photograph shown is that of Rabbi Hagerman, who is not mentioned in the text (Image 29).

Image 29. "July 31, 1940. German police unit publicly abuses and humiliates Rabbi Moshe Yitzchak Hagerman in Olkusz, Poland, on 'Bloody Wednesday'".
Yad Vashem Photo Archives 4613/903

The schoolbook caption reads, "A Jew wraps himself in his Tallit before being murdered", indicating that this man is a specimen of religious Jews who were caught and toyed with by the Germans before being killed. In this case, the caption is simply incorrect. Hagerman was not murdered on that day nor at that place, but two years later, in 1942, in Maidanek death camp in Lublin, Poland.[43] The initial interpretation of this photo was that the town's rabbi requested and was granted permission to say kaddish for his murdered brethren who were lying on the ground. Janina Struk (2004, 201)[44] argues that this incorrect version served Holocaust revisionists' claims regarding false stories about killings that never happened. However, in 1971 one of the men lying on the ground, David Weitzman, told the

---

43. https://www.yadvashem.org/holocaust/this-month/july/1940-2.html
44. *Photographing the Holocaust*

true story.[45] From then on, Yad Vashem and other museums have received numerous testimonies pertaining to this scene, none of which defined it as "a Jew wrapping himself in his Tallit before being murdered." By displaying Hagerman in this way, the textbook turns him into what the Nazis wanted him to become: nameless, voiceless, impersonalized, a unit in a category of many other Jews "just like him." Rabbi Hagerman's true person is obliterated, excluded from the event for which he is remembered, and indeed from history itself, since this is a history textbook.

The facts of this photograph are that following the murder of a policeman by members of the Polish underground in Olkusz, Poland, on Wednesday July 31, 1940, a day remembered as Bloody Wednesday, a German police unit arrived; they gathered all the Jewish men in the main square, and forced them to lie on the ground while the policemen and members of the the Sicherheitsdienst (Security Service), usually called the SD, "registered them." They beat the Jews, and shot one. Rabbi Moshe Yitzhak Hagerman was forced by the Germans to don his defiled tallit (prayer shawl) and tefillin (phylacteries) and to pray barefoot next to the prostrate men of the Jewish community. The Germans took many photos. The most famous one is that of Rabbi Hagerman praying barefoot with a crowd of grinning German soldiers behind him. Hagerman's biography can be accessed at Yad Vashem, along with details of the person who donated the photograph, complete with dates and locations.[46] Nevertheless, the false caption about this scene continues to circulate in Israeli schoolbooks.

In the Museum of Ghetto Fighters in Israel, the same photo bears this caption:

> The Dayan (religious judge) Moshe Ben-Yitzhak Hagerman donning his prayer shawl and phylacteries on a street in the Olkusz ghetto. Also in the photo: Jews (lower right) lying prone on the ground, and Germans (in the background) observing the scene. Photographed on July 31, 1940.

Struk (2011) informs us that the soldiers handed the film to a Polish woman developer named Dabeska, who kept several copies and gave them to Jews who came to search for their families after the war.

The photo of Rabbi Hagerman was the only picture that hung on the wall of the writing-cabin of the prominent Shoah writer Ka-Tzetnik. For Ka-Tzetnik, who had passed through all the circles of hell in Auschwitz, and described them in

---

45. https://he.wikipedia.org/wiki/%D7%94%D7%A9%D7%A4%D7%9C%D7%AA_%D7%90%D7%95%D7%9C%D7%A7%D7%95%D7%A5%27
https://yvng.yadvashem.org/nameDetails.html?language=he&itemId=698476&ind=5
46. Yad Vashem Archives. In the document affirming his identity in Yad Vashem we learn that his three children, Avraham (16), Feigle-Malka (15), and Nathan (12) were murdered as well.
https://yvng.yadvashem.org/nameDetails.html?language=he&itemId=698476&ind=5

graphic detail in his books, this photo depicted the essence of Jewish distinction or even transcendence during the Shoah. It appears on the cover of the English volume of his stories and essays, *Kaddish* and on his last book, *Shivitti* [47]. Ka-Tzetnik was not acquainted with Hagerman nor with the true version of the event surrounding the photo, and believed, as he wrote in his last novel *Shivitti*, that Hagerman was about to be executed, and that the men lying at his feet were already dead. For him, the photographer and the executioner were one and the same, which was probably Hagerman's own thought at that moment. The photograph had a crucial impact on Ka-Tzetnik's life. For years, his wife tried to persuade him to seek treatment from Dr. Bastiaan, the Dutch psychiatrist who treated traumatized Holocaust survivors with LSD,[48] but he was reluctant to do so. The decisive moment that led him to try the treatment was linked to Rabbi Hagerman's photograph. He writes of this as follows:

> The photograph that I had clipped out of a magazine years ago and hung in a frame over my desk now suddenly I couldn't take my eyes away from it, away from the face of the Jew [...] who had been posed against the background of guffawing German soldiers as a souvenir of the event. For the first time I took note that the normally square case of the head Tefillin was spread into three peaks, like the three strokes in the Hebrew letter Sheen." [Which is the first letter of *Shivitti*]. "He was about my age. Any moment now a bullet would dispatch him to join the row of corpses lined at the feet of the rollicking German fraternity of warriors. But it was not the moment of shooting that was of significance here. Anyone could see this, once in touch with the hidden light radiating from the face of the Jew. [...]. I couldn't tear my eyes away from the Jew on the wall. So many times had I been in his situation but never had I attained such a state of transcendence [...] Just look at the serenity on his face, and at those eyes! He looks down at the spot where he will fall in another moment. His hands are folded, defying description, as does the light beaming from his bare feet (*Shivitti*. XIX).

Ka-Tzetnik saw Hagerman in "a state of transcendence." He believed that "anyone could see this, once in touch with the hidden light radiating from the face of the Jew," but I doubt if anyone can see what he saw, least of all twenty-first century children living in a free and highly militarized state such as Israel, where they are taught to revere physical power rather than spiritual strength. Ka-Tzetnik does not speak of humiliation, misery, or murder; they bear no significance for him, nor apparently for Hagerman himself. He casts aside the Germans and focuses on the

---

47. Ka-Tzetnik 135633.1998. *Shivitti: A Vision* Gateways Consciousness Classics. Gateways/ IDHHB Publishers. *Kaddish*- Algemeiner publishers.
48. https://www.haaretz.com/world-news/europe/.premium.MAGAZINE-the-dutch-doctor-who-treated-traumatized-holocaust-survivors-with-lsd-1.8667996

Jew, drawing our attention to a hidden light, which he himself notes he had never seen before the Holocaust:

> I was allowed to see this light face to face in the sealed isolation barracks, stuffed with human skeletons waiting for the crematorium to be cleared to receive us. And [...] it was in the eyes of the rabbi of Shilev as we awaited our turn for the crematorium, that I saw that same hidden light (p. XIX).

It was the Holocaust, the moment before being gassed, that granted him the rare opportunity to attain or at least to witness transcendence. The Rabbi of Shilev also features in Ka-Tzetnik's book *They called him Piepel*, in which he describes how both the tortured young boys, who served as sex toys for the guards, and other tormented Jews in the camp, would do anything to reach the Rabbi and receive one comforting "motherly" look from him, that would sustain them for another day in hell.

For Ka-Tzetnik, the photo is not a sample that represents just any humiliated religious Jewish man who fell victim to the Nazis' perverse and murderous actions, as it is presented in the schoolbook caption, but rather a unique and almost sacred moment of grace, a remnant of a glorious culture and spiritual life that were barbarically assaulted. Ka-Tzetnik's reflections on the photo may evoke in readers not only pity and empathy, but reverence and admiration, which the abundant descriptions of Nazi perversity and cruelty toward Jews that we find in the textbooks, do not evoke. Ronnie Landau (2016, 13) has commented on this emphasis on the pornography of suffering:

> All too often students of the Holocaust confront no other picture of the Jew except one of unrelieved torment and victimization. This can create an obsessive and utterly unbalanced view of the entire Jewish role in history and, for that matter, of all Jews.

When Ka-Tzetnik elevates the suffering Jew and admires his spiritual strength, he treats the barbaric Germans as non-significant, and hence as inferior to the Jewish man glorified by the light beaming from his feet. This light is what Ka-Tzetnik mourns, and it was this light that convinced him to seek a cure for his own trauma. The realistic descriptions and photographs of German perversity and ruthlessness resist mourning, as Hirsch observes, but it is mourning and reverence that post-memory students, who relive the horrors through photographs and texts, need if they are to feel empathy, respect, and an affinity with the photographed sufferers, often defined in the schoolbooks as "our people." Realizing that this man and this light have something to do with me, and are unspeakably valuable in themselves, I can also mourn Rabbi Moshe Hagerman and everything he stands for. Although we, the post-memorial generations, cannot understand nor experience what Ka-Tzetnik felt facing this photograph, we can sense through his writing not only the colossal loss, but also the overwhelming power of faith that can transform the grinning Nazis from cruel tormentors into barbaric insignificant idiots. Reading Ka-Tzetnik, we are able to rid ourselves of the vulgar contemptuous gaze of the German photographer/executioner and audience toward the Jew and toward Jewish culture, and to sense the superiority of human spirit over racism and brutality. This may motivate us to reflect not only upon the photo and the specific event it represents, but also upon similar events that are taking place today in other places, including our own country, and to be transformed from "voyeurs" to cosmopolitan empathic people, in Chouliaraki terms (2006), who care about the suffering of others.

Defining Hagerman as "a Jew praying before being murdered," the photo's caption proceeds with a story about another rabbi, Doniel Movshovitz of Kelm, changing his name to its Hebrew version "Daniel".

The prosperous Jewish community in Kelm suffered numerous massacres until it was annihilated. Rabbi Doniel Movshovitz was the head of a *yeshivah* during the Nazi occupation. He was greatly admired and a most impressive man, so much so that legend has it that Christian women would fall on their knees when they saw him because they believed he was Jesus Christ.[49]

Confounding Moshe Hagerman from Poland with Rabbi Doniel from Lithuania is unaccounted for. Rabbi Doniel of Kelm was murdered with his students on July 29, 1941, while Hagerman was killed in Maidanek in 1942, and the photo was taken on July 31, 1940.

The caption reports about Rabbi Doniel's last moments:

> When the Jews of Kelm were led to the killing ditches, Rabbi Daniel of Kelm requested the Nazis' permission to bid farewell to his students: "Dear Jews. Indeed the time has come that we must honor the commandment of martyrdom (*kiddush hashem*) which we have discussed. To actually perform it. I ask of you only one thing: do not be confused. Accept calmly and honorably this sentence[50].

However, the story about Rabbi Doniel's last "lesson", reported in the caption, is incomplete. The missing part is that after he spoke to his pupils he turned to the German and said, "I have finished, you may start."[51]

---

49. Rabbi Doniel belonged to a particular stream of Judaism called The Mussar (Moral) Movement, which sought to educate the individual to maintain strict ethical standards of behavior, in the spirit of the *halakhah*. https://www.jewishvirtuallibrary.org/the-mussar-movement
50. Quoted from: Ashray, Rabbi Ephraim. 1971. "The Extinction of Lithuania's Jewry." In *Lithuania's Jewry*, edited by Dov Lipatz, p. 351 (Hebrew).
51. https://www.jewishgen.org/yizkor/Lithuania5/lit5_060.html
https://he.wikipedia.org/wiki/%D7%93%D7%A0%D7%99%D7%90%D7%9C_%D7%9E%D7%95%D7%91%D7%A9%D7%95%D7%91%D7%99%D7%A5

Rabbi Doniel's "lesson" reminds one of Socrates' last lesson before being executed. Both celebrate the exemplary nature of true educators, although for Zionists such as Ben Gurion his action may not be regarded as heroism so much as contemptuous surrender.

The caption conceals the meaning of the photograph by anonymizing Rabbi Hagerman, while at the same time concealing the face of Rabbi Doniel. It fails to note who the Jewish man in the picture is, when and where the event depicted in the photograph occurred, or when and where Rabbi Doniel made the speech to his students. Thus, both the picture and the caption conceal information. In both we find the same lacunae, albeit for different reasons: the image does not tell us who the photographed person is because it cannot name persons and place, while the text does not provide any information either about Kelm and Rabbi Doniel, or about Olkusz and the event of Bloody Wednesday even though it could.[52] Hagerman is just a face without a name while Rabbi Doniel is just a name without a face.

Chouliaraki (2006, 106) maintains that the "absence of a person, somebody with a name and a face, deprives the encounter between spectators and sufferers of any sense of humanness." The circumstances, the reasons, the details of time and place, are "the measure of psychological depth necessary for the welling up of emotion." (ibid.) Without the face of Rabbi Doniel and the name of Rabbi Hagerman, and without the story of Bloody Wednesday that goes with the picture, or the story of the Jewish community in Kelm, the viewers fail to communicate with the sufferers, unless one is a Holocaust survivor such as Ka–Tzetnik, who had suffered the same kind of torture, which none of the post-memory students are or can presume to be. In this representation, "the anonymous sufferers are annihilated, no matter what the magnitude or the depth of their suffering is. They remain irrevocably 'Others'." (Chouliaraki, ibid.).

The lack of information about the two rabbis cannot be explained by what Lewis (2001) terms "sloppy scholarship," since the events of Bloody Wednesday are well known and documented, as is the occasion of Rabbi Doniel's final lesson. Therefore, we can only conclude that this omission was motivated by interest. This poses several questions: what was the interest not to attach a photograph of Rabbi Doniel to his own story? Why is his heroic story placed in a marginal caption rather than in the main text? And what drove the designer to place the photo of Hagerman alongside Rabbi Doniel's story and to conceal the story of Bloody Wednesday? Presumably the designer sought an illustration of a "Jew about to be murdered" to illustrate the story of Rabbi Doniel's last moments, which included praying but were not photographed. Hence, the criterial feature for choosing Hagerman's photograph was not his person nor the event of Bloody

---

52. Van Leeuwen, personal communication

Wednesday for which he is known, but the act of praying above the men lying in the street, presumably dead. Devoid of its phenomenology, this picture could represent any rabbi praying over the bodies of dead people, and all the religious Jews who prayed before being murdered and who accepted their death sentence "calmly and honorably". This is the connection between Hagerman and Rabbi Doniel.

The strategy of separating social actors from their own portraits is frequently employed in this schoolbook. Another photo, taken by the official Nazi photographer Ludwig Knobloch, shows a doctor checking a patient in the Warsaw ghetto. The caption reads "medical treatment in Warsaw Ghetto," (Image 30), and then proceeds to tell the story of Dr. Aharon Peretz, a gynecologist who worked in Kovno Ghetto, in Vilnius, Lithuania. Dr. Peretz was also one of the major witnesses at the Eichmann Trial in 1962 and testified to the extreme overcrowding and the hardship he encountered in ghetto hospitals.[53]

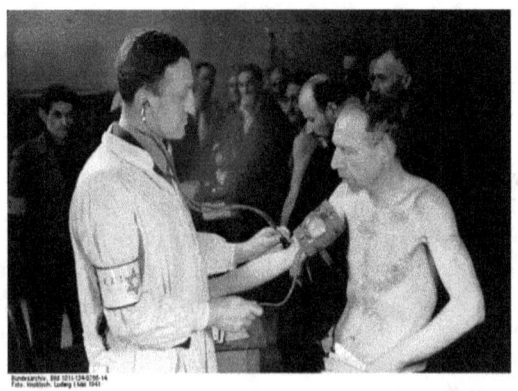

Image 30. Medical Treatment in Warsaw Ghetto (Keren. 1999). Attribution: Bundesarchiv, Bild 101I-134-0766-14 / Knobloch, Ludwig / CC-BY-SA 3.0[54]

Dr. Aharon Peretz is not shown in the book and the Warsaw doctor in the photograph has no identity. The criterial features for choosing this photograph were apparently the doctor's hands, tools, and coat. He is simultaneously anonymized and functionalized. His biography is replaced by another's. The two doctors become one. As in the case of Settela, who was stripped of her identity

---

53. Dr. Aharon Peretz was a Zionist and after the war, he migrated to Israel, where he served as a gynecologist in Rambam hospital in Haifa.
https://www.yadvashem.org/yv/en/exhibitions/eichmann/witnesses.asp
54. https://upload.wikimedia.org/wikipedia/commons/6/64/Bundesarchiv_Bild_101I-134-0766-14%2C_Polen%2C_Ghetto_Warschau%2C_%C3%A4rztliche_Untersuchung.jpg

and biography, and whose function is to represent the boy Avram, and like Rabbi Hagerman who is confounded with Rabbi Doniel of Kelm, so does the doctor of the Warsaw Ghetto become Dr. Peretz of Kovno Ghetto (420 km apart), and Dr. Peretz becomes him. We observe here a trend of anonymizing and using specific persons generically and functionally, in order to represent other persons, as if among those who lived under Nazi rule it did not really matter who was who, since they all succumbed to the same fate. The depicted persons are drained of their own personality and biography whenever someone reads these pages.

In Avieli-Tabibian (2009) the same photo (Image 30) bears a different caption: "blood pressure tests," which seems more accurate than "medical treatment" if we look closely at the photo. The photograph, which is one in a series of photographs taken by Nazi photographer Ludwig Knobloch[55] depicting medical examinations in the ghetto, is definitely not depicting a medical treatment but a test that determined the patient's fate. As Holocaust scholar Sari Segal[56] explains, "Nazi officials required Jewish doctors to perform medical examinations on people in order to determine whether they would be sent to a forced labor camp or to an extermination camp […]. The doctors who were coerced into carrying out this process, had to decide who would be exempt from the transports, and in doing so, they had to determine who would live and who would die."[57]

---

55. https://commons.wikimedia.org/wiki/Category:Photographs_by_Ludwig_Knobloch
56. Siegel, Sari J. 2006. B.A. thesis, the Geoffrey H. Hartman Postdoctoral Fellow at the Fortunoff Archive.
57. See too Offer, Miriam. 2019. "Coping with the Impossible: The Developmental Roots of the Jewish Medical System in the Ghettos." In. *Jewish Medicine and Healthcare in Central Eastern Europe: Shared Identities, Entangled Histories*, edited by Ute Caumanns and Fritz Dross.

Chapter 7. The Question of Pornography

> Let me turn my eyes away. Let me not look.
> (J.M Cotzee. *Elizabeth Costello*, 148)
>
> The camera is a kind of passport that annihilates moral boundaries and social inhibitions, freeing the photographer from any responsibility toward the people photographed. (Susan Sontag, *On Photography*, 41.)

In her study of Holocaust museums, Hannah Holtschneider (2011,76) argues that the difficulty in approaching documentary photographs of Holocaust victims lies precisely in the horrific dehumanization that the images convey, which often renders them obscene. In using such labels as "obscene," "disgusting," and "repulsive," regarding the victims themselves, she argues, "it is as if the viewer reacts to protect himself or herself against the violence of the image, to ward off its 'contamination.'" Intended to shock, "[nude] photographs taken by both perpetrators and liberators not only foregrounded the victims' nakedness, they also emphasized the grotesqueness and ugliness of the bodies of the dead and of surviving victims of the Holocaust, graphically pointing to the horror of the genocide. This strategy makes it difficult for the viewer of such images to empathize with the photographed, even when such photos are employed to state the opposite of their original intention,"[1] namely to incriminate their creators and demonstrate the extent of German perversity and cruelty. Holtschneider contends that these ghastly and painful spectacles disrupt our mechanisms of perception and representation: "Our symbolic modes are emptied, petrified, nearly annihilated, as if they were overwhelmed or destroyed by an all too powerful force" (ibid.). Other scholars also believe that the images of pain may become too painful to bear (Ayab 2020). Holtschneider quotes Kramer (2003),[2] who observed that such representation of dead bodies "breaks with the tradition of presenting the dead in a dignified manner, washed and clothed (ibid.)." She also quotes Brandt and Loewy[3] who argued, "Viewing these photographs constitutes a violation of

---

1. Holtschneider, K. Hannah. *The Holocaust and Representations of Jews*. Routledge Jewish Studies Series, Taylor and Francis, Kindle Edition. 76.
2. Kramer, S. (2003). "Nacktheit in Holocaust-Fotos und -Filmen'". In *Die Shoah im Bild*, 225-248. Augsburg: edition text + kritik. Cited by Holtschneider, ibid. 177.
3. Brandt, K. and Loewy, H. 2003. "Hinter den Bildern: Ausgelöschte Geschichten und die Suche nach ihren Spuren: Recherchen zu den Bildern der Deportierten im Museum Auschwitz-Birkenau." *Fotogeschichte* 23(87). 29–41. Cited by Holtschneider, *The Holocaust and Representations of Jews*, 59-60.

someone else's private sphere, as their lives cannot be reconstructed by the viewer. This violation is enhanced even more when the photos are on public display, where they are employed as examples, standing in for the collectivity of those who were murdered," as is the way Holocaust victims are presented in several museum and in Israeli schoolbooks.

In this section, I examine one such photograph that has become an icon of German perverse sadism in the name of science, that of the naked twin victims of Dr. Yosef Mengele. I compare this image to another photograph of Mengele's twins, which is far less abhorrent and disrespectful, but whose presentation is equally problematic.

Various scholars contend that atrocity photographs showing abused naked victims, and all the more so their exhibition, are a form of pornography (Dean 2004, Lewis 2001, Crane 2008, among others): pornography of evil and pornography of suffering. Some have extensively addressed the links between sadism, racism, Nazism, and pornography.[4] The exhibition and exposure in albums and museums, of abused human beings of all ages, stripped of their humanity and of their human rights to privacy and dignity, is considered by scholars to be undignified, and to violate codes that safeguard respect for the living and for the dead, as well as the laws pertaining to the exposure of children and child abuse.

I adopt the following definition of pornography proposed by Humanitarian photographer Jorgen Lissner[5], who wrote about the use of photographs of starved children in the "third world" by charity and development organizations. Lissner saw these photographs as pornographic for they use "the exhibition of the human body and soul in all its nakedness, without any respect and piety for the person involved." Lissner argues, "The public display of an African child with a bloated kwashiorkor-ridden stomach [...] is pornographic, because it exposes something in human life that is as delicate and deeply personal as sexuality, that is, suffering. It puts people's bodies, their misery, their grief and their fear on display, with all the details and all the indiscretion that a telescopic lens will allow." In his book *The Politics of Altruism* (1977) Lissner defines these images as "negative," demeaning, lacking dignity, and untruthful. Negative images, he argues, are the product of a power imbalance between those representing, in our case museums or schoolbooks on the one hand, and those being represented on the other - the abused, the humiliated, and the voiceless. These images, he contends, demean the

---

4. Steiner, George. 1965. "Night Words." *Encounter* 25, no. 4. 17-18. See also Steiner, George. 1966. "Pornography and Its Consequences." Encounter 36, no. 3. 46-47; and Steiner's letter to the *Times Literary Supplement*, May 26, 1966. 475.
5. Jorgen Lissner is project director of Denmark's leading voluntary aid agency, Danchurchaid, and author of *The Politics of Altruism*, published by the World Council of Churches. The quote is from his article "Merchants of Misery." 1981. *The New Internationalist*, June 1981.

subjects because they represent them as being devoid of dignity. His conclusion is that *negative* images encourage *negative* practice and vice versa.

Applying Lissner's ideas to the representation of Holocaust victims, we may likewise argue that negative images generate a negative attitude toward the victims, manifested in disregard of their names and other biographic details, or of the phenomenology of the photographic event. It takes a Ka-Tzetnik to rise above these feelings of contempt or repulsion and to look at the sufferers with reverence.

Showing an abused, maimed body of a Western child is considered unethical and unlawful in the West, and Israeli law forbids the publishing of nude photos of minors, which qualifies as child abuse. But, as Jorgen Lissner observes, showing naked non-Western children is considered acceptable when it is done to promote a charity, or to jolt the white comfortable "first world" out of its indifference to other people's suffering. The rhetors and designers of Israeli textbooks were probably aware of these laws and norms when they decided to include photographs of naked victims. Therefore, their interest in showing, for example, the naked tormented twin Sinti girls, who were photographed for Mengele just before their death, to jolt students out of their assumed indifference or ignorance, must have outweighed all the counter arguments, and was deemed more important than teaching Israeli schoolchildren to respect the rights of other children. As in "conventional" or sexual pornography, the viewers of these photographs become "voyeurs of the suffering of others, tourists amidst their landscapes of anguish," as Michael Ignatieff (1985) expressed it.[6]

The concepts of the Pornography of Death, the Pornography of Horror, and the Pornography of Suffering and Evil appeared after the First World War (1914-1918) and were used to designate a particular category of specific texts and images that conveyed a potentially objectifying, dehumanizing, and thus morally distorted perception of suffering (Dean 2004). After World War II, atrocity photos that emerged from Iwo Jima were defined as pornographic because they effaced the proper physical and moral distance between the suffering persons and the viewers. They created another, "incurable distance", as James Agee defined it, writing in *The Nation* in 1945[7] about newsreel footage showing the invasion of Iwo Jima. Agee maintained that "we have no business seeing this sort of experience". By creating this "incurable distance", the photograph betrays those with whom we seek to identify. Images of war atrocities, he felt, were thus pornographic because "pornography is invariably degrading to anyone who looks at it or reads it."[8]

---

6. Ignatieff, Michael. 1985. "Is Nothing Sacred? The Ethics of Television." *Daedalus* 114, no. 4, *The Moving Image* (Fall, 1985). 57-78.
7. Agee, James "Films." *Nation*, March 24, 1945, 342.
8. Dean, Carolyn. 2004. *The Fragility of Empathy*. 20.

Proper Distance

Roger Silverstone[9] argues that we can lead a moral life only if we define and maintain a proper distance between others and ourselves. Distance is not merely a material, geographical, or even a social category, but it is a moral category as well. "We 'keep our distance' from strangers (if given the chance), while we get 'close to' our 'nearest and dearest.'" (Van Leeuwen 2008, 138)[10]

The proper distance respects privacy, decency, and dignity, and is one of the unwritten norms that must be followed in every society[11] (D. Tannen 2007). An important element of children's education is to learn to respect the proper distance. There is a difference between spatial and social or moral distance, between intimacy and scrutiny or invasion. Slaves may be very close physically to their abusive masters and yet very far from them socially and morally. Moral and ethical considerations do not apply to them because their masters possess them as objects.

The proper distance that every society defines for itself by unwritten norms of politeness and by actual laws such as those that protect minors, applies to photographs as well. It must be respected in order to establish a proper symbolic relationship between the viewer and the photographed person.

In the analysis of photos portraying human beings, three dimensions come into play: the social distance between the photographed and the viewer, the social relation and the social interaction between the depicted people and the viewer (Van Leeuwen 2008). In all three cases, the relation is symbolic, imaginary. The photograph directs us to see the people depicted as though they were (distanced) strangers, or (close) friends; as though they were "below" us, or "above" us; as though they were interacting with us or not; looking directly into our eyes or avoiding us, irrespective of the actual relations between us and them, or their "kind". People shown in a "long shot," from afar, appear to be strangers; people shown in a "close-up" may either seem like "one of us," or invite scrutiny (Van Leeuwen ibid.). Those who are defined as "others," whether they are immigrants or minorities, such as Palestinians or Ethiopian Jews in Israeli textbooks (chapters 10-13 this volume), are often shown from a great distance, as faceless homogenous groups. The viewer is unable to distinguish individuals among them,

---

9. Silverstone, Roger. 2003. "Proper Distance: Toward an Ethics for Cyberspace." In: *Digital Media Revisited toward an Ethics for Cyberspace, Theoretical and Conceptual Innovation in Digital Domains*. 469-491.
10. *Discourse and Practice*
11. Involvement in discourse. In: *Talking Voices. Repetition, Dialogue, and Imagery in Conversational Discourse*, Cambridge University Press. 25 – 47.

and often looks down at them. Israeli schoolbooks generally refer to these groups as "sectors," "populations," "minorities," "ethnicities," "problems," or "challenges" that the state confronts. On the other hand, effacing distance altogether is tantamount to "crossing the line" of moral behavior. In both pornography and atrocity photographs, the photographed individuals are disempowered not only because we look down at them, but also because we can look into them. Pornographic photos and films show people - usually women - too close spatially. We feel as if we can actually touch them, penetrate them with our eyes. Yet this closeness creates a huge and insurmountable distance, in spite or because of the physical proximity to the photographed person.

Silverstone (2003, 259) argues that the issue is not the media's capacity to get personal, but rather their "capacity to bring people together while simultaneously keeping them apart." It is this ambivalence of mediation, Chouliaraki says, constantly hovering between closeness and distance – that lies at the core of the ethics of mediation. Chouliaraki asks (2006, 102), "Could the use of the visual mode, the very imagery of suffering, enhance proximity with suffering and, thereby, activate a politics of pity?" and she answers: "Not necessarily, because the visualization of suffering does not always humanize the sufferers. Visualization may [...] actually dehumanize them." Although Chouliaraki speaks about television, we can apply her observation to Holocaust photographs shown in schoolbooks as well. The close-up representation of tortured victims annihilates them as subjects. Their human alterity is annulled.

In many instances, individual Holocaust sufferers look into our eyes as they were ordered to gaze at the photographer and at the executioner, yet their proximity, especially if they are undressed or totally naked and bruised, distances them from us socially and morally. As in pornography, the viewer does not feel "close" to the close-up photographed persons, other than as a voyeur.

Carolyn Dean (2004) quotes a number of people who felt they become voyeurs when viewing such images or reading about Nazi obscenities. Among them is Tim Cole (1999, 324), who cites in his book[12] psychologist Israel Charny's reaction to reading about the genocide: "The reading becomes exciting. One murderous incident follows another. My excitement mounts. It is almost a sexual feeling. I flow into the next account of a killing and become one with the murderer."

Cole goes on to describe himself and other secondary witnesses (be they tourists, historians, or commentators) as voyeurs who were vaguely aware of what

---

12. *Images of the Holocaust: The Myth of the Shoah Business* (London: Duckworth, 1999), in *Contemporary Review* 275 (December 1999). 324. In the United States, Cole's book was published under the title *Selling the Holocaust: From Auschwitz to Schindler, How History Is Bought, Packaged, and Sold.* New York: Routledge.

journalist Philip Gourevitch (1993)[13] calls the "potential for excitement and even for seduction by the overwhelmingly powerful imagery." Given the fascination, seduction, and titillation these images may arouse, Gourevitch was skeptical with regard to the expectations of the planners of the Holocaust Museum in Washington "to mobilize morality" by giving people "a proper dose of Holocaust," that "will build up the needed antibodies against totalitarianism, racism, and state-sponsored mass murder," and will serve as "a symbolic orienting event in human history that can prevent recurrence". The feelings regarding photographs that are hard to look at and yet attract the viewer, arouse what Baudrillard[14] calls brute fascination "unencumbered by aesthetic, moral, social or political judgements," which Sontag admits drew her again and again to Holocaust photographs. Sontag states that photographed horror does not necessarily "strengthen conscience and the ability to be compassionate. It can also corrupt them. Once one has seen such images, one has started down the road of seeing more and more. Images transfix. Images anesthetize."[15] Referring to the Holocaust Memorial Museum in Washington, D.C., Dean cites Victoria Barnett, who wrote "A major risk of this kind of museum is that it could degenerate into obscene voyeurism."[16] Speaking of the same museum, American architectural and urban critic, designer, and educator Michael Sorkin, declared, "An excess of detail can neutralize and obscure, commemoration can become entertainment, even pornography."[17]

The cardinal question, therefore, is that which Chouliaraki asks: "Do brute fascination and seduction offer the possibility of ethical relationships? Is there space for connectivity between spectators and sufferers in Baudrillard's thesis? How can the disposition of spectators be shifted from voyeurism to cosmopolitanism, namely to caring about the suffering of others?"[18] She concludes that brute fascination and seduction can make for only a partial relationship with sufferers, since given this total visibility, no space is left for strong emotions of surprise, challenge, or even shock, after the first viewing of such images (p. 51). The sufferers become objects of scrutiny rather than subjects we can relate to, empathize with, or even mourn. As Hirsch explains (2012, 120) "[...] these photos, especially in their endless repetition, resist the work of mourning [...]. They can only be confronted again and again, with the same pain,

---

13. Gourevitch, Philip. 1993. "Behold Now Behemoth. The Holocaust Memorial Museum: One more American theme park." *Harper's Magazine*. July 1993. 55-62.
14. Baudrillard, Jean. 1984. *The Evil Demon of Images*. 27.
15. *On Photography*. 1973. New York: Farrar, Straus and Giroux. 20.
16. Barnett, Victoria. "Bearing Witness." *Christian Century*, May 12, 1993, 509.
17. Sorkin, Michael. 1993. "The Holocaust Museum: Between Beauty and Horror." *Progressive Architecture* 74.
18. Chouliaraki, Lilie. 2006. "Mediation, Meaning and Power." In *The Spectatorship of Suffering*, 51-52.

the same incomprehension, the same distortion of the look, the same mortification. And thus, they no longer represent Nazi genocide but, in their very repetition, they provoke the traumatic effect that this history has had on all who grew up under its shadow." The photos are, as John Berger observed with regard to atrocity pictures from Vietnam, "arresting. We are seized by them" (2017, 42).[19]

Mengele's Naked Twins

A particularly horrific photograph, whose presentation may be termed pornographic, is that of two pairs of naked emaciated twin girls, on whom Mengele performed his monstrous experiments.[20] The photo of the twin girls appears in numerous books and albums as the property of Getty Images, whose logo runs across the girls' knees, as a sign of ownership. The caption reads: "Child prisoners are photographed in the 1940s on the orders of camp physician Josef Mengele who carried out experiments on children and twins. Photo credit should read AFP via Getty Images."

Next to the photograph, the prices are mentioned: Small – 175$, Medium - 375$, Large - 499$. This means that Getty Images allows museums, albums and schoolbooks to exhibit the girls for a fee.[21] Here one must ponder again the difference between ownership and custody. Do Getty Images or the museums truly own the photographs upon transposing them to their sites, or have they become their guardians? More important, do they own the photographed girls as well? Has Getty become the master of the girls after Mengele? Does this mean it can exhibit them however, wherever, and whenever it pleases?

Mengele ordered the photo to be taken as a record of his experiments for further studies. When transposed to schoolbooks, the function of the photo as a teaching resource is preserved, although the nature of what is taught is different. The girls are about thirteen or fourteen years old. In some schoolbooks, we see only their torsos, and in others, their entire naked bodies are exhibited. For instance, in Gutman (2009), we see the torso down to the genitals; in Keren (1999), the entire bodies are displayed; and in the religious textbook (Hertz 2015), only their naked torsos are exposed, down to their waistline.

The criterial features of this photo, both for Mengele who ordered it and for the Israeli schoolbook designers who transposed it from the Nazi archives, or from the Getty collection, are to be found in the anatomy and the physiognomy of the

---

19. Berger, John. 2017. *About Looking*. London: Bloomsbury Publishing.
20. I chose not to display the photo. https://www.gettyimages.com/detail/news-photo/children-prisoners-of-the-nazi-concentration-camp-of-news-photo/51400549?adppopup=true
21. https://www.gettyimages.com/detail/news-photo/children-prisoners-of-the-nazi-concentration-camp-of-news-photo/51400549

girls. It was their anatomy that interested their tormentors, who used them to test the effects of starvation, among other experiments. [22] Their physiognomy subsequently became of interest to those who observed them in albums and museum exhibitions. Their organs were of interest to Mengele; their appearance was of interest to everyone after the war, including schoolbook designers. Their extreme thinness, their shaved heads, and their posture furnish proof of the tortures inflicted upon them. Their function in Mengele's laboratory was to represent metonymically their race and their sub-group of twins. In the schoolbooks, their function is to represent all the children who, like themselves, "served Mengele in his experiments." (Keren 1999, 122). Since they are anonymous, their appearance is indexical of the fate of all minority twins who lived in Europe at the time and ended up in Auschwitz. Such representation, argues Chouliaraki (2006), is a form of "othering," for it distances the viewers from the individual sufferers and stifles pity.

The origins of the girls are not indicated in the Israeli textbooks although they are identified as "gypsies" in many sources, including the photographer's memoirs. The photographer, Wilhelm Brasse, who was twenty-two years old at the time and a prisoner himself, recalled the moment that he photographed the four girls, in an interview he gave to the GUP journal of international photography in 2011.[23] They were so ashamed, he said. Lest he embarrass them even more, Brasse kept his distance from them, and after taking the photo he handed them each a piece of bread. "I cursed God and my mother for giving birth to me," he said.

From Brasse's autobiography[24] and interview we learn that the girls, in their dire condition, still possessed a social sensitivity that made them feel ashamed to be exposed to a man's gaze. Although for them the equation between the camera and the killing instrument was not metaphorical but real, and their reduction by the Nazi gaze that activated Brasse's camera, to "pieces" and "ashes" (Hirsch 2001) was evident, they were still embarrassed to be seen naked by a man. We also learn that they had a moment of affective contact with someone who felt their misery on the cusp of the abyss. Brasse recalls as follows:

---

22. Weindling, Paul. 2014. *Victims and Survivors of Nazi Human Experiments.* Bloomsbury Publishing. Kindle Edition.
23. Peters, Edie. 2011. "The Duty of History," Interview with Wilhelm Brasse in *GUP International Photography Journal*, July 7, 2011.
http://www.gupmagazine.com/articles/the-duty-of-history
The documentary about Brasse, *The Portraitist (Portrecista*, Poland, 2005), directed by Irek Dobrowolski and produced by Anna Dobrowolska, was first shown on the Polish television station TVP1 on January 1, 2006.
24. Anna Dobrowolska. 2015. *The Auschwitz Photographer.* Anna Dobrowolska Publisher. Kindle Edition.

"In all there were about 250-300 of those girls [...] I would instruct [the nurse] how to position the girls [...] I felt uneasy because among the kids there were 13-14-year-old girls who experienced great shame, completely defenseless creatures about whom I knew only that they soon would die. They stood naked, one next to the other, and posed for the photo. There they were, completely exposed, facing a young man. I felt embarrassed. [...] Under such circumstances, I could not look at them as a male. Instead, I experienced the tragedy of the child standing before me [...]. There they stood maimed, naked, disfigured with their hair not merely shaven but pulled out. I feared that all those children would be examined and then sent to the gas. Later, from the nurses and Doctor Mengele I learned that my fears have come true." (Loc. 2316 Kindle edition). This personal account creates what Didi-Huberman calls the event of the photograph and endows the suffering girls with "humaneness" as it does the photographer who, in this case, can no longer be identified with the executioner, and probably risked his own life by giving them bread.

Chouliaraki raises an important question regarding the display of child victims of famine, as she wonders whether these sufferers were still endowed with humanness. Are they still children or is their existence reduced to their body parts, which are the reason for their display? The Sinti twins were surely nothing but "biological machines" (Chouliaraki 2006, 136) to their tormentors, a specimen of a category forged in the "concentrationary universe" of Auschwitz,[25] where the laws and norms of the outside world did not apply. Their bodies were dissected before and after death and organs were cut out of them; they were submitted to acute starvation to investigate how their bodies reacted to hunger. Yet against the backdrop of Brasse's recollections, their photo tells a story, which is particular to them, and as Sontag observes, only photos that narrate, contrary to disconnected depictions of reality, can create meaning. In Brasse's memory of them, the girls cease to be "biological machines," and their photo ceases to be merely a document or a sample. They become subjects. We can interpret their look as a plea not to watch them, to restore their dignity posthumously. This plea is compatible with the Israeli Ministry of Education's call to inspire awe and reverence for the Shoah's victims,[26] a plea that is not always respected in the schoolbooks.

---

25. Rousset, David. 1988. *L'Univers concentrationnaire*. Hachette Littérature.
See also Illsen, About. 2001. "La photographie au service du système concentrationaire national-socialist (1933-1945)." In : *Mémoires des Camps*.
26. https://edu.gov.il/owlHeb/AboutUs/CEO-letters/Pages/mankal-statments.aspx

Image and Words

In the textbooks studied here, the relations between the photo of the tortured twins and the texts in which it is embedded is that of *specification* or *illustration* (Van Leeuwen 2008). The photo illustrates what Mengele's victims looked like and the girls are not the subject of the text that surrounds it. Neither the captions nor the main texts say anything about the twins themselves, or the experiments they went through for that matter. The texts tell about mothers who sent their twin children willingly to Mengele's experiments, believing they would be spared (Hertz, 2015), or describe other cases of children tortured by the Nazis (Gutman, Keren).

The female twins are referred to as two of the "children" or "twins" in the masculine form, which is the generic form in Hebrew, although their femininity is apparent even in the cropped photograph that shows only their torso. This generic representation not only enhances the perception that they are but a specimen of a collective of twin victims, as indeed they were for Mengele, but reflects and instantiates this fact as well.

The meaning of the photograph changes from one text to another according to their educational ideology. For instance, the state-religious Holocaust schoolbook (Hertz 2015) is divided into three main sections, all of which carry titles derived from the Bible that prophesy the most cruel destruction of the people of Israel by its enemies, as punishment for not obeying God. The first section addresses the Growth of antisemitism in Germany and its title is taken from Psalms 35:8: "Let Shoah come upon him unawares."[27] The second section, which contains the photo of the naked twin girls, is titled "And the land of your enemies shall eat you up,"[28] a phrase in Leviticus 26:38, in which God tells the people of Israel, down to the smallest horrifying and gruesome detail, what will befall them should they disobey him. Below this heading, horrifying details and photographs describing and showing Nazi torture and humiliation are presented, as the different sorts of punishment for not observing God's law. The photograph of the girls is one of six photos that illustrate different forms of torture, all of which illustrate the prophecy: selection and gas chambers, excruciating work, morning roll call in the freezing cold, "scientific" experiments, and the psychological torture of musicians forced to accompany their friends and family members to the gas chambers. The text asks the students what appears to be rhetorical questions that pertain to the orchestra: "What did the Germans gain from the performance (of the orchestra) at such a moment? What was their purpose in humiliating and torturing both the

---

27. וְרִשְׁתּוֹ אֲשֶׁר-טָמַן תִּלְכְּדוֹ; בְּשׁוֹאָה, יִפָּל-בָּהּ׃תְּבוֹאֵהוּ שׁוֹאָה, לֹא-יֵדָע. King James Version: "Let destruction come upon him unawares."

28. ואכלה אתכם, ארץ אויביכם

condemned and the orchestra musicians, as well as the prisoners who stood by and watched the performance?"

These questions prompt the students to try to think like Nazi Germans in a calculated manner, weighing up gains and losses, and to adopt their "counter-rationality" which is "inherently impossible to follow [for] it demolishes [...] rationality."[29] This, as Diner (2000) explains, has proven to be impossible even for adult historians. However, in light of the chapters' titles and the texts that surround the pictures, one wonders whether the answer should be that the torturers were merely acting as the tools of God in executing His punishment.

The third section's title is "In thy blood, live – Resurrection and Remembrance" derived from Ezekiel, 17:6: "And when I passed by thee, and saw thee wallowing in thy blood, I said unto thee: in thy blood, live."[30]

In Gutman (2009), the naked twins appear in a window embedded in a horrifying quote from the book *I was Mengele's Assistant: An Auschwitz Doctor's Eyewitness Account*.[31] The author relates how Mengele and his assistants would assemble twins and dwarves for their experiments, and how Mengele ordered him to dissect the children's bodies immediately after their death and record his findings. Thus, the text prompts readers to focus on the girls not as the subject of interest but merely as an illustration. The protagonists of the text are Mengele and his fellow German scientists, and the main story is the process of dissection.

In Keren (1999, 122), where the entire naked bodies of the four girls are exhibited, the caption of the photo reads, "Among Mengele's victims there were pairs of twins who served him in his medical experiments. These twins, Jews and Gypsies, were chosen from among the children, and were allowed to live for this purpose." The word "twins" again appears in the masculine form, which enhances and reflects the status of the girls as a generic sample. The text categorizes the children in terms of *relational identification* (Van Leeuwen 2008): they are defined by the work they did for Mengele, or rather by their servitude to him. Mengele's twins, like slaves, "served" him and his staff very closely, too closely, and yet they were distanced from them to the point of being dehumanized and objectified. The text emphasizes the girls' objectification through the strategy of *passivation*. Passivated persons are represented as "undergoing" the activity (Halliday, 1985. ch.5), or as being "at the receiving end of it" (Van Leeuwen 2008 ibid.). As passivated beings, they are treated as objects that are "chosen," "taken in," or "experimented on" and they are "allowed to live." The verb "allow" evokes and magnifies Mengele's figure as a superhuman being who decided about life and death, and who was served by young naked girls whom he allowed to live for this purpose, until he had done with them. The photograph is embedded in a

---

29. Diner, Dan. 2000. *Historical Understanding and Counterrationality*, 137.
30. https://www.mechon-mamre.org/p/pt/pt1216.htm
31. Miklos Nyiszli. (1946) 2010. *I Was Doctor Mengele's Assistant*. Oswiecim Publisher.

double spread that provides an inventory of perverse and sadistic acts of torture, perpetrated by German doctors and nurses. These include the poisoning of children, a detailed account of a mother who killed her own baby to save herself, and a testimony of a woman whose breasts were tied together by Mengele after she gave birth, in order to observe how long a newborn baby could live without being fed. Descriptions such as these prompted Holocaust historian Yablonka (2021) to observe, as mentioned above, that apart from illustrating the "pornography of evil" there is no educational value in these technical details.

The text adjacent to the naked twins (ibid.) reports that prisoner-doctors were forced to take part in all these abominable experiments, but it also asserts that "the SS scientists joined these dubious experiments with the enthusiasm that characterizes all scientists," adding further horrifying quotes from the book of Mengele's assistant. It concludes by divulging that most of these scientists were not punished, and continued their work after the war, using the organs of Auschwitz prisoners. The list of these hideous acts alongside the incrimination of *all scientists* may well appear to children not only ghastly but also shocking and disturbing, for it creates a most threatening image of scientists and medicine. Would today's scientists also cooperate with a monster such as Mengele for science's sake? They may wonder.

The use of science in the process of extermination deserves elaboration and contextualization. Had this sentence been contextualized it could have offered the students some insight into Western science at the time. Bauman (2013,33)[32] explains that the collaboration of doctors and scientists with the Nazi regime was indeed part of the general "enthusiasm" generated by Hitler's vision of creating a perfect society. Anthropologists, physicians, and biologists were all preoccupied with "healing the national body", and applied the ostensibly scientific criteria of racial purity, fitness, and prowess, calling for the isolation and elimination of defective (*unwerte*) individuals and categories. Likewise, economists, agronomists, and physical planners "felt themselves obliged to sanitize the social structure of the conquered lands." (ibid.) Such insight should definitely be part of a discussion about the relationships between power and science, which is most relevant in this case. The cooperation between German scientists and doctors in the camps and scientific institutions in Germany and abroad is addressed in Wiendling (2014).[33] Wiendling describes the experiments conducted in various camps and the use made of these experiments by the most prestigious research institutions. He furthermore notes the training and financial support the implicated experimenters received from foundations within Germany and beyond. He

---

32. "The Role of Modernity: what was it—and is it—about?" 2013. *Dapim: Studies on the Holocaust*, Vol. 27, No. 1. *The Holocaust: a colonial genocide?* A scholars' forum. 40–73.
33. Weindling, Paul. 2014. *Victims and Survivors of Nazi Human Experiments. Science and Suffering in the Holocaust.* London: Bloomsbury Academic.

mentions, for example, a number of German scientists who received training in Rockefeller laboratories prior to conducting experiments in the Nazi camps. One may thus conclude that cooperation with these experiments did not stem merely from freakish SS "enthusiasm," but was bound up with a general orientation toward science, as explained by historian Mario Biagioli (1992, 185-206).[34] Biagioli argues that Nazi experiments on camp inmates "were not an aberration or a total reversal of the ethics and goals of Western science, but was one of its possible outcomes that carried the very core of its tradition" (p.194). The "processes (though not the results) of Nazi science were not exceptional." Using "other" people as material for study was not an innovation in Europe and Mengele employed, albeit to excess, "anthropological methodologies" that had widespread currency in pre-World War II Europe (1992, 14). Biagioli contends that the medical experiments conducted at Auschwitz were closely linked to modernity and to the assumption that science was "value-free" (ibid. 192). "Western medicine and science in general, with its imperative on experimentation at any price as its incontrovertible raison d'être," actually "led to the possibility of Nazi experiment" (ibid. 185). The concept of "racial hygiene" used to justify the camps and most of the experiments, had emerged before the Third Reich, but it became paramount in the Nazi camps, and lent an aura of science to the norms that regulated life and death (ibid. 201). The discourse of exclusion of which racial hygiene is a part, has always tended to legitimize it and vice versa (ibid. p.205). Hence Nazi doctors did not turn from "the practice of healing to the practice of killing" in Auschwitz, says Biagioli. Mengele's associate doctors and those who were forced to work with him testified that they had merely cooperated, willingly or under coercion, with science that "fell into the wrong hands" and produced "falsehoods." Biagioli offers the example of Dr. Theresa W. who worked with Mengele and testified that his methods were standard for the era, "the normal anthropological work at the time," performed in accordance with "the biological foundation of the social environment" in which she was trained and which eventually took her to Auschwitz. (ibid. p.191) Thus, argues Biagioli, Nazi science paradoxically "proved" the "objectivity" of science because the same methods worked in "normal" and "criminal" situations (p.198). Finally, he asserts that the mechanisms that facilitate and respect the scientific discourse regarding "others" as ethnically inferior, continued to play a crucial role in contemporary Western culture as well (p.204).[35]

---

34. "Science, Modernity and the Final Solution", in *Probing the Limits of Representation*, 1992.
35. In fact, Nazi scientists have been honored after the holocaust as well.
https://forward.com/community/399148/why-are-we-still-honoring-nazis-for-their-medical-discoveries/

Stuart Hall (1997, 272)[36] associates the blatant exposure of body parts of "others" on camera with early racist discourses of pornography. He offers the example of the African woman Saartje (or Sarah) Baartman, known as the Hottentot Venus, or Black Venus, who was brought to England in 1819 from the Cape region of South Africa, and regularly exhibited over five years in London and Paris. In her early "performances," writes Hall, she was displayed naked on a raised stage like a wild beast, coming out of her cage when ordered, "more like a bear on a chain than a human being".[37] Both in London and Paris she gained fame in two quite different circles: among the general public as a popular "spectacle," and "amongst the naturalists and ethnologists, who measured, observed, drew, wrote learned treatises about, modelled, made waxen molds and plaster casts, and scrutinized every detail of her anatomy, dead and alive."

To the scientists obsessed with difference, says Hall, Saartje Baartman became the embodiment of "difference", and her difference was "pathologized". Her body was "read" like a text, for the living evidence it provided of her absolute "otherness", and therefore of an inherent difference between the "races." In the models and casts of her body parts that were preserved in the Musee de L'Homme, she was literally turned into a set of separate organs, into "a collection of sexual parts." She underwent a form of symbolic dismantling or *fragmentation,* another technique familiar from both male and female pornography, although she was neither experimented on nor put to death.

Nazi Germany took this European practice to its monstrous extreme as the German scientists literally dissected and analyzed the bodies they studied. The death camps held museums of human organs, especially deformed ones, of prisoners who were murdered and then dissected and displayed. The body parts, photographs and impressions of the victims, were put on display, for instance in the Museum of the Deported in Dachau (Illsen About 2000), [38] in order to justify for generations to come their exclusion from human society, to reveal and stigmatize the repulsive physical characteristics of the inferior races, and equate their ugly deformed bodies with their equally vile soul, as Friedländer puts it.[39] The photographs served as proof of the value of scientific truth, and of the modernity of these experiments, that were conceived as the camps' contribution to the advancement of human science (About 2000). The very same photographs are

---

36. Hall, Stuart. 1997. "The Spectacle of the 'Other'." in: *Representation: Cultural Representations and Signifying Practices,* edited by Stuart Hall. Sage Publications. 272.
37. Quoted from *The Times,* November 26, 1810.
38. In his *La Photographie au service du système concentrationaire (1933-1945),* Illsen About mentions the Museum of the Deported in Dachau (p. 11). The experiments in Dachau are detailed in Weindling, Paul. 2014. *Victims and Survivors of Nazi Human Experiments: Science and Suffering in the Holocaust.*
39. Friedländer, *The Years of Extermination.*

nowadays exhibited in museums and publications, as well as in schoolbooks, for pedagogic purposes, to demonstrate Nazi perversion and crimes.

These explanations and information are necessary in a discussion about the "scientific" experiments of Mengele because they connect Nazism to the theories and practices of the Western scientific theories since the Enlightenment, and to the scientific work before the Holocaust, as well as to the intricate relations between science and ideology, science and power, which are relevant to this day. Without such a discussion, Keren's negative depiction of the enthusiastic scientists remains opaque, judgmental, and perturbing. Biagioli's observations along with Weindling's and About's reports could help students understand the collaboration of scientists, even of those who were not so "enthusiastic," and to grasp the extent to which Nazi scientific practices "destroyed, once and for all, the tottering belief that science and technology were securely harnessed for the good of humanity." (Landau 2016, 8)[40]

The exhibition of Mengele's girl victims by the Nazis, thus contextualized, is made clearer, but not their exhibition in Israeli schoolbooks, unless we assume that the schoolbook writers also consider them as inferior "others". Observing this photograph denotatively, we see the outcome of starvation and torture, but connotatively we see racism, as it is racism that differentiates between children, and allows perversity and sadism to go to work on those deemed racially inferior. Racism facilitates the exhibition of children in their degrading nakedness. Exposing them to the gaze of schoolchildren in order to exemplify the Nazi racist point of view reproduces this point of view and perpetuates the girls' racialized status. The naked girls are used and abused with every reading and every look, by generation after generation of post-memory students, except that now they are no longer victims of scientific experiments, but of child pornography and the pornography of suffering. As Dean remarks (2004, 16), "a wide variety of critics frequently use the term 'pornography' to describe [...] the exposure of vulnerable people at the moment of their most profound suffering, hence re-victimizing the victims".

These four girls, even after their death and after being transformed from scientific material into icons of German sadism and human suffering, have not regained their right to privacy, dignity, and decency. Abused, naked and exposed, they have forever lost, along with the right to food, health, and life, their right to maintain a proper distance.

In Chouliaraki's words, it is the separation of the humane condition of the torturers and of the viewers (in this case schoolchildren) from the condition of the sufferers, that defines Mengele's twins and all other naked and exposed Holocaust sufferers, as well as today's third world sufferers, as absolute Others. Chouliaraki

---

40. Landau, Ronnie S. 2016. *The Nazi Holocaust, Its History and Meaning*. London: I.B. Tauris.

observes that this visual "othering" sustains powerful hierarchies of human life, because as Lissner notes, such photos of "our children" would never be published.

In conclusion, from the moment the Nazi gaze turned them into objects and functionalized their bodies, the girls fell prey to scrutiny and analysis. Students are prompted to look at these bodies in the same way as the voyeurs who came to gape at Black Venus, lacking information that could humanize and personalize the dying girls, as if Mengele's victims belonged to a different species or were another kind of children. However, unlike museum visitors and curious crowds, schoolchildren do not open their textbooks voluntarily or even willingly but are instructed to do so by the adults who educate them. They are turned into voyeurs as part of their education. They learn from their books that unlike them, some children are not entitled to protection against voyeurism. The symbolic encounter between schoolchildren and the abused twins, all of the same age, degrades both the victims and their viewers, and renders meaningful empathy impossible.

In the Name of Human Privacy, Enough!

Susan Crane (2008, 309) echoes George Steiner's call[41] when she writes "in the name of human privacy, enough!" She observes, "Few, if any, of the victims pictured either in the best known or the least circulated Holocaust atrocity images, were willing subjects." The girls had no choice but to be photographed, just as the photographer Brasse had no choice but to photograph them. They were all trapped in the same cruel net. Yet Brasse was able to recover and regain his life. The girls, on the other hand, have no choice but to be viewed by posterity in their exposed condition, on the verge of death. "Didn't they suffer enough the first time around?" asks Crane. She believes that removing such photos from view or "repatriating" them might serve Holocaust memory better than their reduction to "atrocious objects of banal attention" (p. 310). Crane explains that Holocaust atrocity images may have completed their mission as testimony and may be assigned a new role. She ponders a change in the status of photographs, from incriminating evidence and objects of "a peep show" as Struk defined their exhibitions in museums, to spiritual sacred relics (p.318). Crane insists that the victims should be allowed "to die with dignity at least in the memories of those who know them only posthumously, since their actual deaths were undignified." (ibid.)This may restore human rights to the photographed victims, and prevent their memory from being violated as their bodies were violated.

---

41. Crane, Susan. 2008. George Steiner, "Night Words, High Pornography and Human Privacy." In: *The Pornography Controversy* 17. See also Steiner, "Pornography and Its Consequences," Encounter 36, no. 3 (1966): 46-47; and Steiner's letter to the *Times Literary Supplement*, May 26, 1966, 475.

The photographer confessed that he could not look at them as a man looks at naked women. What do today's adolescents make of this photo? Does it excite them or numb them, or both? We are not Nazis, Crane observes, therefore we do not look at the images in the way Nazis did. Yet, she explains (2008,320), "gaze is shaped interactively within the social, cultural, political and historical context of sharing images, and the meanings associated with photographs (racist in ways specific to each war, in Germany or Iraq) from within collective memories that are never recorded." For a long time, Israeli society regarded Holocaust victims with contempt and disgust. Displaying them in schoolbooks as specimens and exposing them in their nudity is unlikely to evoke respect or empathy, but it can arouse some kind of horrified fascination. We can only assume that the students have probably never seen such bodies in real life or in porn movies, and that after looking and looking away several times they become interested in scrutinizing the bodies of the girls – their bony legs, their well-defined ligaments, the protruding vaginas, and the budding breasts. Schoolgirls may compare themselves to the twins, and the boys to images of naked women in pornographic photographs. We may expect boys to start using black humor and make gross jokes to conceal their embarrassment and the girls to be embarrassed.

Lewis (200, 341)[42] asks, "When photographs are reproduced in books and papers, is the reproduction done responsibly and in a way that is helpful to the reader?" The 2019 Israeli slogan, issued by the Ministry of Education for Holocaust Day, urges students to "remember responsibly," but one must wonder whether the exposure of these two sets of twins helps readers construe a post-memory of the Holocaust that enables them to remember responsibly or to remember at all.

Dr. Nili Keren, in whose 1990 textbook the entire naked and abused bodies of the girls are exhibited, wrote as follows in 2017, twenty seven years after the publication of her schoolbook:

> The writing of a curriculum and study units requires a special skill. It requires, apart from mastery of the subject matter, a profound knowledge of the psychology of children at the relevant age, of the special curriculum, and of textbook language, and of course experience in teaching and in teaching strategies pertaining to the relevant subjects, according to the different age groups. However, in all the years of Israeli education the [Holocaust]

---

42. Lewis, Bryan, F. 2001. "Documentation or Decoration? Uses and Misuses of Photographs in the Historiography of the Holocaust." In *Remembering for the Future: The Holocaust in an Age of Genocide.*

commemoration institutions and departments have never undertaken a thorough examination of these issues (2017, 25).[43]

In light of this statement, one may ask if Dr. Keren and the other schoolbook writers considered the exposure of the girls' naked and abused bodies appropriate for fourteen- or fifteen-year-old students.

Partial Identification

Spectators, argues Chouliaraki (2006), are more likely to be empathic or to care about the sufferers who are construed as being like "us," and they are more likely to turn off the TV or to shun those who do not resemble "us." Heinrich Joest, the Nazi amateur photographer who spent an entire day in Warsaw Ghetto photographing its occupants clandestinely, told Stern magazine in 1982, when his photographs of the ghetto were exhibited, that he hadn't bothered to ask the poor ragged beggars for their permission to photograph them, but had sought the permission of the well-dressed individuals. He respected the proper distance between the well-off Jews and himself but failed to respect the same distance between himself and the disheveled people, whom he treated like phenomena or objects of study and scrutiny. Janina Struk (2011) points out that Jews in Western Europe were not photographed that much because they were considered civilized, whereas the East European Jews, like the Poles themselves, were considered a weird phenomenon that aroused anthropological interest and curiosity. Ethical considerations and good manners thus had no place in interactions with them. The encounter with these eastern Jews merely affirmed German propaganda that deemed them sub-human.

The fact that people are appalled by photographs of Holocaust victims disturbed the Brazilian artist, Marina Amaral. Seeking to humanize them, she created the Faces of Auschwitz Project in which she "re-humanized" victims by concealing their bruises and adding color to their faces. Importantly, in this project, the stories of the victims are told, and the phenomenology of the photographic event is detailed. One of these "re-humanized" victims is a fourteen-year-old young girl, named Czeslawa Kwoka, prisoner number 26947, murdered by Mengele on March 12, 1943, by means of a phenol injection into the heart. Her picture was also taken by Wilhelm Brasse.[44] Marina Amaral added color to her

---

43. In: Geva, Sharon 2017. "Between the chairs: Holocaust teaching in Israel between formal and informal education." In: *Lessons of the Holocaust: Humanistic Pedagogical Perspectives.* Edited by Sharon Geva. Tel Aviv: The Mofet Institute for Educational Research and Hakibbutz Hameuhad Publishers. (Hebrew).
44. https://www.euronews.com/2020/01/28/they-are-no-longer-numbers-or-statistics-how-colour-pictures-are-bringing-auschwitz-to-li

black and white portrait and drew a scarf on her bald head. In a video in which she traces the transformation of the picture, Amaral explains that after this cosmetic procedure, people find it far easier to relate to the girl. When we see the victim as the child she was, we are able to mourn for her. [45]

The following example is a photo that appears in Naveh et al. (2009, 257), of a pair of Mengele's twins who look like any of our little girls.

Image 31. The twin sisters Judith and Lea Čengeri, March 1944. In May 1944, they and their mother were deported to Auschwitz where Mengele conducted experiments on them. The girls and their mother survived. Source: Yad Vashem Photo Archives 6092

L Marina Amaral Photo Colorization / Wilhelm Brasse#oneshot #oneshotnow #photojournalism #documentaryphotography #blackandwhitephotography #reportage #WW2 #holocaust #neverforget #remember
https://www.facebook.com/watch/?v=337415050078856#oneshot #oneshotnow #photojournalism #documentaryphotography #blackandwhitephotography #reportage #WW2 #holocaust #neverforget #remember
https://www.bbc.co.uk/bbcthree/article/7bc68edd-5fb6-4bab-8be3-77089227b8af
45. https://www.youtube.com/watch?v=OHUVmQIHkEE

The above caption does not appear in the schoolbook. In the schoolbook, the photograph is placed in a special yellow "window" embedded in a text that addresses the "monstrous experiments" of Joseph Mengele and his assistants, which ran "contrary to human morality and medical ethics." The text notes that Mengele never expressed regret about his crimes and ends with the sentence: "the twin sisters of the Čengeri family became victims to the experiments of Mengele, who was called the Angel of Death from Auschwitz, or the criminal doctor." The students are required to write an indictment of Mengele and to respond to his claim that he had actually "saved Jews from the gas chambers" and that "his experiments advanced medical research." Here too, the aforementioned articles about the cooperation of scientists with Nazi experiments could have elaborated and clarified this assertion.

Apart from their surname no details which would certainly have endowed them with individuality and uniqueness, including their first names, Yehudit and Lea, are provided. Their provenance, Transylvania, is not mentioned either, nor the fact that they were saved and are still living, thanks primarily to their mother, who risked her own life to care for them in the camp.[46] These details are omitted even though the book of Mengele's assistant, from which most textbooks quote, mentions on p. 395 the names of the two seven year-old Čengeri girls who were among the prisoners liberated by the Soviets. [47]

A-7057 Čengeri L.F. F 7 Jewish Hungary 2 Jun. 1944

A-7058 Čengeri J.T. F 7 Jewish Hungary 2 Jun. 1944

This is a clear case of *partial identification*: we see the girls and we are told their surname and that they were "victims" of the "angel of death," but nothing else. The phrase "became victims" of the "angel of death" denotes one thing only: that they were murdered.

Thus, the transposition of the photo from the family album to the schoolbook, and its re-contextualization in the educational text, has transformed both the biography of the girls and the reading of this photo. The miraculous happy end has turned into an abominable one.

---

46. https://www.yadvashem.org/remembrance/archive/2009/torchlighters/huber.html
https://www.gettyimages.com/detail/news-photo/israeli-twins-lia-huber-and-judith-barnea-who-survived-the-news-photo/909627914
47. https://collections.ushmm.org/search/catalog/pa1155178
https://collections.ushmm.org/search/catalog/pa1155176
https://www.yadvashem.org/he/remembrance/archive/2009/torchlighters/huber.html
interview: https://www.youtube.com/watch?v=MWJyjAYyF8E
https://collections.ushmm.org/search/?q=Barnea%2C%20Yehudit.&search_field=subject
https://www.youtube.com/watch?time_continue=17&v=MWJyjAYyF8E&feature=emb_logo

In Holtschneider's words, the twins are displayed as "orphans," perpetuated on paper in what appears to be one of the last moments in their life before their extermination. Holtschneider objects to showing such detached photographs in Holocaust exhibitions. "Rather than making the fate of those who were to become victims of the Holocaust more accessible by centering on the victims' lives as those of individuals with hopes for the future, dreams and fears, family and friends, in short, as social beings just like the viewers, the lack of information about them renders them more obscure, less individual, merging with a mass of people who ended up as piles of corpses" (pp. 58-59).

As in the case of Rabbi Hagerman, the text does not elucidate the picture but rather conceals information. When I asked textbook co-author Eyal Naveh, why this photo was chosen and whether the authors followed a policy regarding the presentation of Holocaust photos in textbooks, he replied: "we opted against pornography." This decision marks a shift from the choices Naveh made in the past. It certainly did not guide the designer of his 1995 textbook,[48] in which a photograph of naked corpses on a cart occupies the lower section of the title page of the sub-chapter: "For the Final Solution an Effective Death Industry is Established" (p. 140). This photograph is not included in the 2009 schoolbook, which suggests it was what Kress calls a principled semiotic decision.

The twins, who were rescued by the soviets on January 1945, appear in a very well-known Soviet photo of rescued children. According to their own testimony, they are the two girls in the second row, on the right.[49]

The story that includes the photo of old Lea pointing at herself and her twin appeared in an article titled "Lea Huber in Auschwitz: I appreciate every day I stand on my feet," posted on Ynet, a widely accessed Israeli daily news site.[50]

The omission of the girls' story and first names from the schoolbook cannot be incidental or accidental. It must surely be motivated by the interest, to prompt readers to look at these girls not as a particular pair of twins with a unique biography and an exceptional survival story (they both had children, despite the experiments to which they were subjected), but rather as specimens of a larger category of seven hundred and thirty two pairs of twins who, unlike them, perished in Mengele's clinic.[51] When asked why the girls who survived the Holocaust are used to index hundreds of unnamed twins who did not, Naveh revealed that the choice of photographs is subject to "rights and money," and that no policy is in place regarding the transposition of Holocaust photos to

---

48. Naveh. 1995. *The Twentieth. Century a Century that Revolutionized the World Order.*
49. Photograph Number: 85087. United States Holocaust Memorial Museum.
https://collections.ushmm.org/search/catalog/pa13870
50. https://raanana.mynet.co.il/local_news/article/m_203457
51. Weindling, Paul. 2014. *Victims and Survivors of Nazi Human Experiments: Science and Suffering in the Holocaust.* Bloomsbury Academic. An imprint of Bloomsbury Publishing. 159.

schoolbooks. Hence the criterial features governing the transposition of this particular photo were both semiotic and "out of the semiotic" (Chouliaraki 2006), namely the fact that the girls were dressed, and the price of the photo.

Presenting the girls through this familial setting as a special case of survival and telling their story would have created an opportunity to teach children about the life of Jews before the Holocaust. The Čengeri family was wealthy and the girls were photographed at all ages with all the other members of the family.[52] Their family album includes photographs of the parents at their wedding, of the twins with their great-grandmother and their grandparents, cousins, and friends. These photos provide a rich picture of bygone Jewish bourgeois life. Many scholars believe that family photos can be used to restore agency to the victims (Holtschneider, 201, 71). As Marianne Hirsch explains, family photos create a "familial aspect" to post-memory, diminish distance, bridge separation, and facilitate identification and sympathy (2012, 38): "When we inspect photographic images from a long lost world, especially one that has been annihilated, we seek not only information or confirmation, but also intimate material and an affective connection that can convey the affective quality of the events."

Andrea Liss (1998,91) believes that "the photograph as the frozen trace of life would seem to be the fitting artifact of mourning both the life that was lived and its passing in death." The sheer mundane simplicity of living, she observes, grants dignity to those whose memories are evoked in family photographs. (p.93).

Liss believes that mixing family snapshots with atrocity pictures "frames a different point of reference for the viewer's identification with Holocaust victims, that is, different from the positions of pity, horror, disgust, and even indifference that the most difficult of the documentary photographs so terribly risk disseminating."

Plucked out of the family album and out of context, the photo of the twins is nevertheless endearing, and for readers who believe the girls were murdered it is heart breaking. They can mourn the beautiful girls, imagine what happened to their lovely dresses, their beautiful hairdos, their cute dancing shoes, and their sweet innocent smiles. Had the writers added one word to the caption - "saved" or "survived" - or better, had they told the true story, the viewers could have engaged with the photo happily. The photo could have evoked hope and belief in human resilience. As it is, the photo is transformed from a loving memory into a reminder of atrocities and infanticide.

In one of her interviews, Lea Huber recalls that although Mengele preferred older children who would cry less, she and her sister were so enchanting that he

---

52. https://candlesholocaustmuseum.org/file_download/inline/3737e623-9d50-4e9f-af8a-e00a506a54bc

chose them for his experiments. This little recollection could be sufficient to reflect the immensity of the perversion and sadism that drove the criminal doctor, without concealing the fact that the sisters were saved and are still living. [53]

---

53. https://www.yadvashem.org/he/remembrance/archive/2009/torchlighters/huber.html

Chapter 8. The Historical Recount

The historical recount (Coffin 2006), called in other studies the realistic descriptive narrative (Chouliaraki 2006, 99), is best suited to a seemingly dispassionate report, and it is the most common genre of textbook writing about the Holocaust. A descriptive or fact-giving recount is primarily a description of events rather than either narration - telling a story with a plot and characters - or an account, namely a report that incorporates a point of view or value judgments. Consequently, this genre aspires to "objectivity at the expense of emotionality" (Chouliaraki 2006, 111). The quality of "objectivity" tends to create the impression that the events are reported from a "universal" perspective, even if this is patently not the case. As Coffin (2006, 151) asserts, recounts merely appear to be factual reports and their "objectivity is to some extent a rhetorical illusion," because most often the recount is devoid of explicit judgmental tokens. Discursively, the "objectivity" or "factuality" is construed "through the absence of direct, explicit forms of evaluation and the exclusion of competing, alternative interpretations" (ibid.).

The Voice of the Recount

> It is the reality and significance of modern catastrophes that generate the search of a new voice, and not the use of a specific voice which constructs the significance of these catastrophes. (Friedländer 1990, 10).

The voice of the recount is allegedly that of the uninvolved and unaffected "recorder," although "the label of recorder voice refers to reduced authorial intrusion rather than being an indicator of objectivity in any absolute sense." (Coffin 2006, 152). Comments, evaluations and judgments may appear in a recount, but they are rare. One example is Keren's above-mentioned comment "The SS scientists joined in these *dubious* experiments *with the enthusiasm that characterizes all scientists"* (p.122 my italics). This assertion seems factual and neutral although it is judgmental.

The recount seems to bear a greater resemblance to a chronicle than to a narrative, given its seemingly non-intrusive style and its factual, neutral "feel." Thus, it maintains the illusion of "history telling itself" (Barthes 1986)[1] rather than being told by anyone in particular. The author absents her/himself, as if the speech

---

1. Barthes, Roland. 1986. *Rustle of Language Historical Discourse.* 131.

act of the text has what Barthes calls "an empty subject" (ibid.). The objective character of the recount is achieved, inter alia, through the exclusion or suppression of human agency by the use of the passive form or grammatical metaphors. Things happen without anyone willing them to happen or making them happen. Take, for instance, this sentence: "Death in gas trucks was meant to reduce costs and solve the emotional hardship that arose during the direct shooting of Jews" (Naveh et al., 2009, 267). Death and the "emotional hardship" are the principal actors in this sentence, and they act (reduce, solve, arose) on their own volition, as if they were independent of human agency (Van Leeuwen 2008).

Yet, as Barthes argues, the discourse of the chronicle is "discourse that does not signify," for it is "limited to a pure unstructured series of notations" (1986, 131)[2], whereas in the recount, despite appearances, "events are selected, edited and linearized" (Coffin ibid.) within what Hayden White calls "a specific framework of interpretation." (1990, 6)[3]. Unlike the chronicler, the writer of the recount obeys certain rules of re-contextualization dictated by his or her interest, affiliation, or ideology. The recount is designed to inform or to chronicle past events, which are deemed significant in a certain culture at a certain moment. The recount thus differs from the chronicle found, for instance, in the historical Annals, where the author did not know how the future would play out. As Paul Ricoeur explains, "The chronicler has no knowledge of the future and the historian does," and therefore the historical recount "describes past events in light of subsequent ones, unknown to the actors themselves" (1983, 144). Thus, a recount is not a chronicle; it rather proves that facts do not speak for themselves but are constituted by authors, and demonstrates that history is written for someone and by someone (Hayden White, Keith Jenkins).[4]

Facts Do Not Speak for Themselves

> No historical fact is in and of itself meaningful: only its context endows a historical fact with meaning and significance. (Amos Funkenstein 1993, 25)[5]

The recorder's voice, although seemingly neutral and objective, is not value free. Rather, "it captures the way in which writers create their interpersonal position or

---

2. Historical Discourse, in: *Rustle of Language*
3. "Historical Emplotment and the Problem of Truth." In: *Probing the Limits of Representation.*
4. Jenkins, Keith. 1991. Re-thinking History. London: Routledge; White, Hayden. 1978. "Interpretation in History." In White, Hayden. Tropics of Discourse: Essays. In Cultural Criticism. Baltimore, MD: Johns Hopkins University Press.
5. *Perceptions of Jewish History.* 1993. University of California Press. 24-25.

particular interpretation of events in a relatively indirect way, through the selection (or omission) and arrangement of [facts and] tokens of judgment." (Coffin 2006, 151-152).

Let us turn to a text from Naveh et al. (2009), to illustrate the stages and the language of the historical recount. The historical recount unfolds in three stages:

1. *Background or orientation* – provides a summary of previous historical events or conditions: "Having experienced technically and morally killing with gas in the euthanasia operation, in summer 1941, the Nazis began to prepare for the mass extermination of the Jews with gas." (Naveh et al. 2009, 267).

2. *Record of events* – sequencing events as they unfold over time: "In the autumn of 1941 killing began in hermetically sealed gas trucks into which the exhaust pipe of the car was inserted. The Jews were loaded onto the truck, which would drive slowly around the designated area, until it was clear that all its cargo had suffocated and died. From the end of 1941 until this method was discontinued, some 400,000 people, mostly Jews, were murdered in these trucks, in a slow and excruciating method of killing." (ibid.)

3. The last and optional stage of the recount is *Deduction:* drawing out the historical significance of the events recorded. Coffin (2006, 56) states that "often a deduction explicitly interprets the historical meaning of events." She adds that in the deduction stage of recounts "a judgment is made concerning the historical significance of the events recorded, [but] typically, such judgments emerge 'naturally' out of the *record of events* stage," (p. 57) because the recorder voice "assumes or simulates reader alignment with the writer's world view, thus minimizing the amount of explicit interpersonal work to be done, in terms of negotiating with diverse audience positionings" (ibid. 151-152). Naveh et al. (2009, 287) deduce that: "The murder of the Jewish people is unique in the history of mankind and there has never been any massacre like it in the civilized world."

Time is the major dimension according to which the recount is structured (Coffin 2006). The texts unfold with temporal expressions, typically functioning as a point of departure of each thematic unit: in the autumn, in the summer, from the end of 1941 until the discontinuation of this method, etc. Yet the temporal or additive connectors may assume the function of causal links. As Kress explains (2003, 3): "The simple yet profound fact of temporal sequence and its effects are to orient us towards a world of causality [...] and the narrative is the genre that is the culturally most potent formal expression of this." Within the historical recount, one also finds logical and consequential explanations that clarify or constitute the causal unfolding of events, for instance the reasons for moving from execution by shooting to the use of gas trucks in the extract above. The background and the events are linked both temporally and causally. "Having experienced" denotes both chronology and causality, meaning that both "because" and "after" they had experienced killing with gas, the Nazi soldiers could use it more efficiently in the extermination of Jews. As in any other military operation, having been trained to do something technically and to accept it morally, they proceeded to do it efficiently on other occasions.

The recount refers to non-human participants which are often constituted by means of nouns and grammatical metaphors such as "the killing", or "the war", "the methods" that had their "shortcomings", or "the feelings that were forming during the operations."

In terms of context, the "field" (content in Halliday's terms, 1985) of the historical recount consists of "contact between different peoples, conflict and war" (Coffin 2006, 57). The emphasis, observes Coffin, is placed on groups of people, realized through generic participants as in the texts studied here, where the participants in the drama of massacre are Germany and other states, the German soldiers and the Jewish victims, who are presented as homogeneous entities. The victims are referred to in statistical and analytical terms, as numbers and categories, or through informative visuals such as maps and lists that "otherize" them. As Chouliaraki (2006, 89) maintains, "Language may 'Other' sufferers when it subsumes them under the general rule of numerical attributes, collective references or statistics." Such semiotic choices annihilate the sufferers, deprive them of their corporeal and psychological qualities, and remove them from the existential order to which the readers belong.

When the historical recount refers to individuals, their function is usually to represent collective entities and they are mostly defined in terms of their "institutional" or social roles - heads of state or representatives of categories, rather than their domestic or personal life. The recount often revolves around the people who made things happen, such as warlords. When personal stories are added, mostly about the behavior of the assassins, their role is to authenticate the narrative. In the paragraph in Naveh et al. quoted above, the non-human participants are the killing and the exhaust fumes. The human participants are labeled "cargo". Defining human beings as cargo is typical of racist discourse, such as that found in reports about the slave trade. This term entered Nazi terminology as well. In his interview with Gitta Sereny in 1971, Franz Stangl, former Commandant of the Treblinka extermination camp, declared that he regarded the Jews as "cargo" to be dispatched:

"So, you didn't feel they were human beings?" [Asked Sereny].
"Cargo," he said tonelessly. "They were cargo." (Sereny 1974, 216).[6]

Stangl justified this choice of the word by describing the victims as naked, huddled together, and whipped like animals. He compared the Jewish victims to cows that he saw in a slaughterhouse or to lemmings who inexplicably rush to their death.

By labeling the victims "cargo," Naveh et al.'s apparently neutral text adopts the Nazi de-humanizing perspective of them, especially since the word "cargo" is not put in quotations marks. By contrast to the "cargo," the agency of the German killers as a group is foregrounded, both in the clause "having experienced both technically and morally," and in the phrase "excruciating method," which pertains to the killers' capacity to carry out the task and bear hardship. The text hereby stresses that although the Germans were well prepared to murder with gas, this assignment was nevertheless repellent to them, agonizing and unbearable. This description serves to humanize them if not to enlist the reader's sympathy toward them.

In the *Deduction*, appearing to make a factual statement as they conclude the chapter, the authors deliver their judgment on a highly controversial topic, namely the uniqueness of the Holocaust, which has been debated by scholars, among them Naveh himself (2017), for several decades (Blatman 2015). The schoolbook declares that this genocide was unprecedented "in the enlightened world," which probably includes the USA, Australia, and other "enlightened" countries and colonial powers that perpetrated genocides, and goes on to claim that nothing like it had taken place up until 2009, when the textbook was published. Stating that something is "unique" and that "there has never been anything like it" demands an explanation through comparison, for it seems like the conclusion to a debate. Yet, typically of the recount, "there is an absence of negotiation and argumentation, and the writer does not invite the reader to challenge the view of events presented" (Coffin 2006, 58). Readers' acquiescence with this conclusion is neither suggested nor discussed, but simply assumed. Coffin (2006, 56) asserts, "In traditional textbooks, the historical recount has generally been used for presenting mainstream versions of the past." Indeed, the view expressed in this paragraph is aligned with the official stance of the state of Israel. Since textbooks must be approved by the Ministry of Education, they must fall into line with the state's ideology and positions. The book therefore does not deem it necessary to explain why and in what way the Holocaust is considered "unique in the history of mankind," even in 2009, after the world has witnessed the mass murders and genocides perpetrated under Stalin and in the Balkans, in Rwanda, in North Korea,

---

6. Sereny, Gitta. 1974. *Into that Darkness: From Mercy Killing to Mass Murder.*

to mention but a few. Had they not assumed readers' acquiescence with this ideological conclusion, and had they sought to promote critical thinking and universal awareness, the authors could have exposed before them the complexity of this notion, and the arguments that support their view, or oppose it. They could have invited the students to discuss the different views, rather than presenting one view as the definitive conclusion of a debate that has not been settled yet and is not even mentioned.

Landau (2016, 4-5) suggests that such assertions could more usefully be phrased as questions that should be constantly posed but not necessarily answered categorically. One of the questions, he maintains, that dominates Holocaust literature and should be posed in educational contexts is, "Is this catastrophe that overwhelmed the Jews of Europe an incomparably unique historical phenomenon, or is it a case within the category of genocide?" Landau (p.16) recommends inviting students to explore the issue and to consider other genocides, massacres, and ethnic cleansings that employ a similar ideology and justification, be these racist or religious, before reaching their conclusions: "Without doing damage to the uniqueness of the Holocaust, and indeed to the distinctiveness of other examples of genocide in the modern era, it is increasingly important that the ingredients which the different man-made catastrophes have in common be identified. For it is the making, not the breaking, of connections that will enable moral and educational lessons truly to be imparted."

This issue will be further discussed in the epilogue.

Evaluation and Appraisal in Recount

Since the recount professes to be a neutral chronicle of events, appraisal, like judgment, is "buried" in "an array of linguistic techniques that communicate values, create bias and persuade the reader of the truth of whatever message is transmitted" (Coffin 2006, 140). Words such as "cargo" for example, inherently contain evaluation, but since the recount seeks to look like a chronicle, we find only occasional and mostly implicit traces of evaluation. On this point, the recount differs from the account, which contains expressions of evaluation and judgment, as in the following extract from Hertz (2015, 105): "The invasion had an *extremely barbaric, cruel* nature and all the *most murderous passions* were directed against the Jews."

An interesting example of evaluation and appraisal that are buried in seemingly factual phrasing is to be found in Yad Vashem's extra-curricular brochure, titled (as is Joest's book) *A Day in Warsaw Ghetto*. The brochure reproduces Joest's photographs along with extracts from diaries of Warsaw Ghetto Jews, which serve to elucidate them. Regarding photographs that illustrate cultural life in the ghetto, students are asked to answer the following question: "Does the cultural activity in the ghetto reflect spiritual resilience or 'self-numbing,' denial, and negation of reality?" The question offers, as if objectively, a choice between one positive trait - resilience - against three negative ones. This judgmental position stems from the Zionist conception that Jews who remained in Europe, and failed to heed the Zionist call to migrate to Palestine and fulfill the Zionist dream of redemption, "negated reality," were decadent, "self-numbing," and "living in denial," although once they were in the ghetto it was too late. However, inserted into the question, this ideological position does not appear as judgment but rather as an objective assessment.

It is instructive to compare the seemingly objective and neutral texts we find in state schoolbooks with the ultra-orthodox schoolbook, *The History of the Recent Generations* (1998), which does not presume to be "objective," and whose texts are closer to narrative accounts. These texts abound with explicit appraisals and evaluations such as "our brave fighters," "the wicked, hateful enemy," or "it was some comfort to see the ruthless assassins wallowing in their own blood" (p. 201).

Neither of these styles is compatible with the advocacy of Friedländer, Rothberg and LaCapra for involved writing that reflects empathic unsettlement. The dispassionate writing of the recount, which dominates most mainstream secular schoolbooks, teaches the students to remain uninvolved and to approach both the events and the traumatizing photographs of victims in a detached, "scientific" or "agoraic" manner. The seemingly unbiased or bureaucratic discourse of history employed by the schoolbooks engenders the rational inductive questions that prompt readers to focus on situations, phenomena and events, of which people are specimens or indices, rather than on the individual human suffering, starvation, torture and killing, that the photographs illustrate. The following example demonstrates this teaching.

Image 32. *In the ghetto of Warsaw. Heinrich Joest's photograps 9.9.1941*.p.19. [7]
Yad Vashem Archive 50002/7.

The photograph was taken from Heinrich Joest's album: *A Day in the Warsaw Ghetto 1941* (1984). Although we know nothing about the dying child, it is clear that s/he was the reason for shooting the photograph. Joest puts the event into some context:
"On the sidewalk in a side street I saw this tiny child who could no longer pull himself upright. The passersby did not stop. There were too many children like this one." Joest's photograph depicts a tragedy. It displays ghetto residents who look rather poorly themselves, very thin and devastated by the sight of the dying child, unlike the wealthy couple we saw in Image 2, who by passed the dying man on the stairs of the Judenrat building. The woman looks at the child with awe and pity, but the two young men appear to be hurrying away from the awful sight, unwilling or unable to offer assistance.

---

7. 2001. Steidl publishers. UK.

Joest's thoughts and the circumstances in which the photograph was taken are not mentioned in the textbooks that carry this photo. The caption in one textbook (Mishol, 2014) reads, "A boy left lying in the street in Warsaw Ghetto." However, the questions directed at the students do not refer to the child. They are rational inductive questions:

-What can be learned from the reactions of the passersby about the frequency of such a sight in the ghetto?

-Were all the inhabitants of the ghetto equally exposed to hunger?

The child, who is placed at the center of the picture, and constitutes its focus, is referred to as "a sight" and becomes an item on a list of such "sights." The questions prompt the students to see him or her only as a symptom of the dire circumstances that prevailed in the ghetto, and to think of him or her statistically, calculating the "frequency" of "such sights" and guessing how many others like him or her there were in the ghetto. In Naveh et al. (2009) the caption to this photograph reads: "Sights of hunger in the ghetto," implying once again that this little dying child was just one item on a list of "sights."

The questions in Mishol (2014) and the caption in Naveh et al. (2009) teach the students that in a school context the main thing is not to pity or mourn the particular child, but rather to think about him as a specimen of a phenomenon whose prevalence is important historically and should be explored. Doing that, the readers perform what Chouliaraki (2006) names, the ultimate act of "othering."

These questions, typical of the detached style of the recount used in most textbooks, may attest to a certain rhetorical tendency to prevent students from lingering on what the photos prompt us to do, to steer them away from the one instance and to think of the bigger general picture.

Suppression and Exclusion of Social Actors

No representation of a social practice can include all there is to be represented. The question is what is included and what is deleted. Deletion covers both the omission and the suppression of social actors (Van Leeuwen 2008).

The need to select facts and personalities is one of the constraints of every narrative, and especially of re-contextualized and "ideologized" narratives. Lyotard (1992, 90) observes that in grand narratives of emancipation "many events go into the dustbin of history or spirit. An event will be retrieved only if it illustrates the master's views".

As Segev notes (2019, 352), for Ben Gurion and all Zionist leaders after him, it was essential to portray Holocaust victims and survivors as Zionists. Consequently, Israeli schoolbooks fail to mention any public figure, leader, organization, partisan or fighter who were not Zionist.

A striking example is the absence of one of the most prominent Warsaw Ghetto leaders and one of the two major commanders of the uprising, Marek Edelman of the socialist Bund movement. The Bund was very active in the ghetto in the social, the cultural and the educational spheres (Dreifuss 2017). Edelman was second in command to Mordechai Anielewicz during the fighting. His comrades described him as being "unfamiliar with fear," and called him "a man of noble soul" (Zertal 2005). After the crushing of the uprising, Edelman managed to escape and joined the partisans. He always viewed Poland as his homeland and continued to live there, partly, he said, "because it was the place where his friends had died and his people had been felled, and where hundreds of thousands of its sons and daughters were buried in the ground" (Zertal 2005, 35). Besides being a renowned cardiologist, he was a Polish revolutionary and actively opposed the country's postwar Communist regime. He joined the Polish Solidarity movement, led by Lech Wałęsa in the 1990s, and served as a senator in post-communist Polish Republic, lending public support to anti-fascist initiatives and to organizations combatting antisemitism. He was awarded Poland's highest decoration, the Order of the White Eagle and received the French Legion of Honor. Both in Poland and around the world Edelman is admired and honored as one of the leading figures of the Warsaw Ghetto uprising, as a freedom fighter, and a champion of human rights. Edelman was openly anti-Zionist and advocated Palestinian rights. He persistently refused to view the establishment of the State of Israel as conferring "meaning" to the Holocaust. According to him, the Holocaust could have no meaning, ever, either in Israel or elsewhere.[8] Consequently, his narrative of the uprising was silenced in Israel and his role therein was played down. His book *The Ghetto Fights*, published in Warsaw in 1945 by the Bund, was translated into Hebrew only fifty-six years later, in 2001, following a concerted effort on the part of a handful of scholars who refused to accept the Israeli national narrative of the uprisings as their sole narrative (Zertal 2005, 28).

Although both the Israeli education system and the Yad Vashem Holocaust Museum have always commemorated the ghetto fighters and the partisans above all others, and have allotted them far more space than to the other facets of Jewish life in the ghetto (Cole 2006),[9] Edelman is all but absent from educational programs and textbooks. From the outset, the uprising has been presented as a Zionist action and the "realization of Zionist values" (Zertal 2005, 27); the fighters

---

8. Interestingly, this view is echoed by Prof. Yeshayahu Leibovitch, a scientist and an orthodox Jewish scholar, who insisted that the Holocaust had no meaning and bears no lesson but believed that what happened in Germany should be a caution against nationalism, especially in colonial Israel. Ben-Pazi, Hanokh. 2018. "Yeshayahu Leibowitz: The Holocaust as a Sign of Warning against Nationalism." In: Judaica. Year: 2018, Volume: 74, Issue: 3. 263-286
9. Cole, Tim. 2006. "Nativization and Nationalization: A Comparative Landscape Study of Holocaust Museums in Israel, the US and the UK." *Journal of Israeli History: Politics, Society, Culture*, Vol.23, No.1 (Spring) 2006. 130–145.

were all portrayed as Zionists and were elevated to the level of the Jews who committed suicide at Masada or those who fought the Palestinians in Palestine. The figure of Anielewicz has become the icon of heroism and his suicide was viewed with admiration, as is the mass suicide at Masada. When news of the uprising reached Palestine, "Ben-Gurion instantly and publicly drew the affirmative, binding connection between combatant Zionism in Palestine and the Jewish uprising in Poland. Conveying the news about the uprising he said: 'They have learned the lore of the new death decreed to us by the defenders of Tel-Hai.'" (Zertal ibid.)[10] Labor leader Berl Katznelson declared that the uprising "rendered" the ghetto inhabitants closer to "us," to "our concepts."[11] The Warsaw ghetto fighters were thus inducted into the Zionist ethos, since they died fighting, a "beautiful" and worthy death for the homeland - Eretz Israel. Zertal (pp. 34, 36) remarks that the meaning of the nationalization of the ghetto uprisings was also "the expunging of its incompatible, non-Zionist components [...] for the Zionists in Palestine it was convenient to believe that it was solely borne by the young people of the Zionist youth movements. This glossed over and concealed the fact that the rebel groups encompassed the entire spectrum of Jewish political parties; that the Warsaw ghetto uprising was led by a group which did in fact include not only representatives of the Zionists, but also members of the anti-Zionist Bund as well as Communists."

Marek Edelman never shared what Berl Katznelson called "our concepts." After the war, he consistently refused to participate in the project of mythologizing and "Zionizing" the rebels and the uprising. He protested against the collective suicide of Anielewicz and his comrades at Mila 18, as he protested against the suicide of Adam Czerniakow. "Never," he declared, "They should never have done it, even though it was a very good symbol. You don't sacrifice a life for a symbol."[12]

The uprising, as he related it, sounded different to its Zionist version: "Can you even call that an uprising?" he asked. "All it was about finally, was that we didn't just let them slaughter us when our turn came. It was only a choice as to the manner of dying." After all, he said, "humanity had agreed that dying with arms was more beautiful than without arms. Therefore, we followed this consensus" (Krall 1986, 10).

Zertal (2005, 25, 28) comments that "within the flourishing commemoration industry that developed in Israel around the rebellion and its heroes, there was no room for Edelman and his other story. It was not the history that the young Jewish

---

10. Naveh 2017; Zertal 2005. For Tel-Hai see: https://en.wikipedia.org/wiki/Battle_of_Tel_Hai.
11. Katznelson, Berl. "The Common Jewish Destiny, in *Collected Writings*, 1945-1950. Vol. XII, p. 223.
12. Krall, Hanna. 1986. *Shielding the Flame: An Intimate Conversation with Dr. Marek Edelman.* Translated by Joanna Stasinka and Lawrence Weschler, New York, 6.

collective in Palestine/Israel needed, and Edelman himself was not a dead and docile hero to be kneaded into shape according to the political demands of the times. The uprising as a Zionist act became Zionism's 'official' history and all other versions were silenced."

On the occasion of the fiftieth anniversary of the ghetto uprising, the Polish government invited Edelman to speak, but Prime Minister Rabin, who attended the event, objected.

Schoolbooks obscure and suppress Edelman's role, as well as that of other Bund people and institutions. Avieli-Tabibian (2009) mentions his biography in a footnote (p.246). Bar Hillel and Inbar (2010, 195-196) dedicate an entire page to the Bund, but fail to mention its leader Edelman. On page 195, his book *The Ghetto Fights*[13] is referenced, and on page 196, he is referred to as "Marek Edelman, one of the ghetto's residents." The lack of recognition accorded to Edelman is all the more jarring given that this same textbook tells us that the Bund was the largest Jewish party in Poland, describes its relations with the Polish socialist party, and traces its efforts to improve the conditions of the Jews in the ghetto, besides mentioning that it was a non-Zionist movement (p. 60). Hertz (2015) mentions Edelman (p.192) only as Anielewicz's deputy and the head of the Bund in the ghetto, and Keren (1999) likewise identifies him as Anielewicz's deputy (p. 96). Yet in view of the extensive paper time devoted to other fighters and partisans, his exclusion is blatant.

The schoolbooks likewise ignore other prominent Bund institutions and personalities such as Artur Zygielbojm, who was a senior Bund member, fought in Warsaw against the Nazi enemy, served as a member of the first Warsaw committee of the underground Bund, and as a representative of the Bund on the *Judenrat* (Jewish council). From late 1942, Zygielbojm spoke throughout Europe and the USA about Nazi antisemitism, and implored the Polish government to instruct Poles to do all they could to help their Jewish fellow citizens. Finally, on May 12, 1943, he took his own life, believing that this would shock the world into action. Like Edelman, he is venerated as a national hero in Poland and Jewish poets dedicated special poems to him. However, Israeli schoolbooks fail to mention him because he was an anti-Zionist.

Israeli schoolbooks dedicate a whole chapter to the orphanage of Janusz Korczak and his courageous behavior in accompanying the children to their death, but fail to mention the Medem Sanatorium, where Marek Edelman was educated, in spite of its reputation and singular contribution.[14] The Medem Sanatorium was a secular institution that stressed humanity, brotherhood, and solidarity, staffed by highly motivated and committed teachers, trained in modern child psychology and

---

13. https://www.writing.upenn.edu/~afilreis/Holocaust/warsaw-uprising.html
14. https://yivoencyclopedia.org/article.aspx/Medem_Sanatorium

educational theory. It was closely linked to the Bund and was seen as a socialist children's republic that sought to present a foretaste of leftist ideas for the future. It conveyed a specifically Bund-oriented sense of *yidishkayt* (Jewishness), thereby helping to promote a leftist and secular Jewish concept of identity. The facility was run by Anna Broide-Heler, Manie Zygielbojm (wife of Artur Zygielbojm), Sonie Nowogrodska, and Roze Aykhner, who accompanied the children to Treblinka, on August 22, 1942

The ultra-orthodox history textbook (which is not authorized by the Ministry of Education), *The History of the Recent Generations* (1998), mentions only one figure in connection with the Warsaw Ghetto uprising: "Among the voices calling to rebel was that of Rabbi Menahem Zembe, the Rabbi of the city of Warsaw and one of the greatest of his generation" (p.201). No other personality is mentioned.

Chapter 9. The Representation of the Holocaust in Israeli Schoolbooks.

Conclusion for Chapters 1-8.

> After decades of exposure and discussion there is still no clear resolution of the issue of the purpose of looking at atrocity photographs [...]. If any of us believe that atrocity photographs still serve a purpose, how can we, as scholars and teachers, use the images appropriately? These questions raise ethical concerns as well as practical issues of source criticism. (Crane 2008, 310).

In Israeli Holocaust and history textbooks, the photos are mostly used to authenticate the Holocaust narrative. Most photographs are abstracted from their settings and the subjects are stripped of their individuality and their story. They are functionalized and come to represent general phenomena. Some photographed victims are made to represent other people altogether.

Since the origins and the phenomenology of the photographs are not divulged, and since most were taken by German photographers, the Nazi perspective often comes across as objective and factual.

In the examples furnished in chapters 1-8, the students are prompted to think about Holocaust sufferers in an "Agoraic" dispassionate manner (Chouliaraki 2006), and to classify them in categories.

Scholars doubt whether the role of atrocity pictures in documenting the extremities of human cruelty, and offering material evidence for moral lessons, has in fact been completed, and whether new roles are emerging (Crane 2008).[1]

The most common argument made for looking at Holocaust atrocity images is, that we owe it to the victims never to forget their tragedy (Struk 2004). The question is what kind of representation helps us remember. How can third or fourth generation of post-memory students mourn the dead? Or is the rhetors' interest is to make students remember only the horror, and not to mourn for the people?

We mourn life that was lost, cute children whose life was too short, venerated personalities who died before their time. Ka-Tzetnik mourned the light that shone from Hagerman's hands and feet; the poet Kambanellis, in his Song of Songs, mourns the girl he remembers and still seeks, not the skeleton she has become

---

1. Crane, Susan A. 2008. "Choosing Not to Look: Representation, Repatriation, and Holocaust Atrocity Photography." *History and Theory* 47, no. 3. Wiley for Wesleyan University. 309-330.

according to the testimony of her camp friends. And the whole world mourns Anna Frank, the beautiful, clever, gifted girl who was lost to Evil.

Seeking to assess the impact of anonymous Holocaust atrocity photos, Susan Crane asked her students to observe a photo of an undressed woman talking defiantly, or so it seems, to German officers. Crane posed a few guiding questions: did their reading retain the anonymity inscribed on the woman by the Nazified photographer's gaze? Did they regard her as a victim, subhuman, or merely a body, perhaps perversely attractive but denied any subjectivity? If she was "just a victim," did she metonymically represent many others as well as herself? If so, were her unique identity, agency, and experience compromised yet again, first by the Nazi photographer and then by the viewers?

Some of the students "invented" agency for the woman. They imagined her feelings, her words, her imputed stance of defiance, and turned her into a special individual. This was the only way they were able to relate to the photo and to feel empathy toward the woman.

This experiment proves that photographs must be embedded in stories, or rather in histories, if viewers are to relate to them empathically. Scholars such as Janina Struk, Marianne Hirsch, Sybil Milton, Dan Porat, Wendy Lower, and George Didi-Huberman, have demonstrated this beyond doubt. For this reason, I too have sought to embed the photographs wherever possible in their phenomenology, in their circumstances and personal stories, to restore the victims' subjectivity. There is no doubt in my mind that schoolchildren would benefit far more from such a presentation and would be able to feel empathy toward little Hanna Lehrer with her golden star of David, or toward brave and noble Masha Bruskina, had they known their names and stories. They would become acquainted with Rabbi Hagerman through the event of Bloody Wednesday and venerate him through the thoughts of Ka-Tzetnik. Rabbi Doniel would become far more real and memorable if students were to hear his story and learn something about the Jewish community of Kelm. They would come to admire the people who risked their lives to take, preserve and send important photographs such as those of the mother from Ivangorod and the Last Jew of Vinnitsa, were they to become acquainted with their trajectory and with the history of Ivangorod and Vinnitsa. And they would be glad to learn that the twins Lea and Yehudit were saved and are still alive, surrounded by children and grandchildren against all odds. After reading the stories behind the pictures, they could mourn the dead, or rather their lost life.

Struk challenges the notion that viewers can identify emotionally with the victims' experiences by observing their brutalization. The strategy of employing and viewing images, she argues, crosses the boundaries of perspective and experience all too easily, suggesting an affinity where there is distance.[2] Struk is not categorically opposed to showing atrocity pictures, but argues that "the danger of re-victimizing the victims over and over again in contemporary publications, simply by replicating the perpetrators' gaze, should caution us against their uncritical display as illustration".(Cited in Holtschneider 2011, 52). She (2008)[3] believes, like Susan Crane, that it may be time to call a halt to displaying these emotive images, out of respect for those who suffered or died, and to return them to the status of historical documents.

The Nazi gaze produced images intended to be shared among viewers who were sympathetic towards the torturers; this imagined audience excluded the victims or their relatives, or anyone sympathetic toward their suffering (Crane 2008, 318). As Friedländer explains, German films and photos "strove to present the most demeaning and repulsive image of Jews to contemporaries and to posterity."[4] To overcome this gaze one needs not only to "re-humanize" the victims, but to treat them with the utmost respect. This is a challenging educational task since from the outset the viewer is more powerful and therefore tends to be condescending. As Andrea Liss (1998, 4) puts it: "When too much horror is shown, the desired retrospective bond between viewer and pictured can turn into codified positions of the pathetic and the privileged."

Cornelia Brink (2007, 67) ponders whether historians may be able to contextualize images of atrocity so as to establish an ethically sound reason for viewing such violence and shield the photographed victims from a contemporary voyeuristic gaze. Even when the gaze of the photographer, the perspective of the camera, and the vantage point of the contemporary viewer, are carefully distinguished, she is not convinced that it is possible to rescue images that were taken without the consent of the victims, and from an exploitative perspective. Hence, she favors approaches that omit the actual images and describe them to the reader, thereby refraining from implicating today's viewer in the humiliation of the photographed victim. This view is especially important when the viewers are schoolchildren.

Israeli Holocaust historian Havi Dreifuss expressed her view on the matter when referring to her own book, which is not a schoolbook. In the preface to *Warsaw Ghetto-The End*[5] she writes:

> At the peak of the 'actions' and during the crushing of the revolt, atrocities that are hard to verbalize were committed against the Jews. Indeed, some of the

---

2. See also Brink 2007, quoted in Holtschneider, 51-52
3. Friedländer, Saul. *The Years of Extermination: 1939-1945*, 593. Kindle
4. Friedländer, Saul. *The Years of Extermination: 1939-1945*, 593. Kindle.
5. Dreifuss (Ben Sasson), Havi. 2017. *Warsaw Ghetto the End. April 1942-June 1943*. Jerusalem: Yad Vashem.

> documents include verbal and visual descriptions of atrocities that surpass human imagination. On the one hand, I feared that the presentation of things as they were would be too difficult for the readers and might even repel them. As human beings, we are not accustomed to meticulously study such atrocities. On the other hand, this cruelty is an essential part of the events of the Holocaust and of the history of the Jews during the final months of the ghetto's existence. The exclusion or sublimation of these sources would in the end compromise the attempt to understand as far as possible the horrors of those days (p.39).

Dreifuss resolved this dilemma by summarizing the atrocious events in the main text and detailing some of them in the notes. The problem posed by the photos, however, proved far more complex, since Dreifuss felt that reproducing them was degrading and humiliating for the victims themselves, who were photographed naked and abused. She wavered between her duty as a historian not to tamper with the sources, and her human duty to respect the dead. Eventually, after she weighed the options and the consequences, deliberating between the preservation of human dignity and the importance of maintaining historical sources intact, the former gained the upper hand. For instance, (on page 489) Dreifuss relates excruciating sexual torture in the street, of men, women and children, who were falsely accused of hiding ammunition in their undergarments, but quotes the firsthand testimony of an eyewitness in a note, which may be glossed over more easily. She notes that photographs of such events exist and provides the exact location of the sources, but she does not include the photos themselves in the book. Dreifuss' deliberations and decisions are particularly noteworthy in view of the fact that no such process is mentioned in any of the schoolbooks or teachers' guides after the third grade. Yad Vashem educational program for the young children *Down Memory Lanes* is an exception. Dreifuss wrote for adults, not for children, and yet she takes both their sensitivities and limitations into account, and respects the people she writes about. The schoolbooks studied here contain no indication that their authors have considered either the young readers or the victims as she did.

The Impact of Atrocity Images

As noted earlier, despite the immense importance of Holocaust images for the creation of post memory of the Holocaust, no policy has been put in place with regard to the way that such photos are chosen to appear in Israeli textbooks (Keren 2017), or the way that the Shoah is taught. No study has ever been conducted on the impact of Holocaust teaching on children, although this impact can be surmised from testimonies and books, and from the ways Israelis conduct themselves in everyday conversations, public speeches, disputes, and discussions, especially in times of hostilities and extreme fear, such as the Gulf War (Zuckerman 1993).

An important question that arises is, how do Israeli school students relate to these photos and texts? How do they look at the naked twin girl? Do they adopt the Nazi gaze or the gaze of the photographer Brasse whom the books do not mention? In Crane's words, can the Nazified gaze be transformed? Can students respond to the prompting of the books to treat the girls as a generic illustration of both boy and girl victims, both Sinti and Jews? Given the salience of atrocity photos and their life-long traumatizing effect that Susan Sontag and Alice Kaplan[6] attest to, this seems improbable. Both Sontag and Kaplan encountered Holocaust atrocity photographs as children, twenty years apart, and have not gotten over the traumatic effect. Sontag calls this encounter in July 1945 a "negative epiphany." She describes the effect of the photograph as follows:

> Indeed, it seems plausible to me to divide my life into two parts, before I saw those photographs (I was twelve) and after, though it was several years before I understood fully what they were about. What good was served by seeing them? They were only photographs of an event I had scarcely heard of and could do nothing to affect, of suffering I could hardly imagine and could do nothing to relieve. When I looked at those photographs, something broke. Some limit had been reached, and not only that of horror; I felt irrevocably grieved, wounded, but a part of my feelings started to tighten; something went dead, something is still crying.

Susan Sontag was an American child, far removed from Holocaust memories. But Israeli children are introduced to the Holocaust from a very early age and are re-traumatized by these photographs and texts every year of their schooling. One of the most poignant testimonies on this subject is to be found in Noam Hayut's memoir *The Girl Who Stole My Holocaust*. Hayut describes his feelings of disgust, fear, eroticism, and anger that resurfaced upon watching Holocaust films every Holocaust day. He writes about his first exposure to such photographs when he was ten years old, and admits he had his first erection on that day, during the memorial ceremony, while he was crying his heart out, and that this encouraged him to offer his "friendship" to a girl who sat next to him:

> I had an erection, my first as far as I can remember; it was perhaps the first thrill I experienced in relation to the opposite sex. I was in the fourth grade and cried at the ceremony. I cried with pride, as I did at all the Holocaust Memorials of my childhood. I sat next to her and she cried too, her cheeks chubby, red, and wet with enticing tears [...] They showed naked, emaciated human beings piled on top of each other or stuffed into train cars, or standing in endless lines waiting to be incinerated, shot dead or just plain humiliated [...] It was in those Holocaust

---

6. Sontag, Susan. 1989. *On Photography*. New York: Anchor Doubleday, 19-20; Kaplan, Alice. 1993. *French Lessons*. Chicago: University of Chicago Press, 29-30.

films that I was first exposed to the phenomenon of rape [...] Sex and the male sex drive were still unfamiliar to me then, so I resolved the contradiction by embracing the explanation I received from my parents and other authority figures: that the perpetrators were Nazis, the absolute evil, and such evil did not make sense the way normal people's actions did, and if there was no sense, naturally everything was possible.[7]

While some researchers of Holocaust photos maintain that images of atrocity traumatize and re-traumatize the viewers, and do not enable the viewer to work through the trauma, Chouliaraki (2006) observes optimistically that witnessing suffering without being able to help may encourage young people to take action to prevent such atrocities happening again, anywhere, and may turn them into cosmopolitan, caring people. The images may help to educate and act as a deterrent against racism and war. Unfortunately, nobody has ever produced any evidence to support this claim, as Crane argues, least of all the Israelis. Israeli students are not prompted to become cosmopolitan but rather nationalistic and even chauvinistic (Naveh, 2017). This education culminates in the controversial trip high school students make to the death camps in Poland.

Idan Yaron (2018), describing Israeli high school students on their trips to the extermination camps, notes that the Jewish students emerge from these trips, after seeing the crematoria with their own eyes, filled with "national pride." Some teachers affirm that they deliberately educate them to be nationalistic and to believe they are different from youngsters of other nations, because they must forever protect themselves and the state of Israel from real and potential enemies. "This is what makes them walk tall," one of the headmasters explained, "and believe in their own importance: we don't want all the others, neither their wisdom nor their culture", was another headmaster's conclusion. (p. 240).

Noam Hayut describes in his autobiographic book his feelings as a high school musician playing the Israeli anthem on his trumpet in one of the death camps in Poland (2013, 45-46):

> The emotions I felt toward my Holocaust when I was a young child were now replaced by entirely different emotions. Now, in Poland, as a high school adolescent, I began to sense belonging, self-love, power, and pride, and the desire to contribute, to live and be strong, so strong that no one would ever try to hurt me. I remember the tones of "Hatikvah" as I played my trumpet in the death camps of Poland, and a year earlier in the German concentration camp at Buchenwald, which I visited with a German-Israeli friendship delegation of youth. The strongest sensation I had back then was the desire to take revenge. As I played, I took revenge on all those who hated us. If any Nazi villain, I thought, is hiding in Argentina or Brazil, if some miserable train operator of that war is

---

7. Chayut, Noam. 2013. *The Girl Who Stole My Holocaust: A Memoir*. Verso. Kindle Edition. 18.

now sitting in his living room in Germany or Poland, he is surely crazed at the thought that despite all the extermination efforts, our state has come into being. A whole nation was gathered from all corners of the earth to the land of its ancestors, to found a mighty army [...]. And that nation sent me to the country of this Nazi villain to play our national anthem, full of hope, *Tikvah*. Wherever they might be, those scum-of-the-earth criminals, they were now tormented by my vengeful playing, our vengeance in being proud Jewish boys, a vengeance mightier than any court sentence, more painful, even, than the hangman's noose [...] despite the ashes of all those who were incinerated, and the piles of shoes and spectacles and gold teeth pulled out and shipped directly to Switzerland [...] we were strong. And I was here and I was blowing the trumpet [...] "My God, my God, may it never be over / The sand and the sea, the rustling water / The glittering sky, man's prayer.[8]

There are Israeli-Jewish students who voice not only their national pride but their hostility toward the Palestinians, concluding that "they are just like the Nazis, and the only solution is to exterminate them [...] to wipe Gaza off the Earth, until nothing is left, neither places nor people" for they all "deserve four Holocausts, not one." (Yaron, ibid. 241). Yaron does not report any reactions from the teachers that dispute these statements or try to reason with the students. The impact on Arab-Israeli students who join these trips is different. They do not restrict their feelings and thoughts to the Holocaust of the Jewish people, but rather to the suffering of all oppressed minorities, themselves included. In Chouliaraki words, they become more cosmopolitan and more empathic toward human suffering all over the world. One striking example Yaron mentions is the reactions after the murder of Muhamad Abu Khdir by three Israeli Jewish youngsters, who burned him alive in the Jerusalem Forest in 2017[9], a short while after his classmates returned from a trip to the Death Camps, where they travelled with Jewish students. Muhamad excused himself from the trip, saying he was too thin and Poland was a cold country. After the murder, all the teachers and the principal of the school talked to the students about tolerance, fraternity and multiculturalism. They all encouraged the students to refrain from hate, violence and racism, and to remember the friendships that developed in the joint trip. (p. 251).

---

8. *Walking to Caesarea*, a song by the parachutist Hannah Senesz mentioned in chapter 6.
9. https://www.mirror.co.uk/news/world-news/teenager-burned-alive-revenge-killing-3816738

Part II

The Othering of Jewish Ethnicities and Palestinian Minorities

> Nothing has a right to exist just because of the fact that it happens to be around. To be granted the right of survival, every element of reality must justify itself in terms of its utility for the kind of order envisaged in the project [of the perfect state]. (Bauman 1989, 229)

Israel's "Others"

Regarding the representation of "others" in schoolbooks, educational anthropologist Zvi Bekerman (2020, 30)[1] explains that,

> Educational cultural discourses do not provide any innovative solution to inequality but rather offer an alternative space in which tolerance of the cultures of others is suggested as a replacement for equality and even as a justification for its non-existence [...] it provides an appropriate rationalization for inequality.

Autobiographical books such as Noam Hayut's *The Girl Who Stole My Holocaust*, and Avraham Burg's *The Holocaust is Over, It is Time to Rise from its Ashes*, to name but two, compel readers to address the impact of Holocaust remembrance and representation patterns on Israeli youth, and to reflect on the way they mold these youngsters' attitudes toward Palestinians and non-European Jews. The documentary *Izkor - Slaves of Memory* by Eyal Sivan,[2] which focuses on the difficulties that Israeli children encounter when expected to relate to the Shoah through their textbooks and the tedious annual ceremonies, also addresses the impact of Holocaust education on the development of their anti-Palestinian sentiments and their desire to serve in the military and fight "Arabs."

Upon entering an Israeli school, one is immediately struck by slogans that proclaim, "Love the other," "Respect differences," and "The Other Is Me!"[3] However, in view of the fraught inter-group relations prevailing in the country, the

---

1. Bekerman, Zvi. 2020. "Reflection on the Dangers of 'cultural racism' in Intercultural Education." *Journal of New Approaches in Educational Research*, Vol 9, No. 1: 1-14.
2. *Izkor: Slaves of Memory* (1991). IMDb.
3. *The Other is Me* is a nation-wide project launched by the Ministry of Education. See ms.education.gov.il/EducationCMS/Units/ui/

separation between Jewish and Arab schools, the quota set for Ethiopian Jewish children, and the exclusion of children of foreign workers and economic migrants, one may wonder, who are these "others" that Israeli children are encouraged to respect, love and identify with?

Hence, the main questions addressed in this and the next two chapters are these:

- How are contemporary "others" represented in Israeli textbooks?

- What is the nature of their "otherness" and how is this "otherness" de-legitimated verbally and visually in textbooks for different subjects and for different ages?

To answer these questions, I examined the depiction of "others" in Israeli History, Geography, and Civic Studies textbooks issued between 1994 and 2020.[4] They all generated the assumption that Israeli schoolbooks reproduce the hierarchical relations in Israeli society and legitimate Israeli "social engineering" or "gardening". Both Jewish and Arab groups of "others" are marginalized or excluded from the mainstream Israeli narrative. However, while one group - non-European Jews – has been subjected to "enculturation," which actually entails their social exclusion until they can be fully integrated, the other group, the Palestinian natives, has never been considered eligible for integration and assimilation, and is subjected to symbolic, cultural and physical elimination (Massalah 2013, Pappe 2017). This elimination is reproduced and legitimated in schoolbooks. Nonetheless, Civic Studies schoolbooks assure students that a democracy can be an exclusionary and segregationist Ethnocracy: "There is no contradiction between the fact that Israel is a civil nation of citizens [in which] several ethno-cultural minorities live and that the only nationality that enjoys self-determination is the Jewish one." (Diskin 2011, 165).

---

4. There are several streams of education in Israel and I chose only the books most commonly used in state schools. See Peled-Elhanan (2012).

Chapter 10. The "Othering" of Palestinian Citizens

> Victims are not guaranteed to be morally superior to their victimizers, and seldom emerge from the victimization morally ennobled. Martyrdom – whether lived in a real or a virtual reality – is not a warrant for saintliness. (Zygmunt Bauman 2000)[1]

The Holocaust Legitimates Palestinian Discrimination

> The Israeli discourse of power has been perceived in the state public sphere not only as a necessary and inevitable derivative of the reality of the Arab–Israeli conflict, but also as a redemptive act that retroactively assigns meaning to the Holocaust and to the history of the Jewish Diaspora (Loshitzky 2006).

Historians Zimmerman and Zuckerman (2023,11, 84) argue that the attempt to include Israel, Germany and Palestine in the same context – which they call "the un-holy Trinity" - is necessary. Germany – the country of the historical crime, Israel – the refuge and safe haven of the victims, and Palestine – the victims of the victims. Israel that was meant to become the safe haven of the Holocaust survivors perpetrated the collective catastrophe of the Palestinian people. Furthermore, it perpetuates the idea that, these "victims of the victims" are the "new perpetrators" (See Netanyahu's speech on Holocaust Day 2023). the potential exterminators of the Jewish people. Ever since official Israel befriended the "other" Germany[2], the role of the potential exterminators was transferred from European anti-Semites and accorded to the Arabs.[3] It is therefore expected that Holocaust rhetoric and its twin facets, victimhood and power, would impact the representation of Palestinians in textbooks. These two facets are explained by Loshitzky (2006, 328):

> The Arab, and particularly the Palestinian, was to become the container of Jewish fantasies of power and revenge. Jewish powerlessness and vulnerability,

---

1. The Holocaust's Life as a Ghost. In: *Social Theory after the Holocaust* Edited by Fine, Robert and Charles Turner. Liverpool University Press.
2. A term coined by Ben Gurion. Diplomatic relations were established between Germany and Israel on 12 May 1965
3. Naveh 2018; Segev, 1993; Zuckerman, 1993; Zertal 2005.

epitomized by the Holocaust, was transformed into a fantasy of absolute power, exercised against the Palestinian as a substitute for the European goy (gentile).[4]

Israeli education continues to be focused on the relationship between the Holocaust and the need for Jewish sovereignty (Raz-Krakotzkin 2013). Jewish exclusive rights to the land of Palestine are justified in schoolbooks, as in the political and general cultural and social discourse, by the Holocaust, which "proved" that the Jews must have a state of their own to ensure they would no longer be persecuted. As Loshitzky (2006, 8) remarks, "The Zionist view of the Holocaust is predicated on the perception of the state of Israel as [...] the secular redemption" of the Jewish people following the annihilation of European Jewry.

The civic studies schoolbook, *Being Citizens in Israel: A Jewish Democratic State* (2016) reiterates time and again that the Jews must maintain their majority in the land because "our people still bleeds." This schoolbook asserts that "the Holocaust that befell the Jewish people during WWII is proof of the existential need to find a state where the Jews can live in security. [...] The horrors of the Holocaust and the problem of the displaced people proved to the world unequivocally that the Jewish people needs a national home" (pp. 31, 325). This assertion ignores the fact that most victims were not Zionist and that most of the survivors, and those who escaped the Holocaust before it began, did not choose Israel as their national home. It also fails to mention that the "redemption" of the Jewish people in the Land of Palestine was achieved at the expense of the life and freedom of the indigenous Palestinians (Segev 2019).

Israel has nationalized and militarized Holocaust commemoration, and insists that the resurrection of the Jewish people is embodied in the state of Israel and its powerful army (Loshitzky 2001). The army plays a crucial role in the "resurrection" narrative as the true victory over Nazism. A letter penned by the Minister of Education on Holocaust Day 2020 emphasizes:

> Rabbi Amital said: If a traveler should come in a hundred years from now and ask how long it took for this nation to cover the distance from the lonely shoe of a baby girl in Auschwitz to an IDF military tank, three hours distance by plane, this traveler would surely think it took hundreds of years. However, the history of the Israeli people has its own rules indeed. It took only three years! Three years. This is the wonder of resurrection.

As opaque as this declaration is, its meaning is clear: the transition from disaster to redemption is the trajectory from Auschwitz to the Israeli army, from helpless children burnt in furnaces to awesome tanks that spread fire and death unto others;

---

4. Loshitzky, Yosefa. 2006. "Pathologising Memory from the Holocaust to the Intifada." *Third Text* 20 (Issue 3/4, May-July), 327–335.

from absolute victimhood to a great, and as far as the Palestinians are concerned, absolute military power.

The Jewish army as the epitome of Zionism's victorious response to Nazism is heralded in the Minister of Education's communication to teachers and students on September 1, 2020:

> The Zionist movement brought about the most significant transformation in the history of the Jewish people since the destruction of the Temple. It brought about the founding of the state of Israel and the creation of its defense tool, the IDF. The history of the Zionist act and the values it represents - love of the land and of the nation - the importance and uniqueness of the Israeli army including the encouragement of school students to enlist and serve in a significant way, will occupy a far larger slot in educational activity this coming year.

Although both letters were circulated to all teachers and students, they were clearly addressed solely to Jewish students and teachers. The 21% Palestinian-Israeli teachers and students, who are not Zionists and do not enlist, are excluded as addressees, and should be intimidated by these letters.

The Context of Othering Palestinian Citizens and Subjects

> He, who controls the past, controls the future. He who controls the present controls the past. (George Orwell, *1984.*)

> Zionism presents an unparalleled example of deliberate, explicit planning. No campaign of territorial dispossession was ever waged more thoughtfully. (Patrick Wolfe 2012, 137)[5]

Contrary to its self-image and international reputation as a Western liberal democracy, most critical scholars characterize Israel as a colonial settler state[6], as an ethnic democracy (Smooha 2002), and as an Ethnocracy[7] (Yiftachel 2006),

---

5."Purchase by other means. "In: *Past is Present: Settler Colonialism in Palestine*
6. Kimmerling 2001; Lloyd 2012; Wolfe 2006, 2012; Pappe 2017; Piterberg 2008; Zureik 2016 inter alia.
7 Ethnocracies, according to Oren Yiftachel (2006), display some democratic features, such as periodic elections, freedom of religion, legislation, and relative freedom of the media and communications, and they extend significant although partial human and civil rights to minorities. For instance, when Palestinians citizens revolt against their own discrimination, or against the injustice suffered by other Palestinians, they are treated with far less tolerance than their Jewish co-demonstrators, as exemplified in October 2000 and in October 2010 in Um El Fahm and during the 2008 operation against Gaza and again in 2018 when snipers regularly shot demonstrators who approached the fence that encloses Gaza.

which the schoolbook *Values and Citizens* (2014) mentions as an opinion. Israel appropriated the land and turned it into a tool for advancing its national security, demographic dominance, and economic interests. As in other colonized lands, the indigenous inhabitants, some of whom are citizens and most of whom are occupied subjects, are entitled to fewer or no rights at all, depending on their relations with the colonizer. Israel, as do other ethnocracies, extends various kinds of rights to the 1,957,270 Palestinian citizens, labeled "Israel's Arabs," who constitute 21% of the country's population,[8] and are generally perceived as a demographic threat. The Jewish settlers appropriated the territory not only for themselves, but also for their coreligionists living abroad, as specified in *Being Citizens in Israel* (2016):

> The Declaration of Independence states explicitly that Israel is not only a Jewish state, but it is the state [...] of the Jews who do not live in Israel. (p. 34)

This assertion establishes the fact that Israel is a colonial state, whose colonizers live mostly in Western countries although, unlike other colonialists, these colonizers claim their colony as their motherland. This conviction colors the content of history, literacy, and Hebrew schoolbooks as well as the literary anthologies children read at school.

Re-inventing Geography and history

Secular Zionism has turned the Bible into an historical document, transforming its theological and metaphorical texts into factual accounts (Brockhill and Cordell 2019, 8). Relying on the Bible, Zionism has reshaped the history and the geography of the land, denying any alternative version, while re-inventing the past. The "liberated" Palestinian territories on the "redeemed" lands regained their former biblical names (Brockhill and Cordell 2019, 9).

Most Israelis today regard the Bible as a reliable source of historical information of a secular, political kind. As early as in 1937, Zionist leader and future Prime Minister David Ben Gurion waved a copy of the Bible at members of the Peel commission that would decide about the partition of Palestine, exclaiming, "This is our *kushan* (Ottoman document of ownership)." And on February 27, 2017, Naftali Bennet, then the Minister of Education, scolded an Al

---

See, for instance, Yoav Peled. 2004. "The Or Commission Compared to the US Kerner Commission" *Adalah Newsletter*, Volume 6, October 2004.
http://www.huffingtonpost.com/2010/10/27/umm-elfahm-arab-israeli-t_n_774576.html;https://www.thenationalnews.com/world/mena/gaza-s-walking-wounded-israeli-snipers-have-shot-6-392-protesters-in-lower-limbs-this-year-1.800691
8. Israel Central Bureau of Statistics. May 1. 2019.

Jazeera interviewer, saying, "If you claim that this land is not ours you will have to change the Bible. Bring me a new Bible that says the land of Israel does not belong to the Jews."

Being Citizens in Israel (2016, 69, 71) explains, "The Jewish majority is entitled to have its Jewish culture dominate the public sphere." Jewish Israel upholds its rather young dominant culture, imposing its revived language on the entire population, natives and immigrants alike. Palestinians do not learn their own culture in Arab-Israeli schools, nor can they pursue their higher education in their own language, which is spoken and written in twenty-six countries. They must learn the Zionist Israeli culture and history, and the new revived Hebrew, spoken by barely ten million people, in order to live and work in Israel, while only 1% of the Jews speak Arabic (Mendel 2014).

Being Citizens in Israel justifies this situation thus:

> It is easy to perceive the existence of a dominant culture that sets the "main tone" in Israel and alongside it secondary cultures that live in conflict and collaboration at the same time. The dominant culture is influenced by the Jewish majority and the most prominent among the secondary cultures are the Arab one and the Jewish Orthodox one. (ibid. p. 254)

This statement emphasizes the fact that the dominant culture is Jewish but not religious, namely a Zionist secular culture, and that there are in Israel Jewish cultures that are marginalized, just like the "Arab" one. However, the comparison with the Jewish orthodox community, that in reality enjoys privileges beyond any other group in Israel, seems to gloss over the institutional discrimination of Palestinian citizens. Jewish communities such as the Mizrahi or the Ethiopian ones, who are indeed marginalized, are not mentioned, although their discrimination is more similar to that of the Palestinian citizens. The othering of these groups is discussed in chapters 12, 13.

Distancing Palestinian Citizens

Bauman (1989, 65) argues, "Expulsion and destruction are two mutually exchangeable methods of estrangement." From a racist point of view, "Only a physical distance, or a break of communication, fencing them off, or annihilation, may render [the unwanted people] harmless" (ibid.)

Zionism, from the 1930s on, has always argued that excluding the Palestinians was necessary in order to turn Palestine into a safe haven for Jews. "The problem was the very presence of the Palestinians: distancing them, or distancing yourself from them, was always a solution that could be very brutal in the first instance and alluringly peaceful in the second" (Pappe 2012, 52).

As in other colonial regimes, Israeli domination involves "seizing, delimiting, and asserting control over a geographical area [...] writing a new set of social and spatial relations on the ground (territorialization), [which] ultimately amounts to the production of boundaries and hierarchies, zones and enclaves; the subversion of existing property arrangements; the differential classification of people; resource extraction; [...] in short, the exercise of sovereignty." (Achilles Mbembe 2003, 90).[9]

Schoolbooks justify the ongoing endeavor to distance Palestinian citizens from the land by the need to "Jewify" the entire country. For instance,

> [we must] preserve the national land and protect it from illegal invasion by the non-Jewish population, to acquire land for development in order to prevent [the formation of] a territorial sequence of non-Jewish settlements, lest an Arab sequence brings about the detachment of the Galilee from the state of Israel.[10]

These feared Arabs are all citizens of Israel, distanced both physically and symbolically. In the social and cultural spheres, Israeli-Palestinian artists, writers, and poets are never referred to as part of Israeli culture, and Palestinians or rather Palestine has no part in the official history. In history and geography school curricula at all grades, not only is the native population excluded but the land itself is absent (Raz-Krakotzkin 2013, 158): "The land defined as a homeland has no apparent history of its own in Israeli textbooks, especially in upper division high school textbooks." This is because "national consciousness was premised on the active erasure of the history of Palestine" (ibid.). The deletion of the various histories of the land over the past two millennia was imperative for the fabrication of what Pierre Nora calls "the cult of continuity," which serves to justify "our" ways. This cult gives a nation "the certainty of knowing to whom and to what we are indebted for being what we are" (Nora 1999, 12). Nora explains that this cult gives rise to the crucial notion of "origins," which is "that secularized version of myth" that gives a society, "in the process of nationalist secularization its idea and need for the sacred." (ibid.) Since the founding of the state, archaeology has been recruited to reproduce the map of "Ancient Israel," which supports the myth of continuity, according to which the land too was condemned to a sort of exile as long as there was no Jewish sovereignty over it: "it lacked any meaningful or authentic history, awaiting redemption with the return of the Jews." (Piterberg 2008, 32). The familiar Zionist slogan, "a land without a people for a people without a land", does not claim that the land was literally empty, but rather that it was empty of its historic custodians and populated by insignificant intruders

---

9. Although Mbembe refers here to colonial occupation of the past, I have taken the liberty to change all his past-tense verbs into the present tense.
10. *The Geography of the Land of Israel*. 2003, 240.

(ibid.). Thus, the cult of continuity is construed at the expense of the real continuity or the history of the land; and this imagined "continuity" endows the Jews with "natural and historical rights" to the land, as is specified in the Declaration of Independence, and justifies Israel's expansion across its international borders. Therefore, schoolbook maps very rarely show Palestinian cities and national or cultural sites, either within Israel or in Occupied Palestine (Peled Elhanan 2012). Israeli outposts, which segment occupied Palestine into "an archipelago of disconnected compartments" (Lloyd 2012,73) that are impassable for Palestinians, are described in geography textbooks as part of a sequence of Israeli settlements within the country's borders, by virtue of the erasure of the Palestinian towns and villages. As geographer Yoram Bar Gal asserts, the designers of Israel's school curriculum have never resigned themselves to international borders that appear to them an "accidental outcome of cease-fire commands that paralyzed military momentum" (1993a, 125), before it could conquer the entire ancient kingdom. This is why geography schoolbooks are titled *The Land of Israel* rather than the State of Israel. The maps we find in schoolbooks and in all public posters do not depict the state of Israel but "Eretz Israel." (Peled-Elhanan 2009.) Ignoring the borders and the native population is part of a systematic attempt to "de-Arabise" the land and its social geography, but above all its history (Pappe 2017).[11] As Nora (1999, 12) points out, "When we look at the past we take violent possession of what we know is no longer ours."

Schoolbooks legitimate these settler-colonial practices to the younger generation. Legitimation, according to Martin-Rojo and Van Dijk (1997, 560–561), is "the act of 'attributing acceptability to social actors, actions and social relations within the normative order,'" in contexts of "controversial actions, accusations, doubts, critique or conflict over groups' relations, domination and leadership." Since colonialism, oppression and occupation are considered crimes in the Western world, especially after WWII and the Holocaust, Israeli education resorts to very elaborate and sophisticated means of legitimation, in order to motivate its future citizens to carry on these practices.

Palestinians as a Demographic Threat

As detailed in the introduction to this book, "the anxiety of incompleteness" characterizes Israel's dominant Jewish group who feels "incomplete" after the annihilation of European Jewry. The anxiety of incompleteness generates the

---

11. As recently as 13.10.2021, far-right Minister of Finance Bezalel Smotrich shouted at the Arab members of the Israeli Parliament: "You are here by mistake. Ben-Gurion should have finished the job." https://www.timesofisrael.com/smotrich-at-knesset-ben-gurion-should-have-finished-the-job-thrown-out-arabs/

portrayal of Palestinian citizens as a "demographic threat," and a security threat, and justifies their expulsion and killing in 1948, which resolved as one schoolbook emphasizes "a frightening demographic problem." (Barnavi 1998). It also generates a preoccupation with censuses and statistics, suggesting that quantity is quality and expressing the idea that "we are numerous therefore we are safe. Or rather, unless we outnumber them we shall never be safe." (Appadurai 2006, 60). Hence, the constant comparison one finds in the schoolbooks between the Arab and the Jewish populations. Schoolbooks divide all their information about Israeli life into "Arabs vs. Jews," be this in maps, graphs, or texts. Agriculture, urbanization, marriage, the professions, are all divided into two categories: Jews and Arabs (Peled-Elhanan 2012). For example, *Man in the Social and Cultural Space* (2011, 140) informs readers that the highest rate of reproduction is to be found among the Bedouin community.

Since the dominated Palestinians, between the River Jordan and the Mediterranean Sea, already constitute half of the population, the need to maintain a Jewish majority within the borders of the state justifies any measure to insure they remain a minority. One such measure is the Law of Citizenship, according to which Palestinian married couples that constitute of an Israeli citizen and a Palestinian subject from the Occupied Territories, require a permit to live together. The law, which was the first one to be renewed by the new government of 2021, is reproduced in schoolbook, and reiterates the state discourse, which lumps together "exception, emergency, and a fictionalized notion of the eternal enemy" (Mbembe 2003, 69).

Here is one example (Shahar 2010).[12]

> The law denies citizenship to Palestinians who live in Judea and Samaria or Gaza and who marry Israeli citizens. Some defend the law in the name of Israel's Defensive Democracy and Israel's right to eliminate the danger of terror attacks. Some commend the law for nationalist reasons and the need to prevent Palestinian immigration and maintain the Jewish character of the state. Those who oppose the law say it is a racist law that violates the right to family life. The Supreme Court ruled [in 2003] that this law was unconstitutional for it contradicted the fundamental law of human dignity and freedom, yet dismissed the petition against it because it was an emergency law. In 2012, the Supreme Court ruled (by 6 against 5) that the law is constitutional. The minority of judges believed that the law accords excessive weight to the security factor while gravely violating fundamental rights, since it limits the right of Israel's Arabs, and only them, to family life and thereby violates the Equality Law. Yet the

---

12. See Neiman, N. Chairman of the Central Elections Committee of the 11th Knesset 1985. The quote is from Supreme Court Judge Aharon Barak.

פ"ד לט(2) 225, 310, ע"ב 84/2 ניימן נ' יו"ר ועדת הבחירות המרכזית לכנסת האחת עשרה (1985)

majority ruled, "human rights are not a recipe for national suicide because the loss of human life cannot be rectified."

On the matter of this law, *Being Citizens in Israel* (2016, 68) asserts that "the law allows non-Jews to receive Israeli citizenship", before detailing the restrictions imposed on Palestinians who, unlike other non-Jews, jeopardize the Jewish majority and the Jewish nature of the state. It also cites "a politician" who maintains that "a constitution is not a recipe for suicide, and human rights are not the scene for national extermination. A nation's laws must be interpreted on the premise that it seeks to go on existing. Human rights are nourished by the existence of the state and should not be turned into the hatchet that would wipe it out."

The refusal to consider Palestinian citizens as part of Israeli society, into which non-Arab "others" can be integrated, is exemplified in the following diagram found in the geography textbook: *Geography of the Land of Israel* (2003, 303), titled *Age Pyramid: Jewish vs. Arab Population* (Image 33). The data are derived from the *Statistical Abstract of Israel* for 2001.

The "Jewish" pyramid contains "Jews and others." Since in all books the Palestinian citizens or "Israel's Arabs" as they are called, are defined as "the non-Jewish population," we may wonder about these "others" who are attached to the Jewish group. The book does not clarify this question, but the simple conclusion is that they are non-Jews who are not Arabs and are therefore eligible to join "our" group. In fact, these are the approximately 300,000 non-Jewish immigrants from the former Soviet Union, who are indeed defined in the Population Registry as "others." Visually, while the "Jews and others" group is depicted as white Caucasian types with no Jewish characteristics, the Arabs are depicted in racist icons as the imaginary Ali Baba and his camel, with his crouching wife (Van Leeuwen 2000). Although none of the Arabs living in Israel or Palestine look like that, this stereotypical image crops up whenever Arab citizens are mentioned in this book.

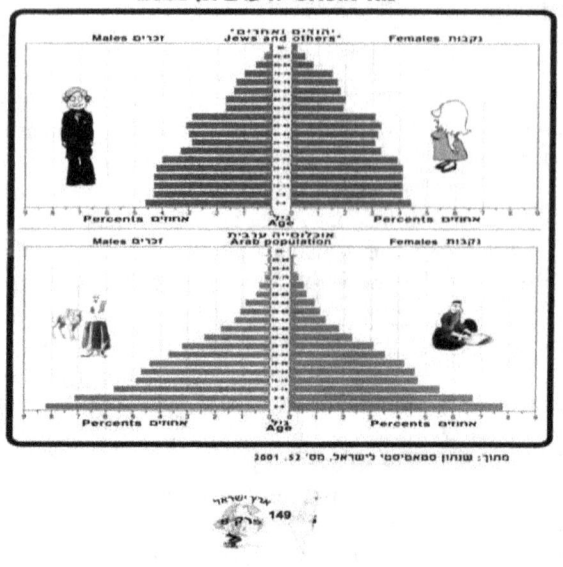

Image 33. Age Pyramid: Jewish versus Arab Population
Lilach Publishers. Tel Aviv.

The visual stereotyping of Palestinian citizens as nomads or primitive farmers, contributes to the perception that they present a "developmental burden" that will never change. Their representation as nomads also suggests that they will not be here for long. Being nomadic Arabs, they can happily wander into any other Arab country with their camels.

Image 34. Aharoni and Sagi 2003, 303: "The Arabs refuse to live in high-rise buildings and insist on living in one-storey land-exploiting houses." Lilach Publishers. Tel Aviv.

Van Leeuwen (2008, 137) reminds us that visual racism can be denied far more easily than its verbal form and dismissed as being "in the eyes of the beholder". Therefore, he advises us "to attend to the visual racism in apparently 'innocent' and 'entertaining' contexts [even more] than to more blatant forms of racism" (ibid. 147). The consideration of images, he maintains, "should have the pride of place in any inquiry into racist discourse. We need to show that images do more than just show what is, we need to make their racist sense explicit."

This imagined "Arab" is presented to Jewish Israeli children who can go through life without ever meeting their Arab co-citizens face to face, although they live next to each other. Israeli children, like most adults, "do not come into contact with the 'real' directly but rather through the medium of the surrounding ideological world" (Shohat and Stam 2014, 180). In this racist icon, the Arab is irreversibly separated from the modern building by the oval frame (Arnheim 1988, 56, 62). The camel - the object-sign of the primitive nomad - turns its stern toward the modern house, which obviously cannot contain it.

The text under the racist drawing read, "In the Jewish sector there is no objection to allocating some of the private lands to public works. In the Arab sector the expectation is that all public services and needs be provided from the state's land reservoir," which is the reservoir of lands confiscated from them.

The primitive Palestinian farmer, refugee, or the nomad with his camel, who are the only representations of Palestinian citizens in schoolbooks, are the "first impressions"[13] of Jews who came to Palestine during the nineteenth century. Although they romanticized these natives and sought to imitate them in many ways, in order to "indigenize" themselves by becoming sun-tanned farmers, horsemen, and keffiya-wearing warriors, this orientalist image has remained unchanged. Pappe (2012, 49) explains Israelis' fixation with this image of a nonexistent Arab: "It seems that when first impressions pertain to questions of 'ethnicity' or 'race', they remain steadfast. When this is accompanied by a harsh conflict and violent reality, of course, the chances of re-evaluating first impressions are even slimmer […] Official Israel, as well as large segments of society, holds on to these first impressions." Neither history nor social changes can change it. Homi Bhabha explains that "The strategy of the stereotype, as a form of (mis)recognition, depends on staging the encounter with 'otherness' in an airless space of fixed coordinates." (Homi Bhabha 1995)[14]

---

13. Pappe, Ilan. 2012. "Shtetl Colonialism: First and Last Impressions of Indigeneity by Colonized Colonizers." *Journal of Settler Colonial Studies* 2, no. 1: *Past is Present: Settler Colonialism in Palestine.*
14. "'Black Male": The Whitney Museum of American Art'. P. 110

Stereotyping and Racism in Colonial Relationships

> Racism sums up and symbolizes the fundamental relation which unites colonialist and colonized. (Albert Memmi 1974, 114)

Because the existence of colonial relationships is not self-evident at all (Bhabha in Huddart 2006), something needs to supply an explanation or legitimation for colonialism. One explanation has often been the supposed inferiority of the colonized people. Through racist representation, the colonizer circulates stereotypes about the laziness, stupidity, lawlessness or murderous instincts of the colonized population, defining them as a problem, danger and threat.

Palestinians are never presented in schoolbooks as human beings with whom we can identify or seek to become close to, and the very few photographs that depict them are invariably "evidence" of terror and backwardness. They are often represented through stereotypes, such as the one in Image 34 (Peled-Elhanan 2012). Their stereotypization fixes them in the unchanging "race" that was assigned to them. As Homi Bhabha explains, "the stereotype impedes the circulation and articulation of the signifier of 'race' as anything other than its *fixity* as racism" (1994, 75). Thus, "colonial discourse fixes identity, and denies it any chance of change." (ibid.)

Stereotyping, or the uniform depiction of a category of social actors, is another way of "not showing" them, or of showing them "as a population of degenerate types on the basis of racial origin, in order to justify conquest and to establish systems of administration and instruction." (Bhabha 1994, 70)

Memmi argues that the only way an elite of usurpers can establish their privileges is by debasing the colonized, denying the title of humanity to the natives, and defining them as animals, not humans. (1974, 22). Dehumanization does not necessarily involve depicting the oppressed as vile, ugly, and dirty. It frequently takes the form of defining and showing "others" to be a different homogenous group that must be handled through a separate bureaucratic system (Pappe 2012). As Yael Berda (2012, 5) observes, the bureaucratic relations between Israeli occupiers and Palestinian occupied are based on race: "The hierarchy of race defines the legal and administrative operation of population control". While Jewish settlers who live in the Palestinian territories enjoy the rights of privileged Israeli citizens, the Palestinian population lives under a military government, subjected to fluctuating military rules, is tried in military courts of justice, and is jailed, at all ages, in military prisons. This policy is presented in the civic studies textbook *Being Citizens in Israel* (2016, 408) in an existential manner, as a note in a sub-chapter on the judicial system in Israel: "In addition there is a system of military courts, which tries the Arab inhabitants of Judea and Samaria who are under the military dominion of Israel." No explanation seems to be needed. Note that even the Palestinians in the Palestinian occupied territories are called "Arabs" and not "Palestinians".

This system is described by Franz Fanon (2005, 37–39)[15]: "The colonial world is a world cut in two. The dividing line, the frontiers are shown by barracks and police stations. In the colonies it is the policeman and the soldier who are the official, instituted go-betweens, the spokesmen of the settler and his rule of oppression [...] the policeman and the soldier, by their immediate presence and their frequent and direct action maintain contact with the native and advise him by means of rifle butts and napalm not to budge [...] The agents of government speak the language of pure force. [...] The zone where the natives live is not complementary to the zone inhabited by the settlers. The two zones are opposed, [and] follow the principle of reciprocal exclusivity. No conciliation is possible, for of the two terms, one is superfluous."

Racism, according to Bauman (1989, 65), "sets apart a certain category of people that cannot be reached (and thus cannot be effectively cultivated) by argument or any other training tools, and hence must remain perpetually alien." It does this by proclaiming "that certain blemishes of a certain category of people cannot be removed or rectified," and therefore "they remain beyond the boundaries of reforming practices, and will do so forever. Not only biological defects but 'the spiritual inability' or 'vice' attributed to the colonized or to the inferior race are articulated as the attribute of heredity or blood" (Bauman 1989, 65; also, Van Leeuwen 2008, 146). Following is an example of this practice:

> The Arab society is traditional and objects to changes by its nature, [it is] reluctant to adopt novelties [...]. The Arabs refuse to live in high-rise buildings and insist on living in one-storey land-exploiting houses. (*Geography of the Land of Israel* 2003, 303).

This statement describes all the Palestinian citizens of Israel as possessing by nature or by heredity these negative attributes. Albert Memmi calls this generalization "the mark of the plural", typical of racist discourse, which projects colonized people as "all the same":

> The colonized is never characterized in an individual manner; he is entitled only to drown in an anonymous collectivity. They are this. They are all the same. (Memmi 1974, 129).[16]

---

15. *The wretched of the Earth*
16. Memmi, A. 1974. *The Colonizer and the Colonized*, Boston: Beacon Press.

No matter what people do, they cannot alter the racist attitude determined by who they are, because in racist discourse man *is* before he *acts* (Bauman 1989). In the Palestinian case, who they are is determined by where they are.

The stereotypes of primitive and vile Palestinians serve to justify Jewish superiority. However, they end up by generating and reinforcing the Jews' anxiety and fear of their neighbors and co-citizens. "In a way the colonizer 'spooks' himself: he fantasizes endless monstrous stereotypes that can only lead to anxiety rather than the desired certainty" (Bhabha in Huddart 2006, 41).

The Logic of Elimination

The process of convincing children, students and the general public, through propaganda or education, that Palestinians are indeed superfluous others, and therefore must be distanced, discriminated, segregated or eliminated, comprises a number of phases that legitimate this "social gardening". Bauman (1989) describes these phases in relation to the German propaganda against Jews. The phases are justified by the need to engineer a perfect society, in Israel's case a pure Jewish one, and viewing the society "as an object of designing, cultivating and weed-poisoning." (ibid. 66).

The first phase is **abstraction**: the whole group is defined as problems and threats. Bauman (1989, 104) contends that abstraction and stereotyping are linked:

> Abstraction is one of the modern mind's principal powers. When applied to humans, that power means effacing the face: whatever marks remain of the face serve as badges of membership, the signs of belonging to a category, and the fate meted out to the owner of the face is nothing more yet nothing less either than the treatment reserved for the *category* of which the owner of the face is but a *specimen*. The overall effect of abstraction is that rules routinely followed in personal interaction, ethical rules most prominent among them, do not interfere where the handling of a category is concerned [...]. (Bauman 1989, 227).

Since Palestinian invisibility has been "institutionalized" (Loshitzky 2006, 8) they are generally invisible in textbooks, unless they are depicted stereotypically. In 2019, Sikuy - the Association for the Advancement of Civic Equality - issued a report showing that Israeli-Palestinian society and culture are excluded from all Israeli textbooks, including those that teach Arabic as a second language. None of the five hundred and twenty nine photographs and none of the texts that addressed various populations, represented Arab-Israeli people.[17] The Palestinian inhabitants on both sides of the unseen international border are missing from maps,

---

17. Representation and foregrounding of the Arab society in school curricula. 2.pdf (sikkuy.org.il).

photographs, and graphs. They are mentioned only in the context of the problems they constitute for Israel (Peled-Elhanan 2012). As Edward Said notes in *The Question of Palestine* (1980), Palestinians are outed or absent even when they are all too present. Said wonders,

> In what world is there no argument when an entire people is told that it is juridically absent, even as armies are led against it, campaigns conducted against even its name, history changed so as to 'prove' its nonexistence? (Introduction, XVII).

Cartographic Silence

The absence of Palestinians from the landscape is best manifested through cartographic silence (Henrikson 1994, 60).

Image 35. The Proliferation of Israel's Arab Population in Israel, by district, 2000.
Israel- Man and Space 2003

This map shows the relative size of the "Arab population," namely of the Palestinian citizens within the state of Israel, without showing a single Arab city, including the mixed cities of Nazareth and Acre. The impression gained is that these "Arabs," abstracted from their locations of dwelling, have no places of their own and therefore they penetrate "our" cities, encroaching upon us. Thus, the map seems like a warning or a call for action. "The alien," says Bauman (1989, 65), in this case the Palestinian citizen, "threatens to penetrate the native group and fuse with it if preventive measures are not set out and vigilantly observed."

The colorless West Bank on this map is depicted in the legend as "an area for which there are no data," in other words it is "terra nullius," empty or vacant land. In this particular population map, it indicates that no Arabs live there or that one cannot know how many live there, which is a rather absurd notion given the regime of occupation that keeps a constant watch on every subject.

Erasing the other from the map is a blatant act of cultural violence (Brockhill & Cordell 2019, 9). This erasure is part of the multimodal "denial of the presence of the Palestinian Arabs on the land destined for colonization, [which is] the single most significant factor in determining the shape taken by the settlers' nation." (Pappe 2012, 42).

In the 2009 geography schoolbook *Israel in the 21st Century*, the same map appears, this time representing the proliferation of the Arab population in 2005. A few Arab cities and towns were added, such as Nazareth, Shfar'am and Um Al Fahem. Students are asked to note three "natural areas" in which Arabs constitute more than half the inhabitants. The West Bank remains "an area without data." In the geography schoolbook: *Man in the Social and Cultural Space* (2011) a map of Israel in 2004, produced by well-known Israeli painter Ruth Modan, is referred to as an example of a country that has diverse landscapes. Yet only Jewish cities are depicted. The map is replete with people of all kinds: soldiers, tourists, farmers, builders. The "Arab" citizens are represented by three figurines, two are in the desert, a shepherd alongside a Bedouin tent and a Bedouin with a camel; a farmer following a primitive plough pulled by two oxen figures in the Galilee. The students are asked to consider how people can change the landscape.

Abstract Occupation

The everyday life of the colonized Palestinians across the border is controlled by a regime of permits and decrees that may change from one moment to the next (Sfard 2018)[18]. This regime denies the conditions required for a normal life and turns people into what Agamben (*Homo Sacer* 1995) defines as "bare life", namely a life that is stripped of its human rights and denied, on the basis of race, the basic conditions needed to sustain itself (see also Lloyd 2012; Berda 2012).

---

18. *The Wall and the Gate*. Metropolitan Books Publishers

Israel deprives the colonized Palestinian people of their human survival needs, their well-being needs, their identity needs, and their freedom needs (Galtung 2013, 43). Galtung notes the negation of each of these needs: "survival needs (negation: death, morbidity); well-being needs (negation: misery, morbidity); identity needs (negation: alienation) and freedom needs (negation: repression)." He defines this practice as Sociocide (2012): "Sociocide is the intended wounding-killing of a society by eliminating the prerequisites for a live, vibrant, dynamic society."[19]

These forms of direct and structural violence are justified in the schoolbooks, which report nothing about Palestinians' everyday life, and hardly ever discuss the occupation or the occupied (Ben Amos 2020).[20] When the occupation is mentioned, it is only in an abstract manner. The civic studies schoolbook: *Going the Civilian Way* (2012), mentions some of its practices abstractly (Peled-Elhanan 2014).

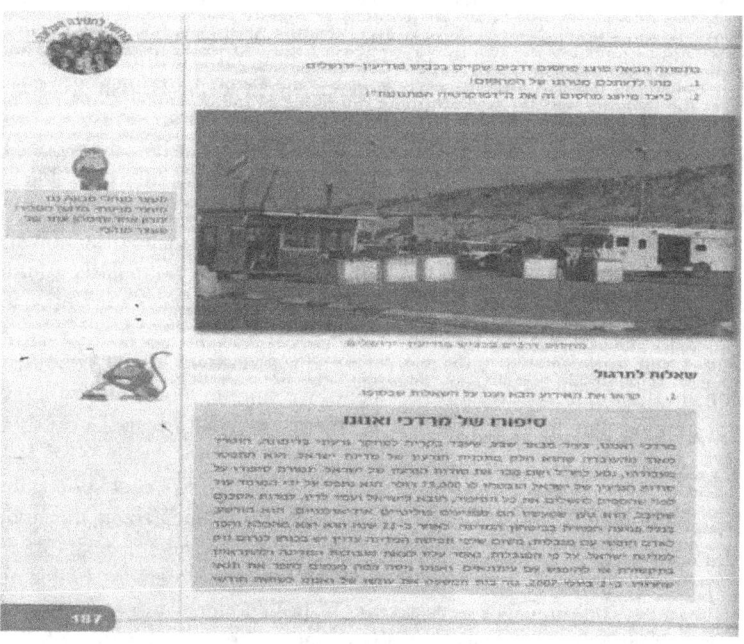

Image 36. *Going the Civilian Way.* 2012, 187. Rehes Publishers.

---

19. *Testimony before the Russell Tribunal on Palestine, NYC, October 7, 2012.*
20. "In Israeli textbooks, the Palestinians are all but invisible." https://www.haaretz.com/israel-news/.premium-in-israeli-textbooks-the-palestinians-are-all-but-invisible-1.8933768 (Hebrew).

This page is the left-hand side of a double spread (pp. 186-187) and is, therefore, the New section (reading from right to left) of a chapter titled: "The right of Democracy to protect itself." Page 186 contains a text that includes a definition of Israel as a defensive democracy, and lists the license this definition grants, thereby preparing the ground for the details on page 187. The text explains that a defensive democracy is entitled to use any measure it deems fit to protect its citizens from potential terrorists and their supporters. The practices of the Occupation such as the separation wall, check-points, targeted assassinations, administrative detention ("detaining a person without trial, without being able to meet a lawyer for an indefinite span of time," ibid.), house demolition, confiscation of land, curfew, and the use of mild physical and psychological pressure ("not torture," ibid.) are explicitly rationalized and legitimated. Page 187 details some of these practices. The left-hand margins of p.187 appear very cheerful and childish, showing a mischievous monkey that toys with the buttons of a nuclear device, hinting at Mordechay Vanunu's betrayal reported in the lower section of the page, in a special window.[21] Vaanunu, an Israeli nuclear technician, revealed details of Israel's nuclear weapons program to the British press in 1986. He spent eighteen years in prison and lives under house arrest to this day. Vaanunu has nothing to do with checkpoints or administrative detention, but he may have something to do with jeopardizing Israel's defensive democracy. Referring to him in this chapter, on the same page that discusses the preventive measures taken against potential terrorists, conveys the message of nation states to their citizens: either act in accord with the prevailing standards of conduct enforced by those in authority, or risk whatever consequences they may wish to impose. (Bauman 1989).

Above the monkey, a wise owl is trying to learn about administrative detention. In the upper section of every page, we find an icon showing a group of Western–looking laughing children who seem very happy to learn about the defensive democracy they live in.

At the center of page 187 is a photograph of a "flying" checkpoint, the type placed at random without warning. The checkpoint is located in the middle of nowhere, between Modi'in and Jerusalem. It comprises several concrete blocks, loosely placed, against which two groups of Israeli soldiers or policemen are leaning leisurely, talking. One sees an empty police van, its doors open, and the Israeli flag flying above a canteen, in the distance the bare slope of a hill. While such defense mechanisms are meant to protect us from "terror," the actual people against whom the checkpoint was erected are neither mentioned nor shown, merely assumed. Concealed, the Palestinians become impersonalized, and more

---

21. https://en.wikipedia.org/wiki/Mordechai_Vanunu

easily identified with the threat of terror. The reality of permanent checkpoints in Israel, which is quite different, is not shown either in Israeli press or in the schoolbooks, where students may be perplexed to see the "enemy" as "people like us."

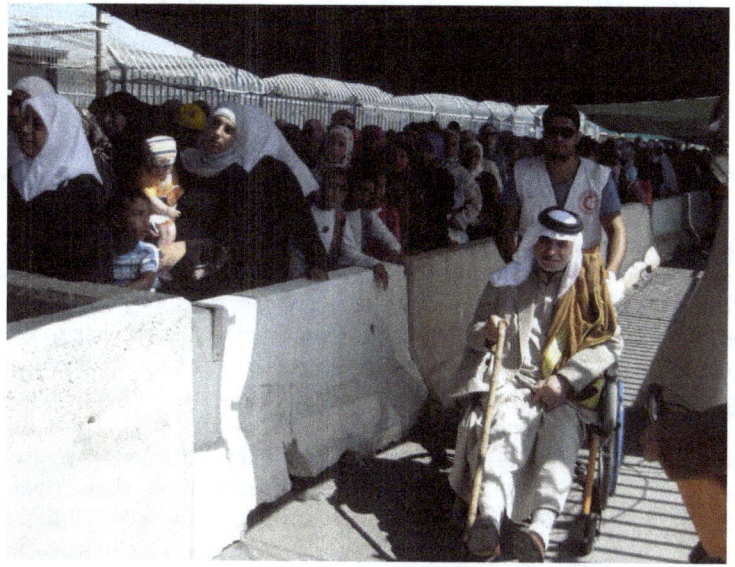

Image 37. Kalandia Checkpoint. Courtesy of Tamar Fleishman

Photographs of real active checkpoints, into which hundreds of people crowd every hour of the day, on their way to work, to school or to the hospital, would convey to students that despite the unbearable conditions and enormous stress they endure daily, in the cramped space between prison-like cages and automatic iron gates that open and lock at whim, the people appear self-possessed, "rational and educated, possessing the positive characteristics Israeli students tend to associate with their own collectives," (Rabinowitz 2001, 76) in short "civilized, stereotype-busting natives" (ibid.). They do not resemble potentially "blood thirsty desperados, yearning for violent revenge, pushed to act against their own interests if they can only harm as many Israelis as they can" (ibid.). Such pictures are liable to raise questions Israeli educationists have no interest in raising, such as: Is this what terrorists look like? How can you tell? Is every Palestinian a potential terrorist, grandparents, children and babies included?

Presenting the practices of occupation in the style of an episode from Winnie the Pooh, with an owl and a monkey (piglet cannot feature in a Jewish schoolbook), and "cool" relaxed soldiers manning an empty checkpoint in a pastoral landscape, portrays the colonial regime as a reasonable, reassuring, non-threatening "procedure" implemented by a defensive democracy. The empty and peaceful checkpoint which appears to be a preventive measure, reassures future soldiers that "doing checkpoints" is not that bad a task. The enemy is nowhere to be seen, may be far away, or hiding among the rocks, but we must be alert.

The questions following this section are rational and based on the criterion of utility:

- What is the purpose of the checkpoint in your opinion?

- How does it represent defensive democracy?

Owl asks the students, "Administration detention is also called preventive detention. Explain why. Name one benefit and one disadvantage of administrative detentions."

Being Citizens in Israel (2016, 268)[22] devotes more than a page to justifying "administrative detention," the indefinite incarceration of people for *seeking* to commit terror attacks, by referring to other countries, especially colonial Britain from whom Israel inherited many colonialist ways of "dealing with" the native population. The argument of "cosi fan tutti" is employed in many instances when the books seek to legitimate unlawful acts on the part of the state. Students are then asked a rhetorical question: "is administrative detention the right tool to fight terrorism?" which is immediately answered: Israel applies this sanction not only against Palestinians *before* they commit terrorist attacks but also against Jews (i.e., Jewish terrorist Noam Feder) *after* they have committed terrorist attacks against Palestinian civilians, though Jewish incarceration is much shorter, as the law requires.

Palestinian citizens as a Problem

> Reference to people by means of a negative quality assigned to them, often realized in an abstract noun that does not include the semantic feature 'human,' for instance as a problem, is typical of racist discourse. (Van Leeuwen 2008, 46).

The situation of Palestinians under Israeli rule is usually referred to as "the Palestinian problem". This is a further facet of "abstraction". By being labeled a problem, "the Other is not only dehumanized but has been successfully converted

---

22. In a previous edition (2001) an entire chapter was devoted to the problematic nature of this measure. This revision attests to the change in the orientation of the Ministry of Education.

into an 'it,' deprived of humanhood, [...] the stage is set for any type of direct violence." Galtung (2013, 294).

Achilles Mbembe (2003, 79) explains that in a colonialist context, the meaning of sovereignty is occupation, and occupation means, "Relegating the colonized to a third zone between subjecthood and objecthood." The colonized are thus dehumanized and "dehumanized objects cannot possibly possess a 'cause,' much less a 'just' one; they have no 'interests' to be considered, indeed no claim to subjectivity." Such human objects become a "nuisance factor" (Bauman 1989, 104), or a problem.

The depiction of Palestinian citizens in authorized Israeli textbooks as a problem-to-be-solved[23] after the Jewish "problem" was meant to be "solved" in the Final Solution, is rather perturbing. This abstraction not only dehumanizes but goes a step further by equating the status of the Palestinians to that of the Jews and other unwanted groups in Nazi Germany, thereby hinting at the possibility of their annihilation.

Confinement and exclusion

> If conditions allow, racism demands that [...] the offending category be removed beyond the territory occupied by the group it offends. (Bauman 1989, 65-66).

The "enemy in our midst," argues Bauman, "triggers a vehement boundary drawing bustle" (ibid.). By defining Palestinians as a problem, Israeli schoolbooks set them in a hierarchy that justifies their removal, or their confinement in clear boundaries, while legitimating Jewish superiority and the privilege of the Israeli colonizer to usurp of indigenous land and goods.

Hence, the next phase is to convince the students of the need to exclude or to fence off the problematic group. Israel has always sought to get rid of its Palestinian citizens. Expelling them was seriously discussed as an alternative to the military regime imposed on them in the years 1948-1966, and is still discussed today (Pappe 2012, 54). The "silent transfer" of Palestinians is an ongoing process.[24] The massacre of Kafr Qassim in 1956 was part of a plan called Plan Mole, to frighten the Palestinian citizens and make them flee the country to Jordan. The details of the plan have been kept secret until 2023.[25]

---

23. See for example Barnavi 1998 184, 244. Quoted in Peled-Elhanan 2012.
24. https://reliefweb.int/report/occupied-palestinian-territory/one-way-ticket-israel-committing-forcible-transfer-protected-persons-occupied-palestinian-territory-and-most-victims-are-women
25. See: Akevot Institute February 2nd, 2023: This is Operation Mole: Following the newly declassified records from the Kafr Qasim Massacre trial. https://www.akevot.org.il/en/article/plan-mole/

The objective of distancing Palestinian citizens from the land legitimates the permanent confinement imposed on both Palestinian citizens and subjects. Schoolbooks justify the siege imposed by the military government of 1948-1966, by the overriding need to keep as much land as possible in Jewish hands:

> The military government helped Jewish settlement all over the country and prevented Arab seizure of vacant lands. (Shahar 2010, 138).

These "vacant lands" or "state land" were the Palestinian confiscated lands.

The Jews in Israel fence themselves in and fence the Palestinian subjects out. The separation wall, built between their homes and their lands, confines Palestinian subjects and creates a dual ghetto, forced on the Palestinians, but entered into voluntarily by the Jews. Both parties live surrounded by a huge concrete wall or barbed-wired fences, guarded by soldiers.[26] Critical Israeli scholars regard this practice as a remnant from the past. Philosopher Haviva Pedaya (2011), a scholar of Jewish mysticism, maintains that during the Middle Ages, the collective punishment for being Jewish was generally expulsion, but in the twentieth century, rather than being thrown out, the Jews were "thrown in", locked away first in ghettos and then in concentration and extermination camps. When East European Jews came to colonize Palestine, their collective memory of being expelled and locked up was so vivid, and their fear of all non-Jews so strong, that they were driven to do exactly what they had been subjected to: to expel and to lock up the native people. Historian Ilan Pappe (2012) calls this practice "shtetl colonialism". Lawrence Davidson (2012) compares the ghettoization of Palestinians within the borders of Israel and in the occupied territories, to the practice of the Russian Czar, who confined the Jewish Russians to designated areas called the "Pale of Settlement," a frontier zone of the Russian Empire, set aside by the government in 1794 for Jewish settlement. Davidson surmises that the people who founded the state of Israel came from these pales and this practice was therefore familiar to them.

---

26. When the writer and Nobel Laureate José Saramago visited Palestine, he gazed from the hills of Ramallah at the Jewish settlement Psagot and said "Just like Auschwitz." Being fiercely castigated for comparing Jews to Nazis, Saramago explained that what he meant to convey was that from the outside the Jewish settlement looked just like a concentration camp, with its high fences topped by electric barbed wire, military-style guard towers, and barriers. However, he did not deny the comparison per se. See https://www.thenation.com/article/archive/misuses-allegory/

The Usurpation of Indigenous Land and "Abandoned" Property

> Israel never sought to achieve equal citizenship between Palestinian Arabs and Jews, nor did it seek the consent of its Arab citizens for the forceful ideological imposition of a Jewish state (Oren Yiftachel 2006, 93).

Unlike the Jews who were "exiled" in Roman times and therefore have the right to return and reclaim their land, Palestinian refugees are presented in all schoolbooks as people who abandoned the land of their own free will, and in so doing lost their right to return. Cleansed Palestinian villages were declared by law in 1950 to be "abandoned property" or "absentees' assets", and were appropriated by the state, although many of the villagers returned after being expelled and presently live in Israel, albeit not on their own land and not in their former homes. The use of the word "abandoned" regarding Palestinian exodus is not random, given a context in which the war over the land is so ferocious. The "abandoned" houses were immediately occupied by Jewish refugees from Europe and later from Arab countries, as noted in all schoolbooks.

The reasons for Palestinian "desertion" are never fully explained. The expulsion of close to 800,000 Palestinians known as *al-Nakba*, the Palestinian national catastrophe, which one textbook (Barnavi 1998) terms the Palestinian Holocaust – is generally presented by the perpetrators as the consequence of spontaneous flight rather than as the outcome of state policy. This version has been adopted by the international community as well.

The Refugees

> Both on the political and on the historiographic levels, Israeli discourse is characterized by the unwillingness to assume responsibility for the refugee problem. (Raz-Krakotzkin 2004, 165)

One of the expressions of Israel's anxiety lest the Jews become a persecuted minority once again, is the refusal to allow Palestinian refugees to return despite Israel's acceptance of the 1948 UN Resolution 194, which stipulates that some 60,000 refugees be allowed to return to their homes. [27] The physical demolition of the villages was accompanied by the destruction of Palestinian agricultural,

---

27. According to the Law of Return, every Jew who comes to Israel can take out citizenship on the spot, whereas Palestinian citizens who leave the country may find themselves unable to return and may lose their rights, as is pointed out in the schoolbook *Going the Civilian Way*, (2012).
https://mfa.gov.il/mfa/mfa-archive/1950-1959/pages/law%20of%20return%205710-1950.aspx

religious, historical and cultural sites. Hence, the Palestinian people was physically, culturally, and symbolically erased from the land. The schoolbook *Going the Civilian Way* (2012, 250) declares:

"Upon the founding of the state of Israel, many Arabs fled the land. The state does not allow them to return and reunite with their families in order to secure the Jewish majority." Here students learn that securing a Jewish majority justifies violating international law and decisions. The schoolbook (p. 471) explains that Israel applies an implicit and explicit policy of "Judaization" of the land through various means. These include confiscation of lands from the Arabs; Jewish settlement designed to curb Arab settlements; discrimination in allocation of resources; and the refusal to allow the refugees to return.

Addressing the refugee problem, the schoolbooks assert that following the 1948 war and the establishment of the state of Israel, people on both sides became refugees. Thus, the Palestinian exodus is made equivalent to the exodus of Jews from Arab countries, as both created refugees as a result of the wars of Israel with the Arab countries. The chapters dealing with these two groups of refugees are usually titled, "The Refugees following the Israeli-Arab Conflict". for instance, *Man in the Social and Cultural Space* (2011, 180) devotes a special "window" to "The Refugees following the Israeli-Arab Conflict," where the Palestinian refugees are represented by an aerial photograph of a huge shanty town that appears unpopulated, identified in the caption as the Balata refugee camp near Nablus (p. 202). The schoolbook asserts that "following the founding of the state of Israel the situation of Jews in Arab countries deteriorated [...] and hundreds of thousands became destitute [...] Their national attachment has always been to Israel and the state absorbed them and took care of them. Today the feeling of 'being refugees' no longer exists." By contrast, "many [Arabs] still feel refugees today because the Arab countries have not recognized them as citizens with equal rights."

Thus, (Shohat 2017, 4), "each argument used to criticize Palestinian dislocation is echoed with a similar argument and phrasing with regards to Arab Jews. The tragedy of 'the Palestinian refugees' is answered with the tragedy of 'the forgotten refugees from Arab countries;' 'the expulsion of Palestinians' is cancelled out by 'the expulsion of Jews from Arab countries;' 'the transfer' and 'ethnic cleansing' of Palestinians is correlated with 'the transfer' and 'ethnic cleansing' of Jews from Arab countries; and even 'the Palestinian Nakba' is retroactively matched with a 'Nakba of Jews from Arab countries.'"

Shohat notes, however, that one of the differences between Arab Jews and Palestinians is that "in the case of the Palestinians, the forced mass exodus easily corresponds to the notion of 'refugees,' since they never wished to evacuate Palestine and have maintained the desire to return, or at least a desire to have the "right" to return." (ibid.). On the other hand, many of the Arab-Jews wished to migrate to Israel and those who did so became citizens, unlike the Palestinians in

Arab countries, which, contrary to the Israeli argument, did not consider them to be part of their own nations.

Another argument, written as the final claim of the text in Bar Hillel and Inbar (2004, 202-205) is the pervasive Israeli message, that the only "real" refugees, who are entitled to the land of Israel, are the Jews who survived the Holocaust:

> The Arab leaders claim that the hostilities cannot be terminated before the refugees are allowed to return to their homes [...] despite what happened in Europe. (p. 204)

Being Citizens in Israel (2016) compares the circumstances that prevailed in Israel to the experience of other countries such as Germany that welcomed back German refugees after World War II (p. 325). The schoolbook explains that the Law of Return, which entitles every Jew in the world to Israeli citizenship upon arrival, serves to safeguard the Jewish majority, because this majority is not secure as long as the borders of the state have not been defined to Israel's satisfaction, and the Palestinians' demand for an equivalent right of return has not been buried. The schoolbook blames the Palestinians and their leaders for their "tragedy" (p.465) explaining that "the tragedy of the refugees is the outcome of the choice made by those who rejected the Partition Plan and started the war." However, the Partition Plan itself has never been translated to Hebrew and is not discussed in any schoolbook (Raz-Krakotzkin 2004).

For their part, the book notes, "the Palestinians argue they have the right to return to their homes" (ibid.). It also mentions (p. 471) that "in the eyes of the Arabs" land confiscation is considered dispossession.

Internal refugees

Man in the Social and Cultural Space (2011, 140) informs readers that during the 1948 war the Arab settlements were destroyed and their inhabitants, who remained, became "internal refugees" who were subjected to military rule that controlled their every move. But today, the schoolbook proceeds, the Israeli government allocates financial support to the Arabs that enhances their integration in Israeli life. They have become a modern, urban, politically engaged population that demands its rights. However, the book fails to mention a single Palestinian-Israeli individual, such as well-known scientists, artists, politicians, nor any political party, or economic, industrial, or cultural achievement of Israeli-Arabs. The entire population of Palestinian citizens form a single homogenous group that lives off the bounty of the state of Israel and reproduces at a high rate.

Being Citizens in Israel (2016) addresses the Palestinian citizens as groups that have mixed identities (Arab, Palestinian, Israeli) and double loyalty, but no history. Neither their own history nor their part in the history of Israel is told. The book emphasizes time and again that Israel's Arabs belong to the great Arab nation. The schoolbook *Values and Citizens* (2014), which unusually addresses the problematic relations between Jewish and Arab citizens in Israel (without ever mentioning the Occupation), asks students the following question, at the end of the chapter dealing with the problematic identity of Israeli Arabs:

> In most of the nation states in the world (for instance in Europe) there are minority groups that have a language, a culture, a religion, and even a nationality that they do not share with the majority. Is there a difference, in your opinion, between these minority groups and the Arab minority in Israel? (p.344)

The answer presumably is that there is a difference, since the Arabs of Israel are loyal to their brethren, who are Israel's enemy.

Legitimating Discrimination and Segregation of Palestinian Citizens

Although *Going the Civilian Way* asserts that "The [Israeli] government made a decision to allocate the same budget to both Jews and Arabs, which proves [its] recognition of the communal Arab right to equality, in addition to the rights of the individual Arab citizen" (p. 249), Palestinian citizens and subjects are segregated by law. Israeli Arab schools are separate from Jewish schools and the budgets allocated to Jewish schools are much greater than those allocated to Palestinian-Israeli schools, according to a graph issued by the Ministry of Education in 2019.[28] Israeli textbooks employ multimodal means to legitimate the ongoing discrimination of Palestinian citizens, and reiterate the conception that as Arabs they can settle in any of the twenty-two Arab countries instead of remaining as a "minority" in "our" Jewish state. Having chosen to remain in Israel, this Arab minority must accept its tragic lot, which, the schoolbooks maintain, it is reluctant to do: "Their painful defeat, Zionist ideals and Israel's definition as the state of the Jewish people make it hard for Israel's Arabs to accept their minority status." (Shahar 2010, 300). "Accept their minority status," means agreeing to be second-class citizens by law.

The schoolbooks justify the segregation of the Arab citizens through the strategy of "existentialization" (Van Leeuwen 2008), which means, "that's the way it is" without further explanation. Following is one example:

---

28. Ministry of Education, Economy and Government Administration September 2020. Cited by Or Kashti in Haaretz.

> Part of the Bedouin population dwells in forty five settlements unrecognized by the authorities. Therefore, they do not receive regular services such as municipal budgets, water, electricity, health and welfare services. (Shahar 2010).

No explanation is given as to how these people, who have lived for centuries in the same area, came to be "unrecognized."

Being Citizens in Israel (2016, 103) links the inadequate services provided to the Bedouins to the fact that they (5.3% of the population) are poor and participate less in the labor market, failing to mention that there are Bedouin officers and soldiers, physicians, surgeons, nurses and scientists, educators, and artists. It reinforces their image as primitive nomads who resist modernization and evade the law. To legitimate or to gloss over the discrimination of native Bedouins, this schoolbook equates their villages with small Israeli illegal outposts that are frequently built across the border, on Palestinian private lands in the West Bank. The book informs us that both types of settlement "claim" they have rights to the land of their ancestors, and are unrecognized by the state. To establish equivalence between illegal Jewish colonial settlers and Bedouin autochthones, the book explains that both types of settlement "are not in the state's master plan" and do not have a municipality. Therefore, every building they build is "necessarily illegal" according to Israeli law. Some of them "are not connected to electricity and water, to sewage or to the telephone network, and no asphalt road leads to them." (p. 103). The fact that the Bedouins have actually lived on the same lands for centuries is presented as their argument, while their "illegal" status earned by not adhering to their colonizer's norms and administrative ways is asserted as fact. The schoolbook justifies the ongoing dismantling of Bedouin villages by asserting that the state "seeks to concentrate the [Bedouins] in pre-planned townships but they refuse to relocate, arguing they are being uprooted from their lands (p. 397)." Bedouin resistance to these measures is presented as ingratitude on their part, which is punished by denying them elementary living conditions and repeatedly demolishing their villages (Nassra 2012).[29] The textbook fails to mention that the Jewish outposts are generally legalized after a while and that only two of them have been dismantled out of several hundreds.[30] Unlike the Bedouins, the Jewish invaders have never been evacuated or "concentrated" in shantytowns. They can live anywhere they choose, but Israel's land custodian, the Jewish National Fund, is permitted by law to refuse to sell or lease land to Palestinian citizens.[31] Furthermore, the text fails to mention that by "concentrating" the Bedouins the state violates their cultural and social rights (Galtung 2013). Their history, their

---

29. https://972mag.com/photos-israel-demolishes-homes-in-umm-el-hiran-amid-violence/124583/
30. https://www.btselem.org/topic/settlements.
See the recent case of the illegal outpost Eviatar: https://www.ynetnews.com/article/SyWv0qY2d
31. https://www.adalah.org/en/content/view/6787

tribal system, and their livelihood are all erased by the bureaucratic jargon of "master plan," "municipality," and "legality," before their settlements are actually razed. Their time-honored ways of affirming and acknowledging ownership are different and therefore unacceptable. This is an example of the colonized citizen being "différend" (Francois Lyotard 1988, 101). Lyotard explains:

> As distinguished from litigation, a différend would be a case of conflict between (at least) two parties, that cannot be equitably resolved for lack of a rule of judgment applicable to both arguments. [...] Applying a single rule of judgment to both in order to settle their différend, as though it were merely a litigation, would wrong (at least) one of them.

The lack of consideration of the Bedouins' land rights is what Lyotard defines as a "wrong." "A wrong result from the fact that the rules of the genre of discourse, by which one judges, are not those of the judged genre or genres of discourse." (ibid.)

Both the inclusion of Jewish settlements, considered illegal under international law, in the state of Israel, and the legitimation of the expulsion of the Bedouins from their lands, are justified by the need to maintain Israeli sovereignty. Thus, the schoolbook teaches that international law and decisions do not apply to "us" when it comes to settling the holy land, and legitimates the forced confinement of Bedouins in townships, promoting the notion that "the aliens ought to be kept beyond closely guarded borders or some sort of boundary-defining device in the passage to modern, 'garden-type' culture." (Bauman 1989, 68)

Legitimating Killing

> Sovereignty means the capacity to define who matters and who does not, who is disposable and who is not. (Achilles Mbembe, 2003, 80).

The last phase of persuasion, according to Bauman, is convincing the public, in our case schoolchildren, of the need to eliminate the alien group. Appadurai (2006, 60) notes that "Majorities can become predatory and ethnocidal [...] when some minorities remind them of the small gap which lies between their condition [...] and the horizon of [...] a pure and untainted national ethnos. [...] The fact of incomplete national purity [may] become susceptible to translation and mobilization in the service of building a predatory identity."

In a documentary titled *The Lab We Sell Weapons*,[32] Israeli former general and arm dealer Amiram Levin is shown addressing young officers regarding the killing of Palestinians. He says:

> Quantity is much more important than quality. You should not think who deserves to die and who doesn't. Most of these guys were born to die anyway so we need to help them.

In order to justify expulsion and killing, racist discourse often resorts to medical terminology and tends to describe the "racialized" as threat to health or an environmental hazard. The logic of this "medicalization" is that one can train and shape "healthy" parts of the body, but not a cancerous growth. The latter can be "improved" only by destroying it. "Cancer, vermin or weed cannot repent." (Bauman 1989, 72)

Israeli Prime minister Ben Gurion, ministers and Knesset members have often compared Palestinians to vermin, cancer, or poisonous snakes and proposed that they be killed (Pappe 2017). To cite but a few recent ones, former Minister of the Interior and of Justice Ayelet Shaked, who is a mother of five, suggested that Palestinian mothers be killed along with their terrorist sons: "They should follow their sons, nothing would be more just. They should go, as should the physical homes in which they raised the snakes. Otherwise, more little snakes will be raised there."[33] During the 2019 election campaign, retired general and former Minister of Defense, Benny Gantz, boasted having ordered, when he was chief of staff, the killing of around 1500 Palestinians in Gaza, among them more than five hundred children.[34] MK Smotrich suggested killing one Palestinian for every rocket launched from Gaza,[35] and former Prime Minister Naftali Bennet kept boasting that he killed many Palestinian with his bare hands, and on more than one occasion encouraged the killing of Palestinian children.[36]

This predatory tendency is exemplified in *Being Citizens in Israel* (2016), in a sub-chapter that addresses presidential amnesty. The schoolbook discusses, as an example, the presidential amnesty granted to the killers in the so-called "affair of

---

32. *The Lab We Sell Weapons*. Yotam Feldman, 2013.
https://www.youtube.com/watch?v=iabky5rvsGk
33. https://www.dailysabah.com/mideast/2014/07/14/mothers-of-all-palestinians-should-also-be-killed-says-israeli-politician; https://www.washingtonpost.com/news/worldviews/wp/2015/05/07/israels-new-justice-minister-considers-all-palestinians-to-be-the-enemy/?utm_term=.3b10cd2dea69
https://archive.is/zWrrG
34. https://www.timesofisrael.com/only-the-strong-survive-gantzs-new-campaign-videos-laud-his-idf-bona-fides/
35. https://www.middleeastmonitor.com/20190507-israel-mk-calls-for-1-palestinian-to-be-killed-for-each-rocket-fired/
See also Akiva Eldar: https://www.haaretz.com/.premium-koshering-the-vermin-1.5168166
36. https://www.timesofisrael.com/bennett-says-idf-should-shoot-to-kill-gazans-who-cross-border/

bus line 300", 1984 (p. 429). The details of the affair are as follows: on April 12, 1984, a bus was highjacked by four young Palestinians. Two died as the army stormed the bus, along with an Israeli female soldier; the other two were beaten to death by security service officers who arrived at the site during the night, upon the order of the head of the security services Avraham Shalom, in what was later described as "a lynching orgy".[37] Nevertheless, the unit reported that the two Palestinians had died in battle, but press photographers Shmuel Rachmani and Alex Levac published a few days later photographs that proved this claim was false (The newspaper that published the photographs was temporarily closed down for bypassing the military censor). The schoolbook report ends rather critically, as follows: "The two remaining terrorists were executed after the Secret Service agents laid hands on them, following the command of the Secret Service chief, contrary to the law that forbids the killing of terrorists who do not constitute a danger to public welfare. Following a series of committees and clarifications, during which the security service officers subverted the investigation, the government attorney recommended that four security service officers be indicted. President Chaim Hertzog pardoned them before the trial could take place."[38]

The questions at the end of the chapter concern the different functions of the president, and the students are not required to address the "affair" of the savage killing, which only serves as the context. Thus, the reader is prompted to ignore the execution of unarmed captured teenagers by fully armed army officers, and focus on the pardon given before trial, which demonstrates the discretion of the president to grant such a pardon. In Kress's terms, the *criterial feature* of the event, which warranted its inclusion in this chapter as an example, is the presidential amnesty. The lack of a credible explanation regarding both the killing and the amnesty, accords with the colonialist view whereby the killing of the "absolute enemy," namely the native or the colonized, is not considered murder and the killers should not be held accountable. (Mbembe 2003, 89).

The Bus 300 affair is mentioned in another schoolbook, *Democratic Values and Judaism* (2009), published by the Hartman Institute that advertises itself as "a Jewish research and education institute that offers pluralistic Jewish thought and education to scholars, rabbis, educators, and Jewish community leaders in Israel and North America" (https://www.hartman.org.il/). The "affair" features in a chapter about human rights, in a sub-chapter titled: "relationships between majority and minority." The section asserts the moral right of Israel to violate human rights when "terrorists" or their supporters are concerned. It starts with a

---

37. Giddi Weitz, Haaretz, February 28, 2013.
https://www.haaretz.com/2013-04-06/ty-article/.premium/how-lies-shielded-israels-secret-service/0000017f-dbc3-db22-a17f-fff3441d0000
38. See also: https://www.haaretz.co.il/magazine/1.1940280#commentsSection

text by Judge Aharon Barak, who affirms the right of the state to violate the law of human dignity and liberty in order to protect itself:

> Human rights are not a stage for national extermination. A constitution is not a recipe for national suicide. (p. 56).

Image 38. The two Palestinian boys who were captured in the Bus 300 affair. Courtesy of the photographer Shmuel Rachmani.

Below this text, at the top of the next page, is the photograph of "The two terrorists captured in the bus no. 300 affair." (Image 38). The photo shows General Itzhak Mordechay, then chief paratrooper commander, holding his gun in one hand and a young boy in another, running and shouting. Another young boy is next to the first one, head bowed, held by secret service man Ehud Yatom (who ordered the murder of the two boys later that night. Zamir 2019[39]); a third soldier pushes this boy from behind. For Israeli readers the photograph contains all the elements that allow a legitimating interpretation. The paratroopers — Israel's greatest role models, and the figure of Mordechay, who was a decorated hero, inspire confidence in the just cause, although it involves murder. For Israeli readers, the "affair" leaves no room for empathy with the Palestinian youngsters who highjacked a bus; nor does the text mention the fact that they were very young (the killers repeatedly called them "boys" and "children" in their investigations, Weitz 2013.). The label "terrorists" justifies the murder, because in

---

39. Prof Yitzhak Zamir, Attorney General of Israel at the time, intimates in his report that Israeli public opinion sided with the murderers and was against the investigation, once the murder was revealed. https://www.gov.il/he/departments/publications/reports/roots_1984. 10.3.2019 (Hebrew).

Israeli social and political discourse Palestinian minors who disrupt order are simply "terrorists" and are treated as such.[40]

In a less biased context, this example may have occupied a less marginal place, and may have raised questions about the murder itself, about the way it was carried out, or about the predatory nature of the killers. It could have prompted a highly relevant discussion about what motivates Palestinian youngsters to undertake such a mission, and would have perhaps led to a comparison between the motivation of young Palestinians to serve their people's struggle and become freedom fighters, and Israeli youngsters' motivation to serve in the army.

Palestinian Death

Eliminating the adversary is not an end in itself, explains Bauman (1989, 91). "It is a means to an end [...]. *The end itself is a grand vision of a better, and radically different, society.*" (Italics in the original). Therefore, most Israeli schoolbooks legitimate the killing of Palestinians by means of *consequential explanations*, namely on the strength of the far-reaching positive consequences for Israel, which are turned a-posteriori into a cause (Peled-Elhanan 2012). This orientation teaches what Elias Canetti (1984) calls the logic of survival: "Each enemy killed makes the survivor feel more secure." Achilles Mbembe, who quotes this phrase of Canetti (2003, IV) adds, "In the logic of survival the horror experienced upon seeing death turns into the satisfaction that the dead person is another. It is the death of the Other, the Other's physical presence as a corpse, that makes the survivor feel unique."

Here are two examples:

Domka et al. (2009, 159)[41] specify that "between 2700 and 5000 Palestinian infiltrators, most of them unarmed, were killed during the years 1949-1956 by the forces of the IDF. PM Moshe Sharet criticized the behavior of the IDF towards these infiltrators". Nevertheless, the chapter ends with the sentence (p. 161): "These actions contributed to the strengthening of the feeling of security among Israeli citizens."

One of the questions following this chapter presents a newspaper from 1956 whose main headline is:

> 50 Egyptians were killed, 40 were taken prisoners – the greatest operation since the War of Independence.

---

40. See: Viterbo, Hedi. 2021. *Problematizing Law, Rights, and Childhood in Israel/Palestine.* Cambridge University Press.
41. Domka Eliezer, Goldberg Tzafrir, and Urbach Hannah 2009.Nationalism - building a state in the Middle East. Shazar Institute Pub. Jerusalem, Israel.

And the questions are:

1) In what way can such a headline influence the morale of Israeli citizens?
2) Why did Israel choose to carry out 'reprisals', though they often involved the killing of innocent people?

The obvious answers, according to Israeli norms, would be retaliation and deterrence, which both contributed to the morale of Israeli citizens according to this book.

In the same line, though less bluntly, Naveh et al. (2009a, 205) pose a question regarding these 'reprisals':

> "Do you think the reprisals were enough to deter the Arabs from acting against Israel?"

Both in schoolbooks and in the media, the language used to report Palestinians' death is not that used for human beings, but for animals or objects. Palestinians are never referred to as "victims," and when soldiers are sent to kill them "they are told to shoot *targets*, which *fall* when they are *hit*." (Bauman 1989, 103) For instance, in Blank's schoolbook (2006:244) we read that in the Kibya massacre and other such "reprisals",

> Most of the raids were aimed at civilian targets, and included stake-outs and incursions deep behind the border lines.

Values and Citizens (2014, 334) addressing the 1929 clashes between Arabs and Jews, concludes that "the events in Hebron terminated the Jewish presence in the city and took sixty seven Jewish lives. Many Arabs were killed as well." Regarding the Jews, the events are personalized. The Arabs actively "took Jewish lives" while the Arabs (and not "Arab lives") were passively killed "as well" in the process. Their death is a side effect of terminating the Jewish presence in Hebron.

Bauman contends that for nation states, during the "gardening" of the desired society, eliminating the superfluous or the threatening others does not destroy anything but rather creates something new and positive. Thus, alongside reports of killings the schoolbooks provide invariably depictions of achievements, improved conditions, and salvation of the Jewish people (Peled-Elhanan 2012).

Representation of the Killers

In Israeli eyes, as in the eyes of other settler-colonizers before them, there is no link between the colonizers' identity and their "predatory" actions toward the natives. Piterberg (2008) argues that Israeli history and identity are divided into two different narratives: who we are is what we find in the Bible and in Zionist utopia. Israelis are heroes, victims and the harbingers of progress. Occupation and ethnic cleansing is what they do. These two narratives that are inextricably intertwined are completely separate in Israeli-Zionist education, as exemplified in the above examples and in testimonies of soldiers who break the silence.[42] Settler-colonial discourse in general (Pappe 2012) focuses on the settlers' intentions rather than on the outcome of their actions. In schoolbooks, Israeli killers are appraised for what they are regardless of what they have done. They are portrayed as moral, good, and loyal to friends and country, although they perform horrible acts when the good of the nation demands it (Peled-Elhanan 2012). When dealing with Palestinians, the "moral color" of the act, in Johan Galtung's words (2013, 292), changes "from red/wrong to green/right or at least to yellow/acceptable." This means that "murder on behalf of the country is right, on behalf of oneself wrong." The educational lesson is that such upstanding patriots could not have done unnecessary wrong. Visually, the killers are always portrayed as legendary figures and role models for Israeli youth. Tall, handsome and clean.

As Bauman (1989, 104) argues, "Dehumanization of the objects and positive moral self-evaluation reinforce each other." This way, young Israelis may "faithfully serve any goal while their moral conscience remains unimpaired."

---

42. See Breaking the Silence.
https://www.amazon.com/Our-Harsh-Logic-Testimonies-Territories/dp/0805095373
http://www.breakingthesilence.org.il/protective-edge

Chapter 11. The Nazification of Palestinians

> There are Thousands of Eichmanns near the borders of Israel. One hundred and fifty meters from the courtroom there is a border, and behind that border thousands of Eichmanns lie in wait, proclaiming explicitly, 'what Eichmann has not completed, we will.' (Davar daily newspaper, June 12, 1961.)[1]

Historian Idit Zertal (2005) cites this statement to show the official Nazification of the Arabs during the Eichmann trial in 1961. In fact, as was mentioned in the introduction, it began earlier, in 1951, when Prime Minister David Ben Gurion justified the reparations agreement with Germany by saying "We do not want the Arab Nazis to come and slaughter us." (Segev 2019, 481). Schoolbooks, which reflect the orientation of the authorities, have adhered to this comparison ever since.

Zimmerman (2023, 32) contends that German nationalism, which served as a model for Jewish nationalism, taught the Jewish nationalists to look for the eternal enemy. The Arabs in the neighboring countries and the Palestinians, especially since they created their own national consciousness, have been conceived as this new enemy, and replaced the European Nazis. Equating the country's Muslim neighbors, its Palestinian citizens and its occupied subjects with Nazis, turns them from "the victims of the victims" to accomplices of the German perpetrators (Zimmerman 2023) and provides a powerful incentive to fight and oppress them. Waging war against the Nazified enemy, and the risk of dying in this battle have become, according to Zertal (2005, 11) l, "the belated vindication of the fathers' helplessness in the face of the Nazi enemy. One enemy was combined with the other. Defense of one's country became a sacred mission endowed with the weight of the ultimate catastrophe."

If Palestinians were not conceived to be mighty Nazis, then risking death while fighting them would not be all that heroic, as the "hereditary victims" of the Holocaust need it to be. As Bauman (2000,19)[2] explains, "in a world haunted by the ghost of the Holocaust such assumed would-be persecutors are guilty in advance, guilty of *being seen* as inclined or able to engage in another genocide. [...] The ethics of hereditary victimhood reverse the logic of the law: the accused remain criminals until they have proven their innocence; and since it is their prosecutors who conduct the hearings and decide the validity of the argument,

---

1. Yosef Almogi, Mapai's Secretary General in an electoral speech during the Eichmann trial in 1961.
2. *The Holocaust's Life as a Ghost. In:* Social Theory after the Holocaust.

they have only a slim chance of having their arguments accepted in court and every chance of staying guilty for a long time to come, whatever they do."

The discourse of Nazification is frequently employed by officers and soldiers who are convinced that whatever they do to Israel's colonized Palestinians will save their country from a second Holocaust.[3]

One of these soldiers and a role model for Israeli youth is Ofer Feniger, who was "one of many, sensitive young 'children of the dream', the golden youths of the Israeli Zionist utopia, the very stuff of which the atoning redemptive discourse was made." (Zertal 2005, 111). The teachers' guide to the Ka-Tzetnik project of the 1990s, in which high school students were asked to write essays following the reading of Ka-Tzetnik's Holocaust novels, begins with a letter that Feniger wrote to his girlfriend:

> I have just finished *The House of Dolls* by Ka-Tzetnik and I feel that from within all this horror and impotence arises in me a tremendous power to be strong: strong to tears. Ferocious. Sharp as a knife. Silent and terrible. No more abyss-deep eyes behind barbed wire [...] we must be strong. Strong, proud Jews! Never again to be led to the slaughter. Is there a better feeling for a soldier than to be quiet, alert, and dangerous?[4]

Ofer Feniger wrote this letter in the wake of the Eichmann trial, just before he was drafted and volunteered to serve in an elite parachutist unit. He was killed on the Ammunition Hill in North Jerusalem during the 1967 war. Zertal points out that "in his life and premature death in the battle of East Jerusalem, the good Israeli soldier-boy Ofer Feniger, like many other young Israelis killed in the war, narrated the teleological story of *Hurban U'ge'ulah* (Destruction and Redemption), forged by Ben-Gurion by means of the Eichmann trial." By 'rescuing' Israel from the allegedly imminent, Holocaust-like destruction it faced on the eve of the war, and by 'liberating' Jerusalem, the sacred, ancient heart of the land of Israel, "Ofer Feniger enacted with his own body the recurring Jewish historical pattern of national revival as the outcome of destruction." (ibid.) His death, like that of all other Israeli combatants, "was thought to have saved the millions who might have been annihilated had Israel not gone to war and won as spectacularly as it did" (p.112). Contrary to Holocaust victims, Ofer and others "hereditary victims" like him died a "beautiful death," namely a "heroic death, in which mortality is traded for immortality." (Lyotard, 1988,100).[5] Lyotard explains the difference between these two types of death (p. 100):

---

3. See the publications of Breaking the Silence
4. Ofer Feniger's letter to his girlfriend Yael, in: Feniger Ofer 1972. *Ha'olam Haya Betokhi* (The World Was Within Me), Tel Aviv. Levin and Epstein Publishers. 52–53.
5. *The Differend*, 1988 University of Minnesota Press. Glossary.

> Public authority (family, state, military) can order its own addressees to die, or at least to prefer to die. The Die needs to be modalized: Die rather than escape (Socrates in prison), Die rather than be enslaved. Die rather than be defeated. [...] This is not the case for "Auschwitz," [where] it is not a Die rather than [...] but simply a Die that the SS authorities address to the deportee, with no alternative [...]. "Auschwitz" is the forbiddance of the beautiful death [...]. The deportee [...] cannot be the addressee of an order to die, because one would have to be capable of giving one's life in order to carry out the order. But one cannot give a life that one doesn't have the right to have. Sacrifice is not available to the deportee, nor for that reason accession to an immortal, collective name." The individual name and the collective name (Jew) must be killed in such a way "that no 'we' bearing this name might remain which could take the deportee's death into itself and eternalize it." Hence, death itself must be killed, "and that is what is worse than death. For, if death can be exterminated, it is because there is nothing to kill. Not even the name Jew."

This is the ugly, humiliating death of the Jews that Ben-Gurion and Israeli education have taught Israeli youth to despise and to rectify with a beautiful death such as Ofer's, the immortalized self-sacrificing Israeli soldier.

Equating Palestinians (and Jewish peace activists) to Nazis brought about the murder of former Prime Minister Rabin, who was likened to Hitler on placards displayed in the demonstrations prior to his assassination. His killer, Yigal Amir, is to this day compared by his admirers to the Jewish partisans during World War II (Zertal 2005, 199). He was also described as "'the salt of the earth,' an ardent Zionist, a reserve soldier, a dedicated, well-educated, lover of Eretz Israel, who undertook to save the homeland from a second Holocaust even at the price of self-sacrifice" (Zertal 2005, 198). Zertal identifies the foundations of Amir's zeal in the educational courses Israeli soldiers attend during their service, such as "The Holocaust and its Significance,"[6] and the "IDF Guide to the Historical Museum".[7] These army educational courses teach that to act in a hopeless situation, to take one's fate into one's own hand, is the true heroism, equal to that of the Jewish partisan who transformed himself "from nothing to a man in charge of his own destiny, and when he was given weapons, he underwent a spiritual transformation beyond description. The weapon not only conferred security, but also restored his personal confidence as a human being." (Zertal, ibid.)

Just as Israeli politicians ignited and stoked the sense of an imminent Shoah in the weeks leading up to the 1967 war, so did they, with the help of the press,

---

6. In: *Basic Texts for Education in the IDF*. Barnea, Aryeh (ed.) Tel Aviv (Manpower Division, Chief Educational Officer) undated, pp. 1–3.
7. Guide to the Historical Museum, a pamphlet prepared for IDF educational personnel. Lapid, Maya (author and editor). Jerusalem. Yad Vashem-Education Department Army Unit. 1–8.

equated Sadam Hussein with Hitler during the 1991 Gulf War.[8] However, contrary to the 1967 war, during the Gulf War Israelis felt they would be deprived of the privilege to die a heroic beautiful death, and would indeed be slaughtered like sheep for being Jewish. This feeling amplified the fear of a new Holocaust and facilitated identification with Holocaust victims, according to Israeli schoolbooks.

The Nazification of Palestinians in Israeli schoolbooks

Schoolbooks explain that Israelis, who always die a "beautiful death," were unable to understand or sympathize with Holocaust victims who died an ugly and degrading one, until they themselves felt that they were about to die an ugly, humiliating "Holocaust-like" death at the hands of the Arab enemies and Palestinian terrorists. Only then could they gain a sense of their vulnerability and helplessness, or in other words, their "Jewishness."

In the 2017 history matriculation exam, the following question appeared in the section titled "The Formation of Holocaust Remembrance":

> Consider the following events:
>
> The murder of (Israeli) athletes in Munich (by Palestinian terrorists 1972), The Yom Kippur War (1973), The (Palestinian) terrorist attack in Maalot (1974).
>
> Choose one of these events and explain its impact on the formation of Holocaust remembrance (10 points).

For every subject on the Israeli curriculum there is a textbook titled *Focus on...*, which summarizes the major topics students are required to study for their final examination (matriculation, A-level) during their last year of high-school. These textbooks are issued each year according to the Ministry's guidelines for the exams. *Focus on History* (2020)[9] gathers together all the chapters the students are required to study toward their final examination in that subject. The chapter about the Holocaust, which they are required to study, is titled "The formation of Holocaust Remembrance in Israel" (pp.134-136). These three pages do not address the Holocaust as such, but rather survey the changes in the conception of the Shoah and its commemoration among the Israeli public. They briefly trace the trajectory of Israeli attitudes toward the Holocaust and Holocaust survivors from the 1950s onward, noting for instance, that 1952 marked the signing of the

---

8. Zuckerman, Moshe. 1993. *Shoah in the Sealed Room*.
9. Cohen, Sagi. 2020. *Mikud History*. Rehes Publishers.

reparation agreement with Germany, and this, the text explains, demonstrates the role of the state of Israel as the representative of all the survivors.

Yet, what primarily led the Israeli public to truly identify with Holocaust victims were several events linked to the Arab countries' aggression and the Palestinians' violent resistance to Israel's occupation of their land, both of which are presented, as in all other schoolbooks, as inexplicable heinous attacks on innocent Jews.

The first of these events, reports *Focus,* is the 1967 war in which Israel conquered parts of Jordan, Syria, and Egypt and occupied the whole of Palestine in just six days. However, during what was termed "the waiting period" - the three weeks of indecision prior to Israel's attacks on its neighbors - a sense of imminent catastrophe prevailed in the country as the Israeli public lived in great fear of being on the verge of extermination again.

Referring to this period, Zertal (2005, 189) quotes the Labor leader Yitzhak Tabenkin as declaring that "the Holocaust that threatened Israel in May–June 1967 was even more devastating than that which the Nazis had inflicted on the Jews of Europe. The pre-fifth of June borders have brought down a Shoah on our heads, and this Shoah is graver than the Nazi Holocaust, because after that Holocaust some Jews remained, capable of rebuilding the nation and establishing the state, whereas if now [Heaven] forbid, the state were to be annihilated, it is doubtful whether the Jewish people could rise again." After the 1967 victory, Tabenkin wrote, "If we had been defeated in the war, we would have been exterminated, as individuals and as a people, and thus, in this war we continued the war of the ghetto fighters."[10]

The 1973 war too is portrayed by *Focus* as an event that made Israelis feel like Holocaust victims. This war, although won by Israel, forced it to "return" some of the territories it had conquered from Syria and Egypt in 1967. In both wars, the text emphasizes, Israelis experienced **"loss, bereavement, and existential danger, which allowed them to identify more easily with Holocaust survivors and allocate a place of honor to their stories in Israeli society"** (p.136, bold in the original).

Other "grave security events" that exposed the "weakness and vulnerability" of the Jews in Israel and led them to identify with Holocaust victims were, according to this textbook, the following: 1. the murder of the Israeli athletes in Munich during the Olympic games in 1972 "on the land of Germany" by a Palestinian terror organization. This event "made room for bereavement and pain and facilitated identification with Holocaust survivors." 2. The Ma'alot attack: "in

---

10. Tabenkin, Yitzhak. 1971. "The Determinant Act." In: The Lesson of the Six Day War: Settling an Undivided Land (Lekah Sheshet Ha'yamim: Yishuva shel Eretz Bilti Mehuleket). Tel Aviv. 44.
Tabenkin, Yitzhak. 1971. "The Lesson of the War without Illusion," In: *The Lesson of the Six-Day War*, p. 19.

1974 terrorists invaded the Jewish settlement Maalot and took hostages: teachers and students. The attempt to rescue them failed and twenty-two of them were killed. This traumatic event exposed the weakness and vulnerability of Israelis in the face of terror and led them to adopt a different attitude toward Holocaust survivors."

One schoolbook, (Barnavi1998, 244), covers the incident more fully, mentioning Prime Minister Rabin's refusal to negotiate with the terrorists from the Democratic Front for the Liberation of Palestine, who took over the school in an attempt to negotiate the release of their twenty three comrades jailed in Israel. The 2020 *Focus* textbook, though it alludes that it was unclear who shot the children, portrays the event as an arbitrary heinous slaughter of Jews by Jew haters.

The third event that made Israelis identify with Holocaust survivors was, according to *Focus*, the hijacking of an Air France aircraft to Entebbe by Palestinian terrorists in 1976. The book asserts: "Like other terrorist attacks this event also exposed the weakness and the vulnerability of the Israelis against their enemies and enabled many Israelis to identify with Holocaust survivors and to be attentive to their stories."

Eleven years prior to the appearance of *Focus* 2020, Avieli-Tabibian (*Journeys in Time*, 2009, 270), reproduced the same text, emphasizing that two of the hijackers were German and that the terrorists separated the Jewish passengers from all the others, and this "reinforced the feeling of persecution."

Avieli-Tabibian does not differentiate between Israeli civilians and soldiers, stressing that it was the 1973 war, which produced photographs of Israeli soldiers being led to Egyptian prisoner of war camps that transformed the self-image of the invincible Israeli into that of the helpless persecuted Jew, once again. (p.271)

In addition to the de-contextualization of the attacks, *Focus* 2020 reiterates, in the description of each of the events, the "exposure of Israeli weakness and vulnerability," thereby prompting students to forget or ignore Israel's powerful army, its nuclear weapons and its remarkable military victories. It conceals the occupation of Palestine and Israel's oppressive rule over five million Palestinians, as well as the collective punishments meted out following the terrorist attacks. The textbook equates both Israeli civilians and soldiers to the helpless, unarmed and unprepared Jewish victims in the ghetto. The Israeli Jews who vowed never to resemble "these other Jews," are once again cast as the victims of murderous, hateful, and gratuitous attacks of anti-Semites. The colonized oppressed Palestinians, who are generally depicted as primitive, vile, lawless and underdeveloped (Peled-Elhanan, 2012), are transformed in the *Focus* chapter into almighty Nazis.

Other means of Palestinian Nazification to be found in the schoolbooks are the equation of Arafat to Hitler (Barnavi 1998 quoting PM Begin), and the recurring reference to the Palestinian Mufti of Jerusalem, Haj Amin Al Husseini, who met with Hitler and allegedly urged him to exterminate the Jews

(Hertz, 2015). In making this assertion, the books fall into line with an ongoing political discourse at the highest level. Prime Minister Ben-Gurion was the first to make this allegation and Prime Minister Netanyahu amplified it decades later, when he actually accused the Mufti of instigating the Final Solution, flying in the face of historical evidence. (Zimmerman 2023, Bauer 2022).[11] However, as Zimmerman and Zuckerman argue, historians become irrelevant when "the target is pre-painted" to suit the nationalistic world view shared by right wing and liberal Zionists. (p.75). This political discourse seems to have more influence on some history schoolbooks.[12]

Enlisting the authority of leaders, the books quote former foreign minister Abba Eban, who spoke of Israel's "Auschwitz borders," and former prime minister Begin, who declared that Israel's attack on Palestinian refugee camps in Lebanon had saved us "from another Treblinka" (Peled-Elhanan 2012).

In conclusion, nothing positive is ever written about the Palestinians or the Arab countries, their cultures are never described, and they are all portrayed as seeking to "exterminate us again," as if they were the direct anti-Semitic successors of Nazi Germany (e.g. Mishol 2014 who writes about "Arab Antisemitism"). In the words of the celebrated Israeli author, David Grossman,

> The Israelis, the citizens of the strongest military power in the region, are once again, with strange enthusiasm, walling themselves up behind their sense of persecution, [seeing themselves as] vulnerable victims. The Palestinian threat, ridiculous in terms of the balance of power, but effective in its results, has returned Israel, with depressing speed, to the experience of living in fear of total destruction. This, of course, justifies a brutal response to the threat.[13]

It therefore appears that the interest of Israeli education as manifested in the *Focus* and other textbooks is to echo the political military discourse and to re-enact the

---

11. Holocaust historian Yehuda Bauer (15.12.2022). "What does Netanyahu know about the Holocaust? Not much". https://www.nytimes.com/2015/10/22/world/middleeast/netanyahu-saying-palestinian-mufti-inspired-holocaust-draws-broad-criticism.html
vol. 26, no. 3/4, 2014, pp. 13–37. *JSTOR*, http://www.jstor.org/stable/43922000.
Bauer, Yehuda 2013. https://www.haaretz.com/2013-02-21/ty-article/.premium/prof-bibi-doesnt-know-history-strategy/0000017f-f824-d2d5-a9ff-f8ac65880000.
Bauer Yehuda 15.12.2022. What does Netanyahu know about the Holocaust? Not much. https://www.haaretz.co.il/opinions/2022-12-15/ty-article-opinion/.premium/00000185-15be-d041-a3ad-15ffa6ff0000
12. See for instance Herf, Jeffrey. "Haj Amin Al-Husseini, the Nazis and the Holocaust: The Origins, Nature and Aftereffects of Collaboration." *Jewish Political Studies Review*, vol. 26, no. 3/4, 2014, pp. 13–37. *JSTOR*, http://www.jstor.org/stable/43922000.
13. Grossman, David. 2002. "Israel Has Won for Now, But What Is Victory When It Brings No Hope?" *The Guardian*, G2, September 30, 2002. 3 – 22.

trauma, while disavowing the Holocaust victims as diasporic Jews whom "we" do not wish to resemble (Yosefa Loshitzky 2006).

As we saw in the teacher's guide for grade 2, the message conveyed in Israeli schoolbooks regarding the threat of another Shoah and the portrayal of Palestinians and Arab countries as potential exterminators, is not confined to high-school textbooks but is inculcated from a very young age.

Yosefa Loshitzky (2006) remarks that "The disavowal of the old Jew and the displacement of the revenge fantasy from the powerful Gentile to the powerless and dispossessed Palestinian, from whom the land was taken by force, resulted ironically in the oppressor turning himself into a victim."[14]

Concluding Remarks

> Israeli Jewish consciousness is characterized by a sense of victimization, a siege mentality, blind patriotism, belligerence, self-righteousness, dehumanization of the Palestinians and insensitivity to their suffering.[15]

This chapter traced the creation of both a "past" and a "present" for future soldiers, through the othering of twenty one percent of Israel's citizens and the entire population of the occupied Palestinian territories, legitimating their exclusion, dehumanization and killing, and equating them with German Nazis. The interest motivating this distorted representation appears to be, to ease the path of the students into military service, during which they will be required to commit acts that contradict all the values and norms they have been taught to respect, especially those regarding human rights to freedom, dignity, and a fair trial. The one-sided, simplistic, and biased presentation of the enduring occupation and the permanent state of exception in which Palestinians live, likewise attests to the interest of the authors to show Israel's future citizens how their state defends itself against accusations on the part of human rights defenders and international law. As Coffin (2006) asserts, textbooks often teach the language of politicians, lawyers and generals, at the expense of disciplinary truth. Schoolbooks in Israel inculcate a settler-colonial logic of exclusion and elimination (Pappe 2012) as the only logic that applies to the relationships with Palestinian co-citizens and colonized neighbors. They employ racist discourse to describe these "others" as deserving confinement, distancing, and elimination, thus promoting "elite racism" (Reisigle and Wodak 2001), which is a strain of racism that is dictated from above

---

14. Loshitzky, Yosefa. 2006. "Pathologising Memory from the Holocaust to the Intifada." Third Text, Vol. 20, Issue 3/4, May/July: 327–335. Third Text ISSN 0952-8822 print/ISSN 1475-5297 online © Third Text (2006) http://www.tandf.co.uk/journals DOI: 10.1080/09528820600853761
15. Bar-Tal and Nets-Zehngut (2008).

and is inculcated through schoolbooks, the press, parliamentary speeches, and history books. This racism inscribes itself in practices - forms of violence, contempt, intolerance, humiliation and exploitation, and in discourses and representations, which express the need to purify the social body, to preserve 'our' identity from all forms of mixing, interbreeding or invasion, and which are articulated around stigmata of otherness (name, skin colour, religious practices) (Balibar 1991), or, as we have seen, the very presence of people where they are not wanted.

Institutionalizing the "otherness" of the Palestinians through the erasure of their memory, their representation as nothing but problems and threat, and the visual depiction of the "terra nullius" narrative, along with the overriding rights endowed to the Jews by the Holocaust and the Bible, provide moral justification for the colonization of Palestine. Such a narrative "suppresses any sense of Israeli guilt and legal or moral responsibility for colonizing the people, violating their rights and needs, or taking the collective punitive actions against them" (Brockhill & Cordell 2019, 12), and leaves no room for questioning.

The Palestinians' portrayal in schoolbooks justifies the direct and structural violence to which they fall victim and renders it acceptable. Therefore, the schoolbooks' texts and visuals can be defined as producing cultural violence: "Cultural violence makes direct and structural violence look, even feel, right or at least not wrong" (Galtung 2013, 292). This cultural violence affects not only Palestinian citizens and subjects but also Israeli schoolchildren. The inculcation of fear and racism with regard to neighbors and co-citizens, and the legitimation of colonialist violence, harm the students by excluding the possibility of empathy towards others, thus turning them into heterophobic beings who regard others as non-human, or at least less human than themselves. It makes them prone to inflict violence without scruples (or sometimes with scruples), once they are drafted into the army, believing this is the way to save their people from another *Shoah*. In order to persuade these youngsters that the transgression of the laws and norms they were taught to respect and obey is legitimate, the books employ a religious and political-legal legitimating discourse while foreclosing the "other version" - that of the victims. That is because, as Naveh (2019, 303)[16] argues, "a genuine and serious discussion of the conflict might shatter some of the hegemonic norms about the righteousness of the Zionist cause and dampen the overall celebratory nature of traditional history education, which praises the Zionist narrative and views it as the only way to inculcate pride and patriotism in the younger generation."

---

16. "Israel" In: *The Palgrave Handbook of Conflict and History Education in the Post-Cold War Era.* Luigi Cajani, Simone Lassing, Maria Repoussi Eds. 297-307.

Hence, it is no surprise that the state of Israel has never encouraged peace education or any official mixing between Jewish and Palestinian-Israeli students. This also explains the prohibition to use the two series of the joint Israeli-Palestinian textbooks that juxtapose the two official narratives against one another. [17] The series were translated into many languages and are used in many European schools as a model of peace education and conflict resolution but were not accepted by the Israeli Ministry of Education and are not allowed in any Jewish or Arab school in Israel. [18]

---

17. Edited by Sami Adwan, Dan Bar-On and Eyal Naveh, and written by Palestinian and Israeli teachers.
18. The two series are: Sami Adwan, Dan Bar-On, Eyal Naveh (editors). 2012. *Side by Side: Parallel Histories of Israel-Palestine*. Peace Research Institute in the Middle East. The New Press; and *Learning about Each Other's Narrative*. 2007. The Van Leer Institute and Al Quds University.

Chapter 12. The Othering of Arab Jews

This chapter addresses the representation of Israelis who came from Muslim countries, in current schoolbooks.

Just as Palestinians feel they have become "the victims of the victims," or "the Jews of the Jews", as Edward Said defined them, so do many non-European Jews who were brought to Israel after the Holocaust. As scholar Shoshana Madmoni-Gerber phrases it, "The [European] Jews, besides being victims, made their own brothers and sisters, other Jews, victims on racist grounds, and this a few years after the Shoah."[1] While Palestinians form a captive nation, Arab Jews or Mizrahim formed a semi-colonized nation-within-the-nation (Shohat 2017, 104).[2]

Arab Jews

> The desire to define Israel as part of the West and in opposition to the Arab world has resulted in the erasure of the histories and traditions of Jews from Muslim countries. (Raz-Krakotzkin 2005,167.)

After the Holocaust and the loss of the European Jews who were to populate the future Jewish state in Palestine, the Zionist leadership encouraged, accepted, and facilitated the mass immigration of Jews from Islamic countries, and subsequently from Ethiopia and the former Soviet Union.[3] "Originally, 'Oriental' Jews were neither included in the Zionist vision, nor in the category of "the Jewish people." (Raz Krakotzkin 2005).[4] Zionism was designed to solve the problems of East-

---

1. Madmoni-Garber, Shoshana. 2019. "Reportage or Whitewash? The Yemenite Children Affair as Reflected in Israeli Media." In *Children of the Heart. The Yemenite Children Affair. Legal, Historical and Cultural Aspects*, edited by Tova Gamliel and Nathan Shifris. Tel Aviv: Resling (Hebrew); Shohat, Ella. "Sephardim in Israel: Zionism from the Standpoint of Its Jewish Victims." *Social Text* no. 19/20 (Autumn, 1988): 1-35; Chetrit, Sami. 2004. *The Mizrahi Struggle in Israel. Between Oppression and Liberation. Identification and Alternative*. Tel Aviv: Am Oved (Hebrew); Shenhav, Yehuda. 2006. *The Arab Jews. A Postcolonial Reading of Nationalism, Religion, and Ethnicity*. Stanford University Press; Derri, David. 2017. *Ancestral Sin*; https://www.youtube.com/watch?v=85_e3tYRyq8; https://www.docaviv.co.il/2017-en/films/the-ancestral-sin/; Yona, Yossi. 2008. "The Palestinian minority in Israel: when common core curriculum in education meets conflicting national narratives." *Journal of Intercultural Education* 19(2). 105-117. https://doi.org/10.1080/14675980801889633
2. *On the Arab-Jew, Palestine, and Other Displacements*. Selected writings. Pluto Press.
3. Segev, Naveh.
4. "Zionist Return to the West and the Mizrachi Jewish Perspective," in: I. Kalmar, D. Pensler Eds. *Orientalism and the Jews*. Waltham Mass.: Brandeis University Press, 2005, 162-181.

European Jews[5] and its ideology, which was secular in nature, "had nothing but contempt for [the Mizrahi] way of life which was considered primitive, feudal and unprogressive" (Kedouri 190, 309).[6] Hence, the Arab-Jews were brought to a place "founded on the explicit rejection of their culture and traditions" (ibid.). Many of the newcomers did not want to adhere to the ideal model of a secular Eurocentric society in the Middle East.[7] They had a hard time adjusting to the harsh conditions in the new state and to its partly Western and partly Bolshevik culture.

Arthur Ruppin, the Zionist leader who is known as the father of Zionist colonization, and the designer of Zionist culture and education (Bloom 2011)[8], was a fervent advocate of Eugenics. He believed that European Jews were a superior Indo-Germanic race, whereas the "oriental" Jews were an inferior Semitic race that fit the descriptions of anti-Semitic theories about the Jews (Bloom 2011, 98-99). As such, they were "an imminent threat to the regeneration of the "new Jew" (Bloom ibid.), and should be brought only to serve the European-Ashkenazi Hebrews. As for Ethiopian Jews, they did not belong to the Jewish race according to Ruppin (ibid. 104). Ruppin's theories have had immense influence on the social discourse of Israel and on its educational discourse.

Israel, like the Zionist leadership before its inception, sought to absorb large numbers of Jews for demographic reasons, with greater urgency following the Holocaust (Segev 2019, Naveh 1995). However, it did not initiate, nor wanted a mass immigration from the Muslim countries or from Ethiopia and in many cases was obliged to accept the immigrants by international and internal pressure (Meir-Glitzenstein 2021)[9]. The veteran Zionist leadership and the state of Israel that replaced it, have always sought to apply selective criteria to Jewish immigration, both prior to the Holocaust and after[10]. This policy was also applied to the immigrants from the "East" (the Mizrahim) and is applied to this day to the immigration from Ethiopia (Peled 2018).

The ideological Zionist narrative depicts Jewish non-European immigrants as rescued victims, although this salvation narrative is contested by many scholars.[11]

---

5. Naveh, Eyal. 1995. *The 20th Century, a Century That Has Upset the World Order*. Tel Aviv Books Publishers. (For high school).
6. Kedourie, Elie. 1970, 309, 311.
7. Derri, David. 2018. *Ancestral Sin*. A documentary film; Amir, Eli. 1983. *Scapegoat*. Am Oved Publishers (Hebrew).
8. Bloom, Etan. *Arthur Ruppin and the production of pre-Israeli culture*. Brill Publishers.
9. "Back to the Question of Arab-Jews' immigration." In: *This Time a Periodical for Political Thought, Culture and Science*. Van Leer Institute. Jerusalem. January 2021.
10. As explained in schoolbooks such as *Being Citizens in Israel* 2016 or Avieli-Tabibian 2009,145
11. Meir- Glitzenstein, Esther. 2004. Zionism in an Arab Country: Jews in Iraq in the 1940s. London and New York: Routledge. Meir-Glitzenstein, Esther. 2002. "Our Dowry: Identity and Memory among Iraqi Immigrants in Israel." *Middle Eastern Studies* 38, no. 2: 165-186; Meir-Glitzenstein, Esther. 2011.

Omri Ben Yehuda (2019, 380)[12] argues, that Israel has never been the savior of Diaspora Jews as it likes to present itself, but is rather "an ordinary immigration state with all its discriminatory features, and suffused with colonial approaches." The conception of Jews as victims of Muslim antisemitism and the "salvation" motif promoted by Israel's leaders and elites (Gamliel 2019) are reproduced in textbooks[13] that portray Israel as the savior of all Jews, from Holocaust survivors to the Ethiopian Jews, but fail to address the particular historical context of these communities.

Shohat (2017, 39) reproduces the Zionist narrative regarding Arab Jews as follows: Zionism took them out of the "primitive conditions" of poverty and superstition they had lived in and ushered them through loving and nurturing into modern Israeli Western society characterized by tolerance, democracy, and "humane values," with which they were but vaguely familiar given the "Levantine environments" from which they came. Within Israel, they have suffered from the problem of "the gap," not simply the gap between their standard of living and that of European Jews, but also because of their inferior minds, which had to be nurtured with great effort so that they could become "fully integrated" into Israeli liberalism and prosperity. Raz-Krakotzkin asserts that the general shared assumption was that the Mizrahim had to be civilized and could not be integrated as they were. Pedagogues, psychologists, and sociologists have debated whether the oriental Jews were innately retarded, in which case it was pointless to try to educate them, or whether they suffered from "secondary retardation" that resulted from their surroundings. The "primitive mentality" of the Mizrahim was compared to "the expression of children, the retarded and the mentally disturbed" (2005, 174). However, all agreed that some Mizrahi children could be rescued were they to be physically extracted from their traditional environment, and that "the north-African should not necessarily remain a north-African." (ibid.).

Arab Jews, asserts Shohat (2006, 222), "have been forbidden to nourish memories of having belonged to the peoples across the River Jordan, across the mountains of Lebanon, and across the Sinai desert and Suez Canal. The persistent narration of a formerly scattered 'one people' rejoined in their 'original homeland' delegitimizes any memory of communal life prior to the State of Israel." Although the culture of Egyptian Jews, North African Jews, Syrian, Iraqi, Lebanese and Libyan Jews, who lived in colonized countries, included more "Western" features than did the culture of East European or Ashkenazi Jews, they were rejected, and denigrated as oriental or "Levantine". They were first called "Jews from Asian

---

"Operation Magic Carpet: Constructing the Myth of the Magical Immigration of Yemenite Jews to Israel." Israel Studies 16, no. 3 (Fall): 149-173.
12. Ben-Yehuda, Omri. 2019. "Ma'abara. Mizraḥim between Shoah and Nakba." In: Bashir and Goldberg, *The Holocaust and the Nakba*.
13. Gamliel, Tova. 2019. *The Children of the Heart*. Tel Aviv: Resling (Hebrew).

and African lands", and more recently Mizrahim, making "Israelis" synonymous with "Ashkenazim" (Raz Krakotzkin 2005). Arab, Iranian, Turkish, Yemenite and North African Jews are classified as a single non-European out-group, Mizrahim. This "imagined community," is a Zionist invention, an attempt to reshape the identity of non-European Jews by erasing their Eastern characteristics and by discriminating against them as a group (Shohat 2017).[14] However, "Despite certain cultural and liturgical similarities among them," the groups that constitute the Mizrahi "ethnicity" have very little in common (Raz Krakotzkin 2005, 173). They, like other "minorities," have been imprisoned in the identity of "others" that was attached to them. Three generations after their immigration, they are still referred to as "ethnicities" while Israelis of European descent are the unmarked group and constitute the norm.

The conditions placed on the inclusion of Arab Jews, namely that they rid themselves of their Arab culture, determined their exclusion (Raz-Krakotzkin 2005). Hence, they were all subjected to a process of cultivation, which proceeded toward secularization (cutting off Yemenite children's side locks in the 1950s).[15] In the process of cultivation "religious artifacts were stolen by Zionist emissaries (with false promises of return), babies were kidnapped, at times literally snatched from their mothers and sold for adoption to Ashkenazim, both in Israel and overseas" (Shohat 2017, 107).[16]

Israeli establishment has systematically sought to suppress Sephardi-Mizrahi cultural memory by marginalizing their history in school curricula. Both Arab and Ethiopian Jews are presented in schoolbooks as passive vessels to be reshaped by the revivifying spirit of "Promethean Zionism" (Shohat 2017). Little mention is made for example, of the fact that major Sephardi texts in philosophy, linguistics, poetry, and medicine were largely written in Arabic and reflect specific Muslim influences as well as a Jewish-Arab cultural identity. Only a small slot in the school literature curriculum is allotted to "ethnic" literature, which is "a demeaning definition born in the colonialist tradition of presenting the dichotomy of culture versus ethnicity." (Haviva Pedaya 2020),[17] Pedaya observes that the

---

14. For a list of publications on the subject of *Mizrahim* in Israel, see Nizri, Yigal S. 2020. "Mizrahim in Israel: History, Politics, and Culture."
CJS340H1 Online Mizrahim_in_Israel_History_Politics_and.pdf. Anne Tanenbaum Centre for Jewish Studies. The Joseph Lebovic Summer Experience in Jewish Studies at the University of Toronto.
15. Segev, *The Seventh Million*. Herzog, Immigrants and Bureaucrats; Tannenbaum-Domanovitz, *Zionism is Color-Blind*. Unpublished Doctoral Dissertation (Hebrew). Shato, Shira. 2011. *The Different Narratives about the Emigration of Ethiopian Jews*. Unpublished Doctoral Dissertation (Hebrew).
16. See also Gamliel and Shifris 2019 *Children of the Heart*. And Shifris. 2019. *Where has my child gone*. Yediot Sfarim Publishers. (Hebrew).
See also The Yemenite, Mizrahi and Balkan Children Affair. https://www.edut-amram.org/en/
17. Pedaya, Haviva. 2020. "Toward Building a Net for Mizrahi Literature." *Haaretz*, September 29, 2020.

relationship between Eurocentric and Mizrahi literature in Israel is that of "cultural oppression experienced as colonialism." The Arab-Jews, she maintains, constitute "an entire collective whose language was exterminated and whose writers' language is nourished by the death of language, its eradication, its severing, its silencing, or nationalizing." Their minority status, she argues, derives not only from the actual language they use, but first and foremost from the missing language, that which Mizrahi writers and poets had to repress, bury, or trample upon in order to use the Hebrew 'paper language', which is slender and poor, but grants entry to the identity of the majority and to the Israelis' celebration of publicity." (ibid.).

Raz-Krakotzkin (2005)[18] maintains that the discourse regarding Arab Jews in Israel echoes the disparaging discourse regarding Jews in Europe. This racist discourse, he suggests, can be elucidated through an examination of Israeli educational discourse.

The representation of Mizrahi Jews from more than six different countries, takes up only a few of the several hundred pages in history schoolbooks, as exemplified in the famous photograph by Meir Gal (1997) "Nine [pages] out of four hundred: the West and the rest."[19] This photograph illustrates the prevalent attitude towards *Mizrahi* Jews in Israeli schoolbooks, as a homogenous group without a history of its own.

The Mizrahi Israelis are generally represented in schoolbooks in a demeaning manner, depicted in photographs that show homogeneous faceless "herds" in nameless places, thus turning them into a phenomenon and a problem. For example, in the same schoolbook two photographs are juxtaposed (Image 39), representing the two big "waves" of immigration – from Muslim countries and from the former Soviet Union. The Soviets are depicted in color; they are well-dressed, independent people, having disembarked from a plane. They stride purposefully ahead, with the blue sky above them. They do not look at the viewer, implying that they need no favors from anyone. The Mizrahi Jews are represented in a black and white photograph showing a dense group of countless Yemenite children who seem to fill the entire world, orphaned, crowded, and similar. While the Russians walk at our side as equals, the Yemenite children are below us, their faces turned upward toward the viewer and their eyes follow us in "demand".

---

18. The Zionist return to the West and the Mizrahi Jewish perspective. In: *Orientalism and the Jews*.
19. http://meirgal.squarespace.com/nine-out-of-four-hundred-the-w/

Image 39. *People in Space*. The Center of Educational Technologies

This representation transmits the very clear message that while the Yemenite Jews were a problem and a burden, the Russians made a welcome contribution to Israel. It is worth noting that the caption under the Russian "Olim" mentions the Ethiopian Jews as well, but the designers of the book chose not to show them.

Eldar and Yaffe (1998, 344) devote an entire chapter to the Yemenite immigrants titled "The Yemenites add a special hue to the landscape." This title singles them out as a distinct group, an exotic ornament in Israel's social landscape. The chapter informs us that "in the years 1881-1882 thousands of [Jewish] people arrived at Jaffa port: from Russia, from Rumania, from the Balkans, and even from far-away Yemen" (p. 269). This attests to the mental maps of Israelis, for whom Europe is closer to Israel than Yemen. The photograph in this chapter shows an art class in the prestigious Jerusalem Betzalel Art School. White students are drawing a Yemenite boy who is sitting on a pedestal above them, as an anthropological curiosity very much like the Black Venus mentioned in Chapter 7. Under the photograph, we find the text of acclaimed painter Nahum Gutman, who describes the Yemenite Jews as biblical figures who lived in wooden boxes.

While schoolbooks generally subscribe to the view that the fundamental inequality of Mizrahi Jews is an inevitable outcome of their encounter with the more advanced and Western Ashkenazis, some note in greater detail the inhumane treatment meted out to them by the Euro-Jewish community in Israel. Regarding the Jewish immigrants from Yemen in the early 1900s, who were brought to replace Palestinian workers by "Hebrew" ones, and to "conquer the labor," Avieli-Tabibian (2009a, 55)[20] suggests the following assignment in her teacher's guide:

> Students should compose an indictment of the veteran Jewish settlers with regard to their attitude toward the Yemenite immigrant.

Avieli-Tabibian proposes holding a discussion regarding the reasons for the atrocious behavior on the part of the Jewish farmer-employers toward their Jewish-Yemenite laborers, who were treated almost like slaves, and enumerates possible cultural, economic, social, ideological, and national reasons for this. However, she suggests no such indictment of the Zionist authorities, thus implying that the way the Yemenite Jews were treated in affluent villages and kibbutzim, was not part of a racist policy toward oriental Jews. This conclusion contradicts scholarship on the topic[21]. The Yemenite Jews themselves are portrayed as naïve, childish, and excessively religious, unlike the secular East European Jews who were the emissaries of progress. Students are then asked to compare the two groups of Jews - Russians and Yemenites - and draw conclusions about the nature of the Yemenite immigration.

Scholars insist that it was cultural oppression that ultimately determined the social marginalization of Mizrahi Jews (Raz Krakotzkin 2005, 173), and not their original culture. In other words, the differences between Mizrahi Jews and the dominant Ashkenazi group were "secondary cultural differences" (John Ogbu 1986, 96–97). Ogbu defines secondary cultural characteristics as "those different cultural features that came into existence after two populations have come into contact, especially in contact involving the subordination of one group to another."

As recent studies show, three generations after their immigration, the gaps in education and in achievements between Ashkenazi and Mizrahi students has widened.[22] These gaps reflect discrimination, low budgeting to peripheral schools and racist criteria for admission and eligibility, not only in education but also in the market.[23]

---

20. *Journeys in Time: Nationality on Trial.* Teacher's Guide. Center of Educational Technologies Publishers.
21. Shohat 2017, Raz Krakotzkin 2005, Gamliel and Shifris 2019
22. Moshe Ben-Atar, Haaretz. August, 4. 2021. "Can a Mizrahi who tries hard succeed? Think again!" https://www.haaretz.co.il/blogs/moshebatar/BLOG-1.10082006
23. Karpel, Dalia. Haaretz Magazine, May 16th, 2014. AN interview with Sami Shalom Chetrit. "In 2014 Mizrahi Children are still discriminated by the Educational System."
https://www.haaretz.co.il/magazine/.premium-1.2322022; Ron, Liat 16.1.2021:" Israeli High-tech: Equal Opportunities to every child or only to the Ashkenazi ones from the Center?"
justhttps://finance.walla.co.il/item/3483064 (Hebrew)

Values and Citizens (2014, 366) reproduces and legitimates the official narrative, and explains that the Mizrahi newcomers who "were influenced by the Muslim culture in their countries of origin were conceived by some of the Zionist leaders as a threat to the Western-European future character of the state". This civic studies schoolbook quotes foreign minister Abba Eban, who warned Israelis that the newcomers from Muslim countries were liable to impact the local culture in an adverse manner: "We should not see these immigrants as a bridge to our integration in the Arabic speaking world. We should imbue them with the Western spirit and not let them drag us into an unnatural Orientalism." (ibid.). The schoolbook also cites Prime Minister David Ben-Gurion, who described the Sephardi immigrants as lacking even "the most rudimentary knowledge" and being "without a trace of Jewish or human education." Ben-Gurion repeatedly expressed contempt for the culture of the Oriental Jews: "We do not want Israelis to become Arabs. We are duty bound to fight against the spirit of the Levant, which corrupts individuals and societies, and to preserve the authentic Jewish values as they crystallized in the Diaspora."[24]

Values and Citizens details the institutionalized acts of discrimination toward the Middle-Eastern Jews in both housing and education, citing protocols of meetings of the Jewish Agency, at which arguments such as the following were articulated: "85% of the 85,000 immigrants from North Africa were sent to development towns at the frontier.... But we cannot send the Polish Jews to such places. We must find for them suitable housing" (p.367).[25] This schoolbook also reproduces the notorious article by respected journalist Arye Gelblum in Haaretz in 1949, replete with racist expressions:

> This is the immigration of a race we have not yet known in the country [...] people whose primitivism is at a peak, whose level of knowledge is one of virtually absolute ignorance, and worse, who have little talent for understanding anything intellectual. They are only slightly better than the general level of the Arabs, Negroes, and Berbers in the same regions. [...] These Jews also lack roots in Judaism, as they are totally subordinated to the play of savage and primitive instincts. [...] Most of them have serious eye, skin and sexual diseases, not to mention robberies and thefts. Chronic laziness and hatred of work [...] *kibbutzim* will not hear of their absorption among them.

Regarding this article, Raz-Krakotzkin (2005, 169) argues that Goldblum's attitude was anything but marginal. Rather, it was reflective of the institutional treatment afforded *Mizrahi* Jews. "Critical research has demonstrated that even had

---

24. Cited in Shohat, Ella. 2017. *On the Arab-Jew, Palestine, and Other Displacements*. Pluto Press.
25. A quote from Chetrit, Sami S. 2004. *The Mizrahi Struggle in Israel 1948-2003*. Am Oved Publishers.

Goldblum's formulation been extreme, it represents the basic Israeli Zionist attitude towards the *Mizrahim* and continues to direct the educational system in its perpetuation of discrimination."

The reproduction of Goldblum article in a schoolbook in 2014 proves this point. While the schoolbook implies that these opinions are not necessarily those of its writers, these observations remain mostly uncontested and gain legitimacy through *authorization* (Van Leeuwen 2007, 97) or by virtue of the institutional authority of the people who expressed them.

The schoolbook attempts to mitigate the harsh judgments by specifying that "often times the immigrants from the Orient, who brought with them a rich culture of philosophy and poetry, literature and liturgical poems (*piut*), did not receive the social recognition that their culture deserved" (p.366). However, it contains no positive assessment of the North African and Arab-Jewish immigrants, nor does it refer to sources from the Jewish Mizrahi communities themselves, that relate to their culture or to the merits of living among Muslims over many centuries.

In the chapter on the Mizrahi groups of Jews brought to Israel, Mishol (2014) quotes extensively from Prime Minister Ben-Gurion and other Zionist leaders who, like Ruppin, considered non-European *olim* as an inferior race, driven by passion and instincts. The textbook commends Prime Minister Ben-Gurion who, despite these obstacles, announced that huge efforts would be required to integrate them as equals. The students are then asked to answer the following questions:

- Enumerate the problems the newcomers suffered from.

- How do Ben Gurion's words express his egalitarian attitude toward the immigrants?

The immigrants from Muslim countries are presented as an impersonalized homogenous "problem." No mention is made of the hardships they encountered nor of their contribution to the country for the last four generations.

In conclusion, the schoolbooks, as Raz-Krakotzkin (2013) observes, instead of discussing the racist stance and its origins, and assuming responsibility for discriminatory policies, reiterate the slander uncritically as fact and teach racism.

Mizrahi Jews and the Holocaust Narrative

The life of Mizrahi Jews in Muslim countries has frequently been equated to the life of East European Jews among the anti-Semitic Christians. As Shohat (2017,

104) [26] asserts, although Mizrahim are considered a-historical people whom Zionism brought back to history, "when Zionist history does acknowledge what might be termed 'Judeo-Islamic history,' it organizes it as a 'pogromization metanarrative,' around a selected series of violent events, moving from pogrom to pogrom, as evidence of relentless hostility toward Jews in the Arab world, presumed to be analogous to those encountered in Europe." , Zionist history has united the entire "Jewish nation" against a common "historical enemy" - the Muslim Arabs, disregarding the very different experience that Middle Eastern Jews had within the Muslim world, utterly distinct from that which haunted the European memories of Ashkenazi Jews. In this way, Arab Jews become part of the persecuted Jewish nation. Shohat (2017, 24) contends that "this selective reading of Jewish history hijacks the Jews of Islam from their Judeo-Islamic history and culture, and subordinates their experience to that of the Ashkenazi-European *shtetl*, presented as a 'universal' Jewish experience." For instance, The Farhud in Iraq is mentioned in the Encyclopedia of the Holocaust, where it is labeled a "pogrom," as are labeled the massacres of Jews in Eastern Europe. However, the author of this item, Esther Meir-Glitzenstein, mentions also the help and the compensation the Jews received from the Iraqi government, as well as the Jewish community's remarkably quick recovery from the two-day assault by anti-British and pro-German Iraqis. Schoolbooks describe the assault but make no mention of the assistance and compensation. They devote considerably more paper time to the 1941 Farhud than to the centuries of Jewish life and to Jewish-Iraqi culture. [27]

Mishol (2014, 195) reports on the Farhud in Iraq in a way that evokes the Nazis' treatment of Jews: "During the Second World War the German ambassador in Iraq circulated anti-Semitic propaganda and published Hilter's book Mein Kampf. The Iraqi government collaborated with this activity and contributed to the distribution of Nazi propaganda, enhancing hostility toward Jews. [...] Pro- Nazi officers organized the revolution [...] Jews were killed, among them women and babies, women were raped."

This rhetoric, maintains Shohat (2017, 103), "incorporates the Arab-Jewish experience into the Shoah, now projected onto a Muslim space that did not produce, or even propose, a Final Solution."

Since the 1980s, when the state decided to turn the Shoah of European Jews into the unifying narrative of all Israelis, and to make it the central component of

---

26. Shohat, Ella. 2017. *On the Arab-Jew, Palestine, and Other Displacements Selected Writings*. Pluto Press.
27. The Farhud (an Arabic term best translated as "violent dispossession") began on June 1 and lasted two days, during the course of which 128 Jews were killed, 210 were injured, and over 1,500 businesses and homes were damaged. Shops were looted and the entire Jewish community suffered an unexpected blow in this country where they were an integral part of the society.

Jewish identity[28], the most prominent question pertaining to Mizrahi Jews in the matriculation exams was in the section on the Holocaust (Raz-Krakotzkin 2013). Students were asked to prove that the final solution was directed at world Jewry, not at European Jewry alone. They had to detail Hitler's plans to annihilate the Jews of the Muslim world as well. Raz-Krakotzkin notes (2013, 170) that this question is particularly strange because it chooses "to focus on those who were not annihilated as a means for constructing a common Jewish history." His conclusion is that the road to integration in Israeli society runs through Auschwitz, "an illustration of just how problematic Holocaust memorialization is in Israel". While the complex and varied histories and experiences of Mizrahi Jews are not discussed, "they are subsumed into a history to which they did not belong, to a catastrophe that was not directly theirs, admitted through the symbolism of hypothetical annihilation."

Nevertheless, the Holocaust narrative that was meant to unite Israelis, consistently excludes the Mizrahi victims. Despite the frequently noted equation between the Muslim and the Nazi regimes, Arab Jews who were deported and murdered in Nazi concentration camps are hardly mentioned. Documentary filmmaker Eyal Sivan explains in the documentary *Ashkenaz*,[29] that during the Eichmann trial, one was told time and again that the Holocaust was the Shoah of European Jewry, an exclusive Ashkenazi catastrophe, and that "the Jewish people" that was exterminated in the Shoah was entirely white.

Although Albert Memmi's novel *The Pillar of Salt* was well received in Israel, and Jewish community leaders in Tunisia and Libya have preserved the memory of Jewish suffering during the Holocaust, their writings were ignored in Israel up until 2000 (Yvonne Kozlovsky-Golan 2015).[30]

Excavations undertaken recently by Israeli archeologist Yoram Haimi and Polish archeologist Wojtek Mazurek in Sobibor extermination camp reveal that hundreds of North African Jews were murdered there, and lists of deported Jews, found in Yad Vashem and the Holocaust Museum in Paris, show that Moroccan Jews were deported to Auschwitz.[31] Libyan Jews were subjected to Nazi atrocities, and transported to Bergen Belsen, where hundreds of them were murdered. However, these Holocaust victims have always been marginalized in the mainstream Shoah commemorative narrative. Their request to testify at the trial of Adolf Eichmann was refused.[32]

---

28. Batya Shimoni 2015.
29. *Ashkenaz*. 2007. Directed by Rachel Lea Jones. Trabelsi Productions. Tel Aviv, Israel.
30. Kozlovsky-Golan, Yvonne. 2015. *Out of the Frame: The Absence of the Holocaust Experience of Mizrahim from the Visual Arts and Media in Israel*. Resling Publishing.
31. Matt Lebovic, Times of Israel June 3, 2019 https://www.timesofisrael.com/with-death-of-last-sobibor-survivor-experts-feud-over-sites-transformation/
32. Khajaj-Liluf, Yaakov. 2020. *The struggle for the Recognition of Libyan Jews as "Holocaust Survivors"* (Hebrew). Organizazione mondiale ebrei de libia. Cento di ricerca e studi sul'ebraismo

Awareness of the suffering of Libyan Jews during the Holocaust has been raised by Yossi Sukary's novel *Benghazi-Bergen Belsen,* published in 2014. More than any learned work, it was this novel that informed Israelis of the Holocaust experiences of Libyan Jews, by relating the story of Sylvana and her family, who were deported to Bergen Belsen. Sukary tells not only of Sylvana's suffering at the hands of the Nazis but of her humiliation at the hands of her European Jewish fellow inmates, who treated her like "a human animal" and brutally abused her. This theme first appeared in Sukary's novela *Emilia* (2008), in which he focuses on his grandmother, whose hatred toward Ashkenazi Jews was kindled in Bergen Belsen, where Jewish inmates of Ashkenazi origin "turned her into dust," only to flare up more strongly in Israel, which, she believed, was dominated by the same oppressive Jews who crushed her in the camp. Indeed, some Israeli Mizrahim define the way they were received in Israel as "a cultural-spiritual Holocaust,"[33]

Textbooks barely mention non-European Jews and their suffering during the Shoah. When they do address them, they do so only in general impersonal terms or through numbers, without testimonies, photographs, or personal stories. For instance, Naveh et al. (2009), in the very detailed chapter devoted to the Final Solution, mention in an off-hand manner that "a few hundred Jews from Libya (who held the status of British residents) were deported to several death camps in Europe" (2009, 239). Gutman (2009) mentions the experience of Libyan Jews in Bergen-Belsen in a single brief sentence: "In 1944 they were transferred to Bergen Belsen concentration camp" (155). Hertz (2015, 126) is equally brief, noting a reduced number of deportees of "about 400." Avieli-Tabibian's sub-chapter on Libyan Jews is titled: "Libyan Jews too are affected by the war" (p. 240) and puts the number at four hundred and seventy six. The contrast between these laconic statements and the detailed descriptions of the suffering of European Jews in the same textbooks is striking, and implies that quantity is the overriding factor that entitles Holocaust victims to be commemorated. It appears that Israeli educators are intent on conveying the impression that North African Jews were not "real" Holocaust victims, or perhaps very minor ones. All the books devote a considerable paper time to the plight of Tunisian Jews under the Vichy regime. Keren (1999), Inbar and Bar-Hillel (2010), Gutman (2009), and Mishol (2014) devote a whole chapter to this topic but ask rhetorically, "Is the history of

---

libico. https://livluv.org.il/%D7%94%D7%9E%D7%90%D7%91%D7%A7-%D7%9C%D7%94%D7%9B%D7%A8%D7%94-%D7%91%D7%99%D7%94%D7%95%D7%93-D7%99-%D7%9C%D7%95%D7%91-%D7%A0%D7%99%D7%A6%D7%95%D7%9C%D7%99-%D7%A9%D7%95%D7%90%D7%94-2/
33, David Benchetrit, creator of the documentary series "Wind of the East," in an interview for YNET August 19, 2002. For further examples, see Ben Yehuda, Omri. 2019. "Ma'abara Mizrahim between Shoah and Nakba." In *The Holocaust and the Nakba A New Grammar of Trauma and History.* Edited by Bashir Bashir and Amos Goldberg. Columbia University Press.

Tunisian Jews during the six months under German rule a Holocaust?" (Inbar and Bar-Hillel, 2010, 251, Mishol 2014, 289-294). Mishol, who devotes an entire chapter to the Jewish community in Tunisia during the Holocaust, offers divergent expert opinions on the matter. The boy from the Warsaw Ghetto, with his hands raised in surrender – the icon of the annihilation of European Jews - appears at the bottom of every page of Mishol's chapter about North African Jews during the Holocaust. Avieli-Tabibian's title of the chapter on Tunisian Jews reads, "The fate of Tunisia's Jews - a Holocaust?!" (2009, 239).

In the 2021 state final examination in history, one of the questions was this: "Historians argue that what happened to North African Jews during World War II is part of the Holocaust of the Jewish people. Find two examples from the "source" below that can justify this argument (12 points)."

The source is the testimony of a British Jewish doctor, Mordekhay Khen (previously Mark Chain),[34] who served in the British army in Libya, and whose driver accidentally entered "a little town called Jado". There he happened to meet a young officer who asked him if he could look into the concentration camp, built by the Italians for Jews from Benghazi, and subsequently used by the Germans to house Jews from other cities. The officer doctor admitted he was at a loss as to what he could do for the inmates of the camp. Dr. Chain describes neglect, typhus, hunger, dirt and stench, a high mortality rate and total despair among the camp's inmates. This testimony provided by an objective foreigner, describes the suffering of Libyan Jews in this Nazi camp and therefore can support the arguments of the "historians" whose names are concealed. No information is given about Bergen Belsen. Although there are studies and testimonies of North African Jews who experienced the Shoah, and who, like Sukary's grandmother, were deported to Nazi camps, the schoolbook does not use any other source except for Chain's testimony.

To compensate for the absence of Mizrahi Jews from the curriculum, and especially from the Holocaust narrative (Yablonka 2009), a special curriculum of the history and literature of Mizrahi Jews has been devised, but it is set apart from the main syllabi and is far from complete.[35]

---

34. http://www.jwmww2.org/soldier.aspx?id=11106
35. https://www.haaretz.co.il/literature/study/1.3014968.

Chapter 13. They Say our Color is Sad (Sintayehu, 10)[1]

Israeli education legitimates the discriminatory policy or rather the institutional racism (Peled, Inbar 2018) of the state and the practices of segregation applied to Ethiopian Jews, or Beta Israel, by relating to them as "natural" facts that require no discussion or explanation. The Ethiopian "prodigal brothers" are presented anthropologically as a distinct homogenous and alienated group, as if they had no history prior to reaching Israel, and no part in Israeli life. As part of the process of "cultivation," Ethiopians are expected to change their names, abandon most of their religious customs, and renounce the authority of their religious leaders.[2] Israeli-Ethiopian children undergo a process of conversion at the religious schools they must attend (Peled 2018).

The schoolbooks maintain that the practices of confinement, segregation, erasure of religious customs, conversion and re-education are implemented for their own good and for the good of the nation. They offer no explanation for this "inner colonialism,"[3] in which Ethiopian Jews are subjected to what Philomena Essed terms "containment in paternalistic relationships," which, she asserts, is the other facet of racism (1991:45).[4]

Unlike the Palestinians, for whom confinement and distancing are considered a permanent measure, Ethiopian Jews, like the Mizrahi Jews before them, are conceived as a "problem" with which the state is obliged to cope through temporary control, monitoring, and distancing, until they are fit for integration. This conception "inherently posits the Ethiopian Israelis as an external factor that needs be integrated." (Peled 2018, 16).

---

1. Syntayehu said that after her classmates refused to be photographed with her at the end of the year. The teacher's solution was that every child would be photographed individually.
2. Ben Eliezer (2008, 944) observes: "In the course of wrenching the Ethiopian community from its special form of Judaism, the establishment totally negated the authority of the *kessim*, their traditional spiritual leaders. In Ethiopia, their authority within the community was absolute but in Israel, they were not allowed to perform their duties, although at the end of 2005 the Prime Minister's Office instructed the religious councils to cease the discrimination against the Ethiopian *kessim*. However, it will take time to show whether the religious establishment will obey that order."
3. Following the definitions of K. Clark, C. Pinderhughes and R. Blauner.
4. Essed, Philomena, 1991. *Understanding Everyday Racism.*

Representation of Ethiopian Jews in Schoolbooks

> Why doesn't anyone know about the history of Ethiopian Jews? What about the alienated identity of a child who learns nothing of his own heritage during all his years at school? [...] If in the 1990s Mizrahi organizations protested against the nine pages of their history in a textbook of 400 pages, the situation of Beta Israel is far worse. (Behar 2012)[5]

Schoolbooks and educational programs follow the official trend by presenting Ethiopian Jews as being culturally and physically problematic. For example, Avieli-Tabibian (2009) asserts that all the cultural traits of Ethiopian Jews, such as respect for elders, the maintenance of parental authority, education toward restraint, and a tolerant conversational culture, constitute obstacles to their integration with an Israeli society that does not share these values. Mishol (2014, 276), asserts that "When the Russians arrived, veteran Israelis feared for their jobs; in the case of Mizrahi-Jews and Ethiopians they feared their primitiveness and potential diseases." A geography schoolbook (2009) tells students that "Ethiopians' culture and ways of life are different from those of Israelis. Their health and their educational levels were low when they arrived."[6]

The few textbooks that mention Ethiopian Jews, report on their "cultivation," which takes the form of name changing, re-conversion, and changes in their choice of partner (Mishol 2014, 312). Some of their traditional customs and one of their festive days may be mentioned, but the extended history of their Jewish life in Ethiopia and their active prolonged struggle to reach Zion are overlooked. The "operations" to bring them "home" are portrayed in detail as courageous clandestine missions that "risked the life of IDF and Mossad operatives" (Mishol 2014, 309, *Being Citizens in Israel*, 2016, 74), but their own memories of this journey are absent. *Being Citizens in Israel* (2016) legitimates institutional and everyday racism through "naturalization," claiming that the "tension" between veterans and newcomers is natural. It then justifies the state by stating that Ethiopians are granted affirmative action everywhere, which is called in Hebrew "corrective discrimination," itself a racist idiom as Kaplan (2013, 461) points out.

The assignments given to students in Mishol (2014, 304) are as follows:

- Describe the difficulties of the Ethiopians' absorption.

- How did the state of Israel cope with these difficulties?

---

5. http://www.iaej.co.il/newsite/Data/UploadedFiles/SitePages/607-sFileRedir.pdf
https://almogbehar.wordpress.com/2013/05/08/from-ethiopia-to-israel/ (Hebrew).
6. Gereizer, Fine and Segev. 2009. *Israel in the 21st Century*.

The books insist that Ethiopians "feel" rejected because of their different culture and skin color, and because of their lack of modernity, and their incapacity to integrate (Mishol 2014, 306). Avieli-Tabibian (2009, 239) for instance states that Ethiopians suffer discrimination because "the cultural gaps and the lack of professional technological training were compounded by another difficulty: the difference in skin color." The books thus mix biological and cultural racism.

Beyond praise for being good soldiers, the achievements of Israeli-Ethiopians are never mentioned. Their writers, lawyers, doctors, teachers and activists, their artists who struggle to be recognized while contending with the predicament of being black in a white racist environment, their poets and their musicians who are admired by young people of all social strata in Israel, are non-existent as far as the schoolbooks are concerned, just as they are non-existent in the Israeli official discourse. They are "explained" and interpreted by Eurocentric psychologists and sociologists who analyze them as a phenomenon. Forty years after their emigration, the representation of Ethiopian-Israelis is based on old studies that nourish the conception that they haven't changed.

Photography is a Wound (R. Barthes)

None of the schoolbooks that depict Ethiopian Jews shows them in Ethiopia where they lived on hill tops, surrounded by green pastures near rivers and lakes, nor in the Israeli landscape or among other Israelis, but only in absorption centers, standing idle or leaning immobile against their shabby caravans (Mishol 2014, 305). They are never shown as active people working, performing, creating. These representations enhance their image as backward, needy, and passive. Avieli-Tabibian (2009, 240-238) displays Ethiopian Jews in a few photographs, all showing them as a uniform group: a procession marching away from the viewer in a nameless desert seen from above; immigrants crowded in an airplane, most of them sitting on the floor with a number stuck on their forehead, like cargo; a packed demonstration protesting the questioning of their Jewishness; and a crowd of "qesotch" (religious leaders) during the Sigd festivity. Ethiopian Jews are very often depicted in aerial photographs, in which we see them sitting on the ground like cattle, and like cattle they are described as "Ethiopians waiting to be rescued at the collecting point" (ibid.).[7]

As we have seen in the case of Palestinian citizens, one of the strategies of racist visual discourse is not to show people where they live and work. Neither Ethiopian Jews, nor Palestinian citizens, are shown on the covers of the *Living*

---

7. Many Israeli students and college teachers believe Ethiopian Jews came from the desert (Peled-Elhanan 2021).

Together in Israel series of books, although the books serve Arab and Jewish children alike.

Image 40. *Living Together in Israel.* Courtesy of the Center for Educational Technologies.

When they are shown in this series, the Ethiopian newcomers are represented, like the Arab Jews, next to Russian newcomers (Image 41). On a double spread from a schoolbook for second grade (Gal et al. 2006, 115), Russian immigrants are represented by the popular theatrical group Gesher. The viewer of the Gesher photograph looks up at the actors, just as the audience in the theatre does. Two cartoon children from the "gang" that accompanies the readers throughout the book offer the actors flowers from below the stage. This "gang" includes the Russian immigrant girl Sasha, who was "fantastically well absorbed" into the gang. Note that Sasha is called by her Russian name. She, unlike Ethiopian children, was not required to change it. The gang includes neither Ethiopian nor Arab children.

Israeli-Ethiopians have theatrical groups, such as Hulugeb ("together" in Amharic) whose productions have won awards and toured abroad (Anteby-Yemini 2019), as mentioned in *Being Citizens in Israel* (2016, 74), a renowned dance group,[8] and successful musical bands, but they are represented on the left as victims of an African "humanitarian crisis." The photograph was not taken in Israel neither in Ethiopia, but in an un-named desert in Sudan, where they stayed for long months, waiting for Israel to rescue them as promised. It shows inactive faceless people. The "gang" of children is not there to welcome them or offer them flowers, as they do to the Russian immigrants. Canetti (1984, 392-394) observes: "A standing man is free and independent [...] Sitting or squatting on the ground denotes an absence of needs[...] The body is rounded and compact as though expecting nothing from the world. Every activity which might require reciprocity is renounced. Since nothing is done, there is nothing for anyone to react to. A man who sits in this attitude [...] no one fears violence from him [...] because he makes do with what he has, however little. [...] squatting or sitting on the ground also implies acceptance of everything which may happen." Both double spreads that show non-European immigrants next to the Russian ones, (Image 39 and Image 41) drive home the message that while Russian immigrants are independent and contribute to Israeli culture, the Ethiopian and Mizrahi Jews are passive, in need of rescue, hence constitute a burden, and have nothing to teach us (Tanenbaum 2015).

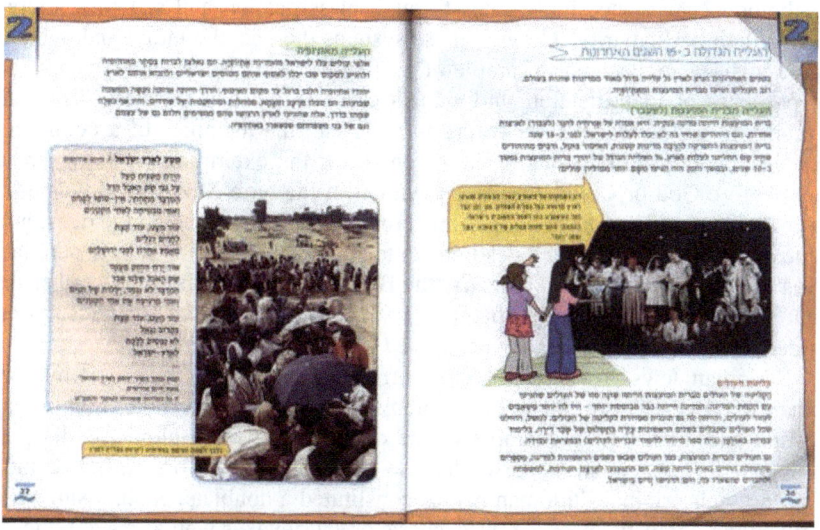

Image 41: "The Great Jewish Immigration (Aliya) over the past 15 years". Courtesy of Gesher Theatre and Aliza Orbach.

---

8. See Baum, Rob. 2009.

When you look into the colonizer's eyes you lose your name. (Kamel Daoud, 2013)

The erasing of individual names, along with the erasing of the names of places and communities, and the imposition of new names, are a familiar colonialist-racist practice (Tuhiwai Smith 2012, 63), meant to deprive people of their collective and private identity and to erase their existence as social actors and as communities. Depriving people of their names smacks not only of colonialist discourse but of anti-Semitic discourse. Israeli psychoanalyst Gavriel Dahan (2021, 106)[9] points to the Hebrew rendering of the term anti-Semitic, which is "anti-shemi," or literally "against the name." Dahan interprets this as being against the "one" or the particular. "The rejection of the name is what we can call the rejection of the one, the 'other'". Colonial regimes have always sought to erase the one, the particular, the minority, which were conceived as dangerous or at least as obstruction, and therefore renamed them. This renaming classified them as "others".[10] "We can assume that the anti-nomination, or anti the human quality of having particular names, [forms] the basis of the relationships of persecution between civilization [and] the individual." (ibid.). Education, the army, the market, and branches of psychology coalescence individuals through classification and statistics, thereby erasing their particularity. Through these systems the one, the individual, who has a particular name, becomes a sample of a category, and his/her name is used only for purposes of identification. Individuals cease to exist in their own right and succumb to the stereotype, according to which all the members of a community are equal before the bureaucrat, the colonizer or the exterminator, as we are all equal before God or Covid19. This is evident in the term Mizrahim, invented by Euro-Zionists, which covers all the Jews from Muslim countries; in the demeaning name given to the country's Palestinian autochthones – Israel's Arabs, or the label given to indigenous Bedouin citizens "the Bedouin Diaspora (pezura)", rather than identify them by their tribal names, in a bid to emphasize their temporary residence on the land where they have lived for generations.

Ethiopian Jews are re-named upon arrival, generally at the airport by some bureaucrat (Ben-Eliezer 2004). Lisa Anteby-Yemini (2019, 24) notes that perhaps the first and most telling example of the denial of Jewish-Ethiopians' diasporic past was the imposition of new Hebrew or Israeli names on the newcomers. "Erasing their original Ethiopian names constituted a double silencing, since each name held a linguistic meaning, in Amharic or Tigrinya, as well as a symbolic one, linked to a specific event at birth. [...] New family names, usually based on the first name of the paternal grandfather, were also imposed on members of what

---

9. *The Body of Love Every day*. Resling Pub. Tel Aviv
10. See also Appadurai 2006: *The Fear of Small Numbers*.

Israeli bureaucrats considered the same 'family,' often going against Ethiopian conceptions of kinship, and blurring genealogical links." Hence, in the act of re-naming the state has taken the place of these people's families - fathers, mothers and grandparents, who are usually the ones who name the children.

The Israeli obsession with Ethiopian names emerges in all schoolbooks, though none of these books relates their history, or discuss their culture. In the textbook *Times for Joy and Memory* [11] that promises to "strengthen our ties with our wonderful tradition and with the state of Israel" (Front Cover), an imaginary Ethiopian girl speaks about the changing of her name. She declares, "I wanted to be like everyone else, so I changed my name. But now I regret having to bear a name that is not really mine! Although it is slightly embarrassing to say that I want to be called by my Ethiopian name. Well, never mind, I'll get over it. And maybe it's good that I have two names now, one for my new life in Israel and one for my ethnicity." (Image 42). This imaginary fragmented girl, whose original name, Kavara, is not translated in the book but means "majestic glory," appears to be very small alongside the huge bubble that conveys her fabricated monologue. Her cartoon-like face expresses the joy of being a split child who leads a double life, permanently different without being unique.[12]

Image 42. *Times for Joy and Memories* 2022

---

11. Of the series *An Opening to the World*, issued by the TALI Educational Fund, whose mission is to promote Jewish values especially in secular schools. Authorized for 2022.
12. Gershoni, A., Teler, D., and Rosenthal-Idan, C. 2009. The Tali Education Fund . The book was authorized for 2022.

Another girl, Gila, features in a booklet in the series *Living Together in Israel* (2005, 35).[13] Gila's photograph is placed in the margin of the page, alongside the heading "An encounter with ..." introduced by an illustration of a white girl who is pointing at her. Gila relates how her parents changed her name, Acham-Yalesh, which means "you are one of a kind," to Gila. The students are invited to discuss why Gila has two names.

Thus, the two girls, Kavara-Maayan and Acham Yelesh-Gila, exonerate the system by taking responsibility for changing their names (or laying it on their parents) and for trying to mold a new identity for them.

Although 80% of Ethiopian-Israeli students are Israeli born (Peled 2018, 17), they are considered as "eternal immigrants". They often study in programs devised especially for them, whether at school, in the army, in nursing school, and in college. One such program is the *Identity Journey*. This program was drawn up in 2012 and has been awarded several prizes, one of them in 2020.[14] It was devised by the department for youth at risk at the Ministry of Education, although the participants are not defined as youth at risk but as "adolescents of Ethiopian ethnicity." The program is based on the assumption that the identity of the students is not yet "integrative" but "heterogeneous," and the "identity journey" is geared to "the empowerment and the consolidation of Ethiopian-Israeli integrative identity" through the study of "Western-Israeli" thought and "values". The program informs Israeli-Ethiopian youth who they are, based on studies conducted – mostly in Ethiopia - fifty years before they were born. It also informs them who they should be through texts written exclusively by non-Ethiopian writers. Thus, the students are required to adopt a negative image of themselves and to accept that their "identity" needs mending by mimicking the imagined Western-Israeli identity, in order to "integrate". In one of the units, these sixteen year old students are asked to explain their Ethiopian names, draw them with colored crayons and write what they do not like about them, an assignment no other student is ever required to do.

Some scholars maintain that the changing of names was convenient for Israelis, who find it difficult to pronounce Ethiopian words. Others assert that this was grasped by Israelis as part of the Ethiopians' process of modernization (Bergman 1986), although most of the Ethiopians received biblical names, as if they had to be "re-named" once they were "reborn" as Israeli Jews. However, none of these explanations really addresses the impact of name changing on the split girls, who lost their names.

---

13. Gal and Goodman 2005; Gal, Fine and Goodman 2006; Fine and Drori 2005. The Center for Educational Technology.
14. https://cms.education.gov.il/EducationCMS/Units/YeledNoarBesikun/machlakot/KidumNoar/tochni t_masa.htm (Hebrew)

Using Bauman's gardening metaphor, [15] Israeli schoolbooks speak of the "gardening" or the "cultivation" of Ethiopian Jews yet neglect to describe the flowers themselves or to give them voice. They reproduce the racist views that inform state policy by emphasizing the "problems" Ethiopian Jews constitute and the ways the state "copes" with them.

---

15. Bauman, Zygmunt. 1989. *Modernity and the Holocaust.*

Part III

Epilogue: The Other is Me

Chapter 14. A Summary of the study

> The paradox of Israel is that it presumed to 'end a Diaspora' characterized by ritualistic nostalgia for the East, only to establish a state ideologically and geopolitically oriented almost entirely toward the West. (Shohat 2017, 105)

Since Jews have often been depicted in anti-Semitic discourse as an alien 'Eastern' people within the West, the dominant Israeli culture has been seeking to westernize itself at all costs, and evolved by distinguishing itself sharply from the East. It downgraded East European Jews, Arab and Ethiopian Jews, and has erased the Palestinian history of the land. As a European national movement, Zionism adopted the Western values of liberalism and humanism, along with the perception that "there is that which is human and then there is the 'other.'" (Bekerman and Zembylas 2018, 59). Through processes of othering, many humans have been considered not to belong to that which is human. The "human" is obviously the powerful, and the "other" is the weak, who is often defined as eastern or "oriental". The powerful "attain the status of essentiality while the weak are reduced to the rank of 'an unfortunate but necessary accident,' e.g., man/woman, Black/White" (ibid.), or in our case, Western / Oriental. This perception, which has nourished the rich Western history of massacres, and served antisemitism, has also served Zionism in many ways, and informs Israeli Education and schoolbooks today. Israeli education inculcates an aversion toward everything "oriental" among the present generation of students, a high percentage of whom are of "oriental" origin.[1] The way Zionist leaders portrayed Jewish cultures both in Eastern Europe and in the Middle East is reminiscent of the way that colonialists described native cultures, namely "in blatant orientalist terms as stagnant, unproductive, and irrational" (Raz Krakotzkin 2005, 167).[2] These "others" were rejected, but continued to nourish the anxiety of incompleteness and the fear of a possible loss of Israel's Western identity. The Israeli Zionist new "Hebrew" man or the "Sabra", was constituted first of all, vis-à-vis the image of the feeble, spiritual Jew, who could not defend himself, and then against non-European Jews who were brought to replace the exterminated Jews of Europe and were marked as primitive, backward and in constant need of acculturation. "The 'redemption of the land,' a term used to denote the transfer of Palestinian lands to Jewish hands, was also its redemption from the East, and its reintegration into the West." (Raz Krakotzkin ibid.)

---

1. See Shohat 2017; Raz Krakotzkin 2005.
2. Piterberg. G. 2008. *The Returns of Zionism: Myths, Politics and Scholarship in Israel*. Verso.

Seeking to forge a united Western nation, Zionism declared "the negation of exile," which means the negation of Jewish histories and the different cultures "within which, and in relation to which, Jews defined themselves as Jews" (Raz-Krakotzkin 2005, 170).[3]

Raz Krakotzkin observes that just as Christianity dismissed Judaism as an historical anachronism, so did Zionism regard the Jews living in "exile" as having been left behind by history. The East, represented by the Arab population, was grasped as either violent, irrational, and evil, or as authentic and antiquated. Both images of the Arab left no room for the Arabs themselves, their contemporary reality, and their rights. East-European Zionists "indigenized" themselves and assumed the role of natives while rendering the autochthonous population obsolete. Israeli schoolbooks display photographs of young East European people, two or three years after arriving in Palestine, as autochthones, labeling them "Eretz-Israeli types": The sun-tanned Russian-Jewish guard riding an Arab horse and wearing a keffiya, or the sun-tanned Russian-Jewish farmer ploughing a field in Palestine.

The Representation of Holocaust Victims

Holocaust victims are depicted in schoolbooks as part of either Nazi or Zionist history. Most individuals who happen to be shown in photographs are presented as illustrations for texts that are rarely about them, and function as samples of the exterminated. Their presence on the page is powerful, but they themselves are absent. Although the Holocaust, as the Israeli "chosen trauma", is the defining feature of Israeli identity, the lives and culture of the people who perished in it remain unknown and unimportant. The people they were are not mourned although their terrible death is foregrounded in a traumatizing manner, as a constant threat, to remind the young readers that this is what happened to Jews when they were stateless. By depriving the sufferers of their names and life stories, the books reproduce the Nazi perspective and the Nazi gaze, which held them as stücke, pieces or cargo.

The schoolbooks transmit a very clear message that these are the Jews we, Israelis, must make sure, every day of our life, never to become again although, as the teachers' guides and schoolbook texts insist, the threat of becoming these Jews once again is hovering above us constantly. Therefore, we must be armed, fearless, ferocious, and we must control, distance, and eliminate our potential exterminators, those who replaced the European Nazis in Israeli discourse and consciousness, and in whose midst we have founded our Jewish state and Jewish

---

3. "The Zionist return to the West and the Mizrahi Jewish perspective".

army. In Dirk Moses' (2021, 13)[4] terms, the schoolbooks perpetuate the idea that Israel must maintain "permanent security," which is "the striving of states, [...] to make themselves invulnerable to threats," in order to prevent another Holocaust.

The Representation of Palestinians

> While the memory of the Holocaust is a pillar of Israeli consciousness, the memory of the Nakba is forbidden today by the state. (Raz-Krakotzkin, 2019, 134).[5]

> In stark contrast to the Australian or United States models, Zionism rigorously refused, as it continues to refuse, any suggestion of Native assimilation. (Patrick Wolfe 2012.)

While the Jews are presented as having endured 2000 years of hardship, pogroms, and Holocaust in their native countries, before being rescued by Zionism and the state of Israel, the Palestinians are denied their suffering and their own Holocaust, the Nakba. The destruction and the ethnic cleansing of Palestine is reported in schoolbooks only by way of its favorable consequences for the Jews (Peled-Elhanan 2012). No room is made for the fate of the surviving victims or their testimony.

School curricula fail to take account of the history of Palestine since the Second Temple period. They present The Promised Land as the provenance of the Jewish-Christian civilization, while denying its Arab-Islamic history, including the four hundred years of Ottoman rule, which are barely mentioned in Israeli schoolbooks. The actual Arab presence on the land is deemed inconsequential, and consequently rejected to the point of obliteration. (Raz-Krakotzkin 2005).

Palestinians have never been candidates for assimilation or integration.[6] Their dehumanization, objectification, and Nazification legitimate their persecution, their exclusion, and their symbolic and physical elimination.

---

4. Moses, Dirk A. 2021. *The Problems of Genocide Permanent Security and the Language of Transgression.* Cambridge University Press.
5. The so-called Nakba Law that was approved by the Knesset on March 22, 2011, officially titled 'Budget Foundations Law (Amendment 40) Reducing Budget or Support for Activity Contrary to the Principles of the State'. The law authorizes the Minister of Finance to relinquish monetary support if... [a] body or institution has made any payment towards an event or action that undermines the 'existence of Israel as a Jewish and democratic state,' violates the symbols of the State, or marks the date of Israel's establishment 'as a day of mourning. The Association for Civil Rights in Israel, "The Nakba Law," updated November 9, 2011. http://www.acri.org.il/en/knesset/nakba-law/.
6. Wolfe, Patrick. 2012. "Past is Present: Settler Colonialism in Palestine." *Settler Colonial Studies* 2(1). 136.

The Representation of Jewish "others"

Paradoxically, the exodus from Europe and the aspiration to create a distinctly Jewish political entity in the East was a means of joining the Christian West, and an expression of identification with the latter's self-perceptions. (Raz Krakotzkin 2005, 168).

Israel has always conceived itself as a "bulwark against Asia, or a Little Europe in the Middle East," as Herzl envisioned the Jewish state, without attempting "to conceal his contempt for the Orient, including its Jews" (Raz Krakotzkin 2005, 170).

The Jews' immigration to Palestine is presented in history schoolbooks as the "return to history," namely the history of the West which includes Jews and Christians, but neither the Islamic East nor Africa (ibid.). Arab and Ethiopian Jews have no history beyond being rescued and constituting a civilizing burden for the state of Israel. They are expected to sever their ties with their former life, language, music, and religious customs, lest they imprint their Arabness of Africanness on Israel's "Western" landscape and levantinize it. They are drawn into the "chosen trauma" of the European Holocaust and learn to appropriate it through education, but the suffering of North African and Libyan Jews in Nazi death camps is downgraded in all schoolbooks.

The representation of "others." Conclusion

In nation-states, "Minorities" and the "ethnicities" are granted a socio-ethnic identity, which allows the dominant group to establish classifications and to 'otherize' them. This group identity is viewed as something static, a-contextual, and ahistorical. It is "reified, so as to consolidate that new generations 'belong' to one [...] group or another and 'differ' from one another. (Bekerman and Zymbalas 2018, 62).[7]

Re-named and un-narrated, present day "minorities", as unnamed Holocaust victims before them, have been silenced in the Israeli social and cultural arena and in schoolbooks, where they do not receive the paper time they deserve, and their voice is not heard. Thus, they are simultaneously present and absent. This, as Stam and Shohat (2014, 198) contend, "is not an error of perception but rather a form of social control, intended to make them what Alice Walker calls 'prisoners of

---

7. For a discussion about different kinds of identity, see Van Leeuwen 2022, 8.

image',"[8] the image given to them by the rhetors and designers of Israeli cultural and educational discourse of ahistorical rescued inferior victims.

However, there are no ahistorical people (Stam and Shohat 2014). There are only people whose history is suppressed for various social and political or economic reasons, and whose claims to humanity, to having a history, have been denied (See also Tuhiwai Smith 2012, 21).[9]

---

8. Quoted in *Prisoners of Image: Ethnic and Gender Stereotypes*. New York: Alternative Museum, 1989.
9. Tuhiwai Smith, Linda. 2012. *Decolonizing Methodologies. Research and Indigenous Peoples.* London and New York: Zed Books.

Chapter 15. A Proposal for an Alternative Joint Narrative

This chapter proposes deconstructing the official "pedagogic" narrative and devising a joint curriculum that would introduce the "other" narratives, which Homi Bhabha (2000) calls "performative".

The deconstruction of the official narrative should reveal the elements that need to be included in the joint curriculum in order to create a "usable past"[1] that would help to cope with the present and envisage a more peaceful future for all parties. Such a joint narrative needs, in the words of LaCapra (2001, 22), "to relate to the past in a manner that helps to make possible a legitimate democratic polity in the present and future."[2] It should be multi-voiced and include not only the Eurocentric perspective of colonial domination that Israeli education has adopted, but all the perspectives that prevail in the country regarding its history, its culture, and its religions, especially the voices of those who have had no power thus far over their own representation and the representation of their own "others", namely their colonizers. Hence, it should abandon the "objective" writing of history that pretends that history tells itself (Barthes 1989)[3] while imposing a single dominant perspective.

Multidirectional Memory

> The attempt to understand the Holocaust through the lens of a national uniqueness approach has reached a dead end (Blatman 2015, 26).

Historians who advocate exploring the possibility of discussing the Holocaust in the context of other twentieth century human catastrophes, such as the Nakba,[4] seek to apply a multidirectional memory (Rothberg 2011) to the human history of suffering and abuse, which includes colonialism, slavery, occupation, and expulsion.[5] Michael Rothberg (2009, 3)[6] believes that unlike the competitive

---

1. Wertsch, J. 2002. *Voices of Collective Remembering*. Cambridge: Cambridge University Press.
2. LaCapra, Dominick. 2013. *Writing History Writing Trauma*. Johns Hopkins University Press.
3. *The Rustle of Language*. Chapter 4, p. 127. University of California Press.
4. Rothberg, Michael. 2009. *Multidirectional Memory: Remembering the Holocaust in the Age of Decolonization*. Stanford, CA: Stanford University Press.
5. Rothberg, Michael. 2011. "From Warsaw to Gaza. Mapping Multidirectional Memory." *Criticism* 53 no. 4. (fall). 523-548.
6. Rothberg, Warsaw Gaza.

memory that generally results in hostility and belligerence, multidirectional memory is subject to ongoing negotiation, cross-referencing, and borrowing. It "has the potential to create new forms of solidarity and new visions of justice." As we have seen, Rothberg compares besieged Gaza to the Warsaw Ghetto without equating the two.

The multidirectional approach relates to the universal nature of Holocaust memory that has become cosmopolitanized, without ceasing to be national and particular.[7] The "cosmopolitanization" of Holocaust memory,[8] or the process of turning it into a part of a transnational memory culture,[9] incorporates it as the defining global event of genocide and trauma in the twentieth century [10] and makes it a part of the "foundational past" of the international community.[11] Goldberg and Hazan (2015, XIII) point out that "Holocaust memory generates a form of common awareness of belonging that creates a very large kind of imagined community, that of the 'global village,' or at least the Western global village [...]. The Holocaust [...] serves as a moral and historical yardstick, as a measure of things human".

This yardstick serves to measure both the cruelty of contemporary oppressors and the suffering of the oppressed. For example, South African freedom fighters imprisoned on Robben Island read Anna Frank's diary and drew imaginative links between their experience of isolated political prisoners and the experiences of a Jewish girl hiding in Nazi-occupied Amsterdam although, as Ahmad Kathrada states: "hers was much worse."(Roni Mikel Arieli 2019, 185)[12].

Marisa Fox-Bevilacqua, a descendant of refugees from the pogroms of Odessa, writes in a Jewish magazine:[13]

---

7. Goldberg, Amos. 2015, int. to Hazan and Goldberg, *Marking Evil*; Goldberg and Bashir 2019.
8. Ilani, Ofri. "Say Goodbye to the Holocaust you have known." https://www.haaretz.com/world-news/europe/.premium-the-crumbling-consensus-that-jews-were-the-ultimate-holocaust-victims-1.5843269
9. Katriel, Tamar. 2015. "Commemorating the Twentieth Century: The Holocaust and Nonviolent Struggle in Global Discourse". In: Hazan, H. and A. Goldberg Eds. *Marking Evil: Holocaust Memory in the Global Age*. Oxford: Berghahn Publishers. 315–343.
10. Introduction to Goldberg and Hazan, *Marking Evil*; Goldberg and Bashir, *The Holocaust and the Nakba*.
11. Confino, Alon. 2012. *Foundational Pasts: The Holocaust as Historical Understanding*. Cambridge: Cambridge University Press.
12. "Reading *The Diary of Anne Frank* on Robben Island: On the Role of Holocaust Memory in Ahmed Kathrada's Struggle against Apartheid."
Journal of Jewish Identities, Volume 12, Number 2, July 2019. Johns Hopkins University Press. 175-195
13. https://forward.com/ August 23, 2021

Delays were deadly during the Holocaust. We cannot repeat that mistake in Afghanistan. We cannot let them meet the same fate as our ancestors who were brutally murdered while an uncaring world looked the other way.

Calling for action, Fox-Bevilacqua argues, "If we can't deploy our legacy as American Jews in the short time before the mass killings start, then what does 'Never Again' actually mean?"

For Marisa Fox-Bevilacqua, the Holocaust has obviously become what Confino (2019) calls a "foundational event," by which she judges the actions of the Taliban today. Her interpretation of "never again" is cosmopolitan and empathic, and places on us a mutual responsibility and response-ability to protect human rights wherever they are violated upon this earth.

This perception contrasts the Israeli point of view, which holds that since the Jews are the ultimate victims of the Holocaust, this lesson cannot apply to Israel. The State of Israel "has made cynical political use of the Holocaust in a bid to divest itself of responsibility for its actions toward the Palestinians, and to suspend the latter people's collective and individual rights." (Bashir and Goldberg 2019, 8).

Nevertheless, the Palestinian Nakba, perpetrated by the Israeli Jews, is frequently measured by the same yardstick. Elias Khoury's novel *Children of the Ghetto - My name is Adam* uses Holocaust language to tell about the massacre of Lydda in 1948 by the Israeli army. Referring to the people who were forced to burn and bury the dead after the massacre in the mosque, Khoury's protagonist, Adam, speaks about "the transformation of the Palestinian youth of the ghetto into a new form of Sonderkommando" (p. 296). He wonders would Claude Lanzmann have been able to imagine an encounter between Jewish Sonderkommando and the men of Lydda, who were forced to burn the corpses of their own people on the orders of Jewish soldiers?

This deliberation brings up the intricate relationship between the Jewish Holocaust and the Palestinian Nakba, and reminds one that the Holocaust of the Jews and the Holocaust of the Palestinians are interwoven, and that both constitute "One Holocaust of the Jewish people. Both stare us straight in the face," as poet Avot Yeshurun put it (2009, 385).[14]

The Seventh Candle

Only one school in Israel "dared" to apply the multidirectional memory on Holocaust Day, in 1995. An alternative ceremony, called "The Seventh Candle",

---

14. Yeshurun Helit and Lilach Lachman Eds. *Milvadata. Selected poems*. Hakibbutz Hameuhad and Siman Kriah: New Library for Poetry.

was performed in the Kedma School in Tel Aviv, in the poor Hatikva quarter, which was an all-Mizrahi neighborhood. Beside the six candles that commemorated the six million Jews murdered by the Nazis, another candle was lit, to commemorate other genocides perpetrated in the course of history, such as the extermination of Native Americans, the slaughter of the Armenians in Turkey, and the genocide in Rwanda. The principal, Sami Shalom Chetrit, explains (2010, 217-219)[15] that the school decided to study the Holocaust from a cosmopolitan point of view, and to try to draw a universal lesson from it; to learn about the conditions and circumstances that gave rise to the "human monster," beyond the persecution of Jews in Christian Europe. The students learned that the conditions for the incubation and growth of the "monster" are lack of cultural tolerance, discrimination on the basis of race and creed, power-mongering and greed, ignorance and xenophobia, fear of the different and the other, persecution and harming of the weak as a way to establish the oppressor's superiority.

Chetrit asserts, "No one aimed to make a unification of all holocausts and genocides in history, and the uniqueness of the genocide of the Jews by the Nazis in an advanced and developed European civilization was emphasized." (p. 118).

But the questions asked at the Kedma school in 1995 were cardinal, and are still relevant: were the Nazi party and its terrible leader a temporary European virus that attacked and exterminated the Jews of Europe, before leaving the world, or can we see them as a model for a potential atrocity that lies deep within any human collective mind? Are we, as Jews and Israelis, with our systematic shunning of the holocausts of other people in the past, and of the suffering of other people in the present, more successful in our mission to remember? The main point of the discussion was how could all these be prevented?
In the ceremony, the students read aloud the following text:

The Seventh Candle:

We, Jews of the third generation of resurrection and independence, do humbly ask to take from the fire of memory of the six million victims of the Jewish holocaust, and make an additional torch to present to the whole world. A Seventh candle.

We have the tragic right to stand here, remember, and warn: There is no people, no culture and no group of humans immune to hatred, racism, persecution and extermination.

Hatred of the other, persecution and extermination of the other, are a social phenomenon that could arise against humanity at any time.

---

15. Intra-Jewish conflict in Israel: white Jews, black Jews. 2010. Routledge

> We intend by no means to belittle the pain of our people's memory, nor to make a comparison between holocausts. We ask only to remind all humans that persecution and extermination of the other is a human monster, created by human mind and hands, as learned also by other races and peoples, of different creeds and populations, over the course of human history. We must remember that only the human can confront this terrible monster.
>
> We, born out of the greatest horror, stand up tall today, in prayer for peace and fellowship between people, creeds, races and cultures.

The event created an uproar at all levels. Prime Minister Rabin scolded the Minister of Education for allowing it.

Chetrit recalls (ibid. 217), "Persecution of the school intensified after that day. Educators and politicians thought that a school in a poor Mizrahi neighborhood had no right to address the issue of the Holocaust, which they considered a European Jewish matter". Knesset member Limor Livnat [16] organized a protest vigil outside the school and called on the minister of education to shut it down. The school was even attacked for playing Hanna Senesz's song "Walking to Caesarea," in an Israeli-Moroccan interpretation. [17] An enraged woman telephoned the school and yelled: "You Moroccans have already stolen everything from us, but this is it! Don't dare touch our holocaust. You will not steal our holocaust with your belly-dancing."

Other voices were heard as well. An editorial in the journal *Hakibbutz* read, "Be mindful of paupers from whom Torah shall issue. Kedma principal has done what none of us had dared. He broke the sanctified framework, created over decades of holocaust remembrance ceremonies, and had the boldness to pour new content into symbols that no one dared touch." Another supportive comment came from a Holocaust survivor: "I bless you for breaking the seal of silence around the genocides committed against Armenians, Gypsies, and others. The power of our outcry as Jews lies in our sensitivity towards other humans, even if they are not Jews." (Chetrit 2010, 218).

In the following year, several educational institutions, including Yad Vashem, requested a video recording of the ceremony and the text "The Seventh Candle". The ceremony at Kedma had become a landmark used by various institutions to discuss the universal question of the Holocaust, a question that has become legitimate.

---

16. Minister of Education 2001-2006 who serves today as the CEO of the welfare foundation of Holocaust victims in Israel.
17. https://www.youtube.com/watch?v=aSyVOI5Cet8

Chetrit asks, "why Kedma? Why did this message come out of the Hatikva neighborhood, rather than from academia, the media, literature, or from any of the state's official pedagogical institutions, or any of the museums and institutes for the study and commemoration of the Holocaust?" The answer lies, he believes, in the school's pedagogy. "Kedma was the epitome of multicultural, postmodern pedagogy, based on faith in the side-by-side existence of multiple histories and narratives, not in one narrative that silences all others [...]. It was precisely from this place that the view of additional, panhuman dimensions of the Jewish Holocaust emerged." (p.219).

The cosmopolitan message of Kedma from 1995 has not reached schoolbooks yet. Israel's pedagogical narrative joins the conventional Western narrative in claiming that the Holocaust was "a unique and incomparable event of ahistorical proportions without a thought for the view of history that gave rise to it" (Raz-Krakotzkin 2019, 102). This position is specifically designed to affirm the Western conception of history that regards the Holocaust as "a catastrophic aberration, a lapse into barbarism," (Bashir and Goldberg 2019, 22) along the progressive continuum of European or Western history, and by no means as a product of the concept of progress itself. The distinction between the Holocaust and the history of the West is made to preserve the West's self-image as "the exclusive bearer of democratization, secularization, and progress", and the Holocaust remains "the only stain on the historical record of the modern West, a record rife, however, with slavery, genocide, dispossession, and destruction" (Raz-Krakotzkin ibid. 103).

The Western and the Zionist perspectives converge. For Israel, the uniqueness of the Holocaust is part of its definition as a Jewish state, and for the West it is part of the European commitment to accept it as such "by way of atonement or redress" (Raz-Krakotzkin 2019, 141).

The conception Israeli education inculcates is clear: the Shoah is a European Jewish catastrophe unlike any other, almost detached from any historical context other than antisemitism, and it is the final phase in the progression from exile to resurrection.

The main article the students were required to read for their final examination[18] in 2021 and in 2022 was written in 1978 by Holocaust historian Yehuda Bauer.[19] In this article Bauer maintains that the uniqueness of the Holocaust lies in its being a total, global, and ideological event. Never before

---

18. https://files.geva.co.il/geva_website/uploads/2021/02/%D7%A9%D7%90%D7%9C%D7%95%D7%9F-22261-1.pdf
19. https://www.yadvashem.org/yv/pdf-drupal/he/education/bauer_yesod.pdf
The article, published by the ministry of Education in 2000, was written previously.

people were murdered because they were born.[20] In another article, Bauer argues that the Rwandan genocide, unlike the Holocaust, was not ideological but "pragmatic" (Bauer 2001, 46, 266). Holocaust historian Dan Stone (2004, 5) responded cynically to this article: "one can breathe again now that the threat to the status of the Holocaust has been removed". The debate has been going on at least until 2019. In an article from August 15, 2019, Bauer explains that the Holocaust was not unique but rather unprecedented. [21] If it were "unique" he argues, it could not have been repeated, in one way or another, in other places. However, he advocates a Judeo-centric view of the Shoah. The students are not aware of the debate of which the article from 1978 is a part, nor of the divergent interpretations that have emerged over the forty years that have elapsed since its publication, even by Bauer himself.

Bauer's 1978 article, reproduced in the 2021 and the 2022 final examinations, is part of a curricular unit issued by Yad Vashem, whose title "How can a Man..." derives from a poem written by an Israeli navy recruit who was subsequently killed in battle, after visiting Auschwitz in 1994. This is a further example of how the Israeli military and Holocaust remembrance are so frequently intertwined, both in the society at large and in education. The photograph below (Image 43) shows an arrangement at the entrance to an Israeli school on Holocaust Day in 2020. The written part, next to the flag of Israel and the star of David on which Holocaust images and a candle are shown, is a quote from a letter written by a soldier, Hadar Goldin, who was killed in 2014 during the Israeli onslaught on Gaza – operation Zuk Eitan (Solid Rock). The letter was written after his trip to the death camps in Poland:

"I am going to the state of Israel. The state that is mine, that is ours. And I understand thanks to you, what this state is giving me, but above all what I have to give of myself to my state." The Shoah, the military and Israeli patriotism are interconnected.

---

20. See Bauer, Yehuda. 1978. "Against Mystification: The Holocaust as a Historical Phenomenon," in Bauer, *The Holocaust in Historical Perspective*. Seattle: University of Seattle Press. 35–36.
21. https://www.haaretz.co.il/opinions/2019-08-15/ty-article-opinion/.premium/0000017f-e9cf-d62c-a1ff-fdffe6760000

Image 43

To redeem Holocaust history from this persistent narrative, Holocaust Scholars have attempted to draw the contours of a new field of inquiry, believing this narrative has run its course and should be replaced by a different, universal, more empathic and responsible one. They propose to place research on the subject within a far broader historical, political and cultural context that defies consensus and closure,[22] arguing that the historiography of the Holocaust calls for a different form of narrative, based on self-conscious writing, that would simultaneously draw us closer to the events and "discourage the facile embrace of closure and coherence found in the typical realist narrative or in the grand master narratives" (Friedländer 1990, 5) such as the Zionist grand narrative of redemption and resurrection that informs Israeli schoolbooks.

Dirk Moses (2007)[23] suggests including the Holocaust in an account of European modernity that links nation-building, imperial competition, international and intra-national racial struggle, to the ideologically driven catastrophes of the twentieth century. Moses also advocates relating each genocide to others in a way that allows them to retain their distinctive features, without appearing completely detached from one another, for example considering colonial genocides alongside the Holocaust. Dan Stone (2004, 128)[24] sees the Holocaust "as part of a

---

22. Blatman, Daniel. 2015. "Holocaust Scholarship: Towards a Post-Uniqueness Era." *Journal of Genocide Research* 17, no. 1. 21–43.
23. Moses, A. 2007. "Conceptual blockages and definitional dilemmas in the 'racial century': genocides of indigenous peoples and the Holocaust." In A. Dirk Moses and Dan Stone (Eds.), *Colonialism and Genocide*, London & New York: Routledge, 148-180.
24. Stone, Dan. 2004. "The historiography of genocide: beyond 'uniqueness' and ethnic competition." In *Rethinking History: The Journal of Theory and Practice*, 8:1: 127-142.

continuum of the history of nation-building on racial, 'ethnic,' political, and developmental grounds, that has permitted the commission of the worst atrocities in the name of 'progress' and 'organic purity.'" These approaches would certainly allow for linkage between the Holocaust and the Nakba. Hannah Yablonka wishes Holocaust studies would teach students how power corrupts and how democracies fall in the face of nationalism and racism (2010). She rejects the idea that the Holocaust was unique, arguing that if it were unique there would be no reason to study it. In a recent interview (2021),[25] she declared that comparisons must be made. Ronnie Landau (2016, 16) recommends that the teaching of the Holocaust "should be approached through the psychology of human prejudice and racism." In this way, it "can serve as a highly effective educational means for sensitizing students to the distinct problem of antisemitism; to the universal issues of minority status and minority identities; to the need most of us have for cultural and national pride; and to the dangers of racial and religious stereotyping and hatred. No study of the Holocaust," he maintains, "would be truly serious, or stand a realistic chance of imparting its educational gravity if it were not related, in some way, to other expressions of man's apparently inexhaustible appetite for killing fellow-members of his species." Landau (ibid. 8) believes that without losing sight of the incomparable uniqueness of the Holocaust as an entire event, it is educationally essential and therefore legitimate to break it down into a range of limited human experiences, motives, crises, and responses, with which it might be easier to identify and which can stand comparison with other situations. For example, the pre-Holocaust Nazi anti-Jewish legislation of 1933–1938 can be considered in the light of attempts by some societies to marginalize entire groups by process of law, as happened in Apartheid South Africa and, one may add, is happening in Israel. The self-righteousness of many of the Nazi perpetrators, and their unwavering belief in the justness and ethics of their bloodthirsty undertaking bears a relation to almost every massacre in human history that has been carried out in the name of a religious or imperial/national mission. Such partial comparisons would help us view the Holocaust as something more than a symbol of Jewish fate and of Jewish unity, and of the need for a Jewish state.

Bashir and Goldberg (2019, 24)[26] propose formulating a new grammar by which to speak and write about the events that shaped Israeli society as it is. This "new grammar" or rather new discourse, places both the Holocaust and the Nakba in the context of a European history of racism, imperialism and colonialism, ethnic cleansing and genocide, of which Zionism is a part. This new grammar would de-

---

25. Alfasi, Moran "Coffee with Hannah Yablonka." February 7, 2021. https://www.onlife.co.il/general/21956
26. Bashir, Bashir and Amos Goldberg (Eds.). 2019. *The Holocaust and the Nakba: A New Grammar of Trauma and History.* Foreword by Elias Khoury. Afterword by Jacqueline Rose. Columbia University Press; *Marking Evil.* 2015.

Zionize the study of the Shoah and would enable the integration of many more voices. De-Zionizing Holocaust discourse and presenting the Holocaust as part of the Western history of racism, is a way of saying that although it was an extreme phenomenon of racism and genocide on an industrial scale, it is not an aberration of western civilization nor is it entirely unique in western history. (Goldberg and Bahir 2019).

Narrating the Land – a Joint Curriculum

> The land was rendered a mythic depiction, and its history the history of messianic-theological images. (Raz-Krakotzkin 2013, 159)

A joint curriculum should relate both Jewish history in the Diaspora and the history of Palestine. The Israeli curriculum, which currently requires Israeli Palestinians to learn Jewish-Zionist history including the Holocaust as a mandatory subject, ignores Palestinian history and culture, as it ignores previous Jewish histories and cultures. A joint curriculum would make a timely contribution toward rectifying this a-symmetrical approach by relating the history of the Jews and the history of the Palestinians.[27] It would go one-step further than the books that juxtapose the two competing narratives.[28]

The Holocaust and the Nakba

> Our Holocaust we cried. Their Holocaust we didn't cry? (Avot Yeshurun 1969. *You Carried Promises with You.*)

Raz-Krakotzkin (2005, 165) asks: "How can we redefine Jewish existence on the basis of the recognition of Palestinian rights and the aspiration for equality between Jews and Arabs?" The obstacle for Israel seems to be the "collective anxiety [that] stems from the fact that answering this question would require a redefinition of the Israeli consciousness."

The first to make the connection between the Holocaust and the Nakba was Hannah Arendt (*The Origins of Totalitarianism*, 290), who linked the phenomenon of Nazi violence directed against Jews to the obsession of the nation-state, constantly engaged in defining who belongs and who must be excluded, thereby turning internal minorities into a "problem" that calls for an urgent

---

27. Raz-Krakotzkin, Amnon. 2013. *History Textbooks and the Limits of Israeli Consciousness.* p. 7.
28. For example, Bar-On and Adwan. 2003. *Learning Each Other's Historical Narrative: Palestinians and Israelis.* Beit Jallah, PNA: A Prime Publication of the Peace Research Institute in the Middle East.

solution. Hitler's solution, she argued, did not solve the problem of minorities and the stateless, and the Zionist solution produced a new category of refugees, the Palestinian Arabs.

Israeli Holocaust rhetoric serves writers and poets in addressing the Nakba.[29] For those who grieve over the Nakba, the Palestinian villagers are the Jews of Eastern Europe, but for those who justify it, the Palestinians are the Nazis.

As was mentioned before, the Holocaust is the "chosen trauma" which defines Israeli Jewish identity and justifies its oppressive practices toward the Palestinians. It is not the chosen trauma of the Palestinian citizens and subjects though it defines their identity as the victims of the victims. Their victimizers equate them to their own victimizers and regard them to be the potential exterminators of the Jewish people. Thus, these two catastrophes visited by European people on "oriental" people are intertwined. As Confino (2019, 216) asserts, "The Holocaust, the Nakba, and the foundation of the State of Israel are the foundational pasts of modern Jewish history." And Elias Khoury contends that the Nakba is the Israeli mirror.[30] One cannot consider the Holocaust in isolation from the Nakba because, as Hanan Hever intimates, (2012, 60) "the Holocaust brought my parents to Palestine and consequently brought the disaster upon the Palestinians. Therefore, the Shoah is the lens I cannot dispose of when I contemplate my responsibility for the Nakba."

The Holocaust and the Nakba are similar in that they are both relevant to the essential struggle of humanity against racism (Bashir and Goldberg 2019, xii). Hence, as Bashir and Goldberg contend, if the memory of the Holocaust is to survive as a collective human memory, it is essential to take an uncompromising stand against expansionist colonial occupation, the Israeli version of which is one of the last remaining examples in today's world (ibid.).

Bashir and Goldberg devote half their book to Elias Khoury's novel *The Children of the Ghetto - My Name is Adam*, which tells the Palestinian version of the expulsion and massacre of Lydda's Palestinian inhabitants. Khoury uses the language of the Holocaust, thus comparing the compound, labeled the ghetto, in which the survivors were detained in years to come, surrounded by barbed wire, to the Warsaw ghetto. The only language that Adam of the Lydda ghetto has to describe his life is that of the Jewish Holocaust, mainly because he learned about the Holocaust at school, but not about the Nakba. He refers to the exodus from

---

29. Stav, Shira. 2012. "Nakba and Shoah. Mechanisms of comparison and denial in the Israeli Narrative." In *The Palestinian Nakba in Cinema and Literature in Israel. A selection of Conference Papers.*
Hever, Hanan. 2012. "'They both look at me straight in the face.' Avot Yeshurun between the Nakba and the Holocaust." In *Papers from the Conference: The Nakba in Israeli Literature and Cinema.*
30. Khoury, Elias. 2008. "The Mirror: Imagining Justice in Palestine." *The Boston Review* July/Aug. 2008.

Lydda as "a death march", and recalls his father, who allegedly fled and left him behind, among the men who went to their death opened-eyed, "like sheep to the slaughter." The day of the massacre is called "bloody Thursday", which reminds one of the lot of Rabbi Hagerman and his fellow Jews in Olkusz, Poland, on Bloody Wednesday.

The saga of the massacre and the expulsion of Lydda's inhabitants, told by Adam, is also reported by Israeli journalist Ari Shavit (2014, 135),[31] who relates the event as an act of revenge taken by the Israeli soldiers, after the wounding of a prominent fighter by the Palestinians besieged in the mosque. Such an act of revenge wrought by the Germans on the Jews resulted in Bloody Wednesday and many further bloody days. Shavit relates only the Israeli perspective as follows:

> Some 3rd regiment soldiers spray the wounded in the mosque with gun-fire. Others toss grenades into neighboring houses. Still others mount machine guns in the streets and shoot at anything that moves. After half an hour of revenge, there are scores of corpses in the streets, seventy corpses in the mosque. The corpses from the mosque are buried at night in a deep hole dug by some nearby Arabs, and a tractor is brought in before morning to cover the hole (p. 135).

For the journalist Shavit, as for Israeli schoolbooks, killed or murdered Palestinians are never victims, they are "corpses". Writing about them, Shavit employs the impersonal passive mode: the corpses "are buried" the tractor "is brought" and the deep hole "is dug". He mentions the Palestinian buriers vaguely and quantitatively as "some nearby Arabs." This is typical of colonial discourse: the colonized have no agency, for they are not social actors but merely "functionalized" people (Van Leeuwen 2008, 40, 42) who have no part in the story and remain "nameless characters [who] fulfill only passing, functional roles".

While the Israeli colonizers have a story, which is narrated and reproduced in the active mode, the colonized do not have a story. Shavit apparently is not concerned with the thoughts and feelings of the colonized Arabs. These are brought alive by Khoury, the novelist who, to borrow Naipaul's words (1995, 77),[32] writes about those "nearby Arabs" "as though they were English people. With the utmost seriousness [...] as though they had that kind of social depth and solidity and rootedness." Khoury's story de-functionalizes and re-humanizes the Arabs, revives their experience, which in Shavit's report is but a lacuna. One of them is Murad al-Alami, who lives in a different time, stuck on that Bloody Thursday whose stench has not left him for fifty years.

---

31. Shavit, Ari. 2014. *My Promised Land the Triumph and Tragedy of Israel*. New York. Spiegel and Grau.
32. *A Way in the World*. Vintage.

Murad tells the untold story, "It was six in the morning of Thursday [...] I'm not certain of the date but I'm sure it was a Thursday. The Israeli officer gathered the youth of the four teams that were working on collecting the bodies and informed us that today would be the last day of work. He ordered the leader of each team to have the bodies gathered together in the garden closest to where he was working. [...] The officer didn't forget to thank us in the name of the Israeli Defense Forces, saying that through this work we had proved our loyalty to the Jewish state and our worthiness to be citizens of that state, which had been established to restore to those in exile their right of return to the land of their fathers and grandfathers.

> We'd piled the bodies in the garden, and the rain poured down, and you can imagine what happened to the thirty corpses or parts of corpses that our team had piled on top of each other. When the rain stopped, the two Israeli soldiers told us to gather the scattered parts together again with the shovels and then one of them gave me a gallon can of kerosene and ordered me to splash it over the parts and the fire started [...] And we, my dear sir, had to wait while the ashes dispersed into the air and then gather the bones and bury them in a small hole (p. 291).

These were the Sonderkommandos of Lydda of whom Claude Lanzmann was ignorant and Ari Shavit did not care to write about. The link between the two groups of Sonderkommando is that they were both the victims of European racism and nationalism.

From diaries written by Israeli soldiers after the massacre, Shavit deduces that they too were appalled by the event and feared the loss of Jewish ethical values and their own resemblance to Nazi soldiers. One of them wrote as follows:

> There is an impression that the quick transition to a state, and to a state of Hebrew power, drove people mad. Otherwise, it is impossible to explain the behavior, the state of mind, the actions of the Hebrew youth, especially the elite youth. The moral code of the nation, forged during thousands of years of weakness, is rapidly degenerating, deteriorating, disintegrating. (p. 135.)

In other words, this soldier felt that power corrupts, that becoming "Nazified" is quite easy. This is the lesson Landau and other scholars wish Israeli schools would emphasize when teaching the Holocaust.

Khoury's story and observations bring about what Bhabha (1994, 139)[33] calls the uncanny "echo of histories that modernity might prefer had remained hidden." He foregrounds "the margins of the modern nation," that return to haunt you and "that you do not want to face again."[34] Khoury brings to the surface the story about what happened between or within the confirmed historical events, and

---

33. *The Location of Culture*. Routledge.
34. Huddart, David. 2006. *Homi Bhabha*. Routledge Critical Thinkers.

focuses on those whom the pedagogical version of history seeks to conceal, or to exclude from the curriculum.

Pedagogical and Performative Narratives

> While travelling theory may focus on the location of those who travel, the attention here is on the people whose bodies, territories, beliefs and values have been travelled through (Tuhiwai Smith 2012, 81).

Homi Bhabha distinguishes between two forms of national narrative: the pedagogical and the performative. The pedagogical narrative is conceived and conveyed by the colonizers. It reflects the meaning made by the dominant group at a certain point in time, in a certain place. Master national narratives such as the Zionist story From Exile to Resurrection are pedagogical. They tell us "that the nation and the people are what they are" and present "the continuist, accumulative temporality of the pedagogical" (Bhabha 1994, 157). The colonized peoples across the world have other stories to tell, that not only call into question the ideals and the practices that the pedagogical narrative generates, but also provide an alternative account of the history and an alternative timeline. The performative narrative does not "celebrate the monumentality of historicist memory, the sociological totality of society, or the homogeneity of cultural experience," (ibid.) but rather breaks up and disrupts the continuity of the pedagogical narrative through alternative and additional versions. Performative narratives introduce a temporality of the "in-between" the known events that form the timeline of the pedagogical narrative (ibid. 148), which features in every schoolbook. A comparison of the Israeli and the Palestinian narratives[35] shows very clearly that each follows its own distinct timeline that defines the nation. This calendrical element of the nation, as Benedict Anderson (1991, 26) maintains, reflects the idea that "each sociological organism moves by its own calendar through homogeneous, empty time." This idea "is a precise analogue of the idea of the nation, which is also conceived as a solid community moving steadily down (or up) history." (ibid.) The performative counter-narratives that disrupt both the timelines and the official narratives are powerful forms of resistance to this steady linear movement in empty time. They demonstrate "the prodigious, living principles of the people as contemporaneity, as that sign of the *present* through which national life is redeemed and iterated as a reproductive process" (Bhabha 1994, 145).

In pedagogical narratives, the people are the historical "objects" of a nationalist pedagogy. As in the historical recount, the text addresses events,

---

35. Adwan, Sami and Baron, Dan. 2012. *Side by Side: Parallel Histories of Israel-Palestine*. The New Press.

procedures, phenomena, and organizations; when a personality is mentioned, it serves metonymically to index an organization such as the state, the army, etc. Minorities and "others" are always objectified.

In the pedagogical narrative, based on the past, the marginalized people are often left to search for the fragments of themselves that were taken, catalogued, studied, stored and reproduced in the history that is presented back to them (Tuhiwai Smith 2012, 45). Such is the narrative presented to Palestinian, Mizrahi or Ethiopian students in Israel.

Edward Said (1978, 3)[36] has shown that in the Western construction of ideas about the Orient, namely Orientalism, a constant interchange takes place between the scholarly and the imaginative. Both the formal scholarly pursuit of knowledge and the informal, imaginative, anecdotal constructions of the Other have been intertwined with each other and with the activity of research. This is how "European culture was able to manage—and even produce—the Orient politically, sociologically, militarily, ideologically, scientifically, and imaginatively during the post-Enlightenment period."

While the pedagogical discourse foregrounds total sociological facts and identities, the performative discourse reminds us that those total facts are always susceptible to change and are subtly altered every day. Hence, as Bhabha contends, the pedagogical narrative is never as stable as it wishes to be. While we are told what the nation is and who is part of it, the national subjects are inventing the nation at every moment, changing its ideas of itself as well as its institutions. Bhabha believes that the problem of the pedagogical narrative lies with the very form of a standardized, falsely consensual national curriculum. As educational theorist Michael W. Apple (1996, 35), citing Bhabha,[37] argues, it is the non-processual nature of that knowledge, which claims to know all it needs to know, to grasp the nation as it is and always will be, (and its "others" as they have always been and always will be), that is the problem. This knowledge allows the powerful to deny the validity of the claim of indigenous peoples and migrants to existence, to land and territories, to the right of self-determination, to the survival of their languages and their forms of cultural knowledge, and to their natural resources and systems for living within their environments (Tuhiwai Smith 2012).

History and Literature

The performative narrative sides with literature, because tales are designed not only to give voice to the voiceless but to preserve people, cultures, and ecosystems. In fact, the performative narrative is often a hybrid text made up of oral and

---

36. Said, E. 1978. *Orientalism*. London: Vintage Books. p. 3
37. Apple, Michael W. 1996. *Cultural Politics and Education*. Buckingham: Open University Press.

written literature, poetry, art and personal memories. It is vital, contends Bhabha, that the artist, who is always on the side of the *performative*, resist the temptations of the static and the self-sameness of the community, namely the *pedagogical* (Huddart 2006, 72). As Elias Khoury asserts, history is fond of closure, while stories are not, just as our life is not.

The performative narrative obeys rules, which do not resemble those of the pedagogical narrative. The rules of literature, for instance, are different from those of historical writing. As Jerome Bruner (1986) observes,[38] literature has to be believable rather than scientifically testable, and it has to create "subjunctivity," namely room for engaging readers and allowing them to find their own interpretations or make their own meanings. The Holocaust picture books Shikhmanter (2014)[39] studied are a good example; they seldom end with a closure such as that found in schoolbooks. They mediate and preserve the meaning of Holocaust symbols but offer readers complex, stimulating representations that create the subjunctivity that Bruner regards as an essential quality of literature.

Both Holocaust and Nakba victims did not leave enough documents for the pedagogical narrative. The alternative ways to narrate the Holocaust and the Nakba, suggested by Goldberg and Bashir and the other participants in their edited volume (2019), are performative in that they include a multitude of voices and employ many forms of narrating both the past Holocaust and the ongoing Nakba, in relation to each other. Thus, they foreground a variety of perspectives and reveal numerous aspects of both catastrophes. This approach is compatible with Bhabha's (1994, 140) notion, that nations do not have to be conceived only in historicist terms, because they are forms of narration.

The difference between historical pedagogical writing and performative, indigenous or migrant literature, is best described by Khoury (p. 169) through a debate between Adam, the protagonist of the novel and its assumed writer, who learns about his own and his people's history from stories, both real and imagined, and an established Palestinian historian, regarding the life and death of his grandfather. The historian is interested in documented facts, because he knows that this is the only way he can refute the accounts of Westernized Zionist historians. All the rest – personal stories, memories, and letters, are of no importance to him.

> He said that [...] History has to rest on written documents, preferably official documents. [...] 'What kind of nonsense is that?' I asked him. 'The whole history of our Nakba is unwritten. Does that mean we don't have a history? That there

---

38. Bruner, Jerome. 1986. "Two Modes of Thought," in: *Actual Minds, Possible Worlds*. Cambridge, Mass.: Harvard University Press.
39. Shikhmanter, Rima. 2014. "Limitations as Possibilities: Uri Orlev's Holocaust Narratives for Children and Young Adults." *Children's Literature*, Volume 42. Johns Hopkins University Press. 1-19.

was no Nakba? Does that make sense?' He said those were the rules of the discipline of history and we could only face the Zionist historians if we had a properly documented past that they could recognize (p. 116).[40]

The colonized historian, who longs for Zionist approval, contemptuously dismisses Adam's personal story as "literature," "because he believed literature wasn't something serious." Adam objects: "I don't know what he meant by serious, but it would seem that his point of departure was the arrogance of the scholar who can see only facts. The man isn't working in the exact but in the human sciences, which remain, in my humble opinion, not far removed from speculation and which resemble literature in many aspects, though they lack its magic and beauty." (ibid.)

Later, after dreaming about the historian, Dr. Hanna Jiryis, Adam concludes that both scientific documents and personal stories and memories are needed to account for what really happened, provided the historians are Palestinian and not Western or Westernized. In this way, the performative and the pedagogical are intertwined, as Bhabha believes they should be. Roland Barthes makes a similar observation regarding history in his article *The Discourse of History*,[41] in which he argues that by reading Tolstoy's War and Peace one learns and remembers much more about Napoleon than by reading a textbook.

Adam does not write for Zionist eyes and therefore can see no hierarchy that places his mother's tales below or above the work of historian Walid Khalidi, although for his own novel it appears he prefers his mother's memories, which to him ring "one hundred percent true."

Therefore, both history and literature should be given more space in the joint curriculum, to include all the historical narratives and all the literary assets that were concealed or destroyed. This would facilitate "the constitution of a narrative authority" for marginal voices and minority cultures (Bhabha 1994, 150).

The official pedagogic narrative found in schoolbooks obeys the imperatives of the dominant political discourse, and serves a political agenda by which, as both Shohat and Tuhiwai Smith contend, cultures were broken, values negated, and key people ignored. This becomes apparent in the struggle waged over textbooks with every change of government, which proves that the academic scientific research underlying the pedagogical narrative is not "an innocent or distant academic exercise, but occurs in a set of political and social conditions" (Tuhiwai Smith 2012, 5).

The pedagogical Holocaust narrative reproduced in Israeli schoolbooks, foregrounds almost exclusively Zionist-affiliated movements, organizations, and persons, while suppressing or excluding those who were not Zionist. It portrays

---

40. Khoury, Elias, 2019. *Children of the Ghetto: My Name is Adam*. Archipelago Publishers.
41. In: *Rustle of Language*

Jewish immigration to Israel as the happy concluding episode of the lengthy return from exile to the homeland. In dealing with indigenous or migrant minorities, it conforms to the rules that dictate the negation of their previous life, hails their "rescue" by the Zionist movement and Israel, and exacerbates their depersonalization, marginalization, and even demonization, whenever the official position requires it. When schoolbooks appropriate literature, poetry and art, they do so to authenticate their pedagogical narrative. This may be the reason why all the "sources" attached in the schoolbooks to the reports about Ethiopian Jews – whether poems, literature, psychological or sociological studies, including the ones Ethiopian-Israeli students are required to read on their *Identity Journey*, are extracts from texts written by non-Ethiopian Jews. The performative dimension of literature, art, and poetry or of personal diaries and memories, are not allowed to disrupt the pedagogical message.

Hence, a joint curriculum should break open the literary canon, which is itself a kind of narrative about what is considered the best that has been thought and written, and reproduces the worldviews of those who rendered it canonical. Israeli literary anthologies for schoolchildren are almost entirely Eurocentric, and Mizrahi, Palestinian and Ethiopian literatures have yet to claim their place in literary anthologies for school. Pedaya (2020)[42] offers some guidelines as to how Jewish-Arab shuttered and rejected "ethnic" literature and poetry can be reinstated and assume its proper place in the realm of Israeli letters. This literature, nourished by ancient Jewish poetry and saga telling, would enable children to become acquainted with the cultural sources of their ancestors. A joint curriculum can take up this initiative and develop it to include other minority literary and poetic works as well.

Alternative Research Regarding "Others"

From the perspective of indigenous and migrant people, the gathering of information by Western scientists is as random, ad hoc, and damaging as that undertaken by amateurs; a scientific research that does not differ from "any other visits by inquisitive and acquisitive strangers." (Tuhiwai Smith 2012, 3).

The confrontation between Western documented narratives and indigenous oral ones is addressed by historian Tuhiwai Smith (2012,14), who writes about Maori's memories, and by Gregg Sarris regarding his own experiences in his native tribe, the Coast Miwok and Pomo Native Americans. Both find it difficult

---

42. Pedaya, Haviva. 2020. "Toward Building a Net for Mizrahi Literature." *Haaretz*, September 29, 2020.

to render these oral histories and culture in the language of Western scholarship.[43] Natives often argue that Westernized scholars cannot speak from a "real" and authentic indigenous position, while those who speak from this position are criticized because they do not make "sense," and their talk is reduced to some "nativist" discourse, dismissed by academic colleagues as naive, contradictory, and illogical. However, as Tuhiwai Smith observes, these "are the stories, values, practices and ways of knowing which continue to inform indigenous pedagogies." (Tuhiwai Smith ibid.).

The demand that historical narratives be written by scholars who do not belong to the ruling group, is raised by indigenous people all over the world and by Israel's Jewish-Ethiopian community as well. Ethiopian Israeli activists and academics, like their Mizrahi counterparts, object time and again to their being "studied scientifically" so that the state and its institutions can better "cope" with them. Recent studies and artistic productions by Ethiopian Israelis "emphasize the need for voices of the Israeli-Ethiopian community to be heard and to rewrite life in Ethiopia, the migration and absorption experiences, from their perspective, not through the eyes of non-Ethiopians. Thus, they aim to restore the memory of Ethiopian Jewry erased during the integration process and increase public awareness of the Beta Israel heritage." (Anteby-Yemini 2019, 46). [44]

Ella Shohat (2017, 121)[45] proposes that a new interdisciplinary research project be launched that would de-Zionize and de-Orientalize Eurocentric research on Israeli "others." Such research should be written by non-Eurocentric scholars and writers. As Tuhiwai Smith asserts, indigenous peoples across the world are longing for such research that would enable them to tell not only their own stories but also the history of the West through the eyes of the colonized. In other words, the history of the represented should be written by them or by their true representatives. Therefore, in a joint curriculum, meant for all children in Israel/Palestine, all parties should be represented by their own representatives, (Bashir and Goldberg 2019, Shohat 2017).

The interdisciplinary field Shohat envisions "would transcend purist notions of national identity to make room for proliferating differences within and beyond nation-states [...]. This field would critique and even bypass the premises of Orientalist representation and Eurocentric discourse and the concomitant demonization of Arab-Muslim culture." (Shohat. Ibid.119)[46]. It would interrupt

---

43. Sarris, Greg. 1993. *Keeping Slug Woman Alive: A Holistic Approach to American Indian Texts.* University of California Press. Berkeley, CA.
44. Anteby-Yemini, Lisa. 2019. "From a Returning Jewish Diaspora to Returns to Diaspora Spaces: Israeli-Ethiopians Today." In *Israel: A Diaspora of Memories*, edited by Michèle Baussant, Dario Miccoli, Esther Schely-Newman, Issue no.16. QUEST. *Issues in Contemporary Jewish History.* Journal of Fondazione CDEC. 46.
45. Shohat, Ella. 2017. *On the Arab-Jew, Palestine, and other Displacements.* Pluto Press. 120
46. "The invention of the Mizrahim." In: *On the Arab-Jew, Palestine, and Other Displacements*

the pedagogical narrative, in which both Jewish minorities and Palestinians have been living "allochronically" in another "time," and have gained entrance into history through Zionism. (Shohat ibid.)

A de-Zionized history of Israel/Palestine will enable us to see Jewish and Palestinian histories forever intertwined by complex and constantly changing intricate links. The history of Arab-Jews, Holocaust victims and survivors, and Nakba victims and survivors, will be addressed in relation to one another.

The de-Zionization of the narrative entails the de-indigenization of Euro-Jews. It can no longer profess exile negation nor seek to negate life in Palestine during the 2000 years "we" have not been there. It should reconnect the descendants of both European and Middle Eastern and African Jews to their origins and their untold history, while reinstating the Palestinian Arabs as autochthones, whose history and culture have been erased both physically and symbolically.

Identity

Talmudic scholar Daniel Boyarin (2023, 57) contends that identity is performance. This definition "challenges the physical, real, or factual existence of a given cultural category, such as gender, and argues for its constructedness by what human actors do." Hence, our social and personal identity may be constantly changing and evolving, and cannot be approached in a rigid, uncompromising manner (Shohat 2017). Identities in Israel, as in other countries of immigrants, have always been defined by hyphens (Shohat 2017, 104). Erasing the non-Jewish side of the hyphen and classifying all Jews according to a unidimensional categorization that places them closer to one another than to the cultures of which they were a part, is tantamount to dismembering a community's identity. To see Arab or Ethiopian Jews, Russian or American Jews as simply Jews or Israeli, would be tantamount to viewing African Americans, despite their complex, conflictual history, as simply American. At the same time, to expect Mizrahim to be simply Arab would be tantamount to reducing African Americans simply to Africans.

Just like other migrant cultures, Israeli culture has always been hybrid. All the identities in this country are hybrid and diasporic (see also Boyarin 2023),[47] even that of the Palestinian natives, who live in a state of internal colonialism and hence in an internal exile, and whose life world and life experience are totally different from those of other Palestinian refugees both in the Occupied Territories and in other countries. Hybridity, according to Bhabha, is not a synthesis of thesis and antithesis. An Arab-Jew is not a constant Arab + a constant Jew, and an Ethiopian

---

47. *The No-State Solution*, Yale University Press.

Israeli is not Ethiopian + Israeli, because each part of the hyphenated identity influences and multiplies the meaning of the other half in new and ever-changing ways. For example, the experience of discrimination and racism of Ethiopian-Israelis has turned their color into a political identity. "As they discover their 'négritude' in Israel [they] begin to identify with other black minorities around the world" (Anteby-Yemini 2019, 40). Israeli-Ethiopian rappers, nourished by African and African-American music, have become very popular and influential entertainers among young Israelis of all social strata.

Realizing that we all have hybrid or hyphenated identities means, as Kristeva (1994, 170) points out, knowing that we are foreigners to ourselves, and it is with the help of this knowledge that we can attempt to live with others.[48] However, realizing that we are all foreigners does not mean that we are all exactly the same (Kristeva 1994, 181–2). It rather means that we cannot assign foreignness to other groups and then dictate their actions or identities. One cannot legitimately require individuals or groups to assimilate into a given culture, as Israel demands of its Jewish migrants and Palestinian colonized society. To be a foreigner among non-foreigners, is obviously to be singled out, as asylum seekers around the world can testify. Yet if we are all foreigners, then it is possible to talk about a general quality of foreignness that defines most people in these global post-modern times. Acknowledging this general quality may lead to tolerance, to empathy, and to the capacity to say and teach that "the other is me."

A New Semiosis

The changes to the existing narrative should not be confined to its topics, although many components of content should be re-considered, along with the "paper time" allocated to certain facts and personalities, and the backgrounding or exclusion of other facts and personalities. The joint curriculum should aim to change language itself and the speech acts regarding "others". The changes should affect lexico-grammar, genre, style and modality. Lexico-grammatical changes should address first of all the way "others" are depicted; the "verbal hygiene"[49] whereby, for instance, the killing of Palestinians is termed "an operation," human beings are referred to as "civilian targets," and ethnic cleansing as "purification", or Holocaust victims as "cargo". They should address all the categories of racist discourse that are used to describe the "others." The changes should address modes (passive mode applied to "others" versus active mode applied to agents of change and control), nominalization (e.g. defining human acts and human caused situations through general grammatical metaphors), qualifications and means of

---

48. Kristeva, Julia. 1994. *Strangers to Ourselves*, trans. Leon S. Roudiez. Columbia University Press.
49. Term coined by Deborah Camron 2012. *Verbal Hygiene*. Routledge.

appraisal, among other structures. Visually, it should incorporate unbiased scientific and artistic visuals such as drawings, paintings, maps, diagrams, photographs, and reconsider the use of cartoons as well as racist and anti-Semitic caricatures.

The joint curriculum should not present human-caused injustice as natural facts, and should replace ideological assertions by suggestions for thought and debate. It cannot articulate a single ideology and cannot follow or rather inculcate the established collective memory, designed and perpetuated by Zionist Israeli education. It should be rid of idées fixes,[50] and offer a dialogic discourse in Bakhtin's (1986) terms, which promotes *an active understanding*, as an antidote to the monologic authoritative discourse that preaches one ultimate "truth" - that of Zionism - and requires *passive understanding* and compliance.

A dialogic narrative will have the potential to "explore the syncretic interaction" (Stam and Shohat 2014, 365) between different groups in faith, in art, in literature, philosophy, social perceptions, technologies and science, and expand students' capacity to cross cultural and individual divides,[51] to engage in a process of cross-cultural intellectual stimulation, and become aware of what Stam and Shohat (ibid. 387) define as "shared contradictions and differentiated commonalities, differences that connect and similarities that separate [...] 'transversalities' (instead of universality), or the hierarchical and lateral syncretisms and dialogisms."

Last Words

Bhabha, in *Narrating the Nation* (2008)[52], contends that like colonial authority, the national pedagogic narrative appears entirely confident of its consistency and coherence, although it is constantly being undermined by its inability to truly "fix" the identity of the people, and limit it to a single overpowering nationality. We should not desire any such end, he argues, because that would force us to accept a fixed and therefore stereotypical notion of any given national identity (Huddart 2006). Since current Israeli textbooks appear to affirm the validity of stereotypical representations of both "us" and "others", a joint curriculum should be written in a way that is "never simply white and never simply black" (Bhabha, *The White Stuff*, 1998, 24). In the Israeli-Palestinian context, a shared narrative can never be simply Western or simply Eastern. The multi-layered Israeli/Palestinian culture cannot be collapsed into a simplistic division of East-versus-West or Arab-versus-Jew, or for that matter, Israel versus Palestine. The joint narrative needs to contest

---

50. *The Rustle of Language*. Chapter 4, p. 127. University of California Press.
51. Holquist, M. 2009. *Dialogism: Bakhtin and His World*. Psychology Press, USA, Routledge.
52. Berghahn Books.

stereotypes and demonstrate, in Bhabha's words, that "there is life outside and beyond the stereotype, even for its victims," (1995, 110)[53] by breaking open the fixed stereotypes and bringing contrasts to life in a shared text, allowing students to contest and construct new, divergent and hybrid identities in an ongoing process.

This curriculum should be polycentric (Stam and Shohat 2014) and represent all the different histories and points of view simultaneously, not as confrontational or competing memories but as one multi-faceted history of the place, an ongoing story of shared life. It should trace the timelines of all the communities that have lived in Israel/Palestine, thereby disrupting the pedagogic narrative sequence through the many performative narratives, concerning events that have been concealed or overlooked, but are central to the history of all the people. It should relate the deeds of the different personalities who marked the trajectory of each group, and highlight the joint initiatives of Jews and Palestinians in all realms of life, such as agriculture, construction, commerce, music and letters.[54] For example, it should focus on the joint history of Jerusalem, Jaffa, Tiberias and Haifa, where Jews and Arabs have lived and worked together for the well-being of all.

The joint curriculum should remedy the negation of exile and the rejection of exilic cultures and exilic languages along with the negation of life in Palestine over the last two millennia. It should celebrate the Jewish cultures that have flourished for hundreds of years in the "Diaspora," in an enriching harmony with the other, especially Muslim cultures.

The joint curriculum should not otherize, but rather celebrate the particular history and culture of all individuals and all groups, and present all the people respectfully, as equal and valuable human beings, rather than as faceless herds or samples. Holocaust sufferers should not be presented as the Jews we do not want to become but as people who had or were deprived of a rich and interesting life where they had dwelt. The girl wearing the yellow badge should become Hanna Lehrer again, and the Jew praying before being murdered should become the Dayan Rabbi Moshe Hagerman again. Masha Bruskina should be defined not only by her Judaism but by her own Communist convictions and her brave deeds. Settela should regain her true name and her true story. Ethiopian and Mizrahi Jews should tell their own history in their own voice and so should the Palestinians and the Bedouins. The joint curriculum should restore the names to the nameless. People, mountains and valleys, cities and villages should regain their identity and

---

53. '"Black Male": The Whitney Museum of American Art'. (1995)
54. Klein, Menachem. 2014. *Lives in Common: Arabs and Jews in Jerusalem, Jaffa and Hebron*. Hurst Pub; Monterescu, Daniel and Dan Rabinowitz, eds. 2007. *Mixed Towns Trapped Communities: Historical Narratives, Spatial Dynamics, Gender Relations and Cultural Encounters in Palestinian Israeli Towns*. Routledge; Elhanan, Yigal. 2020. *From Yaffa to Jaffa to Yaffo*. Rosa Luxemburg Fund Sadaka Reut Arab Jewish Youth Partnership.

their history. Palestinian victims should be represented as human casualties and not as corpses, and the circumstances of their death should be related not from a utilitarian Israeli point of view, but in a way that arouses empathy and unsettlement regarding all victims and all crimes. This "empathic unsettlement" would transform otherness from a problem to be disposed of into a moral and emotional challenge. (Bashir and Goldberg. 2019, 25)

A joint curriculum should be written in the country's two main languages: Hebrew and Arabic. This bilingual curriculum will enable the various groups to narrate themselves in their own voice and to learn each other's language. It should therefore not only celebrate the "revival" of the Hebrew language as a great achievement, but also address the problematics of imposing a foreign language on such a diversity of people and cultures. The joint curriculum should highlight the Palestinian and Jewish Israeli writers and poets who write both in Hebrew and in Arabic, and whose writing reflects the hybridity of their life as Israeli citizens and their use of language as a tool of communication, resistance and defiance.

To conclude, a joint curriculum will differ from the present one both ideologically and semiotically. It will not seek to shock, to traumatize, or to incite revenge. It will not limit the choice of content to pander to this or that ideology but will teach receptiveness toward other versions of history, and toward other languages and cultures, encouraging discussion and celebrating hybridity and the rights of minorities. It will adopt the *theatre mode* of reaction to history, "with its potential for emotional engagement and identification" (Chouliaraki 2006, 179). The alternative curriculum should teach accountability and responsibility, and to observe events in Israel/Palestine through the lenses of multiculturalism and human rights. In the words of Boyarin (2023,130), it should educate children to "care deeply and struggle for the oppressed of other nations as well." Israel/Palestine should be portrayed as a place where a common, multicultural life existed in the past and can exist again.[55] This curriculum will realize the potential of revealing to children the richness, the diversity, and the colorfulness of the place they live in and of the cultures that surround them.

---

55. Klein, Menahem. 2014. *Lives in Common*. Oxford University Press.

INDEX

A

Abendt, Noa, 97, 98
About, Ilsen, 134, 177, 182, 183
Abrahamson, Irving, 41
Abu Khdir, Muhamad, 213
Adorno, Theodor W., 29, 30, 31, 116, 117, 119, 129
Adwan, Sami, 260, 302, 306
African "humanitarian crisis", 279
Agamben, Giorgio, 38, 232
Agee, James, 171
al-Alami, Murad, 304–305
al-Ali, Naji, 100
Al Husseini, Haj Amin, 256
Allach concentration camp, 113
Allied army, 87
Alterman, Nathan, 157
Amalek, 6
Amaral, Marina, 186–187
American Jews, 295
Amery, Jean, 43
Amir, Yigal, 253
Amital, Rabbi, 218
Anderson, Benedict, 306
Anielewicz, Mordechai, 133, 202, 203, 204
Ann Frank Graphic Novel (novel), 46
anonymization, 154–155

through captioning, 155

Anteby-Yemini, Lisa, 278, 280, 311, 313

Antelmes, Robert, 38, 43

anxiety of incompleteness, 7

Apfelfeld, Aharon, 39

Appadurai, Arjun, 7, 244

Apple, Michael W., 307

Arab Jews, 8, 240–242, 249, 270, 271, 278, 287, 312
- cultural identity, 263–265
- defined, 261
- discourse regarding, 265
- ethnicity, 264
- imagined community, 264
- inclusion of, 264
- othering of, 15, 240, 261–269
- "primitive conditions" of poverty and superstition, 263
- representation of, 13–18, 290
- secondary cultural differences, 267
- Zionist narrative regarding, 263

Arendt, Hannah, 30–31, 36, 113, 147, 302

Arkadyev, Lev, 150

Arnheim, R. A., 227

Ashkenaz (documentary), 271

Ashkenazi Jews, 17, 264, 266–267, 270, 272

atrocity images, 43, 107–109
- accoutrements of, 64
- extermination images, 109–128
- impact of, 210–213

verbal text, 128–131

Auschwitz-Birkenau, 84, 87

Auschwitz style, 41, 47, 57, 87–88

Avieli-Tabibian, Ketsia, 72–73, 98–100, 113, 114, 159, 167, 204, 266, 267, 272, 273, 276–277

Ayab, Ruth., 85, 94, 169

Aykhner, Roze, 205

B

Baartman, Saartje, 182

Bak, Samuel, 94, 99, 100

Balata refugee camp, 240

Balibar, Etienne, 259

Ball, Karyn, 41

Barak, Aharon, 247

Barak, Ehud, 15

Bar Gal, Yoram, 223

Bar Hillel, Moshe, 113, 125, 130, 204, 241, 272

Barnett, Victoria, 174

Bar-On, Dan, 260, 302, 306

Bar-Tal, Daniel, 4, 258

Barthes, Roland, 23, 43–44, 94, 156, 194, 277–283, 309

Bartov, Omer, 11, 54, 57

Bashir, Bashir, 6, 301–303, 308

Baudrillard, Jean, 67, 174

Bauer, Yehuda, 298–299

Baum, Rob, 278

Bauman, Zygmunt, 12, 13, 15, 31, 36, 54, 180, 221, 229, 230, 232, 244, 248, 249, 250, 251, 283

Baumel, Judith Tydor, 153

Be'er, Haim, 56

beggars, 136–149

Being Citizens in Israel (2016), 218, 220, 221, 225, 228, 236, 241, 243, 276, 278–279

Bekerman, Zvi, 215, 287, 290

*Benghazi-Bergen Belsen (*Sukary), 272

Ben-Gurion, David, 10–11, 12, 14, 17, 165, 201, 203, 252, 253, 256, 268, 269

Benjamin, Walter, 156

Bennet, Naftali, 221, 245

Ben-Pazi, Ḥanokh, 202

Berda, Yael, 229

Bergen-Belsen, 273

Bergen Belsen concentration camp, 272

Berger, John, 175

Bergman, Ingmar, 95

Bernstein, Basil, 23, 60

*Beyond Words: Translation and Multimodality (*Kress), 59

Bezemer, Jeff, 21, 60

Bhabha, Homi, 18, 227, 228, 293, 305–308, 312, 314–315

Biagioli, Mario, 181, 183

Birkenau, Auschwitz, 66–67

Blanchot, Maurice, 57

Blank, N., 249

Blatman, Daniel, 51

blog, 45–47

Bloody Thursday, 304

Bloody Wednesday, 159, 160, 161, 165, 208, 304

Bloom, Etan, 262

Blösche, Josef, 91, 100

Boltanski, Luc, 128

Bourke-White, Margaret, 43, 75

*Boy–a Holocaust Story, The (*Porat), 91–92

Boyarin, Daniel, 312, 316

Brandt, K., 169

Brasse, Wilhelm, 176, 177, 184, 186

Breslauer, Rudolf, 159

Brink, Cornelia, 84, 209

Brinker, Hans, 142

British army, 273

Britton, J., 57

Brockhill, Aneta, 220, 232, 259

Broide-Heler, Anna, 205

Browning, Christopher, 115, 117, 118–119

Bruner, Jerome, 308

Bruskina, Masha, 150–152, 154, 208, 315

Btozsat, Martin, 34

Bundesarchive, 71

bureaucracy, 31, 33, 117, 135

Burg, Avraham, 128, 215

Burging, Victor, 24

C

Camino, Mercedes, 150, 151, 153

Canetti, Elias, 248, 279

categorization, 133–135

Celan, Paul, 39

Čengeri family, 188, 190

centrifugal memory, 5

Césaire, Aimé, 30

Charny, Israel, 173

Chatterley, Catherine, 39

Chéroux, Clément, 86–87

Chetrit, Sami Shalom, 296–298

chosen trauma, 52–54, 128, 288, 290, 303. *see also* Holocaust

Chouliaraki, Lilie, 38, 42–43, 86, 113, 121, 125, 132, 164, 165, 173, 174, 176, 177, 183–184, 186, 196, 201, 212–213

Christianity, 288

    anti-Semitic, 269

    photographs, 80

Chronicle of a Jewish Family in the Twentieth Century, A (Ka-Tzetnik), 55

civilization, 30

The Clock (Ka-Tzetnik), 58

Coffin, Caroline, 193, 195, 196, 197, 258

cognitive militarism, 4

Cohen, Mor, 11

Cohen Yinon, 16

Cole, Tim, 51, 173–174

colonialism, 6, 10, 13, 16, 30, 197, 293, 301, 306

    colonial Britain, 236

    colonial relationships, stereotyping and racism in, 228–230

    cultural oppression as, 265

discourse, 280, 304
in Europe, 30
inner, 275
internal, 312
Libyan and, 45, 264, 271–273, 290
occupation, 303
in Occupied Palestinian Territories, 25
of Palestine, 96, 100, 219–220, 222–223, 232–233, 243, 252, 256, 259
settler-colonial discourse, 250, 258
shtetl, 238
towards non-Jewish and non-Western citizens, 17
Zionist, 262, 309
Confino, Alon, 295, 303
Cordell, Karl, 220, 232, 259
corrective discrimination, 276
Crane, Susan, 69–70, 184, 185, 208–209, 211, 212
cropped image
  as symbol of annihilation, 88–105
    boy as symbol in Israeli schoolbooks, 98–101
    boy as symbol of Palestinian suffering, 95–97
    childhood in Ghetto, 102–105
    icon, 92–95
cross-cultural intellectual stimulation, 314
Cusian, Albert, 71, 72, 74, 141
Czerniakow, Adam, 73, 138, 139, 141, 142, 203

D
Dahan, Gavriel, 280

Daoud, Kamel, 280

Davidson, Lawrence, 16, 238

Dean, Carolyne, 58, 170, 171, 173, 174, 183

Death Camps, 213

De Beaugrand, Robert, 24

deleted identity, 149–154

de L'Homme, Musee, 182

Democratic Values and Judaism (2009), 246

De-Nur, Yehiel, 55

Derrida, Jacques, 59

Desbois, Father Patrick, 109

Destruction and Heroism (Hertz 2015), 127

Deutsche Soldaten Zeitung, 124

de-Zionization of narrative, 312

dialogic narrative, 314

Diaspora Jews, 49, 53, 263

Didi-Huberman, George, 43, 64–65, 81, 92, 104, 122–123, 125, 138, 177, 208

Diner, Dan, 115, 129, 138, 179

Discourse of History, The (Barthes), 309

Domka, Eliezer, 248

Doniel, Rabbi, 164–167, 208

Down Memory Lane (Vashem), 25, 49, 210

Dreifuss, Havi, 209–210

Duras, Marguerite, 38

Dwork, Deborah, 83

Dworzecki, Mark (Meir), 51

Dubno, Jews of, 118

E

Eban, Abba, 257, 268
Edelman, Marek, 202–204
Egyptian prisoner of war camps, 256
Eichmann, Adolf, 51, 112, 127
Eichmann Trial (1961), 51
Einsatzgruppen massacre, 112, 120, 124
Eldar, Akiva, 15
Eldar, Zipi, 266
Elkana, Y., 4
Elhanan, Yigal. 2020. *From Yaffa to Jaffa to Yaffo*, 325
Emilia (2008), 272
empathic unsettlement, 47, 48, 209, 326
empathy, 5, 6, 38, 45, 46, 69, 80, 93–94, 108, 113, 117, 118, 132, 163, 184, 195, 208, 247, 259, 313, 316
Eshkol, Levi, 51
Essed, Philomena, 20, 275
Ethiopian Jews, 7, 8, 13, 172, 262, 264, 275, 276, 279, 287, 310, 315
    cultivation, 276, 283
    eternal immigrants, 282
    immigration, 279
    photography, 277–283
    representation in schoolbooks, 276–277
ethnicities, 290–291
Eurocentrism, 18
European Jews, 6, 10, 14, 39, 49, 51–52, 84, 186, 198, 216, 238, 261–263, 303
Evron, Ram, 41
exilic Jew, 50

Ezrahi, De-Koven, 4–5
Ezrahi, Sidra De-Koven, 157

F
Fairclough, N., 23
Fanon, Franz, 30, 229
The Farhud, 270
fear
    shudder and, 8
    as unifying element, 6
Felman, Shoshana, 38
Feniger, Ofer, 252
Final Solution, 32, 37, 38, 46, 71, 84, 118, 127, 147, 148, 189, 237, 257, 272
Fink, Ida, 65
Fisk, Robert, 123–125
Focus on History (2020), 264
Fogu, Claudio, 29
Forceville, Charles, 20
Fox-Bevilacqua, Marisa, 294–295
Frank, Anna, 133, 208, 294
Friedländer, Saul, 32–35, 37, 43, 44, 49, 55, 112, 115, 129, 199, 209
functionalization, 134
Funkenstein, Amos, 194
Funny Animals (1972), 75

G
Gal, Meir, 265
Galtung, Johan, 233, 237, 250

Gamliel, Tova, 261, 263, 264, 267

Gantz, Benny, 245

Gauthier, Guy, 93–94

Gaza, 96–98

Gee, James Paul, 19, 21

Gelblum, Arye, 268

genericization, 134

Genette, Gérard, 24

Geography of the Land of Israel (2003), 225

Georg, Willy, 102, 103, 139

German army, 96

German concentration camp, 212

Gershon, Karen, 12

Geva, Sharon, 37, 186

Ghetto Fights, The (Bund), 202

*Girl Who Stole My Holocaust, The (*Hayut), 211, 215

Glasner-Heled, Galia, 56

Gnilka, Ewald, 103

Goebbels, Joseph, 66

Going the Civilian Way (2012), 233, 240

Goldberg, Amos, 6, 56, 294, 301–303, 308

Goldberg Tzafrir, 248

Goldberg, Vicky, 85, 127

Goldin, Hadar, 299

Goldstone, Richard, 96

Gourevitch, Philip, 174

Grass, Gunther, 39

grave security events, 255

Great Patriotic War, 152
Great Synagogue in Warsaw, 89
Green, Avraham, 10, 57–58
Greenberg, Uri Zvi, 39
Grosbard, Ofer, 8
Grossman, David, 38, 257
Grossman, Mendel, 65
Gur-Ze'ev, Ilan, 13
Gutman, Israel, 93, 110, 111, 113, 129, 152, 153, 154, 175, 179, 272

H

Hagerman, Rabbi, 159, 160, 161, 162, 163, 164, 165, 166, 167, 189, 208, 304, 315
Haimi, Yoram, 271
Hall, Stuart, 181–182
Halliday, 35, 189, 196
Handala, 100, 101
Hayut, Noam, 96, 108, 128, 211, 212, 215
Hazan, Haim, 5, 29, 30, 294
Heath, Shirley Brice, 20
Heberer, Patricia, 152
Heled, Galia, 56
Henrikson, A. K., 231
hereditary victims, 13, 54, 251, 252
Hertz, Tehila, 108, 118, 188, 194
Hertzog, Chaim, 246
Hertzog, Esther, 20
Hever, Hanan, 303
Heyman, Eva, 30, 46

Himmler, Heinrich, 89

Hirsch, Marianne, 9, 43–44, 64, 65, 75–76, 87–89, 90, 95–96, 110, 147, 149, 163, 174, 190, 208

History of the Recent Generations, The (1998), 199, 205

Hitler's Willing Executioners (Goldhagen), 35

Hobsbawm, Eric, 31

Hodge, Robert, 133

Holland, Jews of, 44

Holocaust, 3–4, 7–9, 12–15. *see also* Arab Jews; Palestinians
    atrocity images, 42–43, 107–131, 210–213
    as chosen trauma, 52–54, 128, 288, 290, 303
    condescending stance towards victims and survivors, 17
    cosmopolitanization of memory, 294
    cropped image as symbol of annihilation, 88–105
    defined, 12, 32
    desire for, 41–42
    extermination images, 109–128
    foundational event, 295
    ghost, 17
    historical recount, 33 (*see also* recount, historical)
    icons and symbols, 83–88
    individual victims, 133–135
        armband sellers, 136–149
        beggars, 136–149
        image–text relations, 155–167
        indetermination, anonymization, and irreverence, 154–155
        little smugglers, 136–149
        partial information and deleted identity, 149–154

instruction, 49–54

    Ka-Tzetnik Project, 55–58

    from Shoah to Resurrection, 54–55

legitimating Palestinian discrimination, 217–219

and Nakba, 302–306

narrative, Mizrahi Jews and, 269–273

North African and Libyan, 45

photographs, 44, 169–171 (*see also* pornography)

preventing, 7–8

principles of multidirectional memory, 18

representation of victims, 10–12, 29–31, 288–289

    different modes of, 38–41

    photographs, use of, 41–45

    realist and antirealist writing, 35

    transduction, 45–47, 75-82

    visual representation, 41–45

    writing, 32–38

themed ice dance, 46

verbal text, 128–131

visual representation of (*see* visual representation of Holocaust)

WWII and, 223

Holocaust and Heroism Day, 51

Holocaust is Over, It is Time to Rise from its Ashes, The (Burg), 215

Holocaust Memorial Day, 51, 108

Holocaust (NBC 1978), 46

Holocaust Remembrance Day, 54

From Holocaust to Resurrection, 55

Holquist, M., 18, 20, 314

Holtschneider, K. Hannah, 69, 84–85, 169, 189

Hoopes, J. Ed., 85

Horkheimer, Max, 31

horrid fascination, 42

House of Dolls, Piepel, The Clock (Ka-Tzetnik), 55

Huber, Lea, 189–190

Huddart, David, 228, 230, 305, 308, 315

Hulugeb, 278–279

Hussein, Sadam, 253

human debris, 10

humanity, 47

human weeds, 13, 15

I

icons, 83–88
    atrocity, 107–109
        extermination images, 109–128
        impact of, 210–213
        verbal text, 128–131
    of destruction, 112
    documentary images, 84
    and symbols, 83–88

identity
    deleted, 149–154
    "minorities" and "ethnicities", 290–291
    pedagogical and performative narrative, 312–313

Identity Journey program, 282

Ignatieff, Michael, 171

Illouz, Eva, 6
images
    cropped (*see* cropped image)
    of extermination, 109–128
    pornography, 178–184
image–text relations, 155–167
immigrants, 135, 172, 221, 312
    Arab-Jewish, 269
    from the "East", 262
    from Ethiopia, 262
    as ethnicities, 264
    Hebrew Language examination for, 11
    to Israel, 15, 310
    Jewish and Muslim, 16
    of Jews from Islamic countries, 261–262, 265, 269
    non-European, 263
    non-Jewish from former Soviet Union, 225
    from North Africa, 268, 269
    Palestinian, 224, 290
    Russian, 7, 278–279
    Sephardi, 268
    from Yemen, 266–267
    Yemenite, 266–267
imperialism, 301
Imperial War Museum: In the Warsaw Ghetto: Summer 1941 © IWM (HU 060701), 102
Impulevičius-Impulėnas, Antanas, 152
Inbar, Shula, 113, 125, 130, 204, 241, 272

indetermination, 154–155
index, 86
individualization, 133
Infantry Division of the Wehrmacht, 151
instruction, Holocaust, 49–54
  from Shoah to resurrection, 54–55
Instytut Pamieci Narodowej (IPN), 89
intifada, 13
Iraqi Jews, 264
irreverence, 154–155
Israel, Eretz, 253
Israeli army, 119, 218–219, 295
Israel in the 21st Century (2009), 232
Israeli Defense Forces, 305
Israeli Jews, 52, 238, 255, 256, 282, 295
Ivangorod Mother, 120–128
I was Mengele's Assistant: An Auschwitz Doctor's Eyewitness Account (Gutman), 179
Izkor - Slaves of Memory (Sivan), 215

J

Jabotinsky, Ze'ev, 15
Jackson, Justice, 89
Jenkins, Keith, 20
Jerusalem Betzalel Art School, 266
Jewish army, 7, 219
Jewish Cultural Association, 69

Jewish minorities/ethnicities, 3, 153, 173, 227, 281, 290–291. *see also specific Jews*
    culture vs., 265
    Ethiopian, 282
    Mizrahi, 264
    representation of, 13–18
Jewish National Fund, 243
Jewitt, Carey, 19
Jews of Kelm, 164
"Jews and others" group, 225
Jews Revenge, 127
Jima, Iwo, 171
Jiryis, Hanna, 309
Joest, Heinrich, 67, 68–69, 76, 77–79, 103, 141, 143, 144, 146, 186, 198, 200, 201
joint curriculum, 293, 310, 311
    human-caused injustice and, 314
    narrating the land, 302
    space in, 309
joint narrative, 314–316
    changes to existing, 313–314
    empathic unsettlement, 316
    in Hebrew and Arabic languages, 316
    Holocaust and Nakba, 302–306
    joint curriculum, land, 302
    multidirectional memory, 293–302
    pedagogical and performative, 306–307
        alternative research regarding "others", 310–312
        history and literature, 307–310

identity, 312–313
Journey into Memory (1999), 146
Judaism, 17, 164, 246, 268, 275, 288, 315
Judeo-Islamic history, 270
Judenrat, 71, 72, 74, 115, 137, 138, 143, 144, 204

K
Kacharjinsky, Shmerke, 127
Kadari-Ovadia, Shira, 49
Kafr Qassim massacre, 237
Kambanellis, Iakovos, 38, 157
Kansteiner, Wulf, 29
Kaplan, Alice, 211, 276
Kaplan, Steven, 276
Kathrada, Ahmad, 294
Katriel, Tamar, 294
Katzav, 12
Ka-Tzetnik, 36, 41, 43, 47, 55–58, 87, 161, 163–165, 171, 207, 208, 252
Katz, Yaakov, 15, 16–17
Katznelson, Berl, 203
Kedma school, 296
Kedouri, Elie, 262
Keilbach, Judith, 63, 80, 84, 86, 93, 113
Keller, Ulrich, 71, 73
Keren, Nili, 110, 111, 145, 146, 159, 175, 179, 183, 185, 186, 193, 204, 272
Khajaj-Liluf, Yaakov, 271
Khalidi, Walid, 309
Khen, Mordekhay, 273

Khoury, Elias, 41, 295, 303–304, 305, 308

Kibya massacre, 249

Kimmerling, Baruch, 4, 29, 219

Kishka, Michel, 30

Klein, Anna, 147–149

Klein, Jon, 147–149

Klein, Menachem, 315, 316

Knobloch, Erhard Josef, 71, 72, 74, 141

Knobloch, Ludwig, 166, 167

Konrad, Franz, 89, 91

Konzentrationslager, 55

Korczak, Janusz, 204

Korsch, Karl, 30

Kozlovsky-Golan, Yvonne, 45

Krakotzkin, Raz Amnon, , 14, 265, 268, 269, 271, 288, 302

Krall, Hanna, 203

Kramer, S., 169

Kress, Gunther, 21, 22, 24, 45, 56, 59–61, 75, 81, 90, 98, 133, 147, 195, 246

Kristeva, Julia, 313

Kwoka, Czeslawa, 186

L

The Lab We Sell Weapons, 245

LaCapra, Dominick, 5, 37, 38, 129, 199, 293

Lachman, Lilach, 295

land, narrating, 302

Landau, Ronnie, 31, 47, 109, 163, 198, 301

Lanzmann, Claude, 36, 295

Last Jew in Vinnitsa, 111–119
Law of Holocaust and Heroism Remembrance Day, 50
Lazarus, Amit, 16
Łazowertówna, Henryka, 142
Lebanese Jews, 264
Legacy of Abused Children: From Poland to Palestine, The (Rothberg), 97
Lehrer, Hannah, 134, 135, 145, 146–147, 208
Leibovitch, Yeshayahu, 202
Lemke, Jay, 25
Leninist Young Communist League, 150
Levac, Alex, 246
Levin, Amiram, 245
Levi, Nili, 56
Levi, Primo, 38, 43, 135
Lewin-Epstein, Noah, 16
Lewis, Bryan F., 66, 69, 104–105, 121, 156, 165, 185
Libyan Jews, 271–273
Life is Beautiful (Begnini), 46
Life Magazine, 43
Liss, Andrea, 71, 72, 99, 190, 209
Lissner, Jorgen, 81, 170–171
Livnat, Limor, 297
little smugglers, 136–149
Living Together in Israel (2005), 277–278, 282
Lloyd, David, 219, 223, 232
Loewy, Hanno, 66, 169
Loshitzky, Yosefa, 217, 218, 258
Lower, Wendy, 64, 66, 130, 208

Luidor, Yosef, 50
Lybian Jews, 264, 271–272, 290
Lydda ghetto, 295, 303–304
Lyotard, Jean François, 83, 201, 244, 252

M

Ma'alot attack, 255
Machin, David, 19
Machtans, Karolin, 33
Madmoni-Gerber, Shoshana, 261
Magilow, Daniel, 92–93
Maidanek death camp, 160
majoritarianism, 6–8
Man in the Social and Cultural Space (2011), 224, 232, 240, 241
Marking Evil, 5, 294, 301
Martin Rojo, L., 223
Martin, L., 33
Massacre at Liepaja, 109–111
Massalah, Nur, 216
Matner, Walter, 115, 117
MAUS (novel), 46, 75
*Maus (*Spiegelman), 30
Mazurek, Wojtek, 271
Mbembe, Achilles, 20, 29, 222, 224, 237, 244, 246, 248
Medem Sanatorium, 204
Meir-Glitzenstein, Esther, 262, 263, 270
Meir, Golda, 15
Memmi, Albert, 228, 229, 271

Mengele, Joseph, 175–178, 179–180, 188–190
Metamaus, 75
metonymic illustration, 44
Middle-Eastern Jews, 268
Mikel Arieli, Roni, 294
Milner, Iris, 58
Milton, Sybil, 62, 65–67, 69–70, 71, 72, 81, 139, 208
Ministry of Education, 23
minorities, 290–291
Miron, Dan, 57
Mishol, Yigal, 98, 118, 201, 269–270, 272–273, 276–277
Mizrahi Jews, 13, 14, 17, 221, 263, 264, 276, 279, 296–297, 315
    from curriculum, absence of, 273
    and Holocaust Narrative, 269–273
    inequality of, 266
    institutional treatment, 268–269
    in Muslim countries, 269–273
    representation of, 265
    social marginalization of, 267
Mizrahim, 7
Modan, Ruth, 232
Moffie, David, 44
Monmonier, Mark, 131
Monterescu, Daniel, 315
Mordechay, Itzhak, 247
Moroccan Jews, 271
Moses, Dirk A., 289, 300
Moss, Al, 112

Mucha, Stanislav, 87
Museum of Ghetto Fighters, 161
The Mussar (Moral) Movement, 164
multidirectional memory, 293–295
Multimodal Discourse Analysis (MMDA), 22

N

Naipaul, V.S., 304
Nakba Law, 289
Narrating the Nation (2008), 314
Nassra, Mansour, 243
National Archives and Records Administration (NARA), 89
national narrative, 301, 305
    forms of, 306
    German, 251
    Jewish, 251
    pedagogical, 306–313
    performative, 306–313
Naveh, Eyal, 4, 5, 9, 8, 11, 49, 52, 72, 118, 187, 189, 195, 197, 201, 249, 259, 260, 262, 272
Nazi Concentration Camps, 63, 84, 85, 271
Nazi death camps, 96, 182
Nazi extermination camp, 46, 181, 273
Nazification, 12
    discourse of, 252
    in Israeli schoolbooks, 254–258
    of Palestinians, 251–254, 258–260
Nazism, 30, 55, 88, 103, 115, 126, 131, 170, 183, 218, 219

Nazism and Shoah (2010), 103, 126, 131
Neta, Oren, 4
Netanyahu, 257
Nets-Zehngut, Rafi, 4, 258
new grammar, 301
Nichanian, Marc, 39
non-Jewish minorities, 8, 14, 222, 238, 312
    colonialist racist attitude and discriminatory practices towards, 17
    immigrants, 225
    implicitly as, 152
    to receive Israeli citizenship, 225
Nora, Pierre, 222, 223
North African Jews, 264, 271, 273
Nowogrodska, Sonie, 205
Nyiszli, Miklos, 179

O
Occupied Palestinian Territories, 25
Ochayon, Sheryl Silver, 71
Ofer, Dalia, 40
Offer, Miriam, 167
Ogbu, John, 267
Ohlin, Peter, 95
From One Language to Another (Apfelfeld), 39
Oputchinski, Peretz, 142
Orientalism, 268, 307
'Oriental' Jews, 261–263, 267, 268
Orlev, Uri, 40

Oron, Yair, 157

Owusu, Jo-Ann, 61

P

Pagis, Dan, 159

Palestinian refugee camps, 257

Palestinians, 10, 15, 99–101, 277–278, 313–315

    absence of, 231

    abstraction, 230

    abstract occupation, 232–236

    anti-Palestinian sentiments, 215

    Arab-Palestinians, 6, 128, 312

    cartographic silence, 231–232

    catastrophes, 119

    citizens of Israel, 16

    citizens as problem, 236–237

        confinement and exclusion, 237–238

    citizens and subjects, context of othering, 219–221

    death, 248–250

    as demographic threat, 223–227

    desertion, 239

    discrimination, Holocaust legitimating, 217–219

    discrimination and segregation of citizens, 242–244

    distancing citizens, 221–223

    hostility toward, 213

    indigenous, 218

    indigenous land and "abandoned" property, usurpation of, 239

    inhabitants of land, 55

internal refugees, 241–242
  in Israeli schoolbooks, 254–258
  Jews, 172
  killing of, 244–250, 313
  logic of elimination, 230–231
  Nakba, 41
  narratives, 306
  natives, 116
  Nazification of, 251–260
  in occupied territories, 119
  othering of Jewish ethnicities and, 215–216
  in Palestine, 203
  propositional assumptions and, 23–24
  refugees, 8, 239–242, 266, 312
  representation of, 12–13, 289
  rights, 202, 302
  stereotyping and racism in colonial relationships, 228–230
  suffering, boy as symbol of, 95–97
  terror organization, 255–256
Pappe, Ilan, 13, 24, 216, 219, 221, 223, 227, 228, 232, 237, 238, 245, 250, 258
Paterson, Glenn, 113
Payne, Lewis, 94
partial identification, 186–191
partial information and deleted identity, 149–154
pedagogical narrative, 303, 306–307
  alternative research regarding "others", 310–312
  history and literature, 307–310
  identity, 312–313

pedagogic discourse, 60
Pedaya, Haviva, 238, 265, 310
Peled-Elhanan, Nurit, 3, 7, 18–19, 57, 131, 216, 223, 224, 228, 231, 233, 237, 248–250, 256, 257, 277, 289
Peled, Inbar, 17
People in Space (1998), 266
Perec, George, 38
Peretz, Aharon, 166, 167
performative narrative, 303, 306–307. *see also* pedagogical narrative
Persona (Bergman), 95
*Phoenix over the Galilee (*Ka-Tzetnik), 55
Photographing the Holocaust (2004), 70
photographs. *see also* icons; images; specimens of categories
    The Age of Horror and Hope for grades 10–12, 137, 143
    Age Pyramid, 226
    amateur, 67–68
    Arab Jews, 266
    Avieli-Tabibian's Holocaust schoolbook (2009), 99–100
    boy selling armbands in the ghetto, 140
    childhood/girls in Warsaw ghetto, 104
    children begging in the ghetto, 140
    Courtesy Noa Abendt, 98
    cropped photo of Image, 124
    defined, 65, 69–70
    to drawing mode, 75–82
    Einsatzgruppen murdering Jewish civilians in Ivangorod, Ukraine, 120
    forcibly pulled out of bunkers, 88
    front cover of Porat's book, 91

German soldiers searching Jewish boy, 141
Going the Civilian Way, 233
grafiti of Handala, 101
group of destitute boys on a curb in the Warsaw Ghetto, 68
iconic atrocity, 64
ID card, 73, 74
importance of phenomenology of, 64–75
Ivangorod Mother, 120–128
Jewish policemen at the entrance to the Judenrat building, 72, 74
Joest's, 78, 79, 144, 200
Journey into the Past, 2001 for grades 7–9, 136
Kalandia Checkpoint, 235
Lehrer, Hanna, 134, 135, 145, 146, 147, 149, 154, 208, 315
Holocaust of, 41–45
medical treatment in Warsaw Ghetto, 166
as metonymic illustration, 44
mother and twins, 102–103
Nazi, 63–64, 66, 70–75
Nazism and Shoah 2010, 103, 104, 126, 131
Proliferation of Israel's Arab Population, 231
Rabbi Moshe Hagerman, 159–167
Settela as the boy Avram, 157–159
staged, 71–75
studio portrait of Anna and Jon, 148–149
Toward Resurrection and Peace, 77, 80
trajectory of, 62–64
use of, 41–45
in Warsaw Ghetto, 71–75

*Pillar of Salt, The (*Memmi), 271

Pinderhughes, Charles, 275

Piterberg. G., 250

The Planet Auschwitz, 58

Polish Jews, 268, 304

Polonsky, David, 30

Politics of Altruism (1977), 170

Ponar, Jews of, 114

Popovsky, 153, 154, 157, 159

Porat, Dan, 91–92, 98, 208

pornography, 169–171

    defined, 171

    of evil, 41–42

    human privacy, name of, 184–191

    image and words, 178–184

    Mengele's naked twins, 175–177

    proper distance between others and ourselves , 172–175

Pornography of Death, 171

Pornography of Horror, 171

Presner, Todd, 29

The Promised Land, 289

R

Rabin, 297

Rabinowitz, Dan, 133, 235 315

Rachmani, Shmuel, 246, 247

*Racialization of Ethiopian Jews in Israeli Law, The (*Peled), 17

racism, 13, 16, 18, 39, 86, 103, 170, 174, 237, 290, 301, 302, 305

Ashkenazi, 14
  children and, 183
  in colonial relationships, 228–230
  deterrent against, 212
  discourse, 135, 182, 196, 236, 245, 258, 265, 313
  elite, 258
  in Europe, 30
  European history of, 301–302, 305
  everyday, 20, 276
  expressions, 268
  fear and, 259
  German, 143, 146, 156
  hate, violence and, 213
  humanism, 31
  humanity against, 303
  institutional, 275
  nationalism and, 301
  Nazi, 61
  policy, 267
  superiority of human spirit over, 164
  towards non-Jewish and non-Western citizens, 17
  victims of, 132
  visual, 227, 277
Rainiger, Fancesca, 70
recontextualization, changing social sites, 59–62
recount, historical
  evaluation and appraisal in, 198–201
  social actors, suppression and exclusion of, 201–205

stages
- background or orientation, 195
- deduction, 195, 197–198
- record of events, 195
- voice of, 193–194

Red Army, 112

refugees, 8, 227, 239–242, 303, 312
- camp, 240, 257
- in French, 135
- German, 241
- penniless, 10
- from pogroms of Odessa, 294–295
- Zionist solution of, 303

Reisigl, M., 3, 20, 258

relational identification, 179

representation of Holocaust, 10–12, 29–31, 207–213, 288–289
- different modes of, 38–41
- photographs, use of, 41–45
- transduction, 45–47
- visual representation of, 41–45 (*see also* visual representation of Holocaust)
- writing, 32–38

Resnik, Julia, 13, 19, 20, 49, 50, 51–52

rhetoric, 3, 5, 10, 11, 17, 21–22, 33, 37–38, 57, 60, 149, 152, 178, 193, 201, 217, 236, 270, 272, 303

rhetorical model, 37

Ricoeur, Paul, 194

Ringelblum, Emanuel, 142

Roman army, 50

Romkovsky, Haim of Łódź, 138, 139
Ross, Hynrik, 65, 70–71
Rothberg, Michael, 35, 36–37, 97, 100, 129, 199, 293–294
Rousset, David, 177
Ruppin, Arthur, 262
Russians Jews, 238, 288, 312

S
Sadowski, Piotor, 86
Said, Edward, 24, 231, 261, 307
Salamandra (Ka-Tzetnik), 55
Salamon, Hagar, 20
Sarris, Gregg, 310
Sartre, J.P., 31
Schechner, Alan, 97
Schindler's List (film), 46
scholarly sloppiness, 104
schoolbooks
    existential assumptions, 23
    hypertexts, 24
    intertexts, 24
    multimodal schoolbook, 25
    nature of, 22–23
        history and holocaust, 24–25
        ideological common ground and basic assumptions, 23–24
    propositional assumptions, 23–24
    value assumptions, 24
    visual representation of Holocaust in (*see* visual representation of Holocaust)

Schwarberg, Gunther, 67

secondary cultural characteristics, 267

The Second Generation – Things I have not told my Father? (Kishka), 30

secular icons, 85, 90, 127

Segal, Sari, 167

Segev, Tom, 3, 4, 10, 11, 12, 14, 15, 17, 29, 55, 153, 201, 217, 218, 251, 261, 262, 264, 276

Semel, Nava, 40

Semprun, Jose, 29, 38, 43

Senesz, Hannah, 153, 213, 297

Sereny, Gitta, 196

Settela, 157, 159, 166, 315

Settela Steinbach, 158

Sfard, Michael, 232

Shivitti (Ka-Tzetnik), 47

Shaked, Ayelet, 245

Shandler, Jeffrey, 29, 30

Shalom, Avraham, 246

Shapira, Yonatan, 96, 97

Sharet, Moshe, 15

Sharet, Yaakov, 15

Shatzker, Haim, 113

Shavit, Ari, 304, 305

Shcherbatsevicha, Olga, 150–151

Shenhav, Yehouda A., 261

Shifris, Nathan, 261, 263, 264, 267

Shikhmanter, Rima, 40, 81, 308

Shimoni, Batya, 271

Shoah, 5, 33, 35, 36, 38, 40, 54–55, 83, 99, 103, 123, 126, 157, 162, 178, 210, 253, 255, 259, 261, 299, 302, 303

Shohat, Ella, 240–241, 263–264, 269–270, 290, 309, 311, 314

Silverman, Lisa, 92–93

Silverstone, Roger, 172–173

Sivan, Eyal, 215, 271

Small History of Photography, A (1931), 156

Smith, Tuhiwai, 309, 310, 311

Smooha, Sami, 219

Smotrich, MK, 245

Sobibor extermination camp, 271

social semiotic approach, 18–21

Sociocide, 233

Sonderkommando, 295, 305

Sontag, Susan, 64–65, 86, 211

Sorkin, Michael, 174

Soviet Jews, 114, 116, 120

specimens of categories, 133–135, 136–149
    badge as criterial feature, 145–149
    indetermination, anonymization, and irreverence
        anonymization through captioning, 155–157
        impersonalization and irreverence, Rabbi Moshe Hagerman, 159–167

Spiegelman, Art, 30, 75–76, 81, 88

Stam, Robert, 290, 314

Stangl, Franz, 196–197

Stav, Shira, 56, 303

Steiner, George, 30, 39, 40, 170, 184

Stone, Dan, 299, 300–301

Statistical Abstract of Israel (2001), 225
Street, Brian V., 20
Stroop, Jurgen, 89, 91–92
Stroop Report, 89
Struk, Janina, 62, 70, 81, 95, 107–108, 121, 122–124, 128, 160, 161, 184, 186, 208–209
Sukary, Yossi, 272
symbol, 86. *see also* icons
Syrian Jews, 264
Szejnmann, Claus-Christian W., 33
Szymon Pullman, 77

T

Tabenkin, Yitzhak, 255
Tamir, Alexander, 127
Tannen, Deborah, 172
Täubner, Max, 66
Tee, Nechama, 150
textbook style, 49
Theresa, W., 181
Times for Joy and Memory (2022), 281
Tišma, Aleksandar, 94
Tomaszewski, Jerzy, 122
Toward Resurrection and Peace (1999), 55, 77, 80
Traces (Ida Fink), 65
transduction, 45–47
    of photographs to drawings, 60, 75–82
    representation of Holocaust, 45–47

visual representation of Holocaust, 75–82
transformation, 59, 104, 116, 142, 187, 295
   of carpentry, 60
   semiotic changes and, 81
   spiritual, 253
transposition process, 59, 61, 63, 69, 81
   to museums, 85
   of photograph to schoolbooks, 119, 149, 188, 189–190
   to schoolbooks, 85, 142, 149
   of signs, 136
traumatic realism, 36–37
Treblinka extermination camp, 142, 196
Trus, Kiril, 150–151
Tunisian Jews, 272–273

U

Ukraine, Jews in, 124
United Press International (UPI), 112
Urbach Hannah, 248
US Army, 63, 113
US Holocaust Memorial Museum, 68, 148

V

Vaanunu, Mordechay, 234
Values and Citizens (2014), 50, 220, 268, 242
Van Dijk, T.A., 223
Van Leeuwen, Theo, 76, 79, 98, 133–134, 147, 155, 156, 227, 229
van Pelt, Robert Jan, 83

verbal text, 128–131
verbal–visual combination, 42
Vilnius Ghetto, 127
Vinnitsa, Jews of, 112–113, 114
Vinnitsa labor camp, 112
Virgin Mary (Michelangelo), 80
visual representation of Holocaust, 41–45, 75–82
    importance of phenomenology, 64–75
    photo to drawing mode, 75–82
    recontextualization, changing social sites, 59–62
Viterbo, Hedi, 248
Volkan, Vamık D., 52–54, 128
Volkovisky, Leon, 127
    trajectory of photographs, 62–64

W

Wagenaar, Aad, 158
Wałęsa, Lech, 202
Walker, Alice, 290–291
Wallenberg, Raoul, 133
Warsaw, Jews of, 74, 91, 96–98, 198
Warsaw Ghetto, 96–98, 103–104
Warsaw Ghetto-The End (Dreifuss), 209
Warsaw Ghetto uprising, 50–51, 99, 133, 202–203, 205
We Have Not Forgotten (1960), 120, 122, 124
Weindling, Paul, 176, 180, 182, 183, 189
Weisel, Elie, 36, 41
Weiss, Daniel, 150

Weitzman, David, 160–161
Wertsch, J., 23, 142, 293
West Bank, 232
Westerbork transit camp, 159
White, Hayden, 32, 35
Wodak, R., 3, 20, 258
Wolfe, Patrick, 13, 29, 219, 289
woman in Warsaw ghetto, 76–79
writing of Holocaust, 32–38
Writing the Disaster (Blanchot), 57

Y

Yablonka, Hannah, 9, 42, 54, 180, 301
Yad Vashem, 11, 34, 51, 54, 63, 69, 71, 72, 81, 88, 93, 107, 109, 111, 112, 120, 171, 198, 202, 210, 297
Yaffe, Lili, 266
Yaron, Idan, 212
Yatom, Ehud, 247
The Years of Extermination (Friedländer), 33, 35
Yehuda, Omri Ben, 263
Yemenite Jews, 266, 267
Yeshurun, Avot, 39, 295
Yeshurun, Helit, 295
Yiftachel, Oren, 219, 239
Yom Kippur war, 51–52
Young, R.C., 30
Youth Village Hakfar Hayarok, 152

Z

Zagorodka massacre, 114
Zamir, Yitzhak, 247
Zeev, Pisgat, 152
Zelizer, Barbie, 83, 86, 95, 155, 156
Zembe, Rabbi Menahem, 205
Zertal, Idit, 203–204, 251, 255
Zhitomir labor camp, 112
Zimmerman, M., 217, 251, 257
Zionism, 287–288, 289, 301
    designing of, 262
Zionist, 10–11, 15, 303
    anti-Zionist, 202–204
    attitude toward Arab-Palestinians, 6
    authorities, 267
    discourse, 10
    East-European, 288
    emissaries, 264
    Euro-Zionists, 280
    history, 270
    Holocaust narrative, 8
    invention, 264
    Israeli, 53, 221, 250, 252, 269, 287, 314
    Jewish-Zionist, 302
    leadership, 50, 153, 261–262, 268, 287
    movement, 50, 203, 219, 309–310
    narrative, 34, 52, 259, 263, 300
    in Palestine, 14–15

right wing and liberal, 257
Westernized historians, 308
Zionist-Jewish partisan, 152

Zuckerman, M., 9, 217, 257
Zuckerman, Moshe, 6
Zuk Eitan operation, 299
Zygielbojm, Artur, 204
Zygielbojm, Manie, 205

BIBLIOGRAPHY

THE SCHOOLBOOKS

Civic Studies

Alperson, Bilhah, Dubi Tamir, and Dana Shtrakman. 2016. *Being Citizens in Israel a Jewish Democratic State*. Jerusalem: Published by the Ministry of Education.

Diskin, Abraham. 2011. *Israel in Politics and Government*. Maggie Publishers, Israel.

Eden, Yohay and Hefetz Irit. 2009. *Democratic values and Judaism*. Jerusalem. Hartman Institute.

Gal, O., Z. Fine, and S.H. Goodman. 2006. *Living Together in* Israel - Chapters in Civic Studies, Homeland Studies and Geography for 2nd and 3rd Grades. Tel Aviv: The Center for Educational Technology.

Galdi bina, Nisan Naveh and Asaf Motzkin 2012. *Going the Civilian Way* Tel Aviv. Rehes Publishers.

Gershoni, A. Teler, D. and Rosenthal-Idan, C. 2009. Times for Joy and Memory Of the series An Opening to the World, issued by the TALI Fund Jerusalem.

Gershoni, A., D. Teler, Y. Yavnin, D. Yedidya-Kimel, and I. Rosenthal. 2011. *Identity in White and Blue. Identity in a Changing World*. Jerusalem: TALI Fund Publishers.

Rothberg, Naftali. 2011. *Values and Citizens. Civic Studies through Active Learning*. Van Leer Institute and Rehes Publishers.

Shahar, David. 2010. *Citizenship in the State of Israel*. Tel Aviv: Kineret Publishers.

History and Shoah

Avieli-Tabibian, Ketsia. 2001. *The Age of Horror and Hope: Chapters in History for Grades 10–12*. Tel Aviv: The Centre for Educational Technologies.

Avieli-Tabibian. K. 2001a. *A Journey into the Past: the 20th Century in Favor of Liberty*. The Center for Educational Technology.

Avieli-Tabibian, K. 2007. *A Journey into the Past: Selected Topics in History. The 19 and the 20th Century.* Tel Aviv. The Institute for Educational Technologies.

Avieli-Tabibian, K. 2009. *From Peace to War and Shoa.* Shoah Institute for Educational Technologies.

Avieli-Tabibian, K. 2009a. *Journeys in Time: Nationality on Trial.* Tel Aviv: The Center for Educational Technology.

Bar Hillel, Moshe. And Shula Inbar, S. 2009. *A National World Building a State in the Middle East.* Tel Aviv. Lilach Publishers.

Bar Hillel, Moshe and Shula Inbar. 2010. *Nazism and Shoah.* Lilach Publishers.

Barnavi, Eli. 1998. *The 20th Century: A History of the People of Israel in Recent Generations, for Grades 10–12.* Tel Aviv: Sifrei Tel Aviv.

Blank, N. 2006. *The Face of the 20th Century - from Dictatorship to Democracy.* Tel Aviv: Yoel Geva Publisher.

Cohen, Sagi. 2020. *Mikud History.* Tel Aviv. Rehes Publishers.

Domka Eliezer, Goldberg Tzafrir, and Urbach Hannah 2009. *Nationalism - building a state in the Middle East.* Shzar Institute Pub. Jerusalem, Israel.

Eldar, Zipi and Lili Yaffe. 1998. *From Conservatism to Progress.* Jerusalem: Maalot Publishers. The Ministry of Education.

Friedner, Yekutiel. 1968. *The History of Recent Generations. From the First World War Until the Six Days War.* Jerusalem. Yeshurun Publishers.

Gutman, Israel and Haim Shatzker 1990. *The Holocaust and its Significance.* Jerusalem. Shazar Institute Publishers.

Gutman, Israel. 2009. *Totalitarianism and Shoah.* Jerusalem. Yad Vashem and Shazar Institute Publishers.

Hertz, Tehila. 2015. *Destruction and Heroism- Nazism and Shoah.* Crisis and Resurrection series. Har-Brakha Institute. Occupied Palestinian Territories.

Inbar, Shula. 2004. *Fifty Years of Wars and Hopes.* Tel Aviv: Lilach publishers.

Keren, Nili. 1998. *Shoah: A Journey into Memory.* Tel Aviv. Tel Aviv Books Publishers.

Levin, Miriam, Yardena Hadas, Varda Yerushalmi and Yifat Rogner. 1999. *Toward Resurrection and Peace.* Tel Aviv. Ramot Publishers.

Mishol, Yigal 2014. *Nazism, War and Shoa.* High School Publishers. Maaleh Adumin. Occupied Palestinian Territories.

Mishol, Yigal. 2014a. *Building a Jewish Democratic State in the Middle East*. High School Publishers. Maaleh Adumin. Occupied Palestinian Territories.

Naveh, Eyal. 1994. *The 20th Century The Century that Changed the World Order*. Tel Aviv. Tel-Aviv books and Mapa Publishers. Israel.

Naveh, Eyal, Naomi Vered and David Shahar. 2009a. *Nationality in Israel and the Nations. Building a State in the Middle East*. Tel Aviv: Rehes Publishers.

Naveh, Eyal, Naomi Vered and David Shahar. 2009. *Totalitarianism and Shoah*. Rehes Pub.

Rothenberg N. 2011. *Values and Citizens*. Tel Aviv. Rehes Publishers.

Yaakoby, D. et al. (1999) *A World of Changes: A History Book for 9th Grade*. Tel-Aviv. The Curriculum Centre in the Ministry of Education/ Maalot.

Geography

Aharony, Y. and T. Sagi. 2003. *The Geography of the Land of Israel* A Geography textbook for grades 11-12. Tel Aviv: Lilach Pub.

Fine, Z. M. Segev, and R. Lavi. 2002. *Israel- The Man and the Space Selected Chapters in Geography*. Tel Aviv: The Centre for Educational Technologies.

Gal, Ofira, and Ofer Priel. 2011. *Man in the Cultural and Social Space. A Schoolbook in Geography and Environment Development*. For grades 10-12. The Centre for Educational Technologies and Ministry of Education Pub.

Greitzer, I. Z. Fine, and M. Segev. 2009. *Israel in the 21st Century: Selected Chapters in Geography*. For 11-12 grades. Tel Aviv: The Center for Education Technology.

Rap, Esther and Zvia Fine. 1998. *People in Space* a Geography Textbook for 9th grade. Tel Aviv: The Centre for Educational Technologies.

Rap, E. and Iris Shilony-Tzvieli. 1998. I. *Settlements in Space. Chapters in the Geography of Settlements in the World*. Tel Aviv: The Centre for Educational Technologies Pub.

Segev, M. and Z. Fine 2007. *People and Settlements*. Tel-Aviv: The Centre for Educational Technologies.

Va'adya, D., H. Ulman, and Z. Mimoni. 1996. *The Mediterranean Countries* for 5th grade. Tel Aviv: The Ministry of Education and Maalot Publishers.

General References

About Ilsen. 2001. "La photographie au service du système concentrationaire national-socialiste 1933-1945." In: *Memoires des Camps: Photographies des camps de concentration et d'extermination nazi* (1933–1999). Edited by Clément Chéroux. Paris: Marval.

Abrahamson, Irving. 1995. *Against Silence: The Voice and Vision of Elie Wiesel*, Volume 3, 13. Holocaust Library publishers.

Adorno, Theodor W. 2003. *Can One Live After Auschwitz? A Philosophical Reader*. Edited by Rolf Tiedemann, translated by Rodney Livingstone and others. Borders and Boundaries Series. Issue 5. Stanford. Stanford University Press.

Adorno, Theodor 1966/2004. *Negative Dialectics*. Routledge.

Adwan, Sami and Baron, Dan. Naveh Eyal. 2012. *Side by Side: Parallel Histories of Israel-Palestine*. The New Press.

Agamben, Giorgio. 1998. *Homo Sacer Sovereign Power and Bare Life*. Stanford University Press.

Agamben, G. 2005. *State of Exception*. Chicago University Press.

Agee, James "Films." *Nation,* March 24, 1945. The Nation Company Publisher. 342.

Anderson, Benedict. 1991. *Imagined Communities: Reflections on the Origin and Spread of Nationalism*. Verso.

Anteby-Yemini, Lisa. 2019. "From a Returning Jewish Diaspora to Returns to Diaspora Spaces: Israeli-Ethiopians Today." In *Israel: A Diaspora of Memories*, edited by Michèle Baussant, Dario Miccoli, Esther Schely-Newman, Issue no. 16, December 2019. QUEST. *Issues in Contemporary Jewish History*. Journal of Fondazione CDEC.

Anthelme, Robert. 1947. *L'Espèce Humaine*. Editions de la Cité Universelle. (*The Human Race*. Marlboro Press, 1st edition December 9, 1998).

Appadurai, Arjun. 2006. *Fear of Small Numbers: An Essay on the Geography of Anger*. Public Planet Books. Duke University Press.

Apple, Michael W. 1996. *Cultural Politics and Education*. Buckingham: Open University Press.

Arnheim, R. A. 1988. *The Power of the Centre: A study of composition in the visual arts.* Berkeley. University of California Press.

Arendt, Hannah. 1944. "The Jew as Pariah. A Hidden Tradition." *Jewish Social Studies* 6, no. 2 (April 1944): 99-122.

Arendt, Hannah. 1958/2017. *The Origins of Totalitarianism.* Penguin Books Ltd New York.

Ayab, Ruth. "Photographs of Disaster." In *Visual Studies,* 169-193. Routledge, Taylor and Francis.

Balibar, Etienne. 1991. "Is There a 'Neo-Racism'"? In: Balibar, Etienne and Immanuel Wallerstein. *Race, Nation, Class: Ambiguous Identities I.* Verso.

Ball, Karyn. "Unspeakable Differences, Obscene Pleasures: The Holocaust as an Object of Desire." In *Women in German Yearbook* 19: 20-49. University of Nebraska Press.

Bar-On, Dan and Adwan, Sami, Naveh Eyal and Adnan Musallam. 2003. *Learning Each Other's Historical Narrative: Palestinians and Israelis.* Beit Jallah, PNA: A Prime Publication of the Peace Research Institute in the Middle East.

Burg, Avraham. 2008. *The Holocaust Is Over; We Must Rise from its Ashes.* New York: St. Martin Press.

Bar-Gal, Y. 1993. "Boundaries as a Topic in Geographic Education: The Case of Israel." *Political Geography, 12*(5): 421-435.

Bar – Tal Daniel and Rafi Nets – Zehngut. 2008. "Emotions in Conflict: Correlates of Fear and Hope in the Israeli-Jewish Society". In: *Peace and Conflict: Journal of Peace Psychology,* 1532-7949, 14 (3), 2008, pp.233-258 (2008:4).

Barthes, Roland. 1977. *Image, Music, Text.* Fontana Press. An Imprint of Harper Collins Publishers. London. UK.

Barthes, Roland. 1981. *Camera Lucida: Reflections on Photography.* New York. Hill and Wang Publishers.

Barthes, Roland. 1986. *The Rustle of Language.* University of California Press.

Barthes, Roland. 1991. "Rhetoric of Image." In *The Responsibility of Forms,* 28. Berkeley and Los Angeles. University of California Press.

Bartov, Omer. 1996. *Murder in Our Midst: The Holocaust, Industrial Killing, and Representation.* Oxford University Press.

Bartov, Omer. 1997. "Kitsch and Sadism in Ka-Tzetnik's Other Planet: Israeli Youth Imagine the Holocaust." In *Jewish Social Studies New Series 3, no. 2 (winter)*, 42-76. Indiana University Press.

Bashir, Bashir and Amos Goldberg (Eds.). 2019. *The Holocaust and the Nakba: A New Grammar of Trauma and History*. Foreword by Elias Khoury. Afterword by Jacqueline Rose. Columbia University Press.

Baudrillard, Jean. 1984. *The Evil Demon of Images*. Saint Louis, Missouri. Left Bank Books.

Baudrillard. 1981/2005. *Simulacre and Simulation. The Body in Theory: Histories of Cultural Materialism*. University of Michigan Press.

Bauer, Yehuda. 1978. "Against Mystification: The Holocaust as a Historical Phenomenon." In Bauer, Y. *The Holocaust in Historical Perspective*. Seattle: University of Seattle Press, 35–36.

Bauer, Yehuda. 1996. "The influence of the Shoah on the founding of the state of Israel." In: Gutman Israel Ed. *Fundamental Changes in the People of Israel following the Shoah*. Yad Vashem Publishers. 503-509. (Hebrew).

Bauer, Yehuda, 2001. *Rethinking the Holocaust*. Yale University Press.

Baum, Rob. 2009. "Jews, Blood, and Ethiopian Dance in Israel." In: Matzke Christine and Osita Okagbue Eds. *Critical Race Theory & the Postcolonial. African Theatre: Diasporas*. Suffolk, UK: James Currey Publishers, 85-99.

Bauman, Zygmunt. 1989. *Modernity and the Holocaust*. Polity Press.

Bauman Zygmunt 2001. "The Holocaust's Life as a Ghost." In: Fine, Robert and Charles Turner. Eds. *Social Theory after the Holocaust*. Liverpool University Press. 1-7.

Bauman, Zygmunt. 2013. "The Role of Modernity: What was it and is it about?" In: *Dapim: Studies on the Holocaust*, 2013. Vol. 27, No. 1. London and New York. Routledge. Taylor and Francis Group. 40–73.

Baumel, Judith Tydor. 1996. "The Heroism of Hannah Senesz: An Exercise in Creating Collective National Memory in the State of Israel." *Journal of Contemporary History* 31, no. 3. 521-546.

Benjamin, Walter. 1979. "A Small History of Photography." In Benjamin. *One-Way Street and Other Writings*. London and New York: Verso Publishers.

Benjamin, Walter. 2004. "The Work of Art in the Age of Mechanical Reproduction." In Simpson, Philip, Andrew Utterson, and K. J. Sheperdson, Eds. *Film Theory: Critical Concepts in Media and Cultural Studies*. London and New York: Routledge.

Ben-Pazi, Hanokh. 2018. "Yeshayahu Leibowitz: The Holocaust as a Sign of Warning against Nationalism." In: Judaica 2018. Volume 74. Issue 3. 263-286.

Berger, John. 2017. *About Looking*. London: Bloomsbury Publishing.

Biagioli, Mario. 1992. "Science, Modernity and the Final Solution." In: *Probing the Limits of Representation*.

Bekerman, Zvi. 2020. "Reflection on the Dangers of 'Cultural Racism' in Intercultural Education." *Journal of New Approaches in Educational Research*, Vol 9, No. 1: 1-14.

Bekerman Zvi and Michalinos Zembylas. 2018. *Psychologized Language in Education, Denaturalizing a Regime of Truth*. Palgrave Macmillan.

Ben-Eliezer, Uri. 2004. "Becoming a Black Jew: Cultural Racism and Anti-Racism in Contemporary Israel." *Social Identities* 10(2). Taylor and Francis Online. 245-266.

Ben-Eliezer, Uri. 2008. "Multicultural Society and Everyday Cultural Racism: Second Generation of Ethiopian Jews in Israel's 'Crisis of Modernization'." *Ethnic and Racial Studies* 31(5). Taylor and Francis Online. 935-961.

Ben-Yehuda, Omri. 2019. "Ma'abara. Mizrahim between Shoah and Nakba." In: Bashir and Goldberg Eds. *The Holocaust and the Nakba*. 249-275.

Berda, Yael. 2012. *The Bureaucracy of the Occupation: The Permit Regime in the West Bank, 2000-2006*. Jerusalem: Hakibbutz Hameuhad and Van Leer Institute (Hebrew).

Berger, John. 2017. *About Looking*. London: Bloomsbury Publishing.

Bernstein, Basil. 1996. *Pedagogy, symbolic control and identity*. London: Taylor and Francis.

Bezemer, Jeff, and Gunther Kress. 2008. "Writing in Multimodal Texts a Social Semiotic Account of Designs for Learning." In *Written Communication* 25. Sage Publications. 166.

Bhabha, Homi. 1994. *The Location of Culture*. London and New York. Routledge.

Bhabha, Homi. 1995. *A Way in the World*. New York. Vintage Publishers.

Bhabha, Homi K. 1998. "The White Stuff". *Artforum International* 36, no. 9 (1998). New York. Artforum Inc. 21- 23.

Bhabha, Homi. 2008. *Narrating the Nation*. New York. Berghahn Books.

Blanchot, Maurice. 1980. "Our Clandestine Companion." In *Political Writings*, 1953–1993. Translated by Paul Zakir. New York: Fordham University Press, 2010.

Blatman, Daniel. 2015 "Holocaust Scholarship: Towards a Post-Uniqueness Era." *Journal of Genocide Research* 17, no. 1. 21–43.

Blauner, Robert. "Internal Colonialism and Ghetto Revolt." *Social Problems* 16(4): 393-408. Published by University of California Press on behalf of the Society for the Study of Social Problems.

Bloom, Etan. *Arthur Ruppin and the Production of pre-Israeli Culture*. The Netherland. Brill Publishers.

Boltanski Luc 1999. *Distant Suffering. Morality, Media and Politics*. Cambridge MA. Cambridge University Press.

Boyarin. Daniel.2000. "The Colonial Drag Zionism, Gender and Mimicry." In Fawzia Afzal-Khan, Kalpana Seshadri-Crooks, Eds. *The Pre-Occupation of Postcolonial Studies*. Duke University Press Books. 234-265.

Boyarin, Daniel 2023. *The No-State Solution, a Jewish Manifesto*. Yale University Press.

Browning, Christopher. 1995. *The Path to Genocide: Essays on Launching the Final Solution*. Cambridge University Press.

Brink, Cornelia. 2000. "Secular Icons: Looking at Photographs from Nazi Concentration Camps." *History and Memory*, vol. 12, no. 1 (Spring/Summer). Indiana University Press. 135-150.

Britton, J. 1984. "Viewpoints: The distinction between participant and spectator role language in research and practice." *Research in the Teaching of English*. 18(3). UK. NCTE Publishers. 320–331.

Bruner, Jerome. 1986. "Two Modes of Thought," in: *Actual Minds, Possible Worlds*. Cambridge, Mass.: Harvard University Press.

Brockhill, Aneta and Karl Cordell. 2019. "The violence of culture: the legitimation of the Israeli occupation of Palestine." *Third World Quarterly*, Routledge, 1-19.

Btozsat, Martin. 1979. *Hitler and the Genesis of the "Final Solution."* Jerusalem. Israel. Yad Vashem studies 13 (1979), S. 73 – 125.

Burging, Victor. 1982. "Looking at Photographs." In Looking at *Photographs*, edited by V. Burgin. Macmillan.

Camino, Mercedes. 27 June 2022. "War, gender, and lasting emotion: letters and photographs of Masha Bruskina and Olga Bancic, 1941–44." In: *Women's History Review*. Taylor and Francis Online.

Canetti, Elias. 1984. *Crowd and Power*. Farrar, Straus and Giroux Publishers.

Césaire, Aimé. 1972. "Discourse on Colonialism." In: *Monthly Review Press*. New York. 14.

Chatterley, Catherine D. 2011. *Disenchantment: George Steiner & the Meaning of Western Culture after Auschwitz*. Syracuse University Press.

Chayut, Noam. 2013. *The Girl Who Stole My Holocaust: A Memoir*. Verso. Kindle Edition.

Chéroux, Clément. 2001. « Du bon usage des images. » In : Clément Chéroux Ed. *Mémoire des Camps: Photographies des camps de concentration et d'extermination nazi* (1933–1999). Paris. Marval. 13.

Chetrit, Sami, Shalom. 2004. *The Mizrahi Struggle in Israel. Between Oppression and Liberation. Identification and Alternative*. Tel Aviv: Am Oved (Hebrew).

Chetrit, Sami Shalom. 2010. *Intra-Jewish Conflict in Israel: White Jews, Black Jews*. London and New York: Routledge.

Chouliaraki, Lilie. 2004. "Watching 11 September: The Politics of Pity." In: *Discourse & Society* SAGE Publications. London, Thousand Oaks, CA and New Delhi. Vol 15(2–3). 185–198.

Chouliaraki, Lilie. 2006. *The Spectatorship of Suffering*. Sage Publishers.

Cohen Yinon, Noah Lewin-Epstein and Amit Lazarus. 2019. Mizrahi-Ashkenazi Educational Gaps in the Third Generation. In: *Research in Social Stratification and Mobility* 59 (2019) 25–33.

Cole, Tim. *1999. Images of the Holocaust: The Myth of the 'Shoah Business'*. London: Duckworth Publishers. Or: *Selling the Holocaust: From Auschwitz to Schindler, How History is Bought, Packaged, and Sold*. New York. Routledge.

Cole, Tim. 2006. "Nativization and Nationalization: A Comparative Landscape Study of Holocaust Museums in Israel, the US and the UK." *Journal of Israeli History:*

Politics, Society, Culture, Vol.23, No.1 (Spring) 2006. Taylor and Francis Online. 130–145.

Confino, Alon. 2012. *Foundational Pasts: The Holocaust as Historical Understanding*. Cambridge MA. Cambridge University Press.

Crane, Susan A. 2008. "Choosing Not to Look: Representation, Repatriation, and Holocaust Atrocity Photography." *History and Theory* 47, no. 3. USA. Wiley for Wesleyan University. 309-330.

Czerniakow, Adam. 1999. *The Warsaw Diary of Adam Czerniakow: Prelude to Doom*. Edited by Raul Hilberg. Published in association with the United States Holocaust Memorial Museum.

Dahan, Gavriel. 2021. *The Body of Love Everyday*. Tel Aviv. Resling Publishers.

Daoud, Kamel. 2013. *Mersault Contre-Enquete*. Babel. France.

Davidson, Lawrence. 2012. *Cultural Genocide*. New Jersey and London: Rutgers University Press.

Dean, Carolyne. 2004. *The Fragility of Empathy after the Holocaust*. Cornell University Press.

Desbois, Father Patrick. 2009. *The Holocaust by Bullets: A Priest's Journey to Uncover the Truth behind the Murder of 1.5 Million Jews*. St. Martin's Griffin Publisher.

De Beaugrand, Robert. 1980. *Text, Discourse, and Process: Toward a Multidisciplinary Science of Texts*. Ablex Publishers.

DeKoven Ezrahi, Sidra. 1995. "Representing Auschwitz," in: *History and Memory*, Vol. 7, No. 2 (Fall Winter, 1995). Indiana University Press. 121-154.

Derrida, Jacques. 1982. *Writing and Difference*. Chicago: Chicago University Press.

Didi Huberman, George. 2012. *Images in Spite of All*. London and Chicago: University of Chicago Press.

Diner, Dan. 2000. *Beyond the Conceivable: Studies on Germany, Nazism, and the Holocaust*. University of California Press.

Dobrowolska, Anna. 2015. *The Auschwitz Photographer*. Anna Dobrowolska Publisher. Kindle Edition.

Dreifuss (Ben Sasson), Havi. 2017. *Warsaw Ghetto the End. April 1942-June 1943*. Jerusalem: Yad Vashem.

Dwork, Deborah and Robert Jan van Pelt 1994. "Reclaiming Auschwitz," in Geoffrey Hartman, Ed. *Holocaust Remembrance: The Shapes of Memory*, Cambridge University Press. Cambridge, MA, 232-252.

Edelman, 2014. Marek *The Ghetto Fights*. English Edition. Bookmarks Publishers.

Elhanan, Yigal. 2020. *From Yaffa to Jaffa to Yaffo*. Rosa Luxemburg Fund and Sadaka Reut Arab Jewish Youth Partnership.

Elkana, Yehuda.1988. "The need to Forget." *Ha'aretz*, March 2, 1988.

Essed, Philomena. 1991. *Understanding Everyday Racism: An Interdisciplinary Theory*. Sage Series on Race and Ethnic Relations, vol. 2. Sage Publications Inc. New Delhi, London.

Fairclough, N. 2003. *Analyzing Discourse: Textual Analysis for Social Research*. London: Routledge.

Fanon, Franz. 1956. "Racism and Culture." In *Presence Africaine*. The First International Conference of Negro Writers and Artists (PARIS - SORBONNE - 19th -22nd September 1956). 122.

Fanon, Franz. 1967. "The Fact of Blackness." *Chicken Bones: A Journal for Literary & Artistic African-American Themes*. USA. Grove Press.

Fanon, Franz. 2005. *The Wretched of the Earth*. USA. Grove Press / Atlantic Monthly Press.

Feldman, Yael. 1992. "Whose Story Is It, Anyway? Psychology and Ideology in the Representation of the Shoah in Israeli Literature" in *Probing the Limits of Representation*, edited by Shaul Friedländer. Cambridge, Mass: Harvard UP, 223-239.

Felman, Shoshana. 1991. "In an Era of Testimony: Claude Lanzmann's Shoah." *Yale French Studies*, no. 79.1991. *Literature and the Ethical Question*. Yale University Press. 39-81.

Feniger, Ofer. 1972. *Ha'olam Haya Betokhi. Letters by Ofer Feniger*. Tel Aviv. Levin and Epstein Publishers.

Fogu, Claudio, Wulf Kansteiner and Todd Presner Eds. 2016. *Probing the Ethics of Holocaust Culture*. Harvard University Press.

Friedländer, Saul. 1984. *Reflections of Nazism: An Essay on Kitsch and Death*. Harper & Row.

Friedländer, Saul. 1988. *Memory, History*, 42–63. Published by: Indiana University Press.

Friedländer, Saul. 1988. Some Reflections on the Historicization of National Socialism. In: *German Politics & Society* No. 13, The Historikerstreit (February 1988). Oxford and New York. Berghahn Books. 9-21.

Friedländer, Saul. 1992. *Probing the Limits of Representation: Nazism and the "Final Solution"*. Cambridge, MA: Harvard University Press

Friedländer, Saul. 1992. "Trauma, Transference and 'Working through' in writing the history of the 'Shoah.'" In: *History and Memory* 4, no. 1 (Spring Summer).USA. Indiana University Press. 39-59.

Friedländer, Saul. 2000. "History, Memory, and the Historian: Dilemmas and Responsibilities." *New German Critique*, 80 (Special Issue on the Holocaust). Duke University Press. 3-15.

Friedländer, Saul. 2008. *Nazi Germany and the Jews: The Years of Extermination: 1939-1945*. Phoenix. Kindle Edition.

Friedländer, Saul Ed. 1992. *Probing the Limits of Representation*. Cambridge, MA: Harvard University Press.

Forceville, Charles. 2016. "Pictorial and multimodal metaphor." In: Klug Nina-Maria and Hartmut Stöckl. *Handbuch Sprache im multimodalen Kontext [The Language In: Multimodal Contexts Handbook]*. Berlin, Germany. Mouton de Gruyter. 241-261.

Funkenstein, Amos.1993. *Perceptions of Jewish History*. University of California Press.

Galtung, Johan. 1990. "Cultural Violence." *Journal of Peace Research*, vol. 27, 3. Sage Publications. 291-305 .

Galtung Johan and Dietrich Fischer 2013. *Johan Galtung Pioneer of Peace Research.* Springer Publishers.

Gamliel, Tova and Nathan Shifris Eds. 2019. *Children of the Heart. The Yemenite Children Affair. Legal, Historical and Cultural Aspects*. Tel Aviv: Resling (Hebrew).

Gauthier, Guy. 1979. *Initiation à la sémiologie de l'image*. 2nd Ed. Paris: Les cahiers de l'audiovisuel (published by the Service Audiovisuel de la Ligue Française de l'Enseignement et d l'Education Permanente).

Genette, Gérard. 1982. *Palimpseste: La littérature au second degré*. Paris: Editions du Seuil.

Gee, James Paul. Ed. The *Routledge Handbook of Discourse Analysis*. Routledge.

Geva, Sharon 2017. *Lessons of the Holocaust: Humanistic Pedagogical Perspectives*. Tel Aviv: The Mofet Institute for Educational Research and Hakibbutz Hameuhad Publishers.

Glasner-Heled, Galia. 2007. "Reader, Writer, and Holocaust Literature: The Case of Ka-Tzetnik." In: *Israel Studies* 12, no. 3. Indiana University Press. 109-134.

Gluzman, Michael. 2017. "The Two Holocausts of Avot Yeshurun." In: Lazar Rina Ed. *Talking about Evil. Psychoanalytic, Social, and Cultural Perspectives*. Routledge. 69-80.

Goldberg, Amos and Alon Confino. 2020. "To understand Zionism, we must listen to the voices of its victims." In: *972 Magazine. Independent Journalism from Israel-Palestine*.

Goldberg, Amos. 2013. "Body, 'jouissance' and irony in the representation of the Holocaust." In: *Pain in Flesh and Blood*, edited by Stav Shira and Orit Meital. Kineret-Zmora-Dvir Publishers. 61-100.

Goldberg, Amos and Haim Hasan *Marking Evil*. 2015. The Van Leer Jerusalem Institute. Jerusalem. Israel.

Gourevitch, Philip. 1993. "Behold Now Behemoth. The Holocaust Memorial Museum: One more American theme park." *Harper's Magazine*, July issue, 55-62.

Goldberg, Vicky. 1989. *Margaret Bourke White*. Cleveland Museum of Art Publisher.

Goldberg, Vicky. 1993. *The Power of Photography. How Photographs Changed our Lives*. USA. Abbeville Press. Kindle Edition.

Grosbard, Ofer. 2003. *Israel on the Couch. The Psychology of the Peace Process*. Albany USA. State University of New York Press.

Grossman, David. 2002. *See under: Love. A Novel*. Translated by Betsy Rosenberg. Picador Pub.

Gur-Ze'ev, Ilan. 1999. *Philosophy, Politics and Education in Israel*. University of Haifa and Zamora-Bitan Publishers (in Hebrew).

Hall, Stuart Ed.1997. *Representation: Cultural Representations and Signifying Practices*. Sage Publications.

Halliday. 1985. *An Introduction to Functional Grammar*. London and New York. Routledge.

Heath, Shirley Brice and Brian V. Street. 2008. *On ethnography: approaches to language and literacy research*. Teachers College Press, Teachers College, Columbia University.

Henrikson, A. K. 1994. "The power and politics of maps." In: *Reordering the World: Geopolitical Perspective on the 21st Century*. In: G.J. Demko and W.B.Wood Eds. San Francisco: Westview Press. 50-70.

Heberer, Patricia. 2011. *Children during the Holocaust, Documenting Life and Destruction: Holocaust Sources in Context*. Alta Mira Press in association with the United States Holocaust Memorial Museum.

Hertzog, Esther 1999. *"Immigrants and Bureaucrats: Ethiopians in an Israeli Absorption Center*. New Directions in Anthropology, vol. 7. New York and Oxford. Berghahn Books.

Hever, Hanan. 2012. "'They both look at me straight in the face.' Avot Yeshurun between the Nakba and the Holocaust." In *Papers from the Conference: The Nakba in Israeli Literature and Cinema*. Tel Aviv. Israel.

Hirsch, Marianne. 2001. "Postmemory." Yale *Journal of Criticism*. Spring 2001. Johns Hopkins University Press

Hirsch, Marianne. 2001a. "Surviving Images." *The Yale Journal of Criticism*, Volume 14, Number 1, spring 2001. John Hopkins University Press. 5-37.

Hirsch, Marianne. 2002. "Nazi Photographs in Post-Holocaust Art: Gender as an Idiom of Memorialization." In: Bartov, Omer Ed. *Crimes of War: Guilt and Denial in the Twentieth Century*. New York. The New Press. 100-120.

Hirsch, Marianne. 2012. *The Generation of Postmemory: Writing and Visual Culture After the Holocaust*. Columbia University Press.

Hodge Robert and Gunther Kress. 1979. *Language as Ideology*. Routledge and Kegan Paul Publishers.

Holquist, M. 2009. *Dialogism: Bakhtin and His World*. Psychology Press, USA, Routledge.

Holtschneider, K. Hannah. 2011. *The Holocaust and Representations of Jews*. Routledge Jewish Studies Series. Taylor and Francis, Kindle Edition.

Hoopes, J. Ed. 1991. *Pierce on Signs. Writing on Semiotic by Charles Sanders Pierce*. University of North Carolina Press, North Carolina: Chapel Hill.

Horkheimer, Max and Theodor W. Adorno. 2002. *Dialectic of Enlightenment. Philosophical Fragments*, edited by Gunzelin Schmidt Noerr, translated by Edmund Jephcott. Stanford University Press.

Huddart David 2006. *Homi Bhabha*. Routledge Critical Thinkers.

Ignatieff, Michael. 1985. "Is Nothing Sacred? The Ethics of Television." *Daedalus* 114, no. 4, *The Moving Image* (Fall, 1985). 57-78.

Jenkins, Keith. 1991. *Re-thinking History*. London: Routledge;

Jewitt, Carey and Berit Henriksen. 2016. "Social Semiotic Multimodality." Chapter 6 In: Klug Nina-Maria Ed. *Handbuch Sprache im multimodalen Kontext*. Berlin. Germany. De Gruyter.

Kadari-Ovadia, Shira. 2019. "How did the children feel on the way to the gas chambers?" Haaretz 2.5.2019.

Kaplan, Alice. 1993. *French Lessons*. Chicago: University of Chicago Press.

Kaplan, Steven. 2013. "Ethiopian Immigrants in Israel: The Discourses of Intrinsic and Extrinsic Racism." In *Race, Color, Identity: Rethinking Discourses about "Jews" in the Twenty-First Century*. 167-181.

Katriel, Tamar. 2015. "Commemorating the Twentieth Century: The Holocaust and Nonviolent Struggle in Global Discourse." In Hazan H. and A. Goldberg Eds. *Marking Evil: Holocaust Memory in the Global Age*. Oxford: Berghahn Publishers. 315-343.

Ka-Tzetnik. 1966. *Like a Phoenix Rising from the Ashes*. Tel Aviv. Am Oved Publishers.

Ka-Tzetnik. 1999. *Shiviti, a Vision*. California USA. Gateways Books & Tapes, 2nd edition.

Ka-Tzetnik. 1961. *They Called Him Piepel*. London. UK. Anthony Blond Publisher.

Kedouri, Elie. 1970. *The Chatham House Version and Other Middle Eastern Studies*. New York and London. Weidenfeld and Nicolson.

Keller, Ullrich.1984. *The Warsaw Jewish Ghetto in Photographs*. UK. Dover Publications.

Keren, Nili. 2017. "Between the chairs: Holocaust teaching in Israel between formal and informal education." In: Gava Sharon Ed. *Lessons of the Holocaust, Pedagogic Perspectives*. (Hebrew). Mofet Institute Publishers.

Kristeva, Julia. 1994. *Strangers to Ourselves*, trans. Leon S. Roudiez. Columbia University Press.

Khajaj-Liluf, Yaakov. 2020. *The struggle for the Recognition of Libyan Jews as "Holocaust Survivors"* (Hebrew). Organizazione mondiale ebrei de libia. Cento di ricerca e studi sul'ebraismo libico.

Khoury, Elias, 2019. *Children of the Ghetto: My Name is Adam*. New York. Archipelago Publishers.

Kimmerling, Baruch. 2001. *The Invention and Decline of Israeliness: State, Society, and the Military*. Berkeley and Los Angeles. University of California Press.

Klein, Menachem. 2014. *Lives in Common: Arabs and Jews in Jerusalem, Jaffa and Hebron*. UK. Hurst Publishers.

Korsch, Karl. 1942. "Notes on History: The Ambiguities of Totalitarian Ideologies". In: New Essays. A Quarterly Devoted to the Study of Modern Society, Vol. 6 (1942), no 2 (Fall).1-9.

Kozlovsky-Golan, Yvonne. 2015. *Out of the Frame: The Absence of the Holocaust Experience of Mizrahim from the Visual Arts and Media in Israel*. Tel Aviv. Resling Publishing.

Krall, Hanna. 1986. *Shielding the Flame: An Intimate Conversation with Dr. Marek Edelman*. Translated by Joanna Stasinka and Lawrence Weschler. New York. Henry Holt & Company.

Kress, G. 1993. "Against Arbitrariness: The Social Production of the Sign as a Foundational Issue in Critical Discourse Analysis. *Discourse in Society* 4(2). Sage Publications. 169–191.

Kress, G. 2000. "Text as the Punctuation of Semiosis: Pulling at Some Threads." In *Intertextuality and the Media*, edited by Meinhof, U.H. and J. Smith. Manchester: Manchester University Press. 132-155.

Kress, G. 2003. *Literacy in the New Media Age*. London. Routledge.

Kress, Gunther. 2010. *Multimodality: A Social Semiotic Approach to Contemporary Communication*. London: Routledge.

Kress, Gunther. 2012. "Multimodal discourse analysis." In: Gee, James Paul and Michael Handford Eds. *The Routledge Handbook of Discourse Analysis*. Routledge. 35-50.

Kress, Gunther. 2020. "Transposing Meaning: Translation in a Multimodal Semiotic Landscape." In: Boria Monica, Ángeles Carreres, María Noriega-Sánchez and Marcus Tomalin Eds. *Beyond Words: Translation and Multimodality*. Routledge. 24-49.

Kress, Gunther & Theo van Leeuwen. 2006. *Reading Images The Grammar of Visual Design*. Routledge

Landau, Ronnie S. 2016. *The Nazi Holocaust, Its History and Meaning*. London: I.B. Tauris.

League of Fighters for Freedom and Democracy. 1960. *1939-1945. We Have Not Forgotten*. Polonia Publishing House.

Lemke. 1998. "Multiplying Meaning: Visual and verbal semiotics in scientific text." In Martin J.R. & R. Veel Eds. *Reading Science. Critical and functional perspectives on discourses of science*. London: Routledge. 87-113.

Lewis, Bryan F. 2001. "Documentation or Decoration? Uses and Misuses of Photographs in the Historiography of the Holocaust." In: Levy Margot Ed. *Remembering for the Future. The Holocaust in an Age of Genocide*. Editors in Chief John K. Roth and Elisabeth Maxwell. Volume 1. *History*.

Liss, Andrea. 1998. *Trespassing through Shadows: Memory, Photography, and the Holocaust. Visible Evidence*, Volume 3. Minneapolis London: University of Minnesota Press.

Lissner, Jorgen. 1977. *The Politics of Altruism. A Study of the Political Behaviour of Voluntary Development*. Published by the Lutheran World Federation, Department of Studies.

Lissner, Jorgen. 1981. *Merchants of Misery*. UK. New Internationalist. June 1. 1981. UK. Oxford.

Lloyd, David. 2012. Settler Colonialism and the State of Exception: The Example of Israel/Palestine. In: Jabary, Omar; Salamanca, Mezna Qato, Kareem Rabie and Sobhi Samour Eds. *Past is Present: Settler Colonialism in Palestine*. Edited by Australia: Swinburne Institute for Social Research. 59-80.

Loshitzky, Yosefa. 2001. *Identity Politics on the Israeli Screen*. Austin. Texas. University of Texas Press.

Loshitzky, Yosefa. 2006. "Pathologising Memory from the Holocaust to the Intifada." *Third Text* 20 (3/4, May/July). Online Publication. 327–335.

Lower, Wendy. 2021. *The Ravine. A Family, a Photograph, a Holocaust Massacre Revealed*. Apollo Books. Head of Zeus.

Luidor, Yosef. 1967. "Yehuda the Orchard's guard." In Landau, Dov, editor, *Stories*. The Israeli Writers Association. Masada Publishers. 63-90.

Lyotard, Jean François 1984. *Le Différend Phrases in Dispute*. Editions de Minuit.

Madmoni-Garber, Shoshana. 2019. « Reportage or Whitewash? The Yemenite Children Affair as Reflected in Israeli Media." In: Gamliel, Tova and Nathan Shifris. *Children of the Heart. The Yemenite Children Affair. Legal, Historical and Cultural Aspects, edited by* Tel Aviv: Resling (Hebrew).

Magilow, Daniel H. and Lisa Silverman. 2015. *Holocaust Representations in History*. London: Bloomsbury Academic.

Machin, David. 2013. "What is multimodal critical discourse studies?" *Critical Discourse Studies*, 10 (4). Taylor and Francis Online. 347-355.

Machin, David and Andrea Myar. 2012. *How to do Critical Discourse Analysis a Multimodal Introduction*. Sage Publications

Machtans, Karolin. 2006. Friedländer's Historiography of the Shoah. In: Davies Martin L. and Claus-Christian W. Szejnmann Eds. *How the Holocaust Looks Like Today*. New York. Palgrave Macmillan. 199–207.

Martin Rojo, L., and T.A. Van Dijk. 1997. "'There was a Problem and it was Solved!' Legitimating the Expulsion of 'Illegal' Immigrants in Spanish Parliamentary Discourse." *Discourse & Society* 8(4). Sage Publications. 523–567.

Massalah, Nur. 2013. *The Zionist Bible. Biblical Precedent, Colonialism and the Erasure of Memory*. Routledge.

Mbembe, Achilles. 2003. *Necropolitics*. Duke University Press.

Mbembe, Achilles. 2001. *On the Post Colony*. University of California Press.

Mendel, Y. *The Creation of Israeli Arabic: Security and Politics in Arabic Studies in Israel*. Palgrave Macmillan UK, 2014.

Meir-Glitzenstein, Esther. 2002. "Our Dowry: Identity and Memory among Iraqi Immigrants in Israel." *Middle Eastern Studies* 38, no. 2. Taylor and Francis Online.165-186.

Meir- Glitzenstein, Esther. 2004. *Zionism in an Arab Country: Jews in Iraq in the 1940s.* London and New York: Routledge.

Meir-Glitzenstein, Esther. 2011. "Operation Magic Carpet: Constructing the Myth of the Magical Immigration of Yemenite Jews to Israel." *Israel Studies* 16, no. 3 (Fall): 149-173.

Meir-Glitzenstein, Esther. 2021. Back to the Question of Arab Jews' Immigration. In: *Hazman Haze- (This Time) - A Periodical for Political Thought, Culture and Science.* Van Leer Institute. Jerusalem. January 2021.

Memmi, Albert. 1974. *The Colonizer and the Colonized.* Boston: Beacon Press,

Memmi, Albert. 2014. *Racism.* Univ. Of Minnesota Press.

Mikel Arieli, Roni. 2019. "Reading the Diary of Anne Frank on Robben Island: On the Role of Holocaust Memory in Ahmed Kathrada's Struggle Against Apartheid." In: *Journal of Jewish Identities*, Volume 12, Number 2, July 2019, pp. 175-195. Published by Johns Hopkins University Press.

Milton, Sybil. 1984. "The Camera as a Weapon." In: *Simon Wiesenthal Center Annual.* Volume 1, chapter 3.

Milton, Sybil. 1986. "Photographs of the Warsaw Ghetto." In *Simon Wiesenthal Center Annual* 3, 307.

Milton, Sybil. 1986a. "Images of the Holocaust Part I." *Holocaust and Genocide Studies*, Volume 1, Issue 1. UK. Oxford Academic. 27–61.

Miron, Dan. 1994. "Between Books and Ashes. On the Holocaust Literature of Ka-Tzetnik." In *Alpayim* 10, 1196-224. Reprinted in Miron, Dan. 2005. *The Blind Library: Mixed Prose 1980-2005.* Hemed Books, Yediot Aharonot Publishers. 147-183 (Hebrew).

Monmonier, Mark. 1991. *How to Lie With Maps.* Chicago: University of Chicago Press.

Monterescu, Daniel and Dan Rabinowitz, eds. 2007. *Mixed Towns Trapped Communities: Historical Narratives, Spatial Dynamics, Gender Relations and Cultural Encounters in Palestinian Israeli Towns.* Routledge.

Moses, Dirk A. 2007. "Conceptual blockages and definitional dilemmas in the 'racial century': genocides of indigenous peoples and the Holocaust." In Moses A. Dirk and Dan Stone (Eds.), *Colonialism and Genocide*, London & New York: Routledge. 148-180.

Moses, Dirk A. 2021. *The Problems of Genocide Permanent Security and the Language of Transgression*. Cambridge University Press.

Naipaul, V.S. 1994. *A Way in the World*. Penguin Random House

Nasasra, Mansour. 2012. "The Ongoing Judaisation of the Naqab and the Struggle for recognising the Indigenous Rights of the Arab Bedouin People." In: Omar Jabary Salamanca, Mezna Qato, Kareem Rabie and Sobhi Samour eds. *Past is Present: Settler Colonialism in Palestine. Settler Colonial Studies* 2, 1 (2012). 81-107

Naveh, Eyal. 2017. "Holocaust, army and faith as a self-enclosed Identity Foundation of Israeli Education." In: Geva, Sharon. *Lessons of the Holocaust: Humanistic Pedagogical Perspectives*. Hakibutz HaMeuhad (Hebrew).

Naveh, Eyal. 2018. *Past in Turmoil Debates over Historical Issues in Israel*. Tel Aviv: Kav-Adom, Ha-kibbutz Ha-Meuhad. (Hebrew).

Naveh, Eyal. 2019. "Israel". In: Cajani, Luigi, Simone Lassing, Maria Repoussi Eds. *The Palgrave Handbook of Conflict and History Education in the Post-Cold war Era*. Palgrave Macmillan Cham. 297-307.

Nichanian, Marc. 2016. "The Death of the Witness or the Persistence of the Différend." In: *Probing the Ethics of Holocaust Culture*. 141.

Nora, Pierre. 1999. *Rethinking France: Les Lieux de mémoire*, Volume 1: *The State*. University of Chicago Press.

Nyiszli, Miklos. 1946/ 2010. *I Was Doctor Mengele's Assistant*. Oswiecim Publisher.

Ofer, Dalia. 2009. "The Past That Does Not Pass: Israelis and Holocaust Memory." *Israel Studies* Vol. 14, No. 1, *Israelis and the Holocaust: Scars cry out for Healing*. Indiana University Press. 1-35.

Offer, Miriam. 2019. "Coping with the Impossible: The Developmental Roots of the Jewish Medical System in the Ghettos." In: Caumanns. Ute and Fritz Dross Eds. *Jewish Medicine and Healthcare in Central Eastern Europe: Shared Identities. Entangled Histories*. Springer Cham Publishers. 261.

Oppenheimer Yochai. 2010. *"The Holocaust: A Mizrahi PAerspective"*. *Hebrew Studies* 51. Published by the National Association of Professors of Hebrew. USA.

Oron, Yair. 1993. *Jewish-Israeli Identity*. Tel-Aviv. Sifriat HaPoalim. (Hebrew).

Oron, Yair. 2005. *The Pain of Knowledge: Holocaust and Genocide Issues in Education*. University of Chicago Press.

Owusu, Jo-Ann. 2019. "Menstruation and the Holocaust." In: *History Today* 69 (5). History Today Ltd. Publishers.

Pinderhughes, Charles. 2011. "Toward a New Theory of Internal Colonialism." In *Socialism and Democracy*. Published online: June 21, 2011. Routledge.

Pape, Ilan. 2008. *The Ethnic Cleansing of Palestine*. Oneworld Publications.

Pappe, Ilan. 2012. "Shtetl Colonialism: First and Last Impressions of Indigeneity by Colonized Colonizers." *Journal of Settler Colonial Studies,* vol. 2.Issue 1*: Past is Present: Settler Colonialism in Palestine.* 39-58.

Pappe, Ilan. 2017. *Ten Myths about Israel*. Verso.

Pedaya, Haviva. 2011. *Walking Beyond the Trauma*. Tel Avi.: Resling.

Pedaya, Haviva. 2020. "Toward Building a Net for Mizrahi Literature." *Haaretz,* September 29, 2020.

Peled, Inbar. 2018. *From Michael Brown To Yosef Salamsa: The Racialization of Ethiopian Jews in Israeli Law*. Unpublished dissertation for the degree of Master in Law. Toronto University. Faculty of Law.

Peled-Elhanan, Nurit. 2009. "Layout as punctuation of semiosis: some examples from Israeli schoolbooks." *Visual Communication* 8 (1). Sage Publications. 91-114.

Peled-Elhanan, Nurit. 2009a. "The Geography of Hostility Discursive and Semiotic Means of Transforming Realities in Geography Schoolbooks." *Journal of Visual Literacy*, vol. 27 (2). Taylor and Francis Online. 179-208.

Peled-Elhanan, Nurit. 2010. "Legitimation of massacres in Israeli school history books." In *Discourse and Society* 21(4). Sage Publications. 377-404.

Peled-Elhanan, Nurit. 2012. *Palestine in Israeli School Books Ideology and Propaganda in Education*. London: I.B. Tauris.

Peled-Elhanan, Nurit. 2014. "The De-Humanization of Palestinians in Israeli Schoolbooks: A Multimodal Analysis." In *Visual Communication*, edited by D. Machin. Boston, MA. Degruyter Publishing House. 327-340.

Peled-Elhanan, Nurit. 2017. "Writing as Design. Children's Multimodal Writing." In Archer, A. and Breuer E., Eds. *Multimodality in Writing*. Brill, 253-277.

Peters, Edie. 2011. "The Duty of History," Interview with Wilhelm Brasse. *GUP International Photography Journal*, July 7, 2011. http://www.gupmagazine.com/articles/the-duty-of-history.

Piterberg, Gabriel. 2008. *The Returns of Zionism: Myths, Politics and Scholarship in Israel*. Verso.

Polonsky, David. 2018. *Ann Frank Graphic Adaptation* Illustrated. Penguin.

Rabinowitz, D. 2001. "Natives with jackets and degrees. Othering, objectification and the role of Palestinians in the co-existence field in Israel." *Social Anthropology* 9 (1). European Association of Social Anthropologists. 65–80.

Raz-Krakotzkin, Amnon. 1994. "Exile within sovereignty: toward a critique of the 'negation of exile' in Israeli culture." *Theory and Criticism* 5. Jerusalem. Van Leer Publications. 1-113 (Hebrew).

Raz-Krakotzkin, Amnon. 2013. "History Textbooks and the Limits of Israeli Consciousness." In: Shapira, Anita and Penslar, Derek J., Eds. *Israeli Historical Revisionism from Left to Right*. Routledge.155-173.

Raz-Krakotzkin Amnon. 2005. Zionist Return to the West and the Mizrachi Jewish Perspective," in: I. Kalmar, D. Pensler (eds.), *Orientalism and the Jews*. Waltham Mass.: Brandeis University Press. 162-181.

Raz-Krakotzkin, Amnon. 2019. "Walter Benjamin, the Holocaust and the Question of Palestine." In Goldberg, Amos and Bashir, Bashir. 2018. *The Holocaust and the Nakba*. Foreword by Elias Khoury. Afterword by Jacqueline Rose. Columbia University Press. 79-92.

Reisigl, M. and Wodak, R. 2001. *Discourse and Discrimination: Rhetorics of Racism and Antisemitism*. Routledge.

Resnik, Julia. 2003. "'Sites of memory' of the Holocaust: shaping national memory in the education system in Israel." *Nations and Nationalism* 9 (2), 2003. Wiley Online Library. 297–317.

Ringelblum, Emanuel 1992. *Jewish-Polish Relations during the Second World War* USA. Illinois. Northwestern University Press.

Rothberg, Michael. 2000. *Traumatic Realism - the Demands of Holocaust Representation*. Minneapolis, London: University of Minnesota Press.

Rothberg, Michael 2009. *Multidirectional Memory Remembering the Holocaust in the Age of Decolonization*. Stanford, California. Stanford university press.

Rothberg, Michael. 2011. "From Warsaw to Gaza: Mapping Multidirectional Memory." In: *Criticism* Fall 2011, Vol. 53 no. 4 (fall). Wayne State University Press, Detroit, Michigan. 523-548.

Rousset, David. 1988. *L'Univers concentrationnaire*. France. Paris. Hachette Littérature.

Sadowski, Piotr. 2011. "The Iconic Indexicality of Photography." In: Michelucci Pascal, Olga Fischer and Christina Ljungberg Eds. *Semblance and Signification:* [Iconicity in Language and Literature 10]. 353–368.

Said, Edward W. 1978. *Orientalism*. London. Vintage Books.

Said, 1980. *The Question of Palestine*. London. Vintage Books.

Salamon, Hagar. 1998. "Passage from Ethiopia to the Promised Land: Racial Consciousness in Transition." In *Jerusalem Studies in Jewish Folklore*. Mandel Institute for Jewish Studies.

Salamon, Hagar 2003. "Blackness in Transition: Decoding Racial Constructs through Stories of Ethiopian Jews." In *Journal of Folklore Research* 40(1). Indiana University Press. 3-32.

Salamon, Hagar. 2010. "Misplaced Home and Mislaid Meat: Stories Circulating Among Ethiopian Immigrants in Israel." *Callaloo* 33(1): 165-176. The Johns Hopkins University Press.

Sarris, Greg. 1993. *Keeping Slug Woman Alive: A Holistic Approach to American Indian Texts*. Berkeley. CA. University of California Press.

Sartre, J.P. 1976. *Critique of Dialectical Reason. I: Theory of Practical Ensembles*. Trans. Alan Sheridan Smith. London: New Left Books, 752.

Scharf, Rafael F. (Compiler), Willy Georg (Photographer). 1993. *In the Warsaw Ghetto: Summer 1941* Hardcover. New York. Aperture Publishers.

Schwarberg, Gunther, Ed. 2001. *Joest, Heinrich. A Day in the Warsaw Ghetto*. Steidl Publishers. London. UK.

Segev, Tom. 1993. *The Seventh Million: The Israelis and the Holocaust*. New York: Hill and Wang.

Segev, Tom. 2001. *One Palestine, Complete: Jews and Arabs under the British Mandate*. Picador Publishers.

Segev, Tom. 2019. *A State at Any Cost*. Farrar, Straus and Giroux; Illustrated edition.

Sfard, Michael. 2018. *The Wall and the Gate: Israel, Palestine, and the Legal Battle for Human Rights* Macmillan Publishers.

Semel, Nava. 2009. *And the Rat Laughed.* Published by ReadHowYouWant.com.

Sereny, Gitta. 1974. *Into that Darkness: From Mercy Killing to Mass Murder.* McGraw-Hill.

Shandler, Jeffrey. 2017. *Holocaust Memory in the Digital Age: Survivors' Stories and New Media.* Stanford, California. Stanford University Press.

Shavit, Ari. 2014. *My Promised Land - the Triumph and Tragedy of Israel.* New York. Spiegel and Grau.

Shenhav, Yehouda A. 2006. *The Arab Jews: A Postcolonial Reading of Nationalism, Religion, and Ethnicity.* Stanford, California. Stanford University Press, 2006.

Shimoni, Batya. 2015. "Holocaust Envy. Globalizing the Holocaust in Israeli Discourse." In Hazan and Goldberg Eds. *Marking Evil.*

Shifris, Nathan. 2019. *Where has my child gone* 2019. Tel-Aviv. Yediot Sfarim Publishers. (Hebrew).

Shohat, Ella. 1988. "Sephardim in Israel: Zionism from the Standpoint of Its Jewish Victims." *Social Text* no. 19/20 (Autumn, 1988). Duke University Press. 1-35

Shohat, Ella. 2006. *Taboo Memories, Diasporic Voices.* Duke University Press.

Shohat, Ella. 2017. *On the Arab-Jew, Palestine, and Other Displacements Selected Writings.* Pluto Press.

Shohat, Ella and Robert Stam. 2014. *Unthinking Eurocentrism.* London and New York. Routledge.

Silver Ochayon, Sheryl. 2013. "Who Took the Pictures? The Ghetto Photography of Mendel Grossman in Lodz, as Compared with the Ghetto Photography of German 'Ghetto Tourists'." https://www.yadvashem.org/articles/general/who-took-the-pictures.html

Silverstone, Roger. 2003. "Proper Distance: Toward an Ethics for Cyberspace." In: Gunnar, Liestøl, Andrew Morrison, and Terje Rasmussen Eds. *Digital Media Revisited toward an Ethics for Cyberspace, Theoretical and Conceptual Innovation in Digital Domains.* Cambridge, Massachusetts. The MIT Press. 469-491.

Smooha, Sami. 2002. "The model of ethnic democracy: Israel as a Jewish and democratic state." *Nations and Nationalism* 8 (4). Wiley Online Library. 475-503.

Sontag, Susan. 2004. *Regarding the Pain of Others*. Picador.
Sontag, Susan. 1989. *On Photography*. New York: Anchor Doubleday.
Shavit, Ari. 2014. *My Promised Land - the Triumph and Tragedy of Israel*. New York. Spiegel and Grau.
Schwarberg, Gunther. 2001. *In The Ghetto Of Warsaw: Photographs by Heinrich Joest*. London. UK. Steidl Publishers.
Shikhmanter, Rima. 2014. "Limitations as Possibilities: Uri Orlev's Holocaust Narratives for Children and Young Adults." *Children's Literature*, Volume 42. John Hopkins University Press. 1-19.
Sorkin, Michael. 1993. "The Holocaust Museum: Between Beauty and Horror." *Progressive Architecture* 74. Taylor and Francis.
Stav, Shira. 2012. "Nakba and Shoah. Mechanisms of comparison and denial in the Israeli Narrative." In *The Palestinian Nakba in Cinema and Literature in Israel*. A selection of Conference Papers.
Stone, Dan. 2004. "The historiography of genocide: beyond 'uniqueness' and ethnic competition." In *Rethinking History: The Journal of Theory and Practice*, 8:1. Taylor and Francis Online. 127-142.
Spiegelman, Art. 1980. *Maus, a Novel*. New York. Row Publishers.
Spiegelman, Art. 2011. *Metamaus*. London. UK. Viking Pub.
Struk, Janina. 2004. *Photographing the Holocaust. Interpretations of the Evidence*. London. I.B. Tauris Publishers.
Steiner, George. 1966. "Pornography and Its Consequences." *Encounter* 36, no. 3. 46-47.
Steiner, George. 1974. *In Bluebeard's Castle: Some Notes Towards the Redefinition of Culture*. Yale University Press.
Steiner, George. 1975. Night Words: High Pornography and Human Privacy. In:
The Pornography Controversy. 1st Edition. Routledge.
Steiner, George. 1988. "The Long Life of Metaphor: An Approach to the Shoah." In: Lang, Berel Ed. *Writing and the Holocaust* 1. New York: Holmes & Meier.1-54.
Steiner, George. 1998. *Language and Silence. Essays on Language, Literature, and the Inhuman*. Yale University Press.
Struk, Janina. 2008. "Images of Women in Holocaust Photography." *Feminist Review*, No. 88. Palgrave Macmillan Journals. 111-121.

Struk, Janina. 2011. *Private Pictures, Soldiers' Inside View of War*. London: I.B. Tauris.
Sukary Yossi. 2008. *Emilia and the Salt of the Earth. A confession*. Tel Aviv. Babel Publishers.
Sukary Yossi. 2014. *Benghazi-Bergen Belsen*. Tel Aviv. Am Oved Publishers.
Tabenkin, Yitzhak. 1971. *Lekah Sheshet Ha'yamim: Yishuva shel Eretz Bilti Mehuleket.* (The Lesson of the Six Day War: Settling an Undivided Land). Tel Aviv. Hakibbutz Hameuhad Publishers.
Tannen, Deborah. 2007. *Talking Voices*. Cambridge University Press. Online publication date.
Tee, Nechama and Daniel Weiss 1999 Published online: 2015. "The Heroine of Minsk Eight photographs of an execution." In: *History of Photography*. Volume 23. Issue 4. Taylor and Francis. 322-330.
Tuhiwai Smith, Linda. 2012. *Decolonizing Methodologies*. Research and Indigenous Peoples. London and New York: Zed Books.
Van Leeuwen, Theo. 1992. "The schoolbook as a multimodal text." *International Schulbuch Forschung 14*(1). Frankfurt: Diesterweg. 35-58.
Van Leeuwen, Theo. 2000. "Visual Racism". In: M. Reisigl and R. Wodak Eds. *The Semiotics of Racism*. Vienna: Passagen Verlag, 333–350.
Van Leeuwen, Theo. 2005. *Introducing Social Semiotics*. New York: Routledge.
Van Leeuwen, Theo. 2008. *Discourse and Practice: New Tools for Discourse Analysis* (Oxford Studies in Sociolinguistics). Oxford: Oxford University Press.
Van Leeuwen, Theo. 2013. "Critical Analysis of Multimodal Discourse." In *The Encyclopedia of Applied Linguistics*, edited by Carol Chapelle.Wiley-Blackwell. 1-6.
Van Leeuwen, Theo. 2021. *Multimodality and Identity*. Routledge.
Van Leeuwen, Theo, and Gunther Kress. 1995. "Critical Layout Analysis."
Internationale Schulbuchforschung. Vol. 17, No. 1 (1995). Oxford, New York. Berghahn Books Publishers. 25-43.
Van Leeuwen, Theo. and Ruth. Wodak. 1999. "Legitimizing Immigration Control: A Discourse-Historical Analysis." *Discourse Studies* 1(1). Reisigl, Martin and Ruth
Viterbo, Hedi. 2021. *Problematizing Law, Rights, and Childhood in Israel/Palestine*. Cambridge University Press.

Wodak. 2001. *Discourse and Discrimination: Rhetorics of Racism and Antisemitism*. Routledge. 83–118.

Volkan, Vamık D. 2001. "Transgenerational Transmissions and Chosen Traumas: An Aspect of Large-Group Identity." *Group Analysis* 34(1). Sage Publications. 79-97.

Volkan, Vamık D. 2015. *A Nazi Legacy. Depositing, Transgenerational Transmission, Dissociation, and Remembering Through Action*. London, Karnac Books Ltd.

Wagenaar, Aad. 1994. *Settela: The Girl Who Got Her Name Back*. https://www.brabantremembers.com/persecution/het-meisje-met-de-hoofddoek-vindt-haar-naam/?lang=en.

Weindling, Paul. 2014. *Victims and Survivors of Nazi Human Experiments*. Bloomsbury Publishing. Kindle Edition.

Wiesel, Elie. "Now we know," in Richard Arens Ed. *Genocide in Paraguay* Philadelphia: Temple University Press, 1976. p. 165.

Wertsch, J. 2002. *Voices of Collective Remembering*. Cambridge: Cambridge University Press.

White, Hayden. 1978. "Interpretation in History." In: White, Hayden. *Tropics of Discourse: Essays in Cultural Criticism*. Baltimore, MD: Johns Hopkins University Press.

White, Hayden. 1992. "Historical Emplotment and the Problem of Truth." In: Friedländer, Saul Ed. *Probing the Limits of Representation*. Cambridge, Mass: Harvard UP.

White, Hayden. 2016. "Historical Truth, Estrangement and Disbelief." In *Probing the Ethics of Holocaust Culture*, edited by Claudio Fogu, Wulf Kansteiner, and Todd Presner. Cambridge, Massachusetts & London.

Wolfe, Patrick. 2006. "Settler Colonialism and the Elimination of the Native." *Journal of Genocide Research*, 8(4). Taylor and Francis Online. 348-409.

Wolfe, Patrick. 2012. "Purchase by Other Means: The Palestine Nakba and Zionism's Conquest of Economics." In: Jabary, Omar; Salamanca Mezna Qato, Kareem Rabie and Sobhi Samour Eds. *Past is Present: Settler Colonialism in Palestine* 2 (1). Australia. Swinburne Institute for Social Research. 133-171.

Wolfe, Patrick. 2016. *Traces of History. Elementary Structures of Race*. Verso.

Yablonka, Hanna. 1994. *Foreign Brothers 1948-1952*. Jerusalem. Yad Ben Zvi Publishers (Hebrew).

Yablonka, Hanna. 2009. "Oriental Jewry and the Holocaust: A Tri-Generational Perspective." *Israel Studies*. Vol. 14, No. 1, *Israelis and the Holocaust: Scars Cry out for Healing* (Spring, 2009). Indiana University Press. 94-122.

Yaron, Idan, 2018. *The Trips of Israeli Youth to the Death Sites in Poland*. Jerusalem. Carmel Publishers.

Yeshurun, Helit and Lilach Lachman Eds. *Milvadata. Selected poems by Avot Yeshurun*. Tel-Aviv. Hakibbutz Hameuhad and Siman Kriah: New Library for Poetry.

Yiftachel, Oren. 2006. *Ethnocracy Land and Identity Politics in Israel/Palestine*. Philadelphia, PA: University of Pennsylvania Press.

Young, R.C. 2004. *White Mythologies*. Routledge, Abingdon.

Zelizer, Barbie. 1997. "La photo de presse et la libération des camps en 1945: Images et formes de la mémoire." *Vingtième Siècle. Revue d'Histoire* 54 (April - June). Published by Sciences Po. University Press. 61-78.

Zelizer, Barbie, 2000. *Remembering to Forget: Holocaust Memory through the Camera's Eye*. Second Edition. University of Chicago Press Bunko.

Zelizer, Barbie. 2001. *Visual Culture and the Holocaust*. Rutgers University Press.

Zimmerman Moshe and Zuckerman Moshe 2023. *Thinking Germany. An Israeli dialogue*. Tel Aviv. Resling Publishers.

Zuckerman, Moshe. 1993. *Shoa in the Sealed Room: The Shoah in the Israeli Press during the Gulf War*. Zuckerman Publishing.

www.ingramcontent.com/pod-product-compliance
Lightning Source LLC
Chambersburg PA
CBHW071357300426
44114CB00016B/2092